THE OVERSEAS AMERICANS

THE CARNEGIE SERIES IN AMERICAN EDUCATION

The books in this series have resulted from studies supported by grants of the Carnegie Corporation of New York, and are published by McGraw-Hill in recognition of their importance to the future of American education.

The Corporation, a philanthropic foundation established in 1911 by Andrew Carnegie for the advancement and diffusion of knowledge and understanding, has a continuing interest in the improvement of American education. It financed the studies in this series to provide facts and recommendations which would be useful to all those who make or influence the decisions which shape American educational policies and institutions.

The statements made and view expressed in these books are solely the responsibility of the authors.

Books Published

Clark	*The Open Door College: A Case Study*
Cleveland, Mangone, and Adams	*The Overseas Americans*
Conant	*The American High School Today*
Glenny	*Autonomy of Public Colleges*
Henninger	*The Technical Institute in America*
Medsker	*The Junior College: Progress and Prospect*
Pierson	*The Education of American Businessmen*

In Preparation

Berelson	*Graduate Education in the United States*
Corson	*Governance of Colleges and Universities*

THE
OVERSEAS
AMERICANS

Harlan Cleveland
Gerard J. Mangone
John Clarke Adams

McGRAW-HILL BOOK COMPANY, INC.

New York   Toronto   London

THE OVERSEAS AMERICANS

Library of Congress Catalog Card Number: 60-10598

First Edition

11371

Preface · The Carnegie Project

From Osaka to Accra, from Helsinki to Antofagasta, nearly one per cent of our citizens live outside the United States. Some of the overseas Americans are government people who are manning military bases, running embassies, and administering foreign aid. But a third of them are other United States citizens, including wives and children, abroad for a year of study and teaching or for a lifetime of expatriate living in the interests of American business, missionary churches, or philanthropic foundations.

Borne by tides of goodwill and dollars, the United States diplomat and technician, the preacher and the professor, are working to militarize, proselytize, or to reorganize the lives of their foreign cousins. Most of the latter are not unhappy to have these American citizens in their countries; they are, however, often truculent about the behavior and attitudes of their visitors. The face of America we see mirrored in their reactions is not always what we would wish it to be.

The looking glass of alien opinion resembles one of the distortion mirrors that used to be a popular feature at every county fair. The image undeniably looks familiar, but the proportions are awry. The very qualities we regard as our noblest virtues are clearly discernible in foreign comments about us—unfortunately, they are reflected as vices.

An American is a man with energy and drive, Americans say; he is strong and self-confident, yet friendly and straightforward in manner. Alien eyes perceive these same traits. Yet the composite American described by peoples of other cultures is awkward, well-meaning, embarrassingly friendly, and, most irritating of all to them, perpetually impatient and possessed of an annoying sense of superiority.

The image of America held by the peoples of the world is not, of course, all derived from watching Americans overseas at work and play. The image is also shaped by our diplomacy, our military strategy, our Atlas missiles, and our school closings. Federal troops in Little Rock's Central High School and Washington's debates about foreign aid make headlines in every country of the world. Our military efforts to contain the spread of communism typically receive scant attention and less approval in those countries whose political leadership believes the United States is obsessed with the danger of communism and under-impressed with the prior dangers of political instability and economic hopelessness.

Thus it is that the overseas Americans carry with them not only the responsibility for their own behavior but also the guilt for intolerance in Arkansas or bumbling in Washington. They likewise bask in the reflection from great achievements at Cape Canaveral or inspiring acts of leadership in Washington. Businessmen or missionaries, airmen or soldiers, spies, "experts," or diplomats, they are all, like it or not, surrogates for the United States Secretary of State.

Many play the part with a feeling of acute embarrassment. Some learn quickly to relax in the presence of their own power. Not a few take too seriously the notion that their image mirrors America to foreign eyes, and feel they must settle every outstanding issue of American foreign policy every time they talk with a stranger.

Whatever his emotional response, wherever he lives, whatever he does for a living, almost any one of the overseas Americans will tell you that work and life abroad are a liberal education. Most of them will add the regret that more of that education had not been absorbed *before* they took on an overseas assignment. For the next generation of overseas Americans, that regret need not exist.

The Maxwell Graduate School of Citizenship and Public Affairs of Syracuse University began a systematic study of the education of Americans for overseas service in the autumn of 1956, just after President Gamal Abdel Nasser of Egypt had seized the Suez Canal and just before the Soviet Union orbited the first man-made satellite. A grant from the Carnegie Corporation of New York financed the research project, and its working title became "The Carnegie Project."

The frame of the problem was all to clear: more than one and a half million Americans now live and work abroad, but the American educational system has not yet mobilized its imagination and its resources to meet the urgent requirements that this unprecedented fact implies. Generalized exhortations are well received, and new overseas-training programs are springing up all over the country. What has been missing is a general theory of overseas service.

The object of our research was, therefore, to reach for suggestive answers to four main questions about Americans abroad:

- What elements in the education and experience of an American are most relevant to his effective performance on an overseas assignment? (Or, in the question's simplest form: What is so different about living and working abroad?)
- To what extent are these elements central to the education and training processes to which present and prospective overseas Americans are exposed?
- What is now being done to prepare American civilians for overseas service?
- What should the American educational system—and some of its financial sponsors in business, government, and private foundations—be doing in this field?

We first brought together statistics showing the number of Americans at work abroad. With the cooperation of many public and private agencies, sets of figures were developed on United States civilians serving the U.S. Government and international organizations, American business firms, missionary churches, and philanthropic organizations, together with Americans overseas in connection with academic work; this was, curiously enough, the first time such an inventory had been attempted. These statistics, rough as they are, quickly became the standard and have been widely used in college catalogues, official U.S. Government documents, business and religious missionary literature, and articles in journals, periodicals, and newspapers.

More important than the collection of numbers was the analysis of what these Americans were doing abroad. This analysis showed that the United States has come out of the era of arm's-length diplomacy. The work of an American employed outside the United States, whether for a public or a private organization, often involves him in activities that formerly would have been styled the "domestic affairs" of a foreign country. "Foreign operations" is a more comprehensive and descriptive term than "diplomacy" in analyzing American foreign relations today.

To check our preliminary thinking, we assembled at the Maxwell School thirty educators, government officials, foundation executives, businessmen, and international administrators for a three-day conference at Syracuse in March, 1957, on "Americans at Work Abroad." Ten original papers were prepared by practitioners and students of American overseas operations and by members of the Carnegie Project staff. Drawing on these papers, some of which were based on the conference discussions, the first effort to formulate the problem was published in September, 1957, under the title *The Art of Overseasmanship* (edited by Harlan Cleveland and Gerard J. Mangone and published by the Syracuse University Press).*

---

* Other publications from this research have appeared earlier and we gratefully acknowledge permission to use material from them in this volume:
"Education and Training for Public Service Overseas," *Maxwell Graduate School*, October 23, 1956
"One Hundred Thousand Americans at Work Abroad," *Maxwell Graduate School*, January 15, 1957
"American Business and Overseas Employment," *Maxwell Graduate School*, June 15, 1957
"In Asia Reactions Are Even Sharper" by Harlan Cleveland, *Life International*,
(*continued*)

To gather empirical data about the difference between living and working in the United States and in a foreign country—and to discover what the American educational-training institutions could do to prepare Americans to live and work with those differences—a field research project in six selected countries was designed and carried out through a subcontract with Louis Harris and Associates of New York. Louis Harris selected and prepared four interviewers for this part of the project:

A. Doak Barnett, a specialist on China and Asian affairs, formerly an associate of the American Universities Field Staff, Foreign Service officer, correspondent for the *Chicago Daily News,* and research fellow at the Council on Foreign Relations, now a program associate in the Ford Foundation;

Cornelius J. Dwyer, an economist, formerly an Associated Press Bureau Chief, a career Foreign Service officer, and an official of the Economic Cooperation Administration, now a member of the staff of the National Bureau of Economic Research in New York City;

Edward T. Hall, an anthropologist who directed the State Department's Point Four Training Program and is now Director of Overseas Training and Research at the Governmental Affairs Institute in Washington;

February 3, 1958. Excerpts republished by permission from *Life International,* © Time Inc., 1958.
"The Real International World and the Academic Lag" by Harlan Cleveland, *Twenty-Eighth Yearbook of the National Council for the Social Studies, 1958.*
"Education for Overseasmanship" by Harlan Cleveland and Gerard J. Mangone, *Foreign Operations,* 1958
"New Americans in Old Societies" by Gerard J. Mangone, *The Antioch Review,* Winter, 1958
"American Students Abroad: Goodwill Ambassadors?" *Maxwell Graduate School,* January 28, 1958
"The Pretty Americans: How Wives Behave Abroad" by Harlan Cleveland, *Harper's,* March, 1959
"Personnel for Overseas Service" by Harlan Cleveland, *Fifty-eighth Yearbook of the National Society for the Study of Education,* 1959
"The American Overseas," *Hearing* before the Committee on Foreign Relations, United States Senate, February 18, 1959.
"Wanted: Better Business Ambassadors," by Harlan Cleveland, *Dun's Review and Modern Industry,* February, 1960.
"The Option of Study Overseas," by Harlan Cleveland, *National Education Association Journal,* March, 1960.
"Missionaries and the Facts of Life," by Harlan Cleveland, *Overseas Mission Review,* Whitsuntide issue, 1960.

Mottram Torre, M.D., social psychologist, formerly consultant to U.S. Government agencies (ECA, TCA, Department of State, FOA, DOD), now the Assistant Director of the World Federation for Mental Health and psychiatric consultant to the United Nations Medical Service.

After Mr. Harris, with his associate Penn Kimball, had done a pilot study in Mexico, these men visited Yugoslavia, Iran, Ethiopia, Indonesia, and Japan. In all, 244 United States citizens abroad were interviewed. To complement the work of this group, two of the authors of this book traveled to the same countries and, in addition, to Taiwan, India, Egypt, Ethiopia, Ghana, and Brazil, where they interviewed more than 200 foreign nationals about overseas Americans, talked to a host of Americans in government and private work abroad, and also held seminars in six foreign countries with the wives of Americans at work abroad. Most of the quotations in this book have been selected from a mountain of primary and original data developed by research in the field.

With so great a population of Americans in foreign lands, doing so many different things there, we made no attempt to select a "sample." Instead, we sought rather full and coherent impressions about living and working overseas from a sizable number of civilians, attached to different kinds of organizations in different parts of the world, who were on foreign assignment by their own choice.

The countries selected were Mexico, Yugoslavia, Ethiopia, Iran, Indonesia and Japan. The bias against northwestern Europe reflected our observation that the big increase in the outward flow of Americans has been to the non-European areas, and that it is in precisely those areas that a previous unfamiliarity with the history and culture of the country makes it hardest for the American to operate effectively.

In each country an advance agent of the research project was appointed to start the process of identifying those American organizations that might cooperate in the survey project. Arrangements were then made to enlist the help of the director of the relevant American overseas organization. Lists of personnel were drafted by the advance agent in consultation with the heads of the organizations or their deputies. Those selected for interviews, and their immediate superiors, were briefed on the purpose of the project and the scope of its inquiry. From this selection process we obtained the group of 244 United States citizens (at least forty in each of the six countries) employed by a government agency, business firm, church, foundation, or private voluntary agency.

An effort was made to select those people who had been living and working in the country for at least a year, whose work made necessary a good deal of contact with nationals of the host country, and who were in the middle or upper grades of their own organizations and therefore had some discretion in policy matters. Again a bias was introduced: we assumed for the purpose of this study that the most crucial problems of overseas service arise in the more responsible posts held by those Americans who must make some effort to cross cultural barriers in order to do their jobs well. Three basic instruments were utilized to gain information about the 244 respondents: a biographic data sheet, an extended interview, and a set of personality tests.

The biographic sheet consisted of forty-one items covering such background information as family environment, travel experience, language facility, education, previous employment, and special interests. It was completed by each of the 244 men and women a few days before his or her interview by the research team. In so far as possible the information included in the questionnaire was of a character not likely to be materially distorted by pretense. Research teams of two men each then followed up the biographic data sheet with long interviews. These interviews, conducted during the spring and summer of 1957, were all handled by trained observers with considerable experience in interviewing and reporting. Detailed notes were taken and transcribed immediately after the interview, in order to capture as accurately as possible the exact words used by each respondent. Nearly all our interviewees were quite relaxed after they were fully informed about the aims of the project, willing to speak frankly about the simple facts of their lives—birth, education, travel, and the like. We were, of course, less sure about their ability to be completely objective when the information asked them reflected in some way on their status in life or their personal images of what is considered "right and proper," or when the interviewers sought details about their life histories which might be painful or embarrassing to recall. Asking a man about his language

TABLE 1. 244 AMERICANS INTERVIEWED ABROAD
(in Ethiopia, Indonesia, Iran, Japan, Mexico and Yugoslavia)

U.S. GOVERNMENT	BUSINESS
Cultural Officers 5	19 General Administrators
Economic Affairs Officers 14	13 Sales Staff
Internal Administrators 23	3 Personnel Administrators
Librarians 3	3 Lawyers
Labor Officers 2	8 Engineers
Program Administrators 19	5 Bankers
Technical Specialists 11	5 Technical Specialists
Field Investigators 3	1 Business Service Organization Representative
Political Officers 11	**INTERNATIONAL ORGANIZATIONS**
Teachers & Training Officers 12	2 Executives
Scientists 4	2 Technical Specialists
Military Advisors 9	**MISSIONARIES AND VOLUNTARY AGENCIES**
Public Affairs & Information 12	19 Missionaries
Educational Research & Exchange 6	5 General Administrators
Nursing Administrators 4	2 Program Executives
Consular Affairs Officers 14	5 Science and Agricultural Specialists

facility may evoke a reply conditioned either by arrogance or by excessive modesty. Asking him about his wife's attitude toward overseas service nibbles at the nerve ends of his natural defense against exposing himself.

The interviews were "loosely structured"—the interviewers had specific instructions as to what ground must surely be covered during the interview, but were encouraged to guide each conversation according to their own judgment. At least two and quite frequently four hours were spent in private between the interviewers and each respondent. When all the interviews in one country had been completed, the respondents as a group took two brief written psychological tests.

As a corollary to this work, researchers undertook to investigate the foreign language facility and the orientation—both to the United States and to foreign countries—which a college education now affords to Americans. For this purpose more than 500 undergraduates and graduates en route to Europe for the first time were questioned aboard thirteen transatlantic ships during the summer of 1957. Results of this study were published in Congressional hearings and have been widely used by travel organizations, agencies with overseas personnel, and the general public.

While the overseas research was in progress, another group of scholars was classifying and analyzing, from correspondence and personal interviews: (1) area-training programs, "junior year abroad" arrangements, and other major programs in colleges and universities which have a major relevance to the preparation of Americans for international service; (2) all substantial missionary-training programs carried on by churches in the United States; (3) all institutes or orientation plans used by United States business firms to prepare their personnel for work abroad; and (4) the special schools or programs utilized by U.S. Government agencies to orient personnel to work and life overseas.

Those who engage in social research are usually impressed by the willingness of people to go out of their way to cooperate. Students will sit for hours taking intelligence and aptitude tests, housewives will invite the census-taker in for coffee, voters will patiently reply to the imponderable queries of itinerant reporters. Our experience was no exception to the first principle of social science: people like to answer questions about themselves. Each of our 244 subjects contributed several hours of his own time to the project; several hundred nationals of other countries were equally co-operative; and the leadership of every organization or agency involved proved willing to tolerate the inconveniences of probes by outside researchers in the hope that something useful might come out of it all. We are, in fact, not aware of any organization or individual that refused to help when asked.

The reason for this unanimous response is not far to seek. Americans are worried about their overseas performance, and our friends abroad are worried about it too. The general sense of frustration on the subject has produced an intense desire to improve American education so that Americans are better prepared to assume international responsibilities. Because we proposed to study the situation with a view to action, those most concerned were prepared to grant this study a priority claim on their own time and attention.

Our greatest debt, then, is to the—necessarily anonymous—overseas Americans themselves. Among our outside encouragers and consultants, our special thanks go to Deputy Undersecretary of State Loy W. Henderson for having generously conveyed the spirit and purpose of our work to American missions around the world; to Professor David Riesman of Harvard University for many penetrating observations; to Professor Robert Knapp of Wesleyan University for his counsel on psychological tests; to Alexander B. Trowbridge, an executive of Esso, S.A., in Panama, for his large contribution to the chapter on businessmen abroad; to David L. Gordon of the International Bank for Reconstruction and Development, who helped develop the original project; and to Mrs. Dorothy Sickels for editorial guidance.

Many of our colleagues in the Maxwell School faculty helped frame our approach to the research. From Linton Freeman came valuable guidance on methodology. Irving Swerdlow and Mansfield I. Smith counted, checked, corrected, and encouraged us on our way. For many challenging ideas about what the overseas Americans should know about the United States of America, we are grateful to Stuart Gerry Brown. And we are indebted in a very special way to Stephen P. Koff, who worked throughout as a research associate, and who must be credited with much of what has been gathered in this final report.

Finally, a note about three words occurring frequently in this book: "We" generally means any of the participants in the project. "Overseas" means "abroad," and vice versa. We have studied geography and know that it is not necessary to cross water to travel to some foreign lands. But the English language seems to be poorly endowed with adjectives and adverbs describing the state of abroadness, so "overseas" will have to do.

HARLAN CLEVELAND
GERARD J. MANGONE
JOHN CLARKE ADAMS

Syracuse, New York

CONTENTS

Part One
NEW AMERICANS
IN OLD SOCIETIES

1 · International Affairs Are Internal Affairs

According to government figures, there were 1,590,000 American citizens living abroad on March 31, 1959. About one-third of these were civilians and the others were members of the United States Armed Forces and their dependents.

Among civilians, several hundred students and research scholars on foundation and Fulbright grants, together with other categories of undergraduate students and teachers, account for more than 10,000 of our total overseas academic population at any one time. There is also, of course, a shifting population of Americans who like to live outside the United States for reasons ranging from a taste for French wines and Left Bank freedom to a desire to retain a larger proportion of their taxable income than is normally possible at home.

But the typical American civilian overseas is with an organization, and the organization is typically a large one—a government agency, a business firm, a church, a voluntary agency.

More than 100,000 American civilians work with a United States organization overseas; within this group
- about 33,000 are government people
- about 30,000 are missionaries
- about 25,000 are businessmen

What these Americans do is obvious from the scantiest survey of their daily lives: they are involving themselves in the "internal affairs of other nations." As we shall shortly see, the government people are conducting *foreign operations* as well as *foreign relations;* the missionaries are organizing "indigenous" churches; and the businessmen are throwing themselves into that process of modernization which is the economic face of twentieth-century nationalism.

The indictment that overseas Americans are "impatient" and "superior" is, indeed, quite directly the result of the functions they perform in other peoples' countries. They take the initiative in seeking and molding change; they introduce new products, new technical know-how, new political and military entanglements, new means of rapid communication, new definitions of God, and new attitudes toward man.

It was not always so. Hard as it may be for us to remember the fact, we still are only two decades removed from our last "Neutrality Act." In those distant 1930s we had virtually no military forces stationed abroad. We had refused to join either the League of Nations or the World Court. And only about 400,000 Americans, including tourists and naturalized Americans visiting their fatherlands, traveled abroad each year—perhaps one-tenth of the number who will visit abroad in 1960.

The world has changed, and perhaps the United States has changed most of all. The truly revolutionary scientific discoveries and industrial achievements of recent years have opened up startling gaps—between the rich nations with factories and the poor nations without factories, between explosive forces which man could unleash and his invention of institutions to control them, between the fantastic rate of technological change and the "deliberate speed" of social change.

The potentialities of large-scale industrialization have been demonstrated most vividly within the United States. Our gross national product moved from 100 billion dollars in 1910 (at 1950 prices) past the 450 billion dollar level in 1959. The stimulation of World War II, the rise of nationalism, and postwar prosperity have reversed many of the trends which were standbys in social science for decades. One such traditional expectation, for example, was that United States population would tend to level off, and eventually decline, the way the French population already had done, but the development reflected in American population figures belies such predictions. Perhaps most significant of all, the success of Western industry in creating rapidly rising living standards, dramatized for all by American prosperity, has sold to the non-European world the idea of "constant growth"—the most influential social idea of the twentieth century.

For the previous fifty-five hundred years of written history, and probably long before that, it was not "natural" for, say, the Chinese peasant to feel that he could be better off at the end of his life than he was at its beginning, or that his children and grandchildren had any right to expect a better break from the world than he himself had experienced. Indeed, he could consider himself fortunate if his family escaped the "normal" scourges and disasters—flood, famine, and pestilence. But now the idea is everywhere that men have some control of their own destiny, and some right to expect their rulers to improve the condition of the peoples' livelihood. For the first time in most of the world, people are beginning to relate the price of their rice to the nature of their government; they have entered the Triple Revolution of

- rising economic expectations
- rising resentment against inequality
- rising determination to be "free" (or at least to be independent of former masters).

The key political idea of this new era is nationalism; the key economic idea is industrialization. The operation of these two ideas, in achieving independence for a score of countries since World War II, in persuading their leaders to start up industries at all costs and to neglect their own farms and mines as "colonial" kinds of production, has removed from the Europeans a main prop they needed to keep up with the American rate of growth. The survival of Europe has thus come to depend crucially on new regional economic arrangements that make the most of Europe's big internal market. Both in structure and doctrine, the "multilateral" world of pre-1914 (which sturdily lived on in the mythology of the Bretton Woods agreements, the International Monetary Fund, and the United States Treasury) is dead in the real world.

All these varied trends—the growth of United States strength, the Triple Revolution in Asia, Africa, and Latin America, and the weakening of Europe—are to an important degree independent of the increasing military, cultural, and industrial threat to our society that has resulted from the success of the Soviet Union in making over a rather underdeveloped economy into an industrial nation in just forty years. The primary Communist challenge has been not the worker-based attack on the industrial system of the West, but rather the use of political power to bring about an economic transformation in the Soviet Union itself—followed by a vigorous and well-managed attempt to isolate the West from its former dependencies in Asia and Africa.

Faced with a competitor who evidently means to compete, the postwar generation of Americans has gradually become aware that it is not enough to "keep up" with the Russians in basic science and military technology and to "stand firm" against each successive threat to the curiously static ramparts of the non-Communist world. The Soviet threat has quickened our attention, hardened our resolution, speeded up our decision-making process, and increased our appropriations for military defense and foreign aid—and has carried still further the nations' mutual involvement in each others' affairs. The projection of the United States, and of individual Americans, into operations on a global scale in military, economic, social, and psychological fields would surely not have been so rapid if it had been left to unneedled American officials to decide how fast and how far to go in trying to build a world order. But the extraordinary change in the content of our international relations remains more the product of American than of Soviet strength.

The major change in U.S. foreign operations is the switch in emphasis from observation to participation. The emergence of the United States as a major political, military, commercial, and (in a measure) spiritual power has coincided with the blurring of traditional distinctions between internal and international affairs. As John Donne told us long ago, whether we like it or not "no man is an Iland, intire of it selfe," but rather "involved in Mankinde."

At State Department press conferences and in formal diplomatic statements today, there is still much talk about "noninterference in the internal affairs of other nations." But when one examines the true nature of contemporary American overseas operations, this ancient and honorable principle does not describe the present reality. The 160-year-old self-denying ordinance on entangling alliances with other nations was swept aside by the North Atlantic Treaty. The Marshall Plan, which gave economic transfusions to organized governments in Europe, managed to stay just inside a very broad interpretation of "noninterference." But ever since we have begun to deal in earnest with the world's less developed areas, the principle of noninterference has become a manner of speaking rather than a method of action. The weakening of Europe and the rise of Asia and Africa have buried arm's-length diplomacy along with American "neutrality."

Any powerful nation today deeply affects the internal affairs of its many less-powerful neighbors. The broad purposes for which the United States tries to use this influence can be inferred from our national ideals: we want all men to have a rising standard of life and a growing measure of personal freedom. But how this massive influence of ours actually applies to other nations depends mostly on the individual Americans who carry power into action around the globe. Our book is about those Americans.

2 · Why Americans Leave Home

1

The overseas Americans come from all kinds of families and from every region of the United States. They grow to maturity like other Americans: they are dragged to church, sneak off to go fishing, manage the school baseball team, have dates and flirtations, awake to knowledge early or late, go to war, and get married. Somewhere along the line they decide to work overseas. At what stage of their lives do they make the decision—and why?

The timing of the decision to work abroad is fairly clear. Of the 224 overseas Americans who answered the query directly, only 46 said they had decided on overseas service before the age of 20. Most did not decide until they were more than 26 years old—from five to ten years after most youngsters must first solve that universal puzzle of adolescence, "What am I going to do when I grow up?" Overseas service evidently has not been regarded by most young people as a vocational bridge to be crossed at the time that they are deciding on their future occupations. The stereotyped belief is that missionaries supposedly decide on their calling earlier than others, but the biographies of the overseas Americans we interviewed do not support this belief.

When it comes to the *reasons* why Americans work abroad, the evidence from the written questionnaires is less helpful. Each respondent was asked to state the reason for his or her initial in-

terest in overseas service. Of the 288 reasons given (some people
mentioned more than one), many are more like proximate causes
than basic motivations.

Seventy-three interviewees said they took overseas jobs to improve their professional positions, or because they thought they
could be of more "service" than would be possible in America. Of
these, 26 specifically referred to having been persuaded to go overseas by some system of positive recruiting on the part of the church,
firm, or government agency by whom they were employed.

Seventy-two respondents said they wished to resume contacts
with friends or family abroad. A wartime marriage to a foreign-born
bride provided the motive in a few cases, as did parents at missionary or military posts for others. But most of these people were
those whose early memories glow with the stories told by family
friends returning from far-off places or who can quickly trace their
heritage back to Ireland, Germany, Scandinavia, or elsewhere. More
than one-half of all our interviewees had one or more grandparents
born outside the United States, and nearly one-fifth of them were
the children of foreign-born parents. To the extent that the immigration laws in this century have permitted, the United States has
been provided with a pool of Americans whose early experience
enhanced their motivation to work abroad.

Three other motives cited frequently were: wartime experience
abroad (mentioned 41 times), prior travel or a special love for
travel (40 times), and study or reading (33 times). The reasons less
frequently specified, but often implicit in some other responses, were
financial gain, escape, and sheer accident. Many a man went abroad
after reading the Federal income tax laws, and a United States Information Service (USIS) librarian admitted she took a foreign job
because she was "going stale in Baltimore" and had a yen for
exotic places. One man described it as "pure fluke," and another
simply as "chance."

Pasteur once said, in describing the process of scientific discovery,
that "chance favors the mind prepared." When our intensive interviews probed beneath the surface of the formal questionnaires, the
replies took on a little more life and color—and perspective. Time
after time, men and women who said at first that they were abroad

"by accident" revealed a deep-seated desire for travel to foreign places dating back to their earliest childhood experiences:

> *People who had been abroad were around me all my life* [said a USIS research director]. *My father had been in Europe in World War I and loved to talk about it. He had been an escape artist and escaped from prison 16 times. . . . It's funny, you know, I remember that my high-school yearbook, under my picture, said that I would be a Chinese diplomat. How they ever got that idea I don't know. . . .*

> *My father* [said another overseas worker] *had numerous friends who were Arctic explorers and others of the same kind. I met a number of these men when I was small, including Admiral Byrd. These contacts probably stimulated me to read. I did read a lot as a result. In school I was always quite interested in travel and in traveling, much more so than in sports. . . .*

Not every small boy had a chance to meet Admiral Byrd. But an imaginative child does not need so much reality to stimulate his castle-building. One New Englander, groping to explain the love of travel that had brought him to Yugoslavia, came up with a rationale that will seem weak only to those who do not respect the power of a child's dream to motivate the actions of the grown-up he becomes. "I always liked water," he said. "However, I never had anything more than a small rowboat. Maybe I got interested in the Foreign Service just because you have to cross the water to get overseas."

The early influences vary widely, of course, but they are part of a common pattern: an incident or an atmosphere in home or school piques a youthful curiosity and creates a desire to go to unusual places, do unusual things, and see unusual people. A political officer in an embassy had a father who engaged in foreign trade: "We had a lot of foreign visitors come to the house and I was fascinated by some of the stories I heard. History came alive through these stories." A biochemist on an ICA university contract had a father who hauled lumber by ship: "He used to talk about his travels. He traveled the Straits of Magellan three or four times. He visited every port in the world. He'd say he would do it all over again."

Not only people but also things can excite the imagination of a potential young overseasman. "We always had the *National Geographic* all over the house," said the overseas representative of an American publishing house, "and as I look back we were always talking about places." "My father read more newspapers than any man I ever knew," echoed a USIS cultural affairs specialist. "He read an average of five newspapers a day, including the London *Times.*"

If it was not foreign newspapers or travel magazines, it was stamps or postcards. One of our interviewees reminisced, "I remember meeting a man . . . I guess you'd call him an international tramp. At one time he'd been in the French navy. Well, he kept on traveling around and he used to send me back postcards from very many places." Is it "accidental" that the boy who received these cards is now an officer in the United States Navy, working with a military-aid program?

In another case, stamps and foreign friends were obvious landmarks on the road that led to a Foreign Service career: "There was a friend of mine in school who was a Russian Jew. He gave me stamps. He had some family in Moscow. He had a grandmother who didn't speak English at all. I was always going to his home and he to mine."

Books, too, provide the impetus to work abroad. An American pilot was unhappy flying around the United States; wanting to get overseas, he took a job with Ethiopian Air Lines (which is staffed by Trans World Airlines under contract with the Ethiopian Government) to get to Africa. Why did he especially want to get to Africa? "I remember reading as a kid Teddy Roosevelt's book on game hunting in Africa." It was not that as an adult he still wanted to hunt big game; indeed, what this man most wanted was to fly airplanes. But the pull of Africa survived the disappearance of the childhood reason for wanting to go there.

Extending the horizons of the young is the special business of teachers, and it is not surprising to find a number of overseas Americans attributing that first peek beyond the culture curtain to a schoolteacher or college professor.

> *I certainly didn't know anything about other countries when I was a kid* [said a field adviser for an oil company]. *But at Tulane I got some good ideas of foreign countries,*

> *even the Middle East. The history professor dealt with*
> *a lot of countries separately.... From that ... I got in-*
> *terested in the differences among people.*

Not every child has the native imagination to be fascinated by
chance conjunction with the exotic. It is certain, moreover, that for
every person who acts on these early interests, there are many who
do not have enough of the maverick in their make-up to translate
childhood fantasy into overseas employment. But there does seem
to be more than a purely coincidental relationship between vicarious
associations with foreign travel in an American's youth and his decision to work abroad in later life.

                                    2

Given an initial inclination to try working overseas sometime, the
incidents that propel an American into a specific job abroad are almost infinitely varied. Two examples, out of a possible two hundred,
will illustrate how fortuitous are the decisions that determine a
person's life in a free society:

> *I met my wife in February of '45. That's while we were*
> *in the Margeval area. We were unloading a bunch of am-*
> *munition and I was supervising the unloading when a*
> *bunch of girls came along and she was the only one who*
> *could speak English. You know, we were just passing the*
> *time of day....*
>
> *I went to Washington on spring vacation. Called some-*
> *one and he said how about going to Afghanistan. Sheer*
> *coincidence. Did my undergraduate thesis on this country.*
> *Influenced by my roommate from Afghanistan to choose*
> *this subject. I got this roommate because I was the only*
> *person who listed on room form that I had no preferences*
> *racially for a roommate.*

Neither of these reasons for deciding to work overseas is nearly as
accidental as it is represented to be. A young adult who is attracted
to the idea of marrying a foreigner or deliberately seeks an unusual
roommate, is clearly one who is "accident prone" for overseas
service.

For the generation of overseas Americans we studied (their median age was 41), World War II constituted the most universal "accident." Although World War II was an appalling disaster for millions of people, it evidently propelled many of those who survived into careers as overseas Americans. "You know," a Foreign Service officer said with a smile, "maybe war once in a while is a good thing to shake people up. Often what they do afterward is better. After a war you can make a clean break and start in almost anything." The American communities overseas are full of people who would still be rooted to United States soil if a national emergency had not torn them loose and made them available for an "accidental" shove into a career abroad.

The evidence does not go so far as to suggest that the nation's armed forces are a notably efficient device for learning about international relations. "Actually," a former G.I. told us, "being in an infantry outfit of that sort didn't tell you very much about a country. It was like being in a great big boy scout camp. You've got to be able to sit still for more than a couple of days at a time in order to get to know a country."

"In the Navy," said an ex-officer now with the State Department, "none of us were interested in international affairs. I spent what spare time I had reading novels. Looking back I can't imagine, in the Navy, reading books on international affairs in the atmosphere and the environment we were in."

Yet the very fact of being away from home, of being thrown together with all kinds of people, whets the interest of those whose backgrounds incline them to try working abroad at a regular civilian job. And even if there is little occasion to study foreign cultures or diplomatic history, military service does result in some training in political awareness and how to get along in a bureaucracy—training which, as we shall see, is invaluable for every type of overseas career.

The influences of an intermediate factor like World War II, however, should not be overstressed. Many veterans, it is true, sought interesting work abroad, but most Americans promptly returned after the emergency to moorings from which they had been wrenched loose. In any event, it is more important to analyze those

motives that move men and women into overseas service when the
need is not so regrettably clear as it is in wartime.

3

The most common motives that propel overseas Americans into
taking on their first peacetime assignment abroad seem to be these
three: a sense of vocation, the lure of greater financial rewards, and
the desire to escape from uncongenial surroundings at home. (The
motives for remaining in overseas service, as we shall see, are related to, but not the same as, the urge to try it the first time.) Most
overseas jobs are not available to people who merely have a vague
interest in internationalism and in working abroad; they are open
specifically to economists, salesmen, radio technicians, theologians,
political reporters, schoolteachers, and administrators—people who
can do the kinds of work that need to be done.

The initial decision to work abroad is frequently made because of
the possible professional benefits. The overseas job often carries more
responsibility than a comparable position at the same level in America would carry. Young engineers, for example, find that they are
more likely to be placed in charge of a large field construction job
abroad than at home—if they are willing to trade some physical in-
convenience for the opportunity. An American executive hired to
help run a small airline in an underdeveloped country was quite
clear about why he preferred to manage air traffic in Asia or Africa
rather than settling down in a similar job in the United States:

> *You see, one thing about this country is that you do
> everything in a little country. Sometimes you're the only
> one around. You're the one who decides whether an air-
> craft will take off or not, whether the load will make money
> or not. You have an unlimited amount of authority; no one
> tells you what you can do and what you can't do. You have
> responsibility.*
>
> *Back in the States with a big airline, even the district
> manager—he can't change the schedule. He's got to wire
> the home office.*

An equally compelling motive is the desire of many Americans,
apparently frustrated in their drive to make a contribution at home,

to feel that they are needed. In many countries the very environment which repels some Americans—poverty, dirt, disease, ignorance, misunderstanding of America, primitive methods of work—calls others to a mission of uplift and reform. The greater the need, the more intense can be the desire to bring modern techniques, better explanations of United States foreign policy, better schools and hospitals, more food for the starving. The greater the odds against success, the more noble the effort to overcome them. We are accustomed to this paradox in the case of churchmen. What is less commonly known is the existence of a similar sense of service among the practitioners of such worldly professions as private investment, military training, and public administration. The advertising copywriter who first suggested that recruitments for national service could be publicized under the slogan "The U.S. Needs *You*" was tugging at a universal heartstring.

A lively sense of service is to be found also among political appointees to government posts abroad; indeed, a successful businessman can often be recruited for executive work in foreign operations only by persuading him that he has an obligation to serve. Here the obligation may not be to the poor and downtrodden of the underdeveloped world, but to the U.S. Government.

As a Public Affairs officer for the USIS recalls:

> *In the early part of 1950 some friends had been out to the first atomic tests. This was during the Truman Administration. I started cussing out Truman. One man pointed out, "That's fine. That's all well and good to scream and yell, but what are you doing about it? I have seven top jobs in my department. I have three months to fill them in. If I can't fill them, I'm forced to take political hacks. I have talked to lots of people like you. They criticize, but they won't come in."*
>
> *And I said, "I'm not interested. Not at all. I'm not qualified and not interested." Well, many Scotches later he said, "If the Government asked you to serve in these troubled times, would you? . . ." I think they had just announced that Russia had the atomic bomb. . . . I said, "Of course I would," and he came up the next day for brunch. He had the government forms and he said, "I'm going to call your bluff. I'm*

*going to call you on what you said last night." So I filled
out the form and promptly forgot about it.*
Fifteen months later the Scotches had worn off, but the sense of
obligation remained; he went to Egypt. After six years he was still
abroad with USIS and was looking into the possibility of lateral
entry into the regular Foreign Service.

4

In spite of the small number of our interviewees who admitted on
their formal questionnaires that lucre was a lure for them, it seems
likely that, as an inducement to overseas service, financial benefits
rank at least equally with a selfless desire to aid a cause. By and
large, a man is paid more for working abroad than for doing the
comparable job at home—and his family can often live overseas
less expensively.

A candid generalization of this sort is bound to be greeted with
catcalls of rebuke from the overseas Americans as a group. The
exceptions which prove the rule are hereby granted. The American
mother abroad who must maintain and visit her children in a far-
off United States college needs every cent of the family income. So
does the husband who must foot high hospital bills, support distant
relatives, or suffer capital losses due to his inability to supervise his
investments in real estate or the stock market. Vacation periods are
a big financial drain both for families and for single Americans in
corners of the world remote from home.

Nevertheless, in countries where the annual per capita income is
$237 (Japan) or $59 (India), even the normal income of a United
States citizen places him in the category of the gods, in terms of
material if not of spiritual rewards. Government people and businessmen generally have bigger houses, more servants, and access to
cheaper food and liquor than they would have in Long Island or
Long Beach. Private citizens, from missionaries to movie stars, do
not pay Federal income tax on a part of their earned income if they
stay abroad for eighteen months. (Things are getting tougher,
though: a first sign of nascent development in the "underdeveloped
areas" is their tendency to tax resident foreigners at least as heavily

as the foreigners would be taxed at home. Some firms find it necessary to get around the local revenue regulations by depositing "bonus" payments, which are difficult to tax, directly in their executives' bank accounts in the United States.)

Taking everything into account, one American business wife in Indonesia said she and her husband are "spending half as much and saving twice as much" as they would in the United States. One ICA mission chief in another country figured he would lose $10,000 a year if he were transferred back to Washington. A United States information officer in southern Europe, without family, managed to live quite adequately on his overseas allowances, banking his entire salary.

These are, admittedly, extreme cases. But American business and government families generally do live well overseas, and most of them are able to save money—unlike most of their friends at home.

Americans abroad are also pleasantly aware of (and equally reluctant to discuss) such fringe benefits as tax-free housing allowances or company-supplied quarters, post exchange privileges, excise-free luxuries such as liquor, and favorable local currency-exchange rates (though on this score the advantage sometimes runs the other way). The result is a higher standard of living that often costs less than it does at home.

To be sure, the ability to save money on a foreign assignment sometimes has to be paid for in psychic wear and tear—the many anxieties, the adjustments to climate, the monotony and aching legs from too many stand-up cocktail parties, the special frustrations of cross-cultural dealings on and off the job. "It's awfully fatiguing talking to foreigners," says a character in an Agatha Christie story. "I expect it's because they're so polite." Moreover, not all Americans enjoy striking economic advantages abroad. Many of the religious missionaries are paid tiny salaries by American standards—and even so must worry about living on a standard higher than that of the local residents.

A banker with long experience in the Orient summed it up:

> *An American has to be induced to go abroad. After all, if a man is to move his family halfway around the world and go out to a strange place, he has to have a real inducement. Now, I've observed the English and the Dutch. They*

> *came from smaller countries, where there were less oppor-*
> *tunities. Their businessmen seem to go abroad just to be*
> *able to have a job.... But not the people in the United*
> *States.*

5

"Of course I just came abroad to escape! I say so in my questionnaire." So spoke a much-tried American woman in service abroad
after describing her hysterical thrice-married mother, her ne'er-do-
well first husband, her sadistic second husband, an extracurricular
marquis in Spain, and a persistent Englishman in Latin America.
Only she and one other person—the librarian from Baltimore—
volunteered "escape" as a reason for going abroad; the other 242
wrote down less embarrassing explanations, a few even skipping the
question entirely. Yet in the subsequent interviews, most of the overseas Americans indicated in one way or another that they felt pushed
as well as pulled into service abroad.

One of the most successful directors of an American aid mission
in Asia is by his own account "an escapee:" he inherited a farm in
the South and managed it, while hating it, for years. He finally sold
out and went to Washington to get an international job—spurred
by his wife who had always been fascinated by missionary work.
And one cannot help but admire the "escape motivation" of an
architect and his wife who picked up and left Manhattan to design
buildings for the government in Indonesia. "Why are we here?" his
wife repeated. "Well, one year we just got tired designing show-
rooms for brassières!"

"Escape" has come to be a bad word in our lexicon; yet it is, of
course, a very important ingredient in that mixture of motivations
which builds successful careers. Poets and painters often gravitate
into fine arts because they did badly in sixth-grade arithmetic; some
of the leaders in our urban culture are boys for whom there was no
room on a submarginal farm.

The librarian who said she "got fed up with the problems of
disciplining teen-agers" in Baltimore is surely an exception to some
rule: many other librarians and teachers in that city probably feel
quite as resentful of the leather-jacketed young, but they doggedly

continue to live in Baltimore. The Foreign Service officer who "saw no future" in his home town of 5,000 people because "there wasn't very much of anything to do there" was speaking from a rather specialized point of view; most of his fellow townsmen presumably find things to do, but they are not, of course, the things that would appeal to a boy itching to travel. Even the "escape" motive that is the most rational, that activating the man who cannot for the time being find any job in his own community, does not normally project the unemployed into foreign service. How many of the unemployed millions reacted as one engineer did to the recession in 1938?

> *Jobs were tight in the East that summer. I was having a few beers one night that summer with my friend next door when we decided it was South America for us. . . . My friend decided to go back and finish college, but I got a job on a freighter as a purser so that I could get to Argentina for $97. I wanted to go, to see a new place. I made up my mind I was going to like it, and I did, right from the start.*

Personnel officers who recruit for overseas service often say they look for evidence that an applicant is "escaping"—because that is a sure sign he is not the man they want as a representative abroad. The evidence produced from our interviews suggests a sharp second look at any such basis for rejection of overseas personnel. The key lies in what is being escaped *from,* and what attitude the situation has induced in the escaper. If the escape is from a job in which the person was unable to cope with the human relations involved, his chances of a better adjustment abroad are slim. If, however, the escape is from lack of challenge in the job at home, the chances are good that he may be eminently successful in an overseas post. "I wanted to go, to see a new place. I made up my mind I was going to like it." These are healthy reactions to an unhealthy economic situation at home. And if an applicant is escaping from being "average" or "hemmed in" or "intellectually starved," then the escape motivation, far from being considered an unfavorable quality in the applicant, should probably be regarded as a clue to just that out-of-the-ordinary American who may face with unusual zest the special adjustments required of overseas personnel. After all, the American pioneer was an escapist, too.

6

If these factors, in varying combinations, explain why Americans leave home, why do they stay away? For there is no doubt that impressive numbers of Americans are remaining abroad. A successful missionary is almost by definition a fixture in a foreign country until he retires. The main responsibility for American private enterprise abroad is carried by men who remain for many years in a foreign country; this is notably true of banking, manufacturing, mining, and all phases of the oil business (sales and shipping as well as production and refining), and only somewhat less so in the importing and exporting trades. The larger American voluntary agencies and foundations, such as the Ford and Rockefeller Foundations, the Asia Foundation, Radio Free Europe, and the American educational institutions in Egypt, Lebanon, and Turkey, are also increasingly staffed with people who are making a career of overseas work.

Government establishments overseas are likewise built around cadres of career leaders and administrators. Ordinarily, Foreign Service officers are in the diplomatic-consular business for life or at least for twenty years. The other State Department employees on the Foreign Service staff also spend long periods in overseas service; there are secretaries and code clerks who have worked at a dozen different posts and have no intention of returning to America until they are sent. The United States Information Service is so career-minded that there is currently (1959) a vigorous effort to persuade Congress that a special career service should be established for information people abroad. In the technical-assistance and development loan fields, and even among the burgeoning group of government contractors abroad (universities, private firms, and specialized public agencies), there is a large nucleus of people who are fashioning overseas careers by linking two-year assignments together in an infinite series.

"Working abroad is a catching disease," a relief administrator said. "The first time you go it's as if a drop of gypsy gets into your blood," said a woman who works for USIS. Why should this be?

The motivation to stay is a first cousin of the motivation to go in the first place. Elements of the initial drive are there, but exist in altered form. What may have started as a vague delight in the exotic ("The first time I saw the coast of Europe ... it was as though I was touching geography and history") becomes a chronic excitement about life and work in non-American surroundings. "In over a hundred people we have talked to, only two people have not liked it here," said a well-adjusted agricultural adviser in Ethiopia. "Almost all the technicians have taken two terms. There is just something fascinating about this country."

One of his colleagues loved it because he could tramp through the charmingly primitive countryside on weekends. But even the most sedentary official can get excited about the vicissitudes of an overseas bureaucracy:

> *The situation is always changing at any post abroad—there are new agencies and new functions* [an embassy administrative officer said with relish]. *Each year you have either more or less money than the year before, never the same.... Also, every two to four years you have a different post, and each one has different problems. Probably you have a different type of job every two to four years, especially if you're in the upper grades.*

It is the kind of person for whom variety really is the spice of life who finds himself at home abroad.

Other reasons for taking a first overseas job also undergo change. The financial lure has in many cases been converted into tangible assets in a savings account, together with vacation travel that would be unthinkable from a home base in Denver or Indianapolis. The desire to escape from uncongenial people or routine work is transformed into a warm feeling of being "one up" on Americans who sluggishly prefer life in the United States. After describing a recent crisis in his own work, an American working in Mexico City suddenly broke off. "You know," he mused, "it's odd that I have a brother who is content to be a clerk back in the States. Peculiar, isn't it?"

The other important ingredients in the mixed motives of those who stay in overseas service, factors that are not usually appreciated beforehand, are a greatly enhanced sense of service, a gratifying sense of importance, and an altered set of values so cosmopolitan that America begins to look like a good place to visit but not a good place to live.

The sense of service is least evident among businessmen working for their own companies, somewhat more evident among employees of firms and other organizations working for foreign governments, more evident still in government agencies, especially among government field men, and most noticeable of all in the reactions of voluntary-agency and missionary workers. As an agricultural adviser in the Middle East expressed it:

> *The Philippines was my first time out of the United States.... My first contact was in Manila but that was too much like Stateside. You didn't even know you left home. They had neon lights and all. But it was different in the field.*
>
> *I remember my first trip and our first stop in a little barrio. There must have been 700 little faces, standing in the sun, to listen to us. I felt I was starting life back where I had in 1923 in my home state. It left a lasting impression on me. All those eager little faces waiting, first of all, to see an American, and, second, to find out what this 4-H thing was all about. Yes, the eagerness in those faces was striking. You had to ask yourself what you could do for those kids within their barrio surroundings where they stood. In other words, my first impression was "Gosh, what an opportunity to spend a lifetime helping a sea of youth get started with ways of better living that they can use for the next fifty or sixty years."*

An equally important factor in keeping many Americans abroad is a gratifying sense of importance. Many say frankly that they enjoy the feeling of "being a big frog in a little pond." (A half-dozen interviewees volunteered this cliché to explain why they were making a career of overseas service.) "My husband deals with the cabinet ministers here," the wife of an industrial expert told us in one Far Eastern country. "He's just an engineer; if we were home, the Secretary of State wouldn't give him the time of day." In their offices, on their construction jobs, at their air bases and hospitals and trading posts and mission homes, Americans find that the power of the American nation rubs off on them personally. There may, as a foundation officer put it, be "a lot more problems than back home, but they are bigger ones—maybe that's why they don't irritate as much." A perceptive doctor had prescribed overseas service for this man to get him away from the piddling frustration of his position in the United States.

The pure form of bigfrogism was revealed in a comment by a government administrator:

> *There aren't many jobs like this back home. Here, I'm top man in administration. . . . I couldn't hold a top job back in Agriculture. To keep an outfit as large as this mission going, furthermore, is quite something. Being frank, here I am a big shot. Back home now, a man with my salary isn't able to be in a position where he can see the whole picture. There'd be four or five men in the same office. You wouldn't have control of anything. Anyway, to get to the top position, you'd need political pull, and you'd probably last there only a few years. Here there's so much more satisfaction in being in charge of everything. You can do something and know that you did it.*

This statement is unusual only in its frankness. Many other Americans said the same thing less bluntly. Bigfrogism, moreover, is a powerful motive in every category of overseas employment; even the missionaries are not free from the human urge to feel important. A missionary doctor told with zest of his efforts to build a hospital in a remote area: "The last part of the road is seventy-five miles, it had twenty fords in it and two bridges. . . . One time I walked the last hundred miles." His greatest reward may come in heaven, but he also feels that he is being amply repaid on this earth: "I think I have a pretty good name down there. A crowd gathers around, for instance, whenever I go back, and they always tell me that no one will ever replace me. Of course it's their custom, but it makes you feel warm-hearted."

The overseas American comes into every society outside of Western Europe with an automatic membership if not in the local aristocracy at least in a class several notches above his social position at home. His country has bought it for him with its military power, political prestige, and high industrial productivity. He deals not only with governments at top level; he has the kinds of special opportunities which would never come to him at home. Almost at will he—

and his wife—can meet princes, generals, or prime ministers (depending on the form of government at the time). The irrefutable evidence of bigfrog status is the opportunity to rub elbows with important American visitors.

Asked why she liked living in Taipei, one American wife did not hesitate for a moment. "I meet so many important people here—both Chinese and Americans—that I would never meet at home." The same thought was echoed and re-echoed in country after country as an argument for remaining in foreign service: "I've come into contact with Americans overseas that I would never have met in a thousand years at home." And indeed, to any post of any size there come literally hundreds of distinguished circuit riders traveling the international airways from city to city in search of wisdom in "the field" and the prestige of "having been there." If you live and work in Tokyo or Teheran or Tunis, you are indeed much more likely to meet a Senator or the Secretary of State or a famous columnist—or Louis Armstrong or Bob Hope—than you are to meet the same person if you live in the United States, even in Washington, D.C.

To some, the main reason for staying abroad is that the idea of going home is distasteful even to the imagination. "You see, if I were to go back there right now and walk down Broadway I'd have hayseed sticking out of my ears," a businessman reflected. Another did not worry about ridicule but recoiled from boredom: "We have a very nice little business back there, but it's dull as hell. It makes one shudder to think of eating five days a week with all the clients I'd have to eat with." Others are not so sure that even a dull job would be awaiting them at home.

Most Americans periodically develop an acute case of homesickness. The readiest antidote by universal testimony seems to be a trip home. Yet the stories about home leave follow a strikingly uniform pattern: Home loses some of its sweetness because the people there do not seem to share the overseas American's interest in life abroad. "If you've ever come back from even three years abroad and gone to your old home town, you know just how lonesome you can feel. Nobody could be less interested in you." So spoke a businessman in Mexico, and the sudden come-down he describes happens to hundreds of American families every year—and keeps them in overseas work:

> *The first time we got home leave, we rushed around and we saw everyone we knew. It was really one of the most shocking experiences I've ever had. We talked to them about interesting things that were going on in Djakarta and Taipei and what not; they talked about what roses would grow best in the shade. It was just terrible....*
>
> *In my home town there are probably many people who still don't realize that the world is round. I remember when I got home from Moscow people asked me how it was there, but before I could open my mouth, they would begin telling me how Uncle Charlie had broken his arm. They profess interest in things abroad, but they really aren't interested.... Despite all that though, I could probably go back and live perfectly well in the States. In a couple of years I would be just like them. We Americans are pretty smug people.*

This lively disappointment at not being valued at home as you are abroad is hardly a new phenomenon in the world. But the fact that so often the overseas prophet is without honor on his home-town Main Street helps many an American family decide on another tour of duty abroad.

3 · Culture Shock

1

Whatever his background, his motive, and his professional field, the American who has elected to serve overseas faces the necessity of making important physical and psychological adjustments to both the living conditions and the work. The success or failure of his career abroad may depend largely on how well he can make these adjustments.

It is not necessarily the major differences between cultures that bother the newcomer the most. People who go abroad generally expect things to be different in large and predictable ways: there will be unusual scenery, curious garb, a strange tongue, and those major inconveniences which are an expected part of work abroad. What seems to create so much trouble is something more subtle and more intimately subversive—the feeling of inadequacy that results from not knowing quite how to act among strangers who themselves seem to know just how to act. The description of his surroundings by an overseas American is quite likely to sound as if he had wandered through the looking-glass:

> In using a saw, we push but they pull [said an American professor in Japan]. We push a plane along the wood, but they pull it. When a Japanese is given a form to sign, he signs it first and reads it afterward with unquestioning acceptance; an American will read the fine print first before

*signing it. Even academic procedure is different. At com-
mencement ceremonies the Japanese give their degrees out
before the commencement speeches are delivered; in America we make the students wait for their degrees until after
they have heard the speeches.*

The sum of sudden jolts that await the unwary American abroad
is known as "culture shock." Kalervo Oberg, an anthropologist attached to an ICA mission in Brazil, captured the big psychic
trouble that little things can cause when he wrote a memorandum
that has now been used in many overseas-training programs:

*Culture shock is precipitated by the anxiety that results
from losing all our familiar signs and symbols of social
intercourse. These signs or cues include the thousand and
one ways in which we orient ourselves to the situations of
daily life: when to shake hands and what to say when we
meet people, when and how to give tips, how to give orders
to servants, how to make purchases, when to accept and
when to refuse invitations, when to take statements seriously and when not. Now these cues which may be words,
gestures, facial expressions, customs, or norms are acquired
by all of us in the course of growing up and are as much
a part of our culture as the language we speak or the beliefs
we accept. All of us depend for our peace of mind and our
efficiency on hundreds of these cues, most of which we do
not carry on the level of conscious awareness.*

*Now when an individual enters a strange culture, all or
most of these familiar cues are removed. He or she is like
a fish out of water. No matter how broadminded or full of
good will you may be, a series of props have been knocked
out from under you, followed by a feeling of frustration
and anxiety. People react to the frustration in much the
same way. First, they reject the environment which causes
the discomfort: "the ways of the host country are bad because they make us feel bad." When Americans or other
foreigners in a strange land get together to grouse about the
host country and its people—you can be sure they are suffering from culture shock. Another phase of culture shock
is regression. The home environment suddenly assumes a*

tremendous importance. To an American everything American becomes irrationally glorified. All the difficulties and problems are forgotten and only the good things back home are remembered. It usually takes a trip home to bring one back to reality.

Some of the symptoms of culture shock are: excessive washing of the hands; excessive concern over drinking water, food, dishes, and bedding; fear of physical contact with attendants or servants; the absent-minded, far-away stare (sometimes called the tropical stare); a feeling of helplessness and a desire for dependence on long-term residents of one's own nationality; fits of anger over delays and other minor frustrations; excessive fear of being cheated, robbed or injured; great concern over minor pains and eruptions of the skin; and finally, that terrible longing to be back home, to be able to have a good cup of coffee and a piece of apple pie, to walk into that corner drugstore, to visit one's relatives, and, in general, to talk to people who really make sense. . . .

Much of the growing literature on the overseas American deals with the two most extreme, most lurid, and least interesting types of reaction to culture shock—the Americans who "go native" and the Americans abroad who "never left home."

In the mirror of Asians' remarks about the recent American invasion of Asia, the sharpest comments are reserved for the "snugglers"—those Americans who feel that the way to overcome culture shock is to forget America and melt into a new, adopted nationality and culture. Many G.I.'s settled down in Japan after World War II and the Korean War—forming, too hastily, friendships that were often too intense to be lasting. In India there are Americans who profess an exaggerated admiration for everything Indian; their wives wear saris, their homes take on a native air, they lose no occasion to compare American culture unfavorably with the Indian. Sometimes the intoxication is the result of suddenly relaxed moral standards; sometimes it can be traced to the corrupting influence of sudden (relative) wealth, and the illusion that it can buy respect and love.

The snugglers want, quite simply, to belong. They are prepared to pay what they think is the price of belonging—the rejection of their own background as Americans. When they find that they cannot "pass" as Japanese, Indians or Arabs, when they realize they will always be outside looking in, the snugglers may neurotically turn their wrath and resentment on the foreigners who won't permit an American to escape his Americanness.

In popular literature about Americans abroad, the snugglers not infrequently turn up as heroes who, like those featured in *The Ugly American,* love everybody except their own American colleagues. Their capacity for love, moreover, bears a direct correlation to their nearness to the "village level," a phrase which is ordinarily not so much a geographic term as a euphoric state of mind and heart. Among these heroes, sentimentality is equated to goodwill, goodwill to "success" against the all-too-clever Communists. Their motto might be taken from the advice given us by Ghana's Prime Minister Kwame Nkrumah: "In Africa," he said, "love everybody you see." Their willingness to substitute sentiment for analysis makes them first cousins to the beachcomber with his string of mistresses, a staple in our fiction for close to a hundred years.

The "snugglers" thus enshrined in popular literature do, of course, exist in the real world too. A good many missionaries and a few technical-assistance people do in fact live at the "village level" physically or emotionally. But if they really go native they find their effectiveness is blunted; they have been sent, after all, not to embrace the whole of the local culture but to effect fundamental changes in that culture—in the direction of Christ, or modern medical practice, or steel plowshares, or some other aspect of "modernization."

At the opposite extreme from the snugglers are those Americans who in their single-minded ethnocentrism never do learn even the rudiments of adjustment. They do not even try, for they are preoccupied with a different problem: how to adjust the ways of others to the American norm.

It is not that these Americans lack goodwill or even (after their rather specialized fashion) love. What worries some of the current novelists is precisely the dangerous consequences of unleashing a limitless ration of American goodwill in the world. Graham Greene, for example, builds *The Quiet American* around an eager young man whose tendency to charge into unfamiliar territory with ready-made answers leads to his ruin and death.

This literary type, too, has its real-life counterpart. There is the construction foreman who cannot tell the difference between shift-lessness and a tradition of midday relaxation ("Look at those guys out the window there. They haven't moved a muscle for 20 min-utes"). To the mad dogs and Englishmen who traditionally go out in the noonday sun, a good many hardworking Americans must now be added. There is the self-confident driver of an oversized vehicle who complains "these people around here are about fifty years be-hind the times; they don't even know enough to get out of the way of a car." He solves the problem by shouting to the "stupid" peasants at the top of his (or her) voice—in English, of course.

To judge by the comments of America's foreign friends in many lands, the cheerful assumption that "American" is a synonym for "best" is even harder for them to take than snuggling is. The gist of many comments about the overseas Americans by their hosts abroad, comes down to something like this: "We resent your tak-ing for granted that the highest aspiration for any people is their quite natural desire to be American, or at least to be *like* Amer-icans."

It is true that some of the overseas Americans sometimes assume that what we have they could have if they would only work a little harder for it. Plumbing, electricity, macadam roads, clean houses, pretty hair-dos, universal education, freedom of religion, and the right to vote—all these seem to some Americans valid for all as primary goals of personal endeavor and the social process. They are confirmed in that feeling by the often uncritical admiration of West-ern-educated leaders in the newly developing areas, who have equal difficulty distinguishing between the possessions and the pur-poses of industrial society.

A perceptive Jesuit writer has phrased it very well indeed when he wrote:

> *Our own great American achievement has somehow be-come a positive psychological handicap. The United States has been a vast and successful working machine for con-verting into ourselves persons from every nation of the*

world. We have met the entire human race (provided they came to the United States) and have found ourselves able to deal with them successfully. We can make anyone over into ourselves ... [but] we cannot make ourselves over, even imaginatively, into other people. ... Our thoughtlessness is caught in our assumptions that what we do is never chauvinistic or nationalistic, though what others do may well be. Thus, for British missionaries to teach cricket or Canadian missionaries to teach lacrosse would be chauvinistic, but for American missionaries to teach baseball is not spreading American culture but merely enabling the benighted natives to be human beings.*

Fortunately for themselves and the world in which they are intervening, most of the overseas Americans neither go native nor remain blissfully unaware of the relativity of the American Way. With more or less clashing of psychic gears, they do somehow adjust to work in a cross-cultural context. Moreover, their adjustment problems fall into categories so repetitive, so common to all types of activity and to a wide variety of different cultures, that the whole process of adjustment may with further study prove to be reasonably predictable.

Among the culture shocks that are associated with overseas jobs is the discovery that different peoples have widely differing concepts of time. The color line is even more shocking to some. Another shock is the realization that "human relations" are a much bigger part of the job than would be true of the comparable activity at home. Still another is the recognition that such useful American virtues as clarity of expression, equality of treatment, and informality of manner may strike others as neither useful nor virtuous but merely American.

2

A sales engineer in Japan says,
> *Yes, we do have trouble with them sometimes in regard to time. We'll make an appointment, for instance, to go all*

* Walter J. Ong, "That American Way," *America*, November 22, 1958.

the way across the island. Fourteen hours on a train and then when you get there—you'll find that they're not there. I think it's reluctance on the part of our [Japanese employees] to pin those bastards down. Whereas we think we have an appointment at 2:00 sharp, and to them it's actually no appointment at all. We'll call up and say, "Well, we might drop around if it's convenient" and stuff like that, and they make a lot of polite noises and we'll think we have an appointment. We want to be specific and they're not specific.

The world is strewn with the wreckage of collisions like this between the American and other cultures. Appointments to do business (religious and government business as well as sales and manufacturing business) appear to be the most frequent casualty of contrasting concepts of time. If an American is invited to an eight o'clock dinner, the chances are he will arrange to get there between five and fifteen minutes after eight. His Scandinavian friend will have arrived on the dot of eight, very likely carrying a gift. A Latin may politely come to the same dinner at nine, some Ethiopians might come even later, and a Javanese, having courteously accepted the invitation in order to avoid any loss of face on the host's part, may not show up at all. "Time, in this country, is of no importance," said an experienced official of the United States embassy in Addis Ababa. "If you have an appointment at five you might as well show up at six because they're going to keep you an hour waiting anyway and they won't even think anything of it." Edward T. Hall points out in *The Silent Language* * that with us forty-five minutes is an "insult period" to be kept waiting in an outer office, whereas in some Latin countries forty-five minutes would not be at the tail end of the waiting scale but somewhere near its beginning.

A common complaint among the overseas Americans is that it takes so much longer to get anything done than it does (or than they imagine it does) at home.

Things don't go along here quite the way they do in the States—that is, bang, bang, bang [said a banker in Asia who may not have tried to do business with a branch bank in the United States]. It takes time [yet] many Americans

* Edward T. Hall, *The Silent Language*, Doubleday, New York, 1959.

*come out here allowing themselves one week. They end up
not accomplishing anything. You meet for tea and you talk
about generalities, vaguely about what your business is, and
then again you meet about a week later. Still you don't get
anything accomplished. Maybe at the third week and the
third meeting you sign a contract or you get your order.*

The impatience that the American shows under circumstances like
these was caricatured by a European hunter who had led many a
safari into big-game country. "The American is a fast person," he
said. "He expects to see and shoot the rarest gazelle in Africa within
the first half hour."

Even in Europe the pace often seems to Americans to be madden-
ingly leisurely; in Asia, Africa and Latin America it is far more so.
Americans must slow down and swallow their impatience—or risk
not doing any business at all. Many a delicate negotiation, nursed by
a local office for an unconscionable length of time, has been scuttled
by the arrival on the scene of a hard-driving executive sent out by
the home office to "get things moving." You cannot be in Tokyo
many days without being told the story of the New York firm which
sent a man out to Japan to set up a contract, and told him it should
take about two weeks. After he had been there three months, two
vice-presidents of the firm came in and said, "Now we'll take over."
After they had been in Tokyo for a month, they saw the point. "You
get yourself a house," they told their man, "and we'll send your
family out."

From the point of view of the Japanese, the time was not being
"wasted"; it was being used to develop the trust on which a viable
business deal depends. The lunches, geisha parties, and country
weekends that punctuate a sales discussion in Japan are a way of
"getting to know you, getting to know all about you," as the teacher
sings it in *The King and I*. A Japanese businessman inquired of us in
genuine perplexity: "Unless the American with whom I am dealing
gets to know me, how does he know whether I mean what I say?
For that matter," he added after a moment's pause, "unless I know
him rather well, how do I know whether to say what I mean?"

For many American overseas businessmen "time is money," and
this equation makes cultural trouble for them all over the world.
For the government people time is measured not in dollars but in

two-year stints of overseas service; the American tendency to hurry too fast has been institutionalized in the practice of short-term assignments. We are still operating, as Rowland Egger of the University of Virginia has put it, under the handicap of "coping with ten- and twenty-year problems with four- or five-year projects manned by one- or two-year personnel." Government officials too easily develop the "two-year mentality," that determination to "wrap it up" within a time period set by American administrative practice rather than by the natural pace of economic development, military training, or political consent-building.

Just as a quick bargain revolts an Arab wazir, even if it favors him financially, so a negotiation at the government level must often be protracted in order to demonstrate that the matter is worth the attention of the prestigious officials involved. "Anyone will get impatient," said one well-adjusted educational adviser in Ethiopia. "There are times when things can be done with a quick decision, and it's slowed down because it would seem unimportant if things were done too quickly." Where time is not money, it often stands for some other measure of value; it therefore becomes important to learn what concept of time is involved in the business at hand. In Latin America, Dr. Hall points out, one often hears the expressions, "Our time or your time?", "*Hora americana, o hora mejicana?*"

3

For some Americans, the most severe culture shock results from the color line. It can be profoundly disturbing to find how seriously the color line is taken abroad and how impossible it is for a white person to escape *his* color. Our American tradition is to try to "depersonalize" color, to think (or at least to say out loud) that color is only skin-deep, to regard a man's individuality rather than his race as his most relevant characteristic. Americans are discovering all through Asia and Africa that the colored peoples of the world do not share this desire to subordinate the color line.

"We are colorblind," the Prime Minister of Ghana told us, but most Africans and Asians are nothing of the sort. One of the Prime Minister's associates, in fact, spoke in precisely the opposite vein: "If one of my own countrymen says I'm a fool, I will debate the question with him without emotion. But if a white man says I'm a fool, I react instantly and hotly, without thinking." He told of an incident in the Junior Common Room of his Cambridge college when a fellow student mentioned Euripides in some connection and then paused, looking at the African. The African promptly over-reacted: "Yes, I do know about Euripides," he said. "You see, I've climbed *halfway* down out of the trees." That kind of instant de-fensiveness is buried just below the surface of the relations between white and colored peoples all over the world.

For the unsophisticated American, all types of skin color tend to be associated vaguely with American Negroes, and the results of this naïve assumption can be devastating. In Ethiopia a visiting Con-gressman made history in the winter of 1957 by seizing every speech-making occasion to boast of his Negro political associates in a Northern big-city congressional district. "There are no two better ward leaders than those colored boys in the whole district," he would say, unaware that both Ethiopians and Americans were squirming with embarrassment. The Ethiopians do not think of them-selves as Negroes, but rather as a Semitic people who trace their long history back across the Red Sea to the relations between King Solomon and the Queen of Sheba. Indeed, the word they use in their own language for "Negro" is said to be the same word that de-scribes the coal-black slave class on the Sudanese border.

Race prejudice is a subject filled with international political dyna-mite, and a basic tolerance of people who are different in appearance and social background is the beginning of wisdom in overseas service. "If you have an animosity toward any group other than your own, this tends to carry over to all foreign groups, I think," said an ex-perienced missionary in Iran. And dozens of Americans interviewed overseas placed lack of racial prejudice at or near the top of their lists of important personal qualities which anybody, no matter what his job, should possess for service abroad.

The one group that seems least able to forget about race differ-ences is the small minority of American Negroes who now work abroad, most of them with U.S. Government agencies. No figures are available on the number of Negroes now in overseas service, but it is clear that the number is growing. Negroes are especially encouraged to go into some programs, as information officers and ICA technicians, in part because of a widespread, if vaguely expressed, assumption that a colored person has an advantage over other Americans in dealing with the nonwhite peoples of Asia and Africa.

Many Negroes in Asia and Africa will assert, if asked, that it is indeed helpful in their work not to have white skin. Some American Negroes in Indonesia whom we interviewed on this point all regarded it as an advantage. One of them was so light-skinned that he had to keep telling the Indonesians he was really a Negro. "But my wife helps," he added. "She's quite brown-skinned."

"The Indonesians learned a lot from the [Bandung] conference," said another. "They developed a feeling of solidarity with other people with dark skins."

"It's much easier to enter into certain circles," said a third. "They ask us many questions. It's easier to get the Indonesians to talk. For example, if I talk before a group, they all ask question after question. Things like race relations. They relax with me.... You can go anywhere...."

In Ethiopia a Negro member of the ICA mission got involved with an Ethiopian woman, and all concerned agreed he should be sent home. The ICA tried to get the Ethiopian Government to say they did not want him back and ran into a blank wall. "You see," explained the man's American supervisor, "the Ethiopian Government was afraid that someone would accuse them of being prejudiced!"

There are, however, two sides to the question of sending American Negroes into foreign service. While the Negroes abroad on the whole felt their race an asset, their white colleagues were by no means unanimous on the subject. A special investigation of opinion on this point in Indonesia produced several arguments against assigning Negroes there. The Indonesians themselves, according to some white Americans, are prejudiced against darker peoples, and most American Negroes are darker than they. ("The Ethiopian compares himself to the southern gentleman, not to the colored slaves," said an Armenian in Addis Ababa.) Many Indonesians believe, not without cause, that the Negro often is a second-class citizen in the United States. They therefore feel insulted when Negroes are sent out as representatives of America to Indonesia, implying that the

Indonesians themselves are second-class people. They harbor doubts that such "second-class citizens" could be as well qualified as the comparable white American would be, for their image of the Negro is the Southern sharecropper, not the graduate student in New York or Chicago. Some Indonesians feel that Negroes are sent out to Asia merely to prove something which the Indonesians believe to be untrue: namely, that Americans treat Negroes well.

A reverse discrimination results from the morbid interest of colored peoples everywhere in the treatment of the Negro in America. One Negro doctor who worked in China a decade ago used to complain that he could hardly saunter down the streets of any city without somebody stopping him and pleading: "Tell us about the persecution in America!"

And the pretty wife of a Negro Foreign Service officer in Asia asserted that she had never really wished to be white until she met this reverse discrimination. The Indians, she complained, smother you with such maudlin kindness and pity that you find yourself wishing you could be treated like "an ordinary American." If the white Americans are conspicuous in Asia, the American Negroes are far more so. Like other Americans, therefore, they are often uncomfortable in their role as curiosities on parade.

4

For the observant overseas American, the signs of unusual sensitivity to human relations are around him no matter where he finds himself. Universally, it seems, these signposts are, so to speak, printed in larger letters than would be true in the United States: they are more emphatic, more of the essence of life and work. There is the protocol of where to sit, when to leave, how long to carry on the small talk before the real subject of conversation is broached—matters which certainly arise in American social intercourse, but in a more muted and subtle way. To Americans there seems to be an exaggerated insincere obsequiousness in other societies, the bowing and scraping, the flowery introductions and leave-takings, the endless formal handshaking. There is the playing of the "*après-vous,* Alphonse" game every time the American goes through a door. Chinese officials told us how one American in Taiwan resented their insistence that he should get into a car first. "Why," he would complain, "should I climb in and then have to hump myself all the way across the car seat just so some Chinese can get in comfortably?" He never perceived that his Chinese hosts were trying to do him honor by having him go first.

In this environment what passes for American "impatience" is often merely the common American tendency to pay attention to business, to subordinate personal relationships. Despite the contributions made recently to our human relations by the experts in group dynamics, it seems a fair generalization to say that in most parts of the world people set a higher relative value than we do on the niceties of interpersonal relations. It is this, in turn, which misleads so many overseas Americans about what is "falsehood" and what is "truth." Part of culture shock is the discovery that truth, like time, is relative.

After an experience as administrator of the U.N. Relief and Rehabilitation Administration in China a dozen years ago, one of the authors tried to explain how he learned about the importance of interpersonal relations and the relativity of truth.

> *I often observed that, in talking to a Chinese official, I could not count on the official's undivided attention to the substance of the matter under discussion. He often seemed less interested in the subject matter than I, and correspondingly more sensitive to the invisible interpersonal electricity that was generated by our conversation. I would be trying to get agreement that the distribution of wheat would begin in Hunan Province next Tuesday morning at 9 o'clock. But his objective in the same conversation was wholly different: to make me feel good during our conversation, to make sure I did not lose face while he was with me. I wasn't worrying about my "face," but he was worrying about it for both of us. If he guessed that I wanted his agreement about starting next Tuesday morning, he would cheerfully say yes. But his "yes" could not be taken as agreement. It could be taken only for an expression of generalized goodwill toward me, a check drawn against an account that would expire as soon as we parted. Certainly it had nothing whatever to do with what I considered the*

object of the whole exercise, the distribution of relief
supplies in Hunan. For me, "truth" lay in an accurate ex-
pression of our mutual intentions about the relief program.
For him, "truth" was to be measured by my morale, my
"face."

Americans by the thousands have had to learn by embarrassing
experience about the "Oriental yes"—the one that means "yes," or
"maybe," or "no," depending on the circumstances. "These people
will look you straight in the eye and lie in their teeth," was the gist
of dozens of interviews on this point. ("In the East, to say 'no' is
very rare," said an Asian politician with a flair for American slang.
"The greatest crime is not to say an untruth, but to hurt the other
guy.") In some of the languages of Asia, the word for "no" is almost
never used or is the same as the word for "yes." An American investigating the mysteries of Indonesian culture reports this revealing
exchange: "Do you mean to tell me," said the American, "that you
say the same word whether you mean 'no' or 'yes'?" "Certainly," was
the reply, "If I mean 'no,' I will say 'yes' with my mouth and 'no'
with my face—or with my actions later on." (There are, of course,
examples of the "Oriental yes" in reverse. An ICA official in Japan
gave us one example: "You know, it's a funny thing about the Japanese. They'll think things are all set when we tell them we are going to
take it under advisement. They don't realize that we mean 'No'.")

In this atmosphere the American may not accomplish what he
intends to by being his straightforward self. There is no doubt
that easy familiarity is an identifiable American trait. The shock
of adjustment begins when the American overseasman suddenly
realizes that getting familiar is not regarded by most of the world's
peoples as the equivalent of getting friendly.

In the American culture, it is a sign of trust to look a man in the
eye. In Japan, it is more polite to avert your gaze while talking.
To the American, a firm handshake is a sign of warmth and friendship. But to many peoples of other cultures, the very physical contact involved in shaking hands is an unnatural form of intimacy.
Americans are often baffled by the fact that they cannot lean out of
the car window and with a word or two get explicit directions from
a peasant in the road. They fail to realize that they should beat
around the bush a bit, that the peasant in his turn is expected to put

his head on one side, scratch an ear, exhale through his teeth, and make two or three false starts—even if he understands your destination and knows perfectly well how you are to get there. It would not be polite for him to say so right away; that would indicate that the question had been too simple to be worth asking, and the questioner would thereby lose face.

If you tell an American he is "open," "direct," "straightforward," "approachable," he will take these words as compliments. But right on the same continent with us an Indian or a Mexican may regard these same attributes as signs of weakness, hallmarks of the untrustworthy. One Mexican analyst of the Mexican character put it this way:

> *The popular language reflects the idea of defending ourselves against the outside: the idea of "manliness" consists in never "opening ourselves." Those that "open" themselves are cowards. For ourselves, contrary to what occurs with other people, to open oneself is a weakness or treachery. The Mexican can give in, humiliate himself, lower himself, but never open himself; that is, allow the outside world to penetrate his intimate being. The one who is opened is little to be trusted, a traitor or a man of doubtful fidelity, who tells secrets and is incapable of facing dangers as he ought....* *

In spite of the hints with which they are literally surrounded, many overseas Americans seem inclined to believe that their safest course is to be themselves, to stick to the simple straightforward friendliness which is so strong in our American upbringing. Supposedly, friendliness and honesty are what other peoples like best about Americans. Yet because of the thousands of nuances in personal relationships, developed in some cultures over thousands of years of crowded living and preoccupation with "face," the Asian or African is less likely to applaud the American for his friendliness and honesty than to view him askance for his seeming lack of manners or lack of guile. A Western-educated African diplomat put it succinctly: "Americans don't realize that what they consider normal is irritating to others."

* Quoted by John M. Fayerweather, *The Executive Overseas,* Syracuse University Press, Syracuse, New York, 1959, p. 174.

In Indonesia we were told a story that illustrates the special complexity of adapting one's manners to a society given to indirection
and innuendo as a way of life. The story concerned a middle-class
Javanese boy who wanted to marry an upper-class girl. To discuss
the matter, the boy's mother went to the girl's house for tea with
her mother. Arriving for the visit, the middle-class woman did not
broach the subject at the door—we would not permit that even in
our culture of straightforwardness. So they sat down to tea. With
the tea a banana was served—a most unusual procedure. When the
tea was over, the middle-class mother took her leave, still without
having mentioned the subject of the marriage. The visiting woman
had read the sign: just as bananas do not go with tea, so her son
was not regarded as an appropriate mate for the upper-class daughter. Since nobody had mentioned marriage, nobody lost face when
the negative answer was given by indirection.

How many Americans would have read the sign? Is it not more
likely that the average American would have picked up the banana
and started to peel it while he raised the subject of the wedding
date?

5

The whole of American culture seems designed to make it difficult for Americans to move comfortably in many foreign cultures.
We are taught from early youth that clear thinking and lucid ex-
position are very important, that the syllogism is a reliable form of
logic. We treat "equality" as an object of worship; we believe that
all men have similar rights and obligations. A horizontal "man-to-
man" mutuality is better, we think, than any vertical ruler-subject
relationship: many American parents try to be pals to their children,
and the best thing that can be said of a public figure is that he acts
like an ordinary person. As a consequence, a defined protocol and
elaborate formalities are regarded in the United States as vaguely
un-American. In general, form is less important to us than substance,
and we consider them to be antithetical; we have difficulty appreciating the notion that form can be so important that it becomes a
matter of substance.

In all these elements of "culture" other peoples start from different premises. Clarity and cold-blooded logic are less appreciated in some societies than they are in the United States. Equality is often held to be a social vice, not a virtue. Informality is positively offensive in cultures that set great store by the elaborate formalities by which people do business with each other.

Thus in many societies, for example, the syllogism is too embarrassingly obvious to be acceptable as a form of logic. A Jesuit missionary in Japan described how a famous Japanese preacher would "spend thirty minutes describing how beautiful something is and only about five minutes telling them what he really means to tell them. Yet that's just the way they like it." A Protestant missionary told of the difficulty college students had in adapting themselves to Japan—because they had been steeped in rationality.

> *Often it's the "A" students in America who do badly on the language out here because rationality doesn't count at all in studying a language. In Japan the man who is the best speaker is not one who is the clearest but one who can couch his ideas in beautiful phrases that just indicate. You get your ideas across by innuendo rather than by being clear.*

The philosophical strain involved in accepting so un-American a conception is part of what is meant by culture shock. The whole framework of our educational process, in which clear questions are asked in examinations with the purpose of eliciting from the student the single answer that is "right," has "unprepared" us for cross-cultural work. Hundreds of thousands of Americans are having to learn in the field, by the expensive method of trial-and-error, that clarity is not always the highest form of truth.

The error potential of that method is very great; for Americans who deal with non-American systems of logic the danger is not only that of being misunderstood, but of tending to deal only with those foreigners who are "honest" and "trustworthy"—that is, those who know English, have been educated in the West, are therefore the most Westernized, and, thus, the least representative of "true" opinion in the society at large. For millions of Americans, Charles Malik, the Foreign Minister of Lebanon and President of the United Nations General Assembly during 1958–1959, seemed a comprehensible and sensible exponent of Arab nationalism; but to the

majority of Arabs, including many of his colleagues at the American
University in Beirut, Dr. Malik was utterly unrepresentative of the
Arab world: "he talks just like an American now." In Iran one
embassy official had unconsciously fallen into this obvious trap:

> *I do have some very good Iranian friends. It's true that
> contact with Iranians can be discouraging if you are trying
> to get information. They won't respond to you in a direct
> way, they try to respond in a way they think will please
> you. They don't seem to realize that you are just trying
> to sort out the facts and get at the truth, so it's a waste of
> time trying to find out things from the average individual.
> But there are many alert, intelligent Iranians and I con-
> centrate on them.*

For "alert, intelligent Iranians" might be substituted "English-
speaking, Western-type Iranians." The question is whether, in the
operating diplomacy of the twentieth century, the Western-educated
layer in an Eastern society is an adequate source of all information
for an officer of the American embassy. A deeper wisdom was
evidenced by a nursing consultant in Mexico: "You have to be able
to recognize the mechanisms you use to get a 'yes,' because you
can get people to agree to something without there being any
agreement at all."

Our assumption that men are essentially equal likewise gets us
into trouble in organizing work to be done overseas. We tend to
believe that a man is admirable not so much for what he is, but for
what he can do. Moreover, a man should be willing to do any kind
of job required by the common good; work itself is honorable, no
less so if it involves rolled-up sleeves and physical exertion. But
these egalitarian ideas which have worked so well in taming the
American frontier are somehow out of place with the rigid lines of
caste, rank, and specialized function in other societies.

"If you put a truck driver back to wielding a shovel, he will feel
that it is a disgrace," said an American construction man in Iran.
"That's one of the main troubles in a diversified kind of work like
that in the oil fields."

"My God," said an executive of the Near East Foundation, "out
here in the field you often have to set up different kinds of meals for

different kinds of people, and all that sort of thing. It's difficult for Americans, including me, to accept that. The problem is to avoid offending upper-class people who want to be treated differently."

In the Japanese and some other languages, there are different forms for talking to different levels of people. One young American lawyer who married an American girl in Tokyo found that, to his bride's distress, he had to stop addressing her in a form implying equality; when they were with Japanese friends, he had to "kick her around with rough language," and she was expected to address him with elaborate respect.

Perhaps the hardest adjustment of all for Americans who have grown up in this environment is learning to appreciate the place of elaborate formalism in other cultures.

One clue to the significance of form, procedure and protocol is to note what kinds of form must be associated with a matter of substance to ensure that it will be regarded as important. In our society important decisions are often made in an atmosphere of personal informality and, by comparison with other countries, with little time for preliminaries and accompanying ceremonies. In many other cultures the importance of a deal is measured by the amount of formality in which it is encased, and by the duration and complexity of the preliminaries which lead up to it.

An importer in Japan explained how this worked in his own business:

> *Everything here is done by indirection. . . . In the United States, I imagine a very aggressive sales approach probably makes a great impression, while caution and mild-manneredness are probably not good at all, but here the latter are perfect. In America, furthermore, in selling, youth is good. Here a little gray hair makes a great impression. . . . Many times when I, myself, go out on business to make a call, I take a very senior Japanese or an older American whose job often is just to smile and nod. He may not know anything about what we are doing. He doesn't have to play any role, except providing prestige. I have one very old Japanese colleague whom I often take. He makes quite a big impression. All such a person has to do is sit like an*

old bullfrog and just grunt and make an impression. Japanese are also great respecters of scholarship. The more degrees one has the better. This too even helps in business. For example, we have a very senior German on our staff, ...and really his main function is just being around and having his degree. He really impresses the Japanese.

One elderly American in Tokyo described with a tolerant twinkle how he is often asked, "Mr. T——, will you come along with me? We want to use your face to talk on."

And another American, addressing himself to this point during his interview, suddenly broke off and said to the interviewer: "Now, for instance, doctor, if you had been doing it the Japanese way, you would have come here with two or three assistants at least and then a couple of secretaries to take notes. You'd have to have a lot of people around. You certainly wouldn't have come here alone the way you have."

The precise nature and intensity of the culture shock that awaits Americans when they first arrive in a foreign land will vary, of course, not only with the country involved but with the atmosphere in the American community there, its purposes and spirit, its composition, its facilities. But in one form or another, the experience of culture shock is probably common to new recruits in overseas service everywhere.

4· The American Family Abroad

1

Nearly a quarter of a million American wives are now living abroad with husbands who work for the government, business firms, churches, and foundations. Culture shock affects both man and wife when they venture abroad for the first time. But the husband's shock is cushioned by the comfortable continuity of his profession —he spends most of his time soldiering, engineering, teaching, or whatever he has been doing at home. The wife is the one who must transplant family life to new surroundings, build new friendships, adjust to dirt and heat in the home, worry about health and schools, get used to the invasion of her privacy by omnipresent servants, and try to learn a strange tongue in two or three distracted hours a week.

The initial shock is by universal testimony the roughest part of the experience. An agricultural scientist in Mexico described how the burden of adjustment fell on his wife:

> There were maids in the home, but we didn't speak Spanish. We just barely managed to eke out three meals a day. My wife felt terribly deficient and depressed. She wanted desperately for us to pack up and go home the fourth week we were here. I'll never forget it. She just said she didn't see how she'd ever make it. The people were so different in attitude and response. Other members of the staff and their wives helped out. But part of it was my own

fault. I wanted to get off to a running start, and I hit work like a ton of bricks and completely neglected my wife and family in those first days.

The term "culture shock" is often loosely applied to cover all forms of adjustment overseas. But the very first shock is more intimately physical and sensory; it assails the nostrils, the ears, and the eyes. A family can leave New York by air and fifty hours later be on the other side of the world, suddenly turning the clock of civilization back several centuries as measured by American standards of wealth, sanitation practices, and population control.

Consider the psychological adjustment required of a family moved suddenly from Chicago to Calcutta. To the visitor from another land, Chicago has its fantastic aspects, but to the average American woman, in particular, Calcutta is a nightmare of almost sickening intensity. Incredible hordes of people, wrapped, clothed, swathed, scantily covered with flowing robes, white dhotis, billowing pajamas, half-torn shirts, ragged scraps of cloth . . . the heads in turbans, the hoods . . . the saris of green and red and star-studded blue swirling around the frail, barefooted women . . . a red dot on their temples, a red line painted through the part in jet-black hair . . . crowds of people on modern streets, more crowds of people teeming in dirty tenement blocks . . . the wooden hovels, the cheap tin and textile shops jammed in motley rows . . . the taxis and the trolleys, packed with dense humanity, men clinging to doors and window frames . . . people huddled in doorways, stretched out like rags on the sidewalks, sleeping—or dead? . . . bundles of brown bodies in filthy bedclothes on a shred of mattress here and there, by the dozens, by the hundreds, throughout the city millions without a home. . . . The cattle wandering through the city's streets, cows with dried-up udders, placid beasts resting their huge hulks on sidewalks everywhere, stringy cows trailing their bony haunches between the Fiat and Plymouth and Hillman taxis. . . . But most of all the people, a few rich men in great white garments or smart Western suits, contrasting with the hordes of poor, the upstretched palms of withered beggars. It's all a very far cry from the Loop.

I must say that my wife was somewhat shattered when she first arrived [said an embassy officer in Teheran]. *The second day a friend of ours took us in a car to the "colorful native quarter"; it was squalid, poor, unkempt. That was quite a blow to her. She said later to me that she wondered whether we should have come at all. But after we'd gotten to see other people's homes and finally had gotten a nice home of our own, that put a different complexion on it.*

Most American women survive the first wave of revulsion and go on to face subtler forms of adjustment. Many express their initial feelings by waxing indignant in the gripe sessions common to every overseas American community. But a few never get beyond the first few weeks and eventually their husbands are quietly released from their contracts.

2

The frustrations for the American wife, the troubles most frequently mentioned as important in the crucial first few months, have to do with the acquisition and maintenance of a family home. Again, the shock is as much physical as cultural. As one veteran businessman said, many Americans "aren't used to the idea of the shower water running out when you're covered with soap or the lights going out just as you're going to throw a party." Yet these conditions prevail at a good many of the posts at which Americans are now living. The pattern is surprisingly uniform: most Americans are not automatically furnished a satisfactory house, so they must either negotiate with some American controller for an allotted house or search for a home in a tight and expensive rental market. It is difficult in a hurried moment to choose wisely.

The stories of housing trouble during those first few months vary in concrete details, but each one, like the following, tells of the frustration:

> Iran: I *didn't have any surprises when I came here beyond the fact that I had no place to live. I was told that I had a new house all air-conditioned. I got down there; it was 120°, and I said, "Well, I want to go to my house," and my Iranian colleague said, "What house?" I found I had a guest house, a mud house, as dreary as a dungeon. I stayed there several nights. The temperature was 115°, 120°. I*

> *sent my wife back to Teheran.... After a couple of months*
> *we did get a house. Just recently we got a generator: we had*
> *air conditioning, but didn't have any electricity.*

The typical experience is that the American family does eventually get adequately housed, if only because there is a good deal of turn-over in all kinds of overseas missions and the families who are there take over the houses of those who go home, transfer to another country, or die. The Americans we interviewed had generally been overseas for more than a year, and were housed from reasonably to spectacularly well. Even in the best houses, of course, the "little things creep up on you," as a woman Foreign Service officer told us —the bargaining over prices, the ever-present danger of being robbed in some countries, the struggle to maintain modern household appliances in underdeveloped areas:

> *When I first came here I couldn't understand why people*
> *complained about it. But ... you're being frustrated all the*
> *time. My refrigerator works fine in the winter, but not in*
> *the summer. I asked for a new one. I got a new one. Now*
> *I've got two and neither one works. You go to iron, the*
> *electricity goes off and you can't iron, and the pump stops*
> *and you have no water. The food spoils because the re-*
> *frigerator is on the blink. You can't drink the local water.*
> *You ask them to do something. You go away for a week and*
> *they don't do it. I find my gorge rising....*

Under conditions like these, the clue to survival in overseas service is the kind of relax-and-enjoy-it adaptability that takes life as it comes. The professionals in career service abroad are well-nigh unanimous in charging the amateurs with worrying about trifles. "They become too preoccupied with living conditions," said one veteran. "It's simply part of the job." Some, it is true, arrive for a first overseas assignment with a wholly sophisticated attitude. "When I was a kid, after all, I took my bath in a zinc tub with water from a well," said an agricultural technician newly arrived in the Middle East. "One of our people here in the field complained about the lack of adequate baths. I said, 'Hell, if you've got a tin cup and some water, you can have a bath!'"

For most of the wives, the adventure is fun—and there is plenty of social pressure to rise to challenges that do not look funny until

you look back on them later. An American girl is constantly re-
minded (sometimes pointedly by the boss' wife) that she is now a
"goodwill ambassador."

The typical American woman seems to be able to adjust readily
to an oversupply of servants and a shortage of almost everything else.
She can accommodate herself to drafty houses in a European winter
or to permanent perspiration in an equatorial summer. She likes to
make friends abroad as she does at home. Servants present her with
delicate problems of personnel administration, but diligent research
has yet to uncover a single American wife who could not get used
to having some help around the house. So readily does she learn to
boil the water and pretend not to see the grease on the spoons that
these things are seldom mentioned even as minor annoyances by
women who have been abroad for more than a few months. And
she soon catches the spirit of ordering meals and chit-chatting at
parties in a combination of basic English, enthusiastic smiles, ex-
pressive gestures, and a smattering of clichés in the local vernacular.

These changes the American wife takes in her stride. But three
aspects of culture shock are not so easily shaken: the fear of disease,
the chronic worry about schooling for the children, and the frustrat-
ing effort to cross the cultural barrier.

3

In all the countries of Asia, Africa, and Latin America, Americans
are plagued by the "turisticos" (or "Egyptian tummy," "Addisitis,"
"Delhi belly," and so on around the world). This minor dysentery,
which seems to attack the careful eaters and insouciant gluttons
alike, is as much of a medical mystery as the common cold. A survey
published last year showed that one-third of all tourists who went
to Mexico for seven days or more had one or more attacks of diarrhea,
and nearly two-thirds of these became ill during the first week there.
But the same report underlined how mysterious this disease remains:

> Although most physicians are acquainted either through
> personal experience or by hearsay with the bouts of diarrhea
> which afflict travelers abroad, little precise information of
> the subject is available. The cause of the diarrhea of travel-
> ers is not known, nor can it be stated whether one disease

*or several are responsible for the symptoms. Estimates as to
its incidence and severity vary as much as do the picturesque
names which have been applied to it in different countries.**

Everybody knows that in foreign countries "you have to be careful what you eat." But this admonition often stands in direct conflict
with the requirements of diplomacy and public relations. "The hazard
is when you get out in the country," said the sales manager of an
African airline. "Some local governor asks you to eat and you can't
say no. Then you get sick. I draw the line at taking a slice of sheep
cooked with the skin on."

Occasionally, of course, the fears of disease are on the other side.
The wife of one official in Yugoslavia complained that her cook
thought that sore throats came from eating any food cold. "She
thinks, for example, that we are criminal letting our children eat ice
cream. She wants to heat the ice cream before serving it!"

For many overseas Americans, especially businessmen, journalists
and government people, the consumption of substantial amounts of
alcohol is so constant a leisure-time activity that, if long continued,
it becomes a health hazard in itself. Hard work, the annoyances and
disappointments of cross-cultural operations, the requirements of
mutual entertaining, and the tendency to congregate in an American
club after work—all conduce to make one attaché's comment a
nearly universal experience: "We drink too much. We spend too
much time standing around with glasses in our hands, but then that's
part of the racket."

Yet despite the drinking, the dysentery, the gastronomic risks, and
the dilemmas of diplomacy, the general experience overseas is that
very little time is lost through illness. What bothers the overseas wife
is less the reality than the threat of health trouble, the dread of
"what would happen if . . . ," the "deep-down fear of serious illness."
Neurotic fear of disease can create almost as much trouble for the
administrators of overseas programs as the actuality of ill health. In
Chile they still talk about the mining executive who imported his
own drinking water from New York City. Every ship that arrived
with supplies for the mining and refining of copper would have
aboard the inevitable tank of fresh water for the boss.

* B. H. Kean and Somerset Waters, "The Diarrhea of Travelers," *A.M.A. Ar-
chives of Industrial Health,* August, 1958. Vol. 18, p. 148.

Abroad, as at home, the fear of polio is out of proportion to its threat: "There's no iron lung here," we were told with foreboding at several posts. Necessary operations or dental work tend to be postponed until the family gets back to the United States on home leave, but a mother who knows her child should have surgery or orthodontia cannot wholly suppress uneasy pangs of conscience.

"You sometimes wonder," said an embassy assistant in Tokyo. "I mean, for instance, take that ruptured appendix. Maybe it wouldn't have ruptured if the child had been under the care of our family doctor at home. Sometimes you wonder whether people will say maybe just because of your own selfish interests you are not treating the children properly."

Thus the health problem is often less a matter of medicine than of psychology—with overtones of nationalism. When it comes to taking care of their children, American mothers want American doctors. Everywhere there is alleged to be a lack of adequate physicians and hospitals—their adequacy being measured by their American-ness. In Ethiopia they talk about rushing any really ill person to the American Army hospital in Frankfort—a greater distance than from San Francisco to New York. Even in Brussels, serious illness sends Americans scurrying across the German border to the nearest American facility.

4

Overseas wives feel the same way about schools as they do about health: if it is not American, it is not good enough. Most of them feel that the United States should maintain around the world an "educational PX" from kindergarten through twelfth grade. Rare exceptions are the American children put into "indigenous" schools. In New Delhi, only one American boy in 1957 followed the example of Chester Bowles' family and enrolled in an Indian school.

The British, who preceded us on every continent, were willing to ship their children home to boarding school in England at the age of nine or ten. But when Americans go abroad they insist on taking their children with them, even if they have to import an American school system along with baby food. A few hardy souls tutor their own children until they find that doubling as parent and teacher does not work very well. One mother insisted her daughter call her "Mrs. Jones" during class hours. "It's pretty hard to keep up *that* pretense," she confessed. "What do you do when your pupil suddenly hugs you and says, 'Oh, Mummy. I love you. Let's stop now'?"

On four continents during the last fifteen years American wives by the thousands have thrown themselves into the endeavor to meet the educational needs created by their own expectations. In this effort they have had the increasing support of business, private philanthropy, and the educational allowances of government agencies. "We are not going to get and keep enough American employees in foreign posts these days, especially with domestic positions beckoning with all kinds of benefits, unless we provide for the education of their children." * This appraisal by an overseas business executive was echoed in the 1954 Wriston Report on the U.S. Foreign Service:

> *The Committee strongly recommends that an allowance should be instituted to assist Foreign Service Personnel in meeting the abnormal cost of securing a proper education for their minor children. Such an allowance should cover the expenses of transporting such children to and from schools in the U.S. or a country where the educational system matches the American criteria.†*

The effort to "match the American criteria" in foreign parts is one of extraordinary scope and vigor. The missionaries were naturally first to sense the problem and begin to tackle it. In such traditional mission fields as Japan and China, for example, the best schools and colleges for nationals as well as Americans were those started by Catholic and Protestant groups.

The mission schools, in Japan as elsewhere, served well enough the needs of American families when there were but few of them to

---

* The executive's remarks above, and some of the facts about international schools that follow, come from publications of the International Schools Foundation, Inc., 3060 Garrison Street, Washington, D.C. See especially *New Links in Understanding and Cooperation* (Washington and Geneva, September, 1957); "The First Conference of International Schools in Asia," a report by Finley P. Dunne, Jr. (October, 1958); and "International Schools Around the World," an undated Chart of International Schools in Europe, Asia, Africa, and North America. Information about schools in Latin America is available from The Inter-American Schools Service, 1785 Massachusetts Avenue, N.W., Washington 6, D.C.

† Department of State, Report of the Secretary of State's Public Committee on Personnel, May 18, 1954.

be served. But as United States and international agencies began
to spread around the world, the problem of educating the children
of staff members away from their homes was taken in hand by the
parents themselves. When the League of Nations was established at
Geneva after World War I, an experimental school was established
with 9 students, borrowed space, and unpaid teachers, "to provide a
curriculum adapted broadly to the children of all countries." This
school now has more than 800 students from 53 countries, and has
moreover provided the inspiration for similar enterprises elsewhere
in the Eastern Hemisphere.

An American school was created in Rome, shortly after World
War II, by an energetic group of women whose husbands worked
in the Allied occupation, the American Embassy, and the United
Nations relief program. Other schools grew up near the NATO
headquarters outside of Paris, at the seat of the International Court
in The Hague, and in Luxembourg near the Coal-Steel Authority,
first outcropping of the movement for European integration.

Meanwhile in Latin America a most ambitious program called the
Inter-American Schools Service had been developed to assist and
provide professional advice to more than 270 American-sponsored
schools in Latin America. Sponsored by the American Council on
Education, and aided by the State Department with appropriated
funds, it "cooperates with a chain of schools estimated to have a current enrollment of over 103,000 students, a total contact during its
lifetime with over a million Latin American children, and school
property valued at $21,600,000."

After 1945 the expanding communities in Asia and Africa began to
demand something similar. The American School in Tokyo, a nonmissionary institution that had long served the children of American
diplomats, businessmen and missionaries, became both larger and
more international. Good elementary schools were developed by
American initiative, sometimes on the foundation of pre-existing
enterprises, in Manila, Djakarta, New Delhi, and Karachi. Over the
last eight years, again by parental initiative, a large and successful
school has been built on Taiwan where more than 10 thousand Americans are stationed among 10 million Chinese.

A recent inventory of schools in Europe, Asia and Africa, compiled
by the International Schools Foundation, shows 49 schools in 41

countries, with a current enrollment of 13,000 or more. All but five of these institutions (those in Geneva, Beirut, Tokyo, Seoul and Manila) have developed during the past twelve years.

The pattern in places as widely different as Brussels and Djakarta is common to many posts: an international student body (including a fair number of local nationals), receiving instruction in English, following an American curriculum (often the Calvert system), taught by British teachers (because they do not cost as much as our underpaid American teachers). Tuition varies greatly but is generally above $200 a year. Sharp rises in tuition were to be noted as soon as the State Department's allowance schedules were published; each eligible school was naturally anxious to take advantage of the maximum price the government would pay, and some grumbling by nongovernment families was evident for a time. Nevertheless, the cost of such schooling is small compared to maintaining the child in an American boarding school, and has the advantage of having the children remain part of the family at least during their early years of school experience.

Not all the schools for American children are international in scope. On most military posts, the U.S. Army or Air Force maintains an American-style school for Americans alone; the Air Force, indeed, is now said to run the largest single school system in the world.

One way or another, in most places, the school problem for American families is taken care of through the sixth or eighth grade. But at the high school level the shortage is acute, and most families simply assume their children will have to be brought home to college and possibly for preparatory school as well. As a consequence, people with teen-age children—that is, people who are precisely in the age bracket (forty to fifty-five) required for most positions of leadership—are often simply unavailable for overseas work. American business and government agencies report a continual tussle to keep good people in their employ overseas when their children reach high school age; and there is plenty of testimony from younger married couples who say they will stop serving abroad when their children become teen-agers. The religious workers, who often assume they are in service for life, feel the same pinch with even greater intensity.

It is a very serious thing and it is always in the minds of the people here at the mission [said a missionary in Iran].

People try to solve it in various ways. Some try to solve it by taking leave of absence for five years or so, or even resigning when their children are about fifteen and it's time for them to go back to school at home. But some stay on here and let their children go back alone. We, ourselves, keep putting off consideration of what we'll do about the problem. I hate to face it myself. Maybe there will be a revolution in Teheran which will kick out all the foreigners before we have to face that....

Not that there are no good secondary schools. In Europe there are English, Swiss, German, French and even American schools which prepare an American adequately for a United States preparatory school or college. But in the wide expanse from Southeast Asia to West Africa, most of the traditional "foreign" schools are designed to serve British and European needs. They may be just as good as the schools these same children would otherwise attend in Denver or Atlanta or Lincoln, Nebraska; often they make the children work harder than our public schools do. But they are "different," and no parent wants to risk having his child superbly educated yet unable to pass the College Board examinations.

Is it on balance good or bad to raise American children overseas? The answer depends on what the parent thinks is important. The majority of worries on this score have to do with the dangers to a child who grows up as a member of an aristocratic leisure class abroad and then comes home to make his way in an egalitarian society that honors labor and resents "hifalutin airs."

I believe very strongly in equality; I think this is the most wonderful idea in the American system and the lack of this idea in some countries is what worries me most about bringing up my child overseas. [A career commercial officer in Mexico thus expressed a widespread concern.] *My kids have barely begun school and they're already class-conscious ... My wife and I work at this, but it inevitably rubs off from their schoolmates.*

Those who can see no values in education beyond the ones that happen to have been built into the American educational system are those most worried about what is happening to their children under "foreign" influence. Even in American schools abroad, parents worry lest their children may be "missing something." One father told us that once back home his girls had adjusted well to their stint abroad but his son had a harder time. The boy was ahead of his friends in language and literature, but he did not know how to play baseball and he had not been following the comic-strip adventures of Dick Tracy. Once back in America his peers thought him "strange."

Perhaps the most relevant lesson to be learned was expressed by a missionary in Japan.

> *As far as raising children abroad is concerned, whether it is an advantage or not depends on how happy the home is, because the home is so much more important abroad. In most circumstances, the child doesn't have as much to do outside the home, and therefore falls heavily back on the home. The parents really therefore have more responsibilities than in the States.*

The parents who most successfully discharge this responsibility are not those whose concept of the American Way is so superficial that they see no values as enduring for their children unless they are identifiably American. A healthier view about overseas living was expressed by a missionary when she said, "I think that having seen that Japanese are real people, a child raised abroad can realize that French and others are real people too." She is joined in this affirmation of the importance of learning early about cultural pluralism by a heartening number of the parents we interviewed abroad.

"They get and appreciate the advantages of both worlds," said a diplomat in Tokyo. An Air Force attaché in Belgrade reported, with approval, that "we have eighteen nations right here in this school."

"It's true they miss a lot of things, like soda pop and baseball, that they get in high school back home," said another career official. "But they are getting a wonderful understanding of youngsters in other countries and of many of the problems of these countries."

5

"We got into overseas service because we thought it would be restful," one wife told us with a laugh. No doubt a few families naïvely assume that it will be soothing to get away from the hustle and bustle of the American Way of Life. But American wives are caught up almost at once in a highly organized American social whirl.

It is hard to avoid spending most of their "leisure time" in company with other Americans. "The American group has grown larger, you can't ignore them," said an ICA man in Ethiopia. "Otherwise they get hurt. We've been out every night now for the past three weeks."

The tendency of Americans to live in clusters abroad is not one of our more original findings. Many commentators have lampooned what one called "the daily drudgery of bridge parties in the morning, cocktails in the afternoon, dinners in the evening, with philandering thrown in occasionally to break the monotony." Everywhere one travels he can pick up charming stories to illustrate the pathological addiction of some women to the American commissary and the embassy snack bar. (Our favorite tale is about the member of the American church in Rome who was asked to bring a macaroni casserole for the church supper that night. "How can I?" she asked. "I'm out of macaroni, and the commissary is closed today!")

To describe the sociology of America's cultural islands abroad is probably useful and certainly entertaining. More relevant to our present purpose, however, is to analyze why they exist and how they affect what the overseas Americans are sent abroad to do.

Why, to begin with, does the American social whirl develop such intensity, especially in the capital cities around the world? A diagnosis common to all the posts we studied would run like this:

• Because they have servants, the women have an unusual amount of time on their hands.

• There is a lack of familiar and congenial ways of using this time.

• In most societies, especially in the underdeveloped areas, it is extremely hard for Americans to develop activities that truly cross the cultural line.

• The American administrators deliberately promote the social whirl to raise their employees' morale by keeping their families busy.

• There are in any event many occasions, including the coming and going of official visitors, that require American forms of entertainment.

If she is not to spend all her time at bridge parties or the bar of the American Club, the overseas wife has to think seriously about trying to learn enough about the local culture to participate a little in it. It is easy for Americans comfortably rooted in their home-town culture to criticize the failure of Americans overseas to "get along with the local people." But crossing the cultural line is not easy; even in Europe it demands unremitting efforts and elsewhere in the world the odds against success are heavy.

An American woman assumes that the way to become acquainted with people is to exchange visits, to entertain in the home. But if she invites a business associate of her husband, he will seldom bring his wife unless she speaks English or the American wife is fluent in her guest's language. (It is often much more important for the wife of an "operating diplomat" to learn the local language than it is for the husband to do so.) Moreover, in many places social intimacy does not so readily take the form of invitations to share meals at stated times, as it does with us.

In our culture, if we like somebody we will have him or her over to lunch or tea or cocktails or dinner. But, for example, some Indonesians who have passed the line that divides acquaintance from friendship are very likely to drop in on each other unexpectedly. We think it rude for even the best of friends to drop in around mealtime expecting to be fed; with some Indonesians this is not only done, but is regarded as a mark of respect. The point is that if you wait for your friend to invite you to a formal dinner, he then, to do you honor, must serve you enough food to choke a dozen persons. It is thus a kindness to your friends *not* to expect them to lay out a feast in order to attract you into their house. If you call unannounced, you give them an opportunity to entertain you on what Americans would call a potluck basis.

Another problem arises in the convention, especially widespread in the East, that it is bad manners to decline an American invitation but not at all impolite not to attend after accepting. An ICA couple in Ethiopia told this story about their efforts to cross the dinner-party barrier:

> *One time we invited 24 to a dinner and heard from eight of them. Eight turned up, but it wasn't the same eight that we'd heard from. Then again, at another time you'll have*

more than 100% return. You just never can tell. It's been
this way for everyone, from the Ambassador on down. The
Ambassador's secretary has to call up the night before din-
ner to find out whether people are coming or not. If they're
not, of course he has to scratch around to find somebody
to take their place. The thing is that this kind of experience
is pretty wearing. We get pretty tired of trying to be
friendly.

The sentiment is not an attractive one, but it is widely shared by
Americans in many places abroad. Most Americans in the posts
we visited report that their social invitations are seldom returned.
The nationals of most countries cannot afford to entertain as much
as the Americans do; they are ashamed of their homes in comparison
to the grand scale on which many American officials and businessmen live; they often think (mistakenly) that the Americans will eat
only American food, and they are naturally not geared to serve
Western-style meals. Moreover, as an embassy wife said of her own
vigorous efforts to know some Ethiopians in Addis Ababa, "they
know we are doing this because we are supposed to—so there isn't
a sense of personal obligation to invite us back."

The wives' experience in trying to "get along with the nationals"
naturally varies according to the country and the nature of the husband's job. A missionary wife usually has close contact at least with
students or religious associates, while business people are the most
isolated. In Europe friendships are somewhat more readily made
across the cultural barrier; in Latin America a knowledge of the
local language is relatively more essential; in Asia considerations of
caste and hierarchy are more troublesome. It takes hard work anywhere to establish real *rapport* with many people of another culture.
It is a great deal easier to have some congenial American girls over
for bridge and a drink in the afternoon—and avoid the strain and
humiliation of groping in the darkroom of cross-cultural communication.

6

The frustrations of American families add up to a morale problem which the managers of American overseas operations are tackling
with characteristic vigor. To an administrator's eyes, the cocktail cir-

cuit serves a function beyond diplomacy: it can be part of an elaborate and often quite conscious plan to weld the Americans at each post into a closely knit unit. Among the government missions at least, responsible officials are generally anxious to create a desperately full schedule of social functions among the women—parties, clubs, bridge, amateur theatricals, and endless mutual invitations to dinner. The idea is to strengthen the morale of the men at the office by making sure of an adequate ration of "belonging" for their wives. The military services, of course, have attained the highest development in exclusive togetherness. "As a Navy wife," one girl told us with pride, "you're never abroad. You're always just in the Navy."

At any sizable overseas post the "American community" is plural, reflecting the pluralism of American representation. The missionaries see a good deal of each other and very little of the other Americans; the bankers and large businessmen (oil, airlines, big importers) form another group; the small commercial people feel excluded and cling together in their turn; the military officers have their own clubs and social life; and the civilian government people live in an embassy-led social system dominated by a "diplomatic list" that determines which Americans get invited to official parties thrown by the host government or by diplomats from other nations.

Naturally, government people are the ones most criticized in our popular literature for their hyperactive social life abroad. Yet the social whirl has functions more important than keeping wives too busy to interfere with their husbands' work. For one thing, it often represents the most effective form of communication among the civilian agencies in a large U.S. Government establishment. It is also valuable as an arena for status-seeking: the wife's performance in this little society may be her only measure of achievement, and for the husband advancement obviously depends on getting to know his peers, bosses, and prospective bosses in the most informal atmosphere available. Thus in overseas service, "getting along with the Americans" is typically more influential in determining an individual's career than "getting along with the local people." Important among the Americans to be got along with, moreover, are the innumerable supervisors from headquarters, officials from related organizations, and friends and acquaintances from wherever one has previously lived.

Even the missionaries feel the pull of American social life.

I am drawn somewhat into American community relations
[said a missionary teacher in Tokyo]. *This is one of my frus-*
trations now. It makes me sort of a dual personality. In-
stead of being able to spend all my time trying to fit in and
adapt to the Japanese scene, I am constantly being drawn
back out in meetings with other missionaries and relations
with other missionaries. . . . It is too Westernized a city and
there are too many outside American visitors coming
through that you have to see . . .

The government people of course have the same trouble compounded. "We have to spend a terrible amount of time taking care
of American USIS people who come through town," said one of
them. "It's necessary, but it sure takes time. As a result very little
of our social life is with Japanese."

It is the hotly self-conscious new nationalists who make the loud-
est allegations of American exclusiveness. For the new housing
units and the all-American life that grows within them conjures up
memories of yesterday's resentment at "extra-territorial" British,
French and Dutch compounds, enclaves and clubs. "They turned
Maadi [a Cairo suburb] into a Little America," one Egyptian Government official grumbled, "congregating there around their own
school, their club, and their T-bone steaks." In Tokyo, thousands of
Americans live almost as they would in the United States. One area
of Tokyo called Washington Heights is virtually a replica of an American suburban town, complete with supermarket, bowling alley,
movie theater, and a club open only to Americans (filet mignon dinner with all the trimmings, $1.00). This public relations monstrosity
was evidently created by the Army to solve a serious housing problem for its military dependents; but it is a daily reminder to the Japanese that many Americans take Little Americas with them wherever
they go.

An extreme example is a Washington Heights matron who, when
asked if she ever visited the great Oriental metropolis around her,
answered, "I went down to the Ginza once, but it was too crowded
with Japanese." Less extreme but more common is an example from
Addis Ababa. Hundreds of Americans may drink Ethiopian coffee
without complaint. But what the Ethiopians talk about is those Amer-

icans who order hot water in restaurants and produce jars of Nescafé
—in the country that thinks it invented coffee.

The resentment caused by such behavior has prompted a growing number of government agencies and private firms to seek ways
to reduce the appearance or reality of social exclusiveness in their
overseas operations. The head of one local oil company adopted a
policy of giving two parties a year for the Americans on his staff,
but otherwise discouraging social activity among them, or between
them and other American oil people in the area. He found that
this restraint forced the Americans to develop friendships in the
local community—especially since he also insisted on a knowledge
of the local language as a condition of continued employment with
the firm. He believes that the Americans as individuals get much
more out of their overseas experience this way than in operations
where "social life consists of communing with other Americans." He
may be right, not only for his company, but for the overseas Americans
at large.

Part Two
AMERICANS
AT WORK ABROAD

5 · The Government People

The three main groups of civilians overseas—the government people, the missionaries, and the businessmen—share the obligation to involve themselves deeply in the culture and the political economy of the alien peoples among whom they live. But the tasks they perform vary greatly and are strikingly different, too, from what these same groups were doing a generation ago. It will be useful to spend a few moments with each group to bring up to date our somewhat outmoded conceptions about Americans at work abroad.

"I began my job forty-seven years ago," wrote the British career diplomat Lord Vansittart in a *Foreign Affairs* * article not long ago, "and it was a fairly gentlemanly one on the surface. 'The rapine underneath' was there, but it was war . . . in lace." International government representation, until the beginning of the twentieth century, had changed little from the time modern diplomacy was invented during the Renaissance by the Most Serene Republic of Venice. Its purpose was to represent and to report—including the more genteel forms of spying.

It was part of this tradition that the foreign representative must above all be well versed in the aristocratic arts of social behavior. To appear to be a gentleman was the first requisite of diplomacy; and the higher the rank, the more importance that appearance

* *Foreign Affairs,* January, 1950.

assumed. Ideally the diplomat would have brains and education as well as a socially felicitous choice of parents; thus endowed, he could use his social entrée to carry out his reporting function. The nature of this function, however, and the restricted number of persons who made use of his reports, caused it to be subordinate to the splendidly conspicuous one of representation, not only in the eyes of the general public but also in those of many governments less wily, less sober, and less consistently well informed than that of fifteenth-century Venice.

The well-dressed diplomat thus had to be able to charm over a cup of tea and scintillate at a court ball, precisely because his rounds of formal parties kept him in touch with the level of society containing nearly all the people who "mattered" in each country. His companions at these parties ran the country to which he was accredited; and they were also the same people whom visiting American dignitaries might want or need to know. It was by intimate and long social contact with a reasonably stable in-group that the United States diplomat could win the confidence of the rulers, pick up useful intelligence about changes in the power structure, and gain, if not always sympathetic consideration, at least a hearing for the American position on major international issues, and small favors for American residents and tourists, traders and seamen.

It is not our purpose here to assess the degree of proficiency attained in this essentially rarefied art by the long list of Americans who have served their nation without benefit of titles, pedigrees, or fancy-dress uniforms. It is enough to note an ironic twist: just as the United States began to take its international position seriously enough to add to its traditional consular service a body of career diplomats, the whole foundation of arm's-length capital-city aristocrat-level diplomacy began to crumble away.

Rapid communications between capitals made it increasingly possible to bypass or supersede ambassadors. The function of representation vis-à-vis the Foreign Office became more and more ceremonial as the practice developed of having ministers and experts meet and negotiate directly on trade agreements, arrangements for military installations, technical assistance, radio monitoring, atomic energy, and a host of other specialized activities beyond the possible knowledge of the "generalist" Foreign Service officer.

The rise of democracy and the breakdown of the power monopolies formerly in the hands of aristocracies of birth or wealth gradually robbed the teas and court balls of much of their pertinence to government. The function of representing America to whole societies, rather than just to an élite, placed a premium on different qualities. Political reporting began to require the widest imaginable range of contacts with all elements of real power in each society; after all, in a time of rapid political change it might be more relevant to get along with the next government than with the current one.

The expanded range of political reporting accounts, moreover, for less than half of the news reporting that our representatives are called on to submit. Today, in order to keep abreast of the developments in foreign countries, several government agencies in Washington need expert economic reporting as well. The political section of an embassy with its first, second, and third secretaries, which used not only to be the focal point of an embassy's activity but to perform almost all of the embassy's functions, is now overshadowed and overpowered by the economic counselors, the treasury representatives, and the attachés (agricultural, labor, commercial, mining, press, and scientific).

The advent of the labor attaché is an interesting case in point. The United States appointed its first labor attaché in the early 1940s when labor emerged as the predominant political force in some European countries. The men at the political desks at the embassies and in Washington had suddenly found they had no contacts with the upstarts who were ruling the countries to which they were accredited or on which they were specialists. In the few cases where we were lucky enough to have competent ones, the labor attachés, for the most part relatively humble and recently created pariahs of the service, quickly became indispensable links between the U.S. Government and some of the new rulers of Europe.

Most important of all, American *foreign operations* came increasingly to dominate the diplomatic landscape. The subject matter of foreign affairs, from the sixteenth century until World War II, was mostly "international" in the stricter sense of dealing with questions that arose among nations or their sovereigns: dynastic rivalries, territorial claims, commercial exchange, shifting alliances for attack or defense, and the like. Until World War II, America had no foreign aid program and no organized world-wide United States information program. Not only were we not engaged in "operations" abroad, but it would have been contrary to the "no entanglement" doctrine for American government officials to "operate" within foreign countries.

Today, the picture is so different that we can but dimly recall those days of only twenty-one years ago.

2

Before World War II virtually all overseas United States civilian personnel worked for the State Department; today even the recently enlarged Foreign Service accounts for only about one in five of the 32,805 government people working abroad. The 331 American civilians working in foreign countries for the War and Navy Departments in 1938 had by 1958 become the 20,926 Defense Department civilian employees abroad.

A generation ago the great majority of government people abroad would have been found in Europe. Less than 40 per cent of the United States overseas civilians are now assigned to Europe; there are today almost as many American civilians working for government agencies in the Far East as there are in Europe. The 1958 figures show a drop, for the first time in recent years, in the total number of American civilians working for the U.S. Government abroad:

March 1954	29,583
March 1955	31,821
June 1956	33,644
March 1957	34,844
June 1958	32,805

This drop reflects the reduction of 2,500 civilian employees of the Department of Defense, partially offset by small increases in the overseas personnel of the nonmilitary agencies.

The explosion of numbers (see Table 2) reflects not so much the expansion of reporting and of embassy-level negotiation as the addition of major new functions to the still-surviving tasks of pro-

TABLE 2. PAID U.S. CIVILIAN EMPLOYEES OF THE FEDERAL GOVERNMENT IN FOREIGN COUNTRIES, BY AGENCY AND AREA (JUNE 30, 1958)

Areas	All Areas	Africa	Latin America	Europe	Near and Middle East South Asia	Far East and Southeast Asia	Undistributed
Agencies							
All Agencies	32,805	1,840	2,548	13,837	3,172	11,335	73
State	6,462	361	1,096	2,666	1,187	1,149	3
ICA	3,338	349	771	136	893	1,119	70
USIA	1,168	55	134	361	287	331	
Defense	20,926	990	325	10,395	614	8,602	
Treasury	122		10	87	4	21	
Commerce	434	47	103	118	114	52	
HEW	191	24	47	27	49	44	
Agriculture	164	14	62	47	24	17	

Source: "Improvement in Standards of Language Proficiency and in Recruiting for the Foreign Service," *Senate Foreign Relations Committee Hearing on S.1243,* April 16, 1959, page 59.

fessional diplomacy. It is our foreign operations—the postwar reliance on overseas bases and military aid to other nations' forces, the spreading of clandestine operations, the increased functions of the United States Information Service, and the new programs of economic and technical assistance—that largely account for the presence of U.S. Government offices in more than one hundred countries and territories.

Massive garrison forces have placed United States troops semipermanently in Germany, England, and Japan, reflecting a decision in each of these countries that its domestic "self-defense" cannot be carried on without American soldiers, sailors, and airmen. A recent report of the U.S. Operations Coordinating Board showed one-quarter of all overseas Americans to be in Germany. In many other countries, such as Turkey, Iran, Pakistan, Thailand, Taiwan, and South Korea, American military strength takes the form of equipment and training personnel, but it is no less crucial to the defensive development of the nations concerned. The ring of bases around the Soviet periphery creates large and often essentially insoluble problems of public relations for the United States, notably in Morocco and Okinawa as this is written.

In all of these cases, and others too, the military build-up has massive political implications. Everywhere it strengthens the hands of the political "ins"; outside Western Europe military aid helps develop military officers in their expanding role as a new and often revolutionary middle class.

In Ethiopia, as in some of the Latin American nations, the military-aid mission has a primarily political function; its role (sometimes unknown to the American officers who are doing the job) is that of organizing an officer corps that will have the technical knowledge of weaponry and the sense of modern military organization to become a major factor in the politics of succession when existing leaders die or otherwise lose their grip.

Until twelve years ago the United States had no continuing civilian intelligence agency—and the military ones were not notably efficient when it came to nonmilitary information. Early in World War II, just before the invasion of that island from bases in North Africa, a group of economists was trying to put together some advice for the Army on civil government in Sicily. A member of the Washington research team was dispatched to the Office of Naval Intelligence to look up Sicily in their files; the latest entry (this was in 1943) was an unclassified consular report on commercial trends dated 1924!

Since its establishment in 1947 as the successor to the wartime Office of Strategic Services, the Central Intelligence Agency has been absorbing a constantly growing proportion of the foreign reporting and operating tasks of government—and tucking them behind a security curtain that obscures both successes and failures from foreign eyes and from serious Congressional review. Its expanding work, which until 1958 required a larger overseas staff in each successive year, would add to Table 2 several thousand overseas Americans. The exact number is an official secret.

Like other foreign operations, the Government's clandestine intelligence operations represent an unannounced revision of the principle of "noninterference." So, for that matter, does the intelligence work of other nations in the United States. One reason why a growing proportion of our foreign relations is being carried on in clandestine channels, perhaps, is that we need to hide what we are doing not only from others but also (in view of verbal adherence to "noninterference") from ourselves.

3

The spread of equalitarian enthusiasm has also led our foreign representatives deep into a function that hardly existed in our government at all a generation ago, that of propaganda and political advertising. It is no longer enough to impress only those who attend official receptions; the masses must be impressed too, and a number of new jobs have been created specifically for this purpose—press attachés, cultural attachés, librarians, technical specialists in the media of modern communication, and a growing number of researchers (some of them on government contracts) who take continuous soundings of foreign attitudes toward "the image of America."

The function of the United States Information Service in more than eighty countries consists of an effort to use the nation's communication network to get across certain ideas and attitudes. Those segments of foreign populations that are least favorably impressed by our efforts have often found in USIS buildings and American libraries a convenient target for brickbats.

The current involvement of whole societies in each other's daily lives is far beyond the control of government, if not beyond its concern. American-produced movies occupy more than 50 per cent of the *total* screen time in *each* of the world's major regions. American fast communication media pour forth each day between one and two million words for foreign consumption; the United States produces about 10 per cent of the world's books each year.* According to a recent compilation by the State Department, every year some 4,421,000 American tourists travel abroad; the United Nations says there are 64 million international tourists in all each year.

Considering its limitations—$100 million a year and only 1,168 overseas American employees—the problem for the U.S. Information Service is to make itself heard at all in the midst of this hubbub of international interaction. Its daily output is impressive: the USIA wireless file is 40,000 to 50,000 words a day, or 4 to 5 per cent of the million words a day produced by the world's major wire services. The Voice of America is on the air for a little more than 5 per cent of the international total of 10,000 weekly hours of radio broadcasting. USIA maintains libraries in 77 countries with 2,542,275 books and about 1,100 program films on display, produces 68 foreign magazines or editions of magazines (18 in English and 50 in other languages), and maintains 225 permanent exhibits.

Compared to Soviet propaganda or even to private business operations, this output is less impressive than it seems at first glance. Soviet efforts, reputed to cost billions of dollars, reflect the Soviet view that the whole government apparatus is a propaganda vehicle; it employs 370,000 propagandists full time, according to a Senate Foreign Relations Committee report in 1958. In the field of American private enterprise, as Edward L. Bernays has noted, one company (Unilever) spent approximately $232,000,000 in 1957 for advertising, to communicate with 1,800,000,000 consumers in the free world.

But the chief limitation of any United States propaganda operation is that it represents a wildly pluralistic society in which it **is**

* The Soviet Union produces about 18 per cent.

not anybody's official business to say authoritatively what America's purposes are and how they will be pursued. An accurate reflection of such a society is a multiple image. An undistorted echo of its politics is not a Voice but a babel of voices raised in democratic argument. It is hard for the government to "sell America," because the American people have not delegated to their government the authority to put it up for sale. Increasingly, therefore, the function of USIS in every country is to seek out all elements of the population and try to make sure they understand the nature of American society and have a sound basis for an understanding of American foreign policy from day to day. Other countries do the same work in the United States: the nations' intervention in each other's opinion-making processes is energetically reciprocal.

<h1 style="text-align:center">4</h1>

On the economic side of the government's overseas establishment, it is even clearer that a technical-assistance and public-investment program implies the deepest kind of involvement in the internal affairs of other nations—with their permission and within limits which their governments ultimately must set.

"There are some people," said the late Reverend A. Powell Davies, a Unitarian minister in Washington, D.C., "who still trot out the trite canard that loving our neighbor means what we do in direct relationship with him and that we cannot love him through acts of Congress. This is just a tired platitude. In the modern world we cannot even do our ordinary duty to our neighbor except through acts of Congress. This is true within our own country, as we have begun to recognize, and it is also true of our duty to the world."

Technical assistance, which the historian Arnold Toynbee has called "the greatest single idea in foreign policy to emerge from the twentieth century," brings Americans into contact with thousands of local and provincial leaders and with specialists in many fields who are far removed from the recipient nation's Foreign Office. These Americans deal with a society at its most sensitive point, at the very center of its rising expectations—teaching people to recognize their needs, helping them to be more articulate in demanding what they want from their own political leaders. By demonstrating what people can do for themselves once they set their minds to the task, technical assistance in the first instance increases the very gap between reality and expectations which is a prime cause of political ferment in every "underdeveloped" area. An investment program, moreover, requires attention to the whole of a nation's most sovereign process—the decisions as to how the nation's resources will be used, how the national budget will be allocated among purposes, what changes in the structure of public administration will be required to accomplish the modernization on which the leaders of the newly developing countries have generally set their hopes.

In 1958 the International Cooperation Administration, which administers most of the United States economic and technical aid abroad, had 3,338 Americans on its own payroll in more than 60 countries. In addition, there were more than 2,235 Americans overseas, representing private business firms and universities under contract to the ICA. Ten years ago, when the first of these figures was much smaller and the use of government contracts had barely started, nearly all the foreign-aid people had an arm's-length relationship with the governments to which they were accredited. But in Latin America the *servicios*—agreements by which Americans were placed as operating personnel inside Latin American governments—had already suggested a principle which the intervening years have dramatized again and again: that the more "underdeveloped" the country, the more inappropriate is mere cool advice, the more necessary an active role by the advisers in actual operations. As more countries emerge from colonial rule, especially in Africa, the need for operators rather than advisers becomes more acute, and is accompanied by the need for a clearer understanding on our own part of the role that Americans in the foreign-aid program actually play in foreign countries. In Ghana, first of the new African republics, there were, at the time of independence in 1957, just 80 architects of whom only 4 were Africans; only 20 to 30 per cent of all the engineers in Ghana were African; and hardly any of the young Ghanaians studying in Europe or America were taking any kind of technical course. In these circumstances the first job of a "technical adviser" often is to get something started; the next job to train nationals to perform subordinate tasks; the third stage is to select and train an "opposite number" who can gradually take

over operating responsibility; then and only then can the American
retire to a truly advisory role.

It is a slow business, and hundreds of foreign-aid officials have
learned that it cannot be rushed. As an ICA man in the Middle
East explained:

> At first we tried to do much more than they could
> assimilate here. I'm afraid some of our newer technicians
> don't understand this. They come out dewy-eyed and want
> to get things done. But the technical assistance program is
> a long-term program. Maybe you could say each project
> will go through three periods—the first five years getting
> started, the second five years of helping them, and the
> third five years of getting out of here.

This overseas veteran's time sense is wholly consistent with the
original concept of technical assistance as a U.S. Government activity. "We are here embarking," President Truman said in his first
message to Congress about the Point Four program, "on a venture
that extends far into the future. We are at the beginning of a rising
curve of activity, private, governmental and international, that will
continue for many years to come." In a remarkable outcropping of
administrative courage, an Assistant Secretary of State later told
an inquiring Congressman in a public hearing that technical aid
might go on for fifty years or more. The program, indeed, made no
sense except in very long-range terms.

Yet today, with the first ten years of world-wide technical assistance behind us, the continuity of United States interest in economic
development in the less-developed nations can be deduced from the
fact that it continues, somehow, from year to year. That continuity
is not yet formalized in our foreign-aid legislation, in the status of
the government agency that administers foreign aid, or in the method
of providing most of the investment funds and all of the technical
services.

The foreign-aid program, financed though it is by year-to-year
appropriations to an agency which would expire unless authorization were renewed each year, is a permanent aid program *de facto*
if not *de jure*. The most striking evidence of ICA's permanence can
be seen in the agency's own personnel policies.

Visiting the U.S. Operations Mission in Djakarta, we learned that
more than a third of that 96-member mission had been on a field

assignment with the foreign-aid program for more than four years—in other words, already at least on their third tour of duty. More than a quarter of all ICA employees in Indonesia had been in the field for more than five years. Other missions seemed to have comparable records; and percentages like these are the more remarkable since these missions typically include a good many short-term technicians sent out on spot assignments outside of the regular ICA employment system and an uncertain number of secretaries whose career ambition—to find a man—is fulfilled during their first tour of overseas duty.

The facts in the field are in the process of being institutionalized at headquarters. In the absence of cabinet-level leadership in the matter, the civil servants in the International Cooperation Administration began in 1957 a wholesale reform of personnel procedures designed to create in fact, in the absence of legislation, a viable career system for ICA's field staff. The scope of this undertaking was impressive: it meant, as ICA's personnel director put it to his staff at the time, "staffing some 4,200 positions in 60-odd countries encompassing a diversity of economic, cultural and political situations to stagger the imagination." In fashioning careers for its staff, ICA was encouraged by the parallel decision in the U.S. Information Agency to build a foreign information service on a career basis; USIA has been seeking for the last two years to get a Congressional imprimatur on the system it has already established by administrative action.

In short, ICA and USIA are not agencies which regard themselves as temporary aberrations from a norm of nineteenth-century diplomacy. The overseas Americans who make up the bulk of their staffs already know what the Budget Bureau and Congress do not yet officially admit: that foreign operations, enveloping and complicating United States foreign relations, are here to stay.

5

From this quick inventory of overseas government activity, it is once again evident that the United States already has its fingers in the political pastry of many countries, whether the American people like it or not, or, indeed, whether they know it or not. Judging from our interviews—and from the chronic malaise in our own country about United States foreign policy—these fingers are partly paralyzed by official reluctance to admit that the United States is interested in "domestic" political developments beyond our own shores.

The military-aid program is an example: The generals and colonels in charge of most military-assistance advisory groups abroad, many of them able soldiers with excellent records as combat leaders and peacetime administrators, usually believe their function to be limited to the training of troops in the use of modern weapons and advising on military organization and tactics. Yet in a dozen countries or more the foreign military officers we have trained are almost bound to have a powerful (or as we have recently seen in the Middle East, a controlling) voice in determining the political composition of their own civilian government, its foreign-policy posture, and the direction of its economic-development programs.

Similarly, United States technical and economic aid has very important impacts on the domestic politics of several dozen nations. In this progress-conscious era, a Minister of Health may ride to the premiership not on a white horse but on a malaria-eradication program or a network of carefully placed rural health clinics. Yet if you ask civilian technicians or economic-aid officials to describe the central purpose of their mission, they will most often formulate it either in vague clichés about soliciting friendship or in the narrow language of the official's specialty.

Pressed to define the object of his work, one United States information officer at a small African post summed it up this way: "To create among these people an understanding of Americans by allaying their suspicions of the United States and getting them to give full support to their own government, which is pro-Western." Members of ICA missions typically pin their faith on "economic development" or "economic growth" or "improvement in living standards" or "getting people better educated" or "getting our aid out to the village level." Too seldom do they make the connection between these intermediate goals and the development of political institutions strong enough to survive in a turbulent world and free enough to be compatible with our own institutions in a peaceful world order. A typical statement of purpose follows.

I suppose the general purposes of U.S. policy here in Mexico are to make Mexico a better prospect to sell or buy from. We're probably interested, out of every $100 spent, in $1 of brotherly love and $99 to benefit the U.S. Of course, in benefiting us we will also benefit the Mexicans. That's the way I'd sum up the purpose of our foreign policy as it applies to Mexico. Our job is that of being technicians in trying to give them some help.

On the military side the responses are equally devoid of political content; there are many references to foiling Russian aggression, a few mentions of internal security, and silence on political institution-building—although in most of the non-European countries in which we have military-aid programs, the actual priority of significance is precisely the opposite. If you ask directly about political impacts, you will generally be told that these are matters for the "political people" over at the embassy. The jurisdictional sensitivity thereby displayed is charming, but the referral is simple evasion. It is not the "political people" who are in day-to-day contact with the rising "middle class" of Army officers and economic planners. Moreover, some of our ambassadors are ill-equipped by training or inclination to provide the executive leadership to United States elements outside the embassy proper that would be necessary if the operation of military, economic, and information programs were to be shifted to the shoulders of the ambassadors. Nor is it clear that the President or Congress want our ambassadors to assume any such responsibility. In United States foreign operations to date, pluralism is still the order of the day.

The many overseas programs the United States sponsors—information and intelligence agencies, military and economic aid, international and private philanthropy, business and educational contacts by the thousands—give our government an unmatched opportunity to bring the United States into close and friendly touch with the coming leadership of all but a dozen nations in the world. But, while the government does many admirable things around the globe, it has yet to relate them effectively to each other and to the central purposes of American foreign policy.

The rapid changes in United States foreign operations have, moreover, not been accompanied by a bold enough look at the place of the diplomatic service itself in the scheme of things. Deep United States involvement in the internal affairs of other societies, for example, has called seriously into question the historic policy of sending most men for only two, three, or four years to each post. The acute need for people who can become intimately familiar with the language, culture, politics, and administrative workways of every country is so great that the old policy, which was based on a fear that Foreign Service officers might "go native" if left in one place too long, is under widespread attack within, as well as outside of, the State Department's career service.

The need for specialists in the Foreign Service has forced a wholesale reorganization in which the career men, who had resisted the lateral entry of economists, labor and agricultural experts, and professional administrators, found themselves engulfed by the sudden merger of the Foreign Service with the civil servants in the State Department's Washington headquarters. Having strained at a series of gnats, the career officers finally had to swallow a camel; and it is altogether possible that two or more large groups of officials, the career people in USIA and ICA, will likewise be merged with the Foreign Service before the ferment about the government's overseas-personnel policy quiets down.

Above all, the new facts of diplomatic life have raised serious questions about a system which projects men whose main experience has been in reporting and negotiation into most of the nation's ambassadorships, just when the ambassador's task has come to be that of a large-scale public executive. In the era of foreign operations that is now upon us, the ambassador's constitutional position as the President's man abroad is now being reinterpreted to include the task of presiding over the whole range of United States governmental activities in the country to which he is assigned.

The effective ambassador, therefore, needs not only diplomatic but also executive qualities of the first order. If the trend of filling all but the "rich men's posts" (like Paris and London) from the career service continues, the career service will have to make sure that its members have been given ample opportunity to acquire executive experience by working in the foreign-operations agencies.

6 · The Missionaries

1

When Christ told his followers, "Go ye therefore and teach all nations," he was talking about a contemporary world populated by 250 million people; the field for evangelism has increased tenfold since then. He did not say to his disciples "Go West," but His words were interpreted to imply the Western migration of a Word which came to dominate the Mediterranean, Roman, and North European worlds and was brought to the American continent by the first settlers from Spain, England, and France. The propagation of the faith has since been an important element of every American church's activity.

There are more American missionaries abroad today than at any other moment in our history. Of the total 29,609 Americans and Canadians, the Roman Catholics accounted for 5,753 in 1958.* The Protestant figure of 23,856 represents an all-time high; it constitutes two-thirds of the world-wide total of 38,606 Protestant missionaries of all nationalities. The world-wide missionary effort of the Roman Catholics probably exceeds the Protestants in numbers of missionaries at work outside their own countries. The growth of the total effort is marked if not spectacular: the current missionary population is three times the number reported in 1903 and about

---

* These and other figures on missionary activity are, except as otherwise noted, adapted from data cheerfully and efficiently supplied by the Missionary Research Library in New York City. See Table 3, page 89.

50 per cent more than the figures for 1936. Each year more than 1,000 Americans pack up and depart to serve some church activity in a foreign country.

The missionary effort is concentrated, as is the U.S. Government's foreign-aid program, in the world's underdeveloped regions: 28 per cent of the American and Canadian missionaries are in Asia, 23½ per cent are in Latin America, 22½ per cent are in Africa. Fewer than 3 per cent have tackled the Middle East where Islam is by universal testimony Christianity's toughest competitor.

The Protestant missionary more often than not is a woman. Most of the boards appoint wives as missionaries along with their husbands, and there are a great many more unmarried women than unmarried men in the field. When the unmarried Roman Catholic priests are added in, however, the balance probably turns somewhat in favor of the men. The Missionary Research Library's figures on the sex of American Protestant missionaries are incomplete. On the basis of those agencies reporting, however, there are 8,459 men and 12,828 women serving, a 2-to-3 ratio. Of the male missionaries, 6.3 per cent are unmarried. The proportion of married women to single women has shown a marked increase in recent years. The figures do not indicate whether the unmarried women are giving up posts to wives brought in from the United States or whether the single women are luring the single men into marriage.

North American Protestant missionaries' agencies collected a total of $147,282,881.47 in 1957, and spent 78 per cent of it overseas—the rest, presumably, on administration and fund-raising. If the total income for Protestant foreign missions in 1957 is divided by the reported church membership of that year, it appears that Protestant churches of the United States and Canada gave an average of $2.34 per member for the world-wide mission of the church. Roman Catholic expenditures for foreign missions amount to more than $50,-000,000 per year.

Even the least evangelistic missionary remains a distinctive element in the American overseas population for three main reasons: his standard of living, his length of service within one culture, and his reason for being there.

Because of his style of living—he is usually ineligible for such conveniences as the embassy commissary or the military post exchange,

and avoids on principle the social life of the American community—
the missionary normally lives closer to the people; there are few
barriers between him and the natives other than those which they set
up and he must patiently demolish. His salary is low, his benefits
few, his vacations spaced far apart. Jesuit missionaries are maintained for about $1,500 per annum, and get no furloughs at all.
The conservative Baptists give couples $1,800 plus rent, travel, and
health insurance. The Southern Baptists estimate they spend around
$100,000 for a lifetime—perhaps $2,500 per year—on a career missionary and his equipment. (To maintain a comparable person,
probably less well educated, in an American business abroad could
easily cost $100,000 in three or four years.)

Low as it is, this standard of living cannot be raised. Not only
are mission boards' funds limited, but the typical missionary's present standard of living already exceeds that of his native colleagues
by a margin sufficient to cause envy and invidious comparison. The
seriousness of the problem is shown by the Kenyon E. Moyer report,
published by the Missionary Research Library in 1957, where 37
per cent of 838 answers to the question "Would you advocate
simpler living for the missionary?" were "Yes." (A number of the
"no" answers stressed the difficulty Americans would have in living
on a lower standard; others reasoned that cultural differences,
rather than disparities in living standards, are the main barriers to
effective missionary work.)

The missionary is generally expected to make a career out of
serving at a single post or at least in a single area. There are several
sound reasons for this. It is, for instance, usually necessary that a
missionary to serve effectively master the local language; if he were
subsequently sent to another language area several years of effective
service would be lost while he learned the new language. In many
parts of the world, respect and influence are in good part associated
with age and length of service. Then too, if a missionary is satisfied
and acclimatized in one area, the board runs the risk of losing him
if it transfers him. Many boards feel that a missionary should identify himself with the local culture and forget he is an American.
Moreover, the assumption is that only if he knows he is going to
dedicate his entire life to the evangelization of one people will the
missionary devote his whole energy to comprehension of and iden-

tification with a foreign culture. The only large group of missionaries that has gone into a second area seem to be those who were forced out of China, and a very large number of them are working on the crowded islands of Taiwan and Hong Kong.

Why, in spite of the hardships, do so many Americans choose the missionary vocation? Their total number rose by 25 per cent between 1952 and 1956, and again by about 7 per cent from 1956 to 1958. Religious inspiration is surely a major part of the answer, but missionaries share with other Americans several of the motivations for choosing overseas service—the wish to escape, the delight in the exotic, and excitement of travel; these qualities move them, once having selected religion as their vocation, to preach to the unchurched in darkest Africa rather than in the almost equally dark corners of Manhattan's silk-stocking district or Mississippi's rural slums.

2

The historic tendency of American missionary enterprise has been to retain a distinctively American character. As an alien minority trying to magnetize a heathen majority, missionaries have historically appealed with the trappings of Western culture as well as with their Western religion. As evangelists for schooling and sanitation, for seed selection and farm machinery, for economic development and individual freedom, the missionaries everywhere made friends for "progress," measured in material and political terms—and for the United States. They have been a distinctive but integral part of American cultural imperialism.

It is not our purpose here to assess the effectiveness of American religious salesmanship, but there is no doubt that, measured as cultural evangelism, the missionary movement has been extremely successful. The Triple Revolution in underdeveloped areas stems directly from what Asians, Africans, and Latin Americans have learned about the West, and if they connected the West with Christianity, this was no more than the Christian missionaries themselves were doing.

That the missionary is an integral part of the apparatus which has been Westernizing Asia is not open to question.

*He is the advance guard in the ideological field, as the
soldier was in that of power, as the foreign Asian was in
that of commerce. Trade follows the flag; but equally the
convert often makes a better businessman than his uncon-
verted brother.* *

For better or worse, Christianity came to be associated with Western-style architecture, Western dress, medicine, jeeps, ideas about
freedom, and the English language. An educational administrator
in Iran, himself the product of an American mission school, stated
it bluntly: "We Persians do not think of these churches as Christian,
we think of them as American."

Protestant or Catholic, conservative or fundamentalist, the missionaries therefore have shared a common dilemma: Should they
resist the awakening revolution and the nationalists who ride it, or
find some way to join them? The almost universal answer now is to
join them. If anything is clear in this age of doctrinal confusion, it is
that Christianity can no longer be paraded in Western cultural
clothing and survive in the East.

This conclusion is the product of much traumatic experience in
recent years. In dozens of countries nationalist feelings have been
vented on the local representatives of a Christian faith. In Iran,
American missionaries had been educating Persians since 1830;
many middle-aged Persians remember with nostalgia Dr. Jordan,
the saintly American who ran a secondary school and spoke their
language better than they. But during the 1930s the Reza Shah, the
tough and dictatorial father of the present Shah, became worried
about Russian influence and decided to close all foreign schools—
since he could not merely close the Russian schools without being
discriminatory. Of all the foreigners who had established schools in
Iran, the Americans took the Reza Shah's order the most seriously:
they packed up and went home. (Others, like the British, stalled
awhile; then World War II came along, and those who delayed
compliance with the old man's orders are still to be found operating
in Iran.)

Most traumatic of all for the American mission field was the

---

* Leslie H. Palmier, "Changing Outposts: The Western Communities in Southeast Asia," *Yale Review*, XLVII (March, 1958), p. 405. Copyright Yale University Press.

experience in China. Here the investment of missionary zeal, good-will, faith, and funds was huge, and among American churchgoers the strange troubles of dedicated doctors and teachers abroad, graphically described in pulpit and parish house, could be trusted to produce tears of sympathy and increased budgetary contributions every time. Many of America's outstanding experts on Chinese history, culture, and politics were missionaries; some saw the meaning of communism and worked against it, but most of them were so disgusted with the Nationalist regime that they assumed they could get along with the Communists. For a hundred years they had occupied themselves with the welfare and salvation of individuals, as near to the village level as they could get. But the attack came at the level of politics and government, and the extraordinary investment of spirit and cash in a people-to-people relationship turned out to be not enough, not nearly enough.

The great exodus of missionaries from China ten years ago (a few still remain, under house arrest or worse) is full of poignant stories of personal disappointment. Men and women who had spent the best part of their lives building relationships with Chinese communities found themselves cut off even from their own converts. The director of Church World Service, veteran of 32 years of service in China, wanted to stay and do what he could even after the Communists took over, but his Chinese chairman finally persuaded him to go. "It is useless for you to stay in China. You will not be allowed to do any work, to preach, to teach, nor to help with relief. Besides," he added with persuasive but crushing frankness, "if you stay, you will jeopardize the life of every Chinese who has been associated with you." *

Christianity survives in China, especially in the cities where the Bible is still printed and church music is composed. There is even a Chinese bishop serving as part-time apologist for Communist foreign policy. But what remains is only a small residue of the total missionary investment. The "loss" of China has been felt more deeply by the missionaries than by any group of Americans. And every missionary body is trying in one way or another to find in every area a satisfying answer to the deceptive but plausible Chinese

* Robert T. Henry, "What Is Happening to the Church in China?" *World Outlook,* May, 1958, p. 41.

Communist proposal: that the church in China be self-supporting, self-governing, and self-propagating.

3

The word "missionary" still conjures up in many minds the image of a patriarchal, soul-saving preacher, quite certain of the superior righteousness of his own personal faith and of the Western church. But there have been two revolutions in missionary work since the Crusaders sacked Jerusalem, butchering Moslems and burning Jews, or Pizzaro promised the Inca of Peru death by strangling rather than by fire if he accepted baptism. One revolution, which has been going on for many decades, has created the social-service missionary; the other, the revolution of nationalism, has created the fraternal worker sent as a religious technical-assistance expert to a native church.

Schools and medicine have proved to be effective introductions to religious faith throughout the modern era; the string of modern hospitals maintained by the Seventh-Day Adventists, for example, have gained that denomination much favor in Asia. Many churches in the United States found places for agricultural experts in the villages of Asia and Africa where most of their time is spent on problems of productivity and marketing or actually working in the fields. Good works have thus come to be considered potent missionary strategy: they help illustrate Christian living and win adherents by example rather than conversion. Missionary teachers include not only the dedicated young woman drilling African tribal children on English pronunciation but the distinguished professor of biology advising Japanese graduate students on their Ph.D. dissertations. Only about half of all American missionaries overseas today are primarily evangelists; the others are engaged in some form of church-sponsored social service, relief work, or educational endeavor.

In spite of the fact that the social-service content of missions has been growing, it is probably fair to say that until World War II most missionaries were engaged in purveying Christianity to Asians and Africans in Western trappings and in building institutions to be headed usually by Americans or Europeans. But today Chris-

tianity, where it thrives, is finding ways to become an expression
not only of a universal faith but of local nationalism, the drive for
racial equality, and the hunger for rapid economic development.

TABLE 3. NORTH AMERICAN MISSIONARIES BY AREAS [1]

Area	Protestant	Catholic	Total	Percentage of All North American Missionaries
North America	394		394	1.3
Latin America	4,825	1,944	6,769	23.5
Europe	416	106	522	1.7
North Africa (*Including Near and Middle East*)	694	103	797	2.7
Africa (*South of Sahara*)	6,240	421	6,661	22.5
Asia	6,709	1,639	8,348	28.0
Pacific Ocean (*Oceania*)	203	809	1,012	3.4
Undistributed by countries	4,375	731	5,106	17.3
Total All Areas	23,856 [2]	5,753	29,609	100. [3]

[1] Data supplied by the Missionary Research Library.
[2] Including 475 Canadian Protestants.
[3] Total exceeds 100% due to rounding.

Though this was not necessarily true of him, the nineteenth-century
evangelist could go his solitary way bringing the word of God to
the heathen with little more knowledge of or respect for the native
culture than that of St. Augustine for the rites, beliefs, and ideals
of the former inhabitants of Great Britain or of the early Puritans

for the quaint and curious habits of the American Indians. The change was summed up by one mission executive in these words: "I had the more patriarchal concept in the old days, I fear. I was working for the poor benighted African. Now I feel ... the necessity of working with the African and letting him take responsibilities even if he makes mistakes."

The present-day missionary could often benefit from some of the supererogatory fervor of his predecessors, but he is also required to cultivate other qualities that in the past were not so clearly required. The modern evangelist is often working within a national church, either in the initial stages of its organization and establishment or in the later stages when it is being strengthened and prepared to function independently. In either case the missionary's intercommunication with the natives can no longer be in the slightest degree patronizing. Rather, the relationships he builds must be rooted in fraternal equality and cooperation.

More and more governments are now imposing formal restrictions on the numbers and kinds of missionaries who can be admitted, feeling about them a little the way the United States Congress felt about foreign Communists when the McCarran-Walter Immigration Act was passed. India, for example, is making it increasingly difficult for a purely religious missionary to get a visa; those who bring technical and material aid are still welcomed, but the Indian Government does not relish the thought of spiritual guidance from America these days. The Belgians and the Portuguese, fearful of the disruptive effect of missionary endeavor in their African territories, have usually required specialized training to be taken in the home country before missionaries can serve in Africa. This change is also reflected in Indonesia where the 31 church bodies now contain 3,000,000 Christians but only 100 Christian missionaries from foreign countries. On the other hand there are 3,000 missionaries for the 300,000 Protestants in Japan.

The missionary is involved, moreover, in the process of establishing, maintaining, and orienting institutions. With respect to the local church leadership, then, the missionary is *servus servorum dei* in a situation in which the *servi* he serves are often disconcertingly black, brown, or yellow. Such worldly skills as politics and administration, which the old-fashioned missionary could afford to shun, are necessary to the present-day evangelist's church-building mission and equally essential to those modern missionaries who are serving as public health advisers, school principals, and agricultural technicians.

The evidence of these changes in attitude and emphasis is to be found in every missionary church but naturally differs in form. The Roman Church, as befits its Catholicism, has tended to react not by grasping the new nationalisms to its bosom but by further internationalizing its approach. "We're here for 500 years," said one Roman Catholic, "we can't try to fit in precisely with every secular fad that comes along."

Among the Protestants there are naturally a good many cross-currents. Some observers suggest that the most logical stand for American churches is to go the whole way and declare that technical assistance, not religious conversion, should be the prime activity of Americans active in overseas church work. But most of the fundamentalist churches, where activity is vigorously Bible-centered, put their primary effort into evangelism as such.

The effect of a revolutionary world on organized Christianity is nowhere better exemplified than in the gradual change in attitude toward the word "missionary" (Latin: to send). Some of the mission boards have spent hours discussing this word, fearing that in many parts of the world the term is still symbolic of a bygone pose of superiority. The reasoning is that the new passion for equality in the newly developing areas makes their leadership peculiarly sensitive to any implication of American moral or spiritual preeminence —and that the traditional term carries just such an implication. In any event, the Pentecostal groups now generally advise their new missionaries against having this word appear on their American passports.

4

Before World War I, in 1911, most of the missionary effort from the United States was sponsored by a few of the larger denominations, which cooperated with each other by exchanging information and pooling their resources on many projects. The form and some of the substance of this cooperation is preserved today in the Division of Foreign Missions of the National Council of Churches, but by 1956 the groups cooperating in the National Council accounted for only 42½ per cent of the total Protestant effort in the mission field.

Gazing thoughtfully around him recently, a missionary of one of the cooperating churches thus described the scene:

> *The noncooperative "faith" missions, and evangelicals, rigidly fundamentalists, holding the view that there is a literal hell to which men without Christ are doomed, have nearly 10,000 missionaries. Pentecostal adherents alone are estimated at over eight million.... In addition to all this, the rise in Africa and Asia of powerful indigenous sects, almost invariably fundamentalist, millenarianist and condemnatory of other Christian bodies, witnesses to the divisions of Christianity....*
>
> *It is sadly true that the several divisions of Christianity have felt it their task, sometimes, one might think, their primary task, to bring their creeds, liturgies, prayers, hymns, methods of Church government, church architecture, music, and art, familiar to the missionary, not as gifts to be set aside if something better evolved to take their place, but as something rigidly to be adhered to, something obligatory and fundamental to the faith.*

The confusing result at the country level may be typified by the situation on Taiwan. There are at least 57 Protestant missions on the island, and a total of 444 missionaries. Some of the missions are of course very small, such as the American Soul Clinic and the Evangelize China Fellowship (which consists of only one missionary). The list, however, also includes virtually all of the major Protestant sects. There are, in addition, some established Protestant activities not locally considered as "missions," such as churches for the Americans in Taiwan and the YMCA, YWCA, and Church World Service. Taipei is also headquarters for a Roman Catholic archdiocese with four apostolic prefectures, twelve principal institu-

---

* D. Howard Smith, "A Critique of Foreign Missions," *The Witness*, December 11, 1958, pp. 11–12. Pentecostalism is defined by Webster as "Religious excitement accompanied by ecstatic utterances, interpreted as the gift of tongues, as at Pentecost." The Biblical reference is Acts 2:1–13.

tions staffed with Benedictine and Carmelite sisters and priests from
the Franciscan, Dominican, and Jesuit orders among others. The
Roman Catholics also maintain three schools, three hospitals, and a
welfare operation.

In many countries, there is a coordinating group which includes
many or most of the Protestant sects. In Taiwan, however, there is
no such coordinating group, and no recognized center or dean of
the Protestant missionary community. There is a good deal of rather
cheerful competition among the regular Protestant sects, and some
very bitter competition among them and the more fundamentalist
and evangelical missions.

The confusion resulting from missionary multiplicity must be
very great. We talked to one cultured Chinese woman who said
that she was not a Christian, but was very much interested in becoming one. The trouble was she simply could not decide which of
Taiwan's many institutions was the true Christian Church. In this
one case, the 57 varieties proved to be rather too many.

The proliferation of Christian sects in Taiwan is an extreme case,
but it does not stand alone. Ninety-seven North American missionary societies are represented in Japan, 95 in India, 51 in Brazil, 49 in
the Philippines, 46 in Hong Kong, 34 in the Belgian Congo, 29 in
Colombia, and 28 in Nigeria.

5

Since most mission boards maintain only a small number of missions abroad, they tend to specialize in the type of missions they
staff. They seek to find a correlation between the types they are
best able and most eager to operate and the needs and legal requirements of the various countries.

In general, the fundamentalists prefer the more primitive environments where their evangelistic approach is relatively more
palatable and effective. They lack the money to supply services and
they try to make up for it with energy and conviction. One of these
groups, the New Tribes, is proud to say that as a matter of policy
it sends its missionaries to the most difficult parts of the world to
work under the worst possible conditions. Among the mission boards
more concerned with education that specialize in primitive groups

is the Christian and Missionary Alliance board, which trains Ph.D.s in linguistics to transcribe previously unwritten languages.

In the highly developed areas there are often established national churches through which the missionaries representing the National Council churches are expected to operate; in these situations, co-operation in the field often goes well beyond the formal agreements in New York. The amount of American help needed by and acceptable to these churches depends on several factors, but nationalist pressures are prominent among them.

In Japan, for example, the combination of denominations is known as the United Church of Christ. The formation of this church was the result of a restrictive act passed by the Japanese Diet in 1940. Since the end of World War II, it has been supported by a consortium of North American mission boards. As things now stand, the Japanese church has the cooperation of the Methodists, the Northern Presbyterians, the Church of Christ (Congregationalists and Evangelical & Reformed Church), Disciples of Christ, Evangelical United Brethren, the Reformed Church, and the United Church of Canada. Among the American churches, the Lutherans, Baptists and Episcopalians do not cooperate in the venture; on the Japanese side, the Japanese Lutherans and Episcopalians as well as most of the Japanese Baptists and the Japanese Church of the Nazarene have left the United Church, as have some of the Presbyterians. We have exported not only our faith but our pleuralism.

Where there is a united Protestant church there are actually three broad categories of missionaries: those who support the united church, those who support an independent church (*e.g.*, the Episcopalians and the Lutherans generally, and the Baptists often), and those of the fundamentalist churches. The functions in each of these categories are quite distinct. The missionaries of the first group have something like a religious technical-assistance program to administer. They are servicing a going local institution. Since this institution is interdenominational, emphasis on doctrinaire theology is actually a detriment to the effectiveness of this type of missionary. It should also be borne in mind that these united churches may be affiliated among themselves as well as with American churches. The Indonesian Council of Churches for instance is affiliated with Japanese, Filipino, Australian, and New Zealand groups. This council is trying to increase the ratio of Japanese and Filipino missionaries on the grounds that nonwhite missionaries are more acceptable to Indonesians.

The independent groups tend to go their own way in peace, neither cooperating with the united groups nor interfering with them. Their differences are usually theological, at least this is so in the more hierarchically organized churches such as the Episcopalians and the Lutherans, or are the result of local situations in the highly decentralized groups such as the Baptists. In Japan some congregations have left the United Church because they wanted to get along on their own without foreign influence.

The third group of Protestants is a thorn in the side of the first two groups. In country after country the latter complain that the evangelical enthusiasm of this group leads it to raid the converted rather than convert the heathen. From this point of view the major "disturbing" elements are the three highly organized fundamentalist churches: the Southern Baptists, the Seventh-Day Adventists, and Jehovah's Witnesses. After 39 Southern Baptist missionaries arrived in Indonesia, the Reverend Winburn Thomas, Field Representative for Indonesia in the Division of Foreign Missions of the National Council of Churches, asked the following question in the name of the Indonesian Protestant churches: "Are there no Christians in America interested in strengthening the church? Most of those who come out here are intent upon disturbing it."

6

Faced with nationalist resistance and internecine warfare in the prosecution of "normal" missionary work, some missionaries are beginning to talk about a wholly different strategy: the possibility of providing religious training to the thousands of overseas Christian laymen engaged in secular employment. The trouble here was succinctly stated by a Lutheran: "The concept is no longer that of a Christian West bringing light to a heathen East. Now we know the West is not Christian." Perhaps overseas evangelism should start with the overseas Americans.

In the early Church "many of the ordained clergy and even bishops supported themselves by gainful employment," according to one observer. The implication is clear: that Americans might do what the Swiss are already doing. Switzerland's missionary council, noting that there are 65,000 Swiss abroad in secular occupations as against 300 missionaries, has adopted a plan for the training of laymen for Christian service abroad at nonmissionary posts. If the "tiny bands" of Christians sponsored by North American missionary boards cannot readily expand, so the argument runs, why should not the laymen who are overseas anyway—for business, government, and voluntary agencies—carry a larger proportion of the missionary load?

It is a possible avenue, and will doubtless be explored. The evidence to date does not support the proposition that the overseas Americans are likely to be more oriented toward organized religion than their stay-at-home compatriots.

> *I have had the opportunity of watching the behavior and deterioration of more than one U.S. citizen in a foreign place* [so reads a letter from a Protestant pastor in one of the capital cities of Latin America]. *Golf, hunting, cocktail parties, and social climbing take precedence over church, much more so than at home; and one's perspective easily becomes warped and distorted.*

> *There is certainly a great apathy among the American Protestants with regard to Christianity. It is a real problem. Some of our people have grown so accustomed to doing other things on Sundays that getting them to change would be something of a miracle, though not an impossibility.*

But as in most communities in the United States, the social pressure to belong to the American community by belonging to its American church is very great.

The effect of adherence to an overseas American church may be to build one more wall around the Americans that will interfere with the development of cross-cultural communication with the nationals of the host country. The pastor of an American church overseas has not only the problem of getting the overseas Americans into his church on Sundays; he must also worry about whether they are coming because it is Christian or because it is American. The pastor of one Overseas Union Church frowned with deep concern when he

remarked: "So many people say, after church service on Sunday
'Thank you so much. It was just like being home for an hour!' "

The Overseas Union Churches are not truly a part of the missionary movement.* The 93 churches now affiliated with the National Council of Churches, with a membership of 12,000 to 15,000
in 45 countries, are established and maintained primarily as a service
to the American communities, not as a means of evangelizing the
Asians, Africans, and Latin Americans who surround the "little
Americas" of which these churches form an integral part. Another
10,000 or 15,000 Americans actively participate in the life and worship of these churches although they are not members of them.

The hope nevertheless persists, in some quarters, that by bringing
more overseas Americans to Christ, their faith would somehow rub
off on the non-Christian people with whom they deal. As a minimum,
some missionaries would hope by educating overseas laymen to
reduce the adverse effect of the "other Americans" on the missionary
movement as such. For, as D. Howard Smith has bluntly stated it:

> *The failure of the Church to substantiate the claim that
> Christianity is the faith for the world is due, more than
> anything else, to the fact that the multitudes of Asia and
> Africa have failed to see in the lives of those who have
> come to them from the Christian West any compelling
> reason why they should forsake their own spiritual and
> moral values for those of Christianity.*

* The Overseas Union Churches mainly serve members of churches belonging
to the National Council. The following figures, from a 1958 survey of a number of the larger Overseas Union Churches, illustrate the point:

Methodist	1,545	Evang. United Brethren	44
Presbyterian	1,484	Angelican	38
Baptist	884	Unitarian	31
Lutheran	578	United Church of Canada	29
Congregational	492	Greek Orthodox	21
Episcopal	438	Mennonite	20
Disciples of Christ	242	Church of Christ	17
Union or Community	218	Church of the Brethren	14
Reformed	92	Quaker	13
Evang.-Reformed	44	Mormon	13
		Other and unclassified	341
		TOTAL:	6,598

The "other" category includes a wide variety of smaller sects, together with
13 Roman Catholics and 4 Jews. National Council of Churches, "Department
of Overseas Union Churches: Denominational Backgrounds of Members,"
June 20, 1958.

7 · The Businessmen

1

The American geologist was just finishing his dessert, served up from the galley of the houseboat anchored in a river of Burma's Irrawaddy Delta, when the shots first split the evening silence. He and his fellow technicians, with their Burmese assistants, hit the deck in tangled confusion. Moments later they heard the roar of returning fire, followed by the excited commands of a Burmese army officer as he gathered his troops to head for shore in small boats to take up the pursuit of the intruders. This American, employed by one of his country's best geophysical-survey companies, which was under contract to the Burmese Government to explore the Irrawaddy Delta for oil structures, was caught in the crossfire of the continuing struggle for pacification of Burma's rural areas. The Government, intent on pushing forward its search for natural resources, had provided an armed escort for the survey team, and the presence of the army troops had stirred the local bandit groups into starting this nocturnal skirmish. Before the survey was completed, it became commonplace to have dinner thus rudely interrupted. The sight of 50-caliber tracers was just another occupational hazard for the geological team.

Not all overseas American businessmen have quite so exciting a time, but an inventory of United States business activity abroad confirms the image of American private enterprise as enterprising—

even if in an era of government contracts it is no longer so private. The American accountant figuring the overhead for a Japanese supplier, the engineer crash-landing his plane near an Asian village damaged by earthquake, the oil executive trying to tell his Iranian boss that in a modern organization the head man does not personally open all the mail—these and more than 25,000 other Americans work abroad, searching for new business or managing established sources of profits for American investors.

American businessmen have had the capital and enterprise to venture into foreign lands since the days the Salem Clipper sailed to China and have been a major factor in foreign markets since Commodore Matthew Perry forcibly opened the Japanese market with two steamships and six sailing vessels. Early in the twentieth century, as the United States slowed down its rate of capital imports for its own development and started exporting capital on a big scale, some of the largest American companies, especially those in mining and food production, began to make direct investments abroad under the tacit protection of the U.S. Government.

At first the concern of these companies for the welfare of the native population and for the building of effective governments in foreign countries was easily outweighed by the desire for quick returns and high profits on their investment. But the Triple Revolution has been as influential in shaping business policy as it has been in changing government programs and molding missionary attitudes. Foreign markets are limited by enforceable government regulations; in an era of nationalist enthusiasm the specter of having your business nationalized is never further away than the next change in political leadership.

American firms face not only the normal competition of the open market but also the handicap of operating as "foreign" enterprises. Their most important trademark, for better or worse, is the competence and conduct of their American employees, and the way these employees treat the local employees who often outnumber the American by 15 (or more) to 1. Consequently, the men who produce and distribute oil, mine copper, grow rubber, sell and install machinery, establish retail outlets, or buy handicrafts for the American market find they cannot do business in foreign countries without engaging in vigorous and expensive programs of community relations. His task immensely complicated by nationalism, racism, and rising expectations all around him, the businessman discovers that his ability to create and maintain a profitable enterprise with a long life ahead of it depends on his becoming a contributing partner in meeting the demands which the world-wide revolution of attitudes has brought to the surface.

"The customer is always right" is an old slogan in American business life. Now that the customer is, in effect, the world, the old slogan has taken on a new complexity. To get at the customer, the businessman cannot merely look across the counter and ask, "May I help you, sir?" If he did, he might hear the customer say: "Yes, you may—if you split your profits with me, if you hire and train the citizens of my country to work in your company, if you help develop the health, education, and sanitation facilities in my country, and if you generally behave like a responsible citizen when you come to do business with me!" Faced with this strings-attached welcome, the American businessman, like the government worker and the missionary, has drifted into a deep involvement in the domestic affairs of other nations. Local sources of supply and machine shops must be developed, and firms established that are owned partly (and in many countries predominantly) by local people. American firms are forced to lean with the nationalist winds on such questions as the number of Americans who can be brought in to work and the margin of profit that can be taken out. Companies like Firestone in Liberia, Creole Petroleum in Venezuela, Sears, Roebuck in Mexico, the Philippine American Life Insurance Company in Manila, the Arabian American Oil Company in Saudi Arabia, and United Fruit in Costa Rica have deliberately involved themselves in national economic-development programs as a matter of public relations and business survival. And while business leaders protest that they do not interfere in politics, they must make their own business decisions with a wary eye for political repercussions, studying carefully the nationalist ideology or even the possible corruptibility of the men in each country who can make or break an American business by passing a law or inciting a mob.

2

American private enterprise is found everywhere, even behind the Iron Curtain. It takes many forms, from the huge corporation whose single influence can bring a small country from the ox-cart era into a Cadillac economy in thirty short years to the one-man "buyer" who specializes in the development of indigenous handicrafts for export. American businessmen abroad are selling insurance and bulldozers, mining quicksilver and cutting timber, manufacturing pencils and penicillin, building dams and laying pipe. They are found in the capital cities of the world or, like the geologist in Burma, "out in the boondocks." They go abroad to live, to set up business operations, and to manage those operations in a manner designed to fulfill the basic requirement of any commercial enterprise: to earn a profit.

It is not the presence of American business overseas, but the extent of it, that is the recent phenomenon. United States direct investment abroad was already on the increase before World War II, has risen from $.6 billion in 1897 to $7.9 billion in 1943. As might be expected, investment capital flowed at first to markets already developed and considered safe: 90 per cent of the direct investment by 1943 had been placed in Canada, Europe, or Latin America.

The war and its aftermath produced a striking increase in United States foreign investment. By 1950, the value of direct investments abroad had reached $11.8 billion and by 1957 the total was up to $25.3 billion—this does not include the billions of dollars in government grants and loans to foreign countries, much of which American businessmen also helped manage. From 1950, when the annual net private capital outflow was $1.3 billion, the rate almost tripled to an annual figure of $3.2 billion in 1957. Henry Kearns, then Assistant Secretary of Commerce for International Affairs, told Congress when he presented these figures:

> *The close and intimate relationship . . . between trade and investment . . . can be seen* [from the facts that] *the total value of our direct private investments abroad, in the period 1950 to 1957, has increased 114 per cent. Direct private investments abroad in manufacturing industries during that*

period *increased 107 per cent. At the same time ... the
annual increase in total United States exports amounted to
93 per cent. The bunching of these percentages is more
than coincidental.*

The only part of the picture which had not radically changed was
the geographical pattern of this outflow. The lion's share, 86 per
cent of the 1957 pie, was still cut in favor of Canada, Europe, and
Latin America.

The impact of this overseas investment is heavy. In 1958, United
States exports of goods and commodities were about 17 billion
dollars while American plants abroad were selling to the foreign
markets goods and services estimated at 30 billion dollars. The total
foreign sales of American business and industry, therefore, added
up to 47 billion dollars. This figure may not seem too impressive
compared to an American gross national product of more than 400
billion dollars, but it is more than our annual defense spending
in the United States; it is equivalent to the gross national product
of the United Kingdom and twice the gross product of Canada.

TABLE 4. AMERICAN BUSINESS

Type of Firm and number in group	544 Manufacturing Sales and Service		30 Oil	
Geographic Region	U.S. *Citizens*	*Foreign Nationals*	U.S. *Citizens*	*Foreign Nationals*
Latin America	2,597	232,228	5,534	81,398
Middle East and North Africa	216	9,448	3,504	41,892
Far East	992	57,241	875	37,888
Europe	1,560	340,353	273	65,760
Canada	810	91,455	518	2,007
Central and South Africa	188	12,873	136	12,365
Totals	6,363	743,598	10,840	241,310

Source: Overseas Training Project, Maxwell Graduate School of Citizenship and
Public Affairs, Syracuse University, 1957.

Why is such a large amount of investment capital and business effort being exported? Basically it is because American companies have found that in spite of the difficulties and dangers of doing business in strange places and under demanding conditions, profits are still rewardingly high. In a 1957 survey by Milton M. Mandell and Alexander O. Stanley, of 93 major United States companies which have plant investment abroad, more than half reported receiving up to 20 per cent of their total net profits from their overseas operations, and over 30 per cent of the companies reported that they derive from 40 to 100 per cent of their net profits from their foreign affiliates. Sometimes American companies, when building a plant or establishing a distribution market overseas, are able to proceed on the basis that the investment can be completely paid off within four to five years; from then on the operation is pure profit.

Clearly then the dollars are coming back in proportions that tend to accelerate further growth of American international business

AND OVERSEAS EMPLOYMENT

49 Engineering and Construction		23 Raw Material Procurement		Totals 646 Companies	
U.S. Citizens	Foreign Nationals	U.S. Citizens	Foreign Nationals	U.S. Citizens	Foreign Nationals
1,086	16,843	1,276	156,298	10,493	486,767
1,400	16,680	7	0	5,127	68,020
814	25,760	568	13,622	3,249	134,511
1,004	6,737	123	11,270	2,960	424,120
589	10,336	141	10,397	2,058	114,195
1	126	150	27,719	475	53,083
4,894	76,482	2,265	219,306	* 24,659	1,280,696

* Includes 297 who work in more than one region.

operations. To guide and manage the investments, people too are going out and coming back: people to oversee and administer, people to build and to buy, people to negotiate and to train. The small entrepreneur, the ex-G.I. who thinks he can make a new start abroad, and the sharp trader who is looking for a quick profit are also going overseas, though in small numbers. As United States economic growth slowed its pace, businessmen have been gazing at new vistas of opportunity beyond the water's edge. In 1957, the 646 American companies that replied to a survey questionnaire sent out by the Maxwell School reported 24,659 United States citizens and 1,280,000 foreign nationals at work for their firms in overseas establishments. Counting wives and families, the total American business population living abroad certainly exceeds 100,000. (To be added to this total are the thousands of home-based American executives who make fortnightly to semestral excursions abroad—to explore, to investigate, or to trouble-shoot.) Forty-four per cent of the American businessmen working abroad are connected with the oil industry, while 26 per cent are engaged in manufacturing, sales, and service. Engineering and construction firms employ 21 per cent, and companies engaged in raw material procurement account for 9 per cent. (See Table 4.)

It does not seem possible to estimate the number of individual Americans overseas engaged in contract work for foreign governments or foreign companies, or running their own offices as consultants or lawyers or public relations men, or merely drifting around picking up odd jobs and taking advantage of opportunities as they present themselves. These individuals, free from any corporate control, cannot be catalogued and in many cases can hardly be classified as overseas Americans, for many have severed all connections with their homeland and have become permanent expatriates.

With the opportunities go many challenges. Nationalism is one. The United States executive, accustomed to the warm camaraderie of the Rotary luncheon or the monthly get-together with the like-minded at the Chamber of Commerce, may suddenly find himself in a spotlight with the label "economic imperialist" hanging around his neck. Not many of the familiar rules apply; he must learn, as some of the most successful companies have learned, the technique of "philanthropy with a profit motive," and the lesson that "altruism pays." Moreover, no matter how little he may know of international diplomacy, he must learn or invent a new kind of business ethics appropriate to the era of deep transcultural involvement.

Finally, he finds himself playing, perhaps a little self-consciously, an important role in his country's program of meeting and beating the vast new challenge of Soviet economic welfare. The oil executive who suddenly realizes that 5 to 6 per cent of the Western European petroleum market is now buying Soviet fuels (at low "political" prices for high-quality products) or the steelman who sees the political effects of a Soviet steel mill in India, does not need a political scientist to tell him the potential danger not only to his business but also to the free economy in which he plays a part. Soviet enterprise is not private, but it is a nonetheless enterprising form of business. On arriving at a trade fair in Leipzig in early 1959, Soviet Premier Nikita Khrushchev denied that he came as an official representative of his government. "I represent business circles of the U.S.S.R.," he announced.

3

What has been the response of American international businessmen in the postwar era to these challenges of nationalism, unfriendly political identification, and the Soviet economic threat? Some venture forth with interest, and recoil in horror from what they find. A businessman told a group at Harvard,

> One company I know of decided to investigate the foreign market and sent its superintendent to do the job because he knew the product line and had been with the firm for twenty years. But this man did not know a single thing about either foreign business or the international economic and political situation. He came back with a three months' expense account and a report which read in substance: "These fellows do things differently in Europe. Let's stay where we are"! *

* By permission from *Management Guide to Overseas Operations*, by Dan H. Fenn, Jr., Copyright 1957, McGraw-Hill Book Company, Inc., p. 83.

Other companies engage in overseas ventures, either extensively or as relative sidelines to their domestic operations, and after a few years find them not worth continuing. Many establish their operations, get their machines running and their products into the market, and continue to run their overseas businesses pretty much as if they were in Hometown, U.S.A. Their overseas affiliates make a profit, their businesses expand, and things look good—the only problem being that if they truly consider their overseas operation as a mere extension of Hometown, U.S.A., they are probably operating on borrowed time.

The success stories to date prove the need for more searching analyses of foreign business operations on the part of the average American business organization. Such success stories, covering the experience of eight large U.S. firms, are described in a remarkable series of case studies of *United States Business Performance Abroad,* published over the past six years by the National Planning Association (NPA).* From these studies American business can draw some general conclusions concerning the evolution of company policies toward their overseas business operations, their relationships with the local communities in which they are working, and their development programs for both American and local personnel.

A principal ingredient of success has been the willingness to equate company interest with the interest of the country in which the company operates. "What is good for the country is good for business," say most successful enterprisers, without demanding that the reverse be *ipso facto* true. Creole Petroleum Corporation in Venezuela has found that it is in the interest of both company and country to develop wider world markets for Creole's products and to conserve the country's oil resources in order to maximize their long-range yield. Creole's contribution to the building of a skilled, literate labor group in Venezuela benefits both Venezuela and the

---

* The National Planning Association has put out the following case studies of *United States Business Performance Abroad:*
1. Sears, Roebuck de Mexico, S.A. May, 1953. 88 pp.
2. Casa Grace in Peru. November, 1954. 112 pp.
3. The Philippine American Life Insurance Company. March, 1955. 94 pp.
4. The Creole Petroleum Corporation in Venezuela. December, 1955. 116 pp.
5. The Firestone Operations in Liberia. December, 1956. 140 pp.
6. Stanvac in Indonesia. June, 1957. 144 pp.
7. The United Fruit Company in Latin America. June, 1958. 316 pp.
8. TWA's Services to Ethiopia. April, 1959. 80 pp.

company, as does their cooperative effort to diversify other aspects of the economy. In retailing its refined products within the Venezuelan local market, Creole finds that strict government price controls make this domestic market unprofitable. Yet the company has decided to continue this marketing in order to maintain its good relations with the government and people on whose toleration the exploitation and export of Venezuelan petroleum ultimately depend.

Companies going abroad at this time must do so with a long-range plan for settling down. Dr. Harold Hutcheson of IBM World Trade Corporation remarked to the National Foreign Trade Convention in 1957: "It is not any longer possible to arrive one night, and next morning make a quick profit and a quick exit the next afternoon. You [may even] have to consider having a sustained loss on your investment for perhaps ten or twenty years before you have firmly established your business."

The story of the Standard Vacuum Oil Company in Indonesia helps illustrate the validity of the long-range outlook. In 1946, with prewar refinery and producing areas in shambles from consecutive Dutch, Japanese, and Allied poundings, and Indonesia in the throes of both rehabilitation and a war to oust Dutch rule, Stanvac faced the decision of risking at least 65 million dollars on the reconstruction of its business. Although there were several factors that seemed to justify such a risk, such as the proved existence of oil reserves and experience with oil development in that region, the future was filled with political uncertainties. But, with confidence in Indonesia, the company proceeded with its rebuilding program. So far, the intervening years have proved their decision wise: the company has prospered, and relations with the Indonesian Government have been better than were to be expected in so turbulent a period in Indonesian history. During the abortive civil war of 1957–1958 between the central government and the Sumatra-based rebels, word was apparently passed by President Sukarno and agreed to by the rebels that, no matter what happened in the fighting, "Let's leave the oil companies alone."

Another major company policy which is undergoing constant evaluation is the question of repatriation or reinvestment of profits. This is, of course, largely based on the laws of the particular country, and the status of its dollar reserves at any given moment. There are some success stories, however, which show that reinvestment of profits abroad will return both political and monetary profits from the goodwill and the economic development created. The Philippine American Life Insurance Company, when formed in 1947, was faced with no restrictions on the amount of capital it could export or with any shortage of dollars in the Philippine Central Bank. But, guessing that this would not always be the case and that the faint whispers of nationalism would soon grow louder, the company decided to make investments in the country commensurate with the amount of business being done there. Since then its business has progressed handsomely. The company's practice of investing capital in local middle-income housing developments has been beneficial to the country, and it has also been helpful in selling insurance to the tenants. Within six years of its formation, Philamlife had 120,000 policies in good standing, with 175 million dollars worth of insurance in force. Philamlife now insures about half of all policyholders in the Philippines.

4

The progression of American companies through the various stages of international trade has depended upon the type of business and the degree of the market's prior development. One of two historical routes has generally been taken, the first by raw-material developers and extractors and the second by manufacturers. The former have gone directly into foreign operations with large investments and large numbers of Americans living in American-style company camps.

The manufacturing companies, on the other hand, have normally started overseas operations through a small export department, sometimes sending out multi-lingual salesmen to travel the trade routes with their order blanks. They next arrange with foreign distributors to handle the company's products; if things go well, this is followed by the establishment of a company sales office overseas. The next step may be the construction of assembly plants and even full-scale manufacturing facilities. Sometimes this is accomplished through joint capitalization of the investment with local entrepreneurs and often does not entail the permanent employment of large numbers of Americans abroad after production is in full swing. Some companies go only so far as to make a licensing agreement in which the American group supplies technical know-how during a training period, but takes little or no financial risk; others invest abroad in partnership with overseas capital; still others have their wholly owned subsidiaries producing for them overseas.

A third route has developed recently to project American private enterprise into overseas operations—the acceptance of no-risk government contracts for specific projects abroad. The International Cooperation Administration had, at the beginning of 1959, a total of eighty-four active technical service contracts with business firms, most of which are American companies. The Defense Department, through contracts with some of its major suppliers, posts technicians around the world to assist with the construction of facilities, the maintenance of equipment, and the training of local personnel in its use. American companies have contracts with foreign governments throughout the world, primarily in the engineering and technical fields, and Americans travel abroad under these contracts on tours of duty both long and short.

As a company extends itself abroad, it must release more and more control to the field. The men on the spot, responsible for producing within a local context, insist on increased authority to decide which policies are the most appropriate for their particular organization. American business has been learning, often very painfully, that what is good in Toledo or Terre Haute is not automatically going to be successful in Tunis or Timbuktu. Yet many of the major companies have proved to be very flexible and resourceful when it comes to meeting the demands of the markets in which they operate. When the European Common Market scheme was under negotiation, many American companies realized that by uniting to reduce trade barriers among themselves, the countries of Western Europe would in effect be creating several barriers to American trade in that market. Some observers anticipated a wave of anguished cries from the American business community abroad and were rather surprised by the unexpected silence. Rather than organizing in opposition to the European Common Market, the business community, in domestic study groups and talks with European firms, tried to determine how American enterprise, by leaping the new barriers with dollar investment, could gain for itself a place in the new market.

Just as the successful businessman is capable of flexibility in his mode of operations, so must he be adaptable in gearing his product to the local market. Take an example out of the files of the National Cash Register Company:

> *Egypt ... is undergoing a powerful wave of nationalism today. This sense of independence extends right down to the matter of record-keeping. The Egyptians take pride in keeping their books in Arabic and sturdily refuse to adopt a less cumbersome system. Out of respect for this attitude, we are making bookkeeping machines for Egypt which speak mathematical Arabic. You can imagine the initial difficulties. Like Chinese, the Arabic language reads from right to left, and so do Arabic record-keeping entries. The English alphabet has 26 characters; the Arabic language has 72 characters or variations of characters. If you should ask me how we managed to design a machine that would suit the Egyptian customers, I would only say that our people did not know that it could not be done—and so they went ahead and did it!* *

One of the approaches that bring success to foreign operations has been the adoption of policies designed to stimulate segments of the local economy beyond the immediate confines of the industry involved. Sears, Roebuck de Mexico, S.A., opened in 1947. Six years later it had gross sales of over $15 million per year and was one of the twelve largest private corporations of the country. Instead of importing all of its merchandise from the United States, a procedure rendered difficult by Mexico's shortage of foreign exchange, Sears set out deliberately to establish a wide variety of local suppliers. By 1953, according to the NPA report, "Sears was buying 80 per cent of all its merchandise from 1,295 Mexican suppliers. It had helped many of these manufacturers to expand or diversify their lines, others to pioneer on new products. Through financial and technical assistance given to hundreds of these manufacturers, it had played a direct and active role in accelerating the general industrial development of the country."

* Fenn, *op. cit.*, p. 69.

W. R. Grace and Co., a leader in the sugar-producing industry of Peru, had, like most others, used bagasse (the cane fiber residue left over after cane milling) as fuel in steam-generating boilers. But, with other locally produced fuels becoming available, Grace engineers in 1932 started experiments which led, seven years later, to the use of bagasse as the basic raw material in the manufacture of paper. Today Casa Grace produces papers of all kinds containing 75 per cent bagasse, thus stimulating other domestic industries and saving foreign exchange, as well as adding a profitable product to its sales line. Both Sears and Grace, having found that their business will prosper in direct relation to the over-all development of the economy, have exerted special effort to contribute to the development beyond the limited confines of their own particular bailiwicks.

Once the American company has established itself abroad, its capital and its people at work, it rapidly becomes aware that it must work out its relationship to the host community. The 646 companies that answered our 1957 questionnaire revealed that between 3 and 4 per cent of their overseas personnel were engaged primarily in community-relations work, with the percentages rising in the less-developed areas. One wise overseas manager said, "All our men are in the community relations business—but we also have to make a living." The Arabian–American Oil Company, which operates a vast enterprise in Saudi Arabia, usually has between sixty and seventy Americans in its "Government Relations Department," men who speak Arabic, live all around the country, and deal with Saudi officials at every level. Aramco, in fact, maintains in Cairo a staff whose task, according to a staff member, is to convince Arab leadership everywhere that Aramco has no motive other than to produce oil, that it wants to benefit the people, and is very much in favor of Arab nationalism. Other sizable companies generally have public relations officers, though for obvious reasons the trend is toward filling that responsible job with a qualified local national rather than an American. Most firms, however, still prefer to make "government relations" a function of each line executive rather than to establish a separate group of staff specialists.

American enterprisers operating abroad have adopted one cardinal rule that is based on hard, and sometimes bitter, experience.

They insist that they do not and will not interfere in the political affairs of the host nation, although they all admittedly pay close attention to those affairs. In terms of outright intervention, they undoubtedly mean what they say. But the line is not easy to draw, for in some cases the company is the prime economic influence in the nation and almost anything it does has political implications. Similarly, there are cases where the host government, when considering a political decision, cannot afford to overlook the impact which such a decision will have on its American guest. Whether or not American companies operating abroad are willing to admit it, they are deeply involved by their very presence in the other country's domestic politics.

5

In order to get at the oil or the minerals or the planting areas, the raw-material-producing companies must often open up virgin countryside, haul in their production facilities, and build company camps. These new self-sufficient communities in the jungle or the desert not only provide housing for their employees, but they soon begin to run hospitals, schools, commissaries, and to supply all manner of public services.

The standards used by these companies in providing such community facilities have been extremely high and the companies have contributed much to the welfare of their employees and to the surrounding communities which spring up around the company operations. The results of such paternalism, however, are a cause for concern. In Latin America the company finds itself assuming the position of the "patron" who is now expected to care for all the needs of each member of every employee's family. In the Far East the company becomes the focal point for many family decisions, and the demands upon it to provide ever-increasing services tend to multiply very rapidly once it has demonstrated a willingness to be paternalistic. Not only does paternalism seem to create more problems than it solves, but it is of course tremendously expensive. Casa Grace in Peru estimates that its paid cash wages amount to only 40 per cent of its total labor cost. Creole Petroleum figures its total cost per laborer at three times the man's salary.

The difficulty is that once a company is in the business of running a community, it cannot easily extricate itself: the more given, the more expected. As the egalitarian revolution takes hold in each newly developing country, the company must be careful not to give its American or European staff advantages not available (at least in principle) to the nationals as well. One British mining firm in Ghana found it impossible, as a matter of public relations, to build a swimming pool for its British staff without building an identical one for the African employees. (The Africans showed no special interest in integrated use of a single facility; they are still in the "separate but equal" phase of racial self-consciousness.)

Many American companies, faced with the mounting cost of their own paternalism, are now making serious efforts to relinquish their "patron" role. It is more than a matter of cost accounting. Those firms which think of their overseas business in long-range terms realize that the long-term interests of the host country can hardly be advanced by a system that eliminates individual initiative and fails to develop voluntary group action in solving community problems. Gradually, therefore, they are introducing new management techniques into their company camps, such as contracting many services to such local businessmen as are capable of handling them. Instead of building homes in tediously uniform styles and assigning them to employees according to rank and family size, they are offering assistance in the form of housing loans to be used by the individual to build his home to his own liking. Without withdrawing any benefits previously granted, companies are redirecting their programs with the hope that eventually the essential community services will be self-supporting and self-generating. It is a slow and painful process: employees who have become accustomed to living in a company town, that commercial version of the welfare state, are usually reluctant to assume responsibilities for which they have had no previous experience.

An important part of the effort to integrate company and community interests has been the creation of a skilled labor force. Here the companies also face many difficulties. The success stories outlined in the National Planning Association case studies show leadership in the pattern of wage scales, tempered by the recognition that each company gives to the danger of upsetting established wage patterns in other segments of the economy. But each extra benefit

granted to their own labor force brings demands for greater concessions, and a "share-the-wealth" philosophy grows hand in hand
with the growth of nationalist-minded trade unions. Particularly in
the underdeveloped areas, moreover, the trend is toward greater
government influence at the bargaining table. The increase of labor's
productivity is rarely as rapid as the rise in organized labor's ability
to extract greater concessions. "Cheap foreign labor" as an incentive
to produce or manufacture abroad is increasingly open to question.

In spite of the increasing labor costs of natives in overseas establishments, however, the employment of Americans is more expensive
by far. Moreover, the savings to be gained from training and
promoting of local personnel are to be counted in political as well
as monetary currency. American companies are therefore evolving
ambitious development programs for local personnel.

In an increasing number of countries, it is politically essential to
emphasize the indigenous character of the business organization;
in both India and Japan, for example, the objective of the Standard
Vacuum Co. is to eliminate all (in India) or virtually all (in Japan)
the American supervisory and executive personnel. To be heavily
staffed with foreigners in an overseas business is to invite constant
identification as a "foreign company" and suffer the slings and arrows
of rising nationalism. For reasons akin to those which prompt the
missionaries to develop "fraternal worker" relationships, the successful American companies abroad feel compelled to rely more heavily
on their native employees. The speed and extent of this trend, of
course, vary with the country's level of economic development. In
some countries the shift has been already completed: many overseas
American firms—even wholly owned subsidiaries—employ no American citizens at all.

The proportion of United States citizens to total employment in
the American overseas firms that answered our questionnaire is
lowest in the highly industrialized countries (a ratio of 1:143 in
Europe, on the average) and highest in underdeveloped areas (in
the Middle East and North Africa, the ratio is 1:13). By broadly
classifying the Far and Middle East and Africa as relatively underdeveloped, identifying Latin America as semideveloped, and considering Canada and Europe as developed, the ratios of American to
native personnel are:

Underdeveloped regions   1:29
Semideveloped regions   1:47
Developed regions   1:107

We can see that, on the average, American companies (except engineering and construction firms where little variation apparently applies, perhaps due to the relatively short duration of their operations in any single place) require double the number of American citizens to accomplish a given task as they move their operations from a developed area to the "semideveloped" world, and need to increase this number even more for the less-developed areas.

Although most countries require by law that the number of foreign staff employees be held within a certain percentage of the total, the successful Americans firms working abroad are safely below the legal requirements. W. R. Grace and Co., operating in South America, says "In most countries, the law compels a firm to employ at least 85 per cent nationals; . . . we employ 98.6 per cent nationals and only 1.4 per cent Americans and Europeans in all of our Latin American operations." Casa Grace in Peru, limited to a 20 per cent foreign staff, operates with less than 1 per cent of foreign staff employees of which fewer than half are Americans. National Cash Register Company reported in 1955 that it conducted an overseas business volume of $100 million—40 per cent of their total volume—with an organization of approximately 18,000 employees, only 6 of whom were Americans.

As to the range of jobs open to foreign nationals there seems to be no limit. They are being used as managers, salesmen, clerks, skilled tradesmen, and lawyers. If one were to attempt to summarize the attitude of American business on this whole question, it would be that a company should use the minimum number of Americans necessary to protect the interests of the owners and hire the maximum number of foreign nationals. And if qualified local candidates are not available, training programs should be conducted. *

Attitudes on this question are, of course, tempered by the industry

* Milton M. Mandell and Alexander O. Stanley, "International Markets: The Vanishing American in Overseas Plants," *Dun's Review and Modern Industry,* April, 1957, p. 130.

involved, the kinds of specialized skills required, and the existing
business code of ethics prevailing in a given area. An interview in
Cairo, for instance, brought forth this comment:

> ... *There seems to be no trend in the Middle East to
> reduce further the number of Americans in executive posi-
> tions in the oil companies. . . . Even those who believe that
> Americans should be fewer do not believe that they can
> be eliminated entirely from the American operation abroad:
> there have to be* some *if only as an antidote to the tenden-
> cies toward nepotism and family benefits.*

But, with few exceptions, the records of those companies that have
been successful abroad include strong emphasis on training, development, and promotion of local employees.

It stands to reason that American firms operating in the less-
developed areas would have to place a relatively greater emphasis
on training native employees. But the company that tries to create a
skilled labor force where one did not exist before has to face basic
problems of education and social outlook. In South America, for
instance, the difficulties encountered in training laborers are
almost everywhere the same: lack of education, lack of initiative, an
unwillingness to assume responsibility. When looking for middle-
group managerial talent, many companies have found a deficiency
caused by the inelastic social structure, deep-seated interpersonal
rivalries and suspicions, and a concept of work as a means of reaching the point where you no longer have to work. Some of these
shortcomings may be caused by lack of understanding on the part
of the Americans; in any case they appear to be capable of correc-
tion over a period of time by good leadership. The American supervisors, who often feel that the training they give to local personnel
will merely eliminate themselves from a job, are sometimes reluctant
to fulfill their training function. But the companies with the best
records in developing local talent have also made sure that the
training skill of an American staff member is rewarded by transfer
to another post at a higher rank or pay rate.

Not every American businessman going into overseas service today will be in the position of a supervisor with only other Americans as superiors. The policy of promoting local nationals means
that the overseas American is taking orders from someone of dif-

ferent nationality, background, education, and (in Asia and Africa) race. In addition, an American may go abroad as a representative of his company's interest in a joint venture or sometimes as a member of a multinational executive unit, such as the consortium which controls the oil interests in Iran. This gives the American no more power than the proportion of his company's investment share to the total. He may think his way of doing things best, but he lacks the power to enforce his ideas over those of the other shareholders. Such an American is being continually tested on his ability to maintain patience, to convince others in their language rather than his own, and to appreciate other points of view. This is naturally more difficult for an American in a mixed operation than it is for one whose firm retains exclusive managerial rights.

6

In this age of world-wide American influence, the American businessman is usually not lonely for other Americans when he lives abroad. If he is not in a large company camp with many company associates, he is likely to be in the capital or some major city of the country. Like Americans everywhere, businessmen tend to cling together with other members of the American overseas community, sometimes to the virtual exclusion of social contact either with the citizens of the country or with groups of other Americans, such as the missionaries. A natural tendency to take the path of least resistance causes them to cluster into groups consisting of Americans of similar income, language, background, social interests, and drinking habits.

Within the typical American overseas community, however, there is one area of partially hidden conflict that augurs ill for the American position in a number of countries. The traditional American view that "We need less government in business and more business in government" has been extended abroad. The lack of understanding that exists between Americans working for the government and Americans working for private enterprise is seen in the gap between the business community and the government community at many overseas posts. At its worst, the two groups look at each other as if each were in the country solely to thwart the interests of the other. The extreme business view holds that U.S. Government offices abroad are there to hinder business operations, not to help. The extreme government view would be that the average American business is operating to the detriment of the United States, for the object of business is to extract rather than contribute.

An interesting instance of this conflict between conceptions of private versus national interest is the story told by an American mining company executive of a labor dispute in an iron ore mine that was managed by American mining engineers in a Southeast Asian country. Strikes and labor problems had become common at the mine under the guidance of a strong union organization. The American general manager of the mine knew most of the union leaders, and had confidence in his ability to outbargain them at the conference table. But in one dispute he noticed the union leaders had suddenly become very erudite and were able to cite previous precedents in labor settlements in favor of their position. He could not understand how they had come upon their new ability until the day the union team piled some books on the table, all of which were marked "Borrowed from the International Cooperation Administration Labor Library." In telling the story, the American mine manager was indignant: "Now who the hell are these guys supposed to be working for over here, anyway?"

The hazy line between concepts of national interest is easily seen in this episode, for if the ICA labor adviser were to say to the mine manager, "Don't you agree that it is a good idea for the United States to help the development of strong democratic institutions in this country?" the mine manager might reply, "Yes, I'll go along with that, but not when it comes to the point where you are making it harder for me to run my business." At best they would probably agree to disagree and see as little as possible of each other.

Opposing conceptions of American responsibility abroad, as well as differences in living standards between official and private American people abroad, maintain a gulf between government and business overseas. Where both the U.S. Government staff and the American business community are large, fundamental divisions sometimes exist.

Yet beneath these differences there is a community of interest between United States business and government agencies overseas that is sometimes seen more clearly by non-Americans than by the Americans. The contacts and assistance of the government representative can be of tremendous aid to a business manager abroad. The vast amounts of nonclassified information gathered by the embassies on current political and economic problems can be very useful to the business community as it makes its long-range plans. The business representative, conversely, has much to offer the embassy informally. The nature of his work often makes it mandatory for him to travel throughout the country, and he gets a picture of events outside the capital which often is not available to the government analyst. His close working knowledge of the economy can make him a useful expert and, because he is "nonofficial," he can sometimes talk with greater freedom to citizens of the host country who are reluctant to discuss issues frankly with officials of the Government that "carries the H-bomb in its pocket." In the American interest, there is every reason for liaison between business and government representatives abroad.

Top executives of two large American companies overseas were asked: "To what extent does your company stress upon its overseas American executives the importance of closely studying the political and economic factors in the countries where they are working? Do your men overseas focus attention on the 'government relations' character of their job?" One man, an experienced "Old Far East hand" who directs his company's activities throughout South and Southeast Asia, replied: "Mister, we do business *in spite of* governments." A second executive, who directs his company's operations in the Caribbean and Central America, replied: "We not only expect, but insist, that our men pay close attention to this context in which we all work. After all, I don't care how black or white a man is, how educated or illiterate, how developed or undeveloped his economy—his country and mine still have the same number of votes in the United Nations."

The majority of American businessmen abroad work for established corporations, and their personal attitudes are deeply affected by the policies and attitudes of the "leadership element" in their own companies. The attitudes of such top business leaders will naturally reach down into their organizations. They will have a bearing on what the companies accomplish in the selection, training, and development of their American personnel for foreign service. And they will set the tone as the individual American businessman settles down at his job overseas.

Part Three
THE ELEMENTS OF
EFFECTIVE PERFORMANCE

8 · The Gauge of Success

1

Despite the many intelligent policies that government, religious, and commercial enterprises have evolved in recent years to meet the challenge of revolutionary nationalism, the fact remains that little systematic effort has been made to define the qualities these organizations should seek in the personnel hired to implement their policies. It may well be that some of the very motives that prompt Americans to enter overseas service constitute a kind of preliminary natural selection of individuals potentially qualified for such service. But, unfortunately, this factor is by no means enough.

In our research, therefore, we reached for a definition of the elements of effective overseas performance as a first step toward better selection and training of Americans for service abroad. While taking into account the differences between countries and the special problems of each group, we looked particularly for the *common factors*, the universals of overseas experience. In this search the interviews proved especially valuable.

The interviewers' final notes on each of the respondents were based in part on the testimony of the person interviewed and in part on comments solicited from co-workers balanced by the judgment of the interviewer himself. The detailed report of each interview, including the summary by the interviewer of all the possibly relevant factors in each case, was then brought back to the New York office of Louis Harris and Associates for further analysis. There the many factors considered for each individual were fully examined and clustered into five general elements that seemed notably relevant to overseas performance:

- Technical Skill
- Belief in Mission
- Cultural Empathy
- A Sense for Politics
- Organization Ability

Each individual was rated by the Harris Associates on each of these elements. The problem then was to determine whether these elements actually could be correlated with performance. For this purpose, some over-all measure of performance was required.

To gauge the general performance of a person on any job is a complex matter. Who rates whom—and by what standards? The more responsible the job and the more it requires in the way of authority, discretion, or imagination, the more the mark of success or failure must be qualified, thereby increasing doubt about the accuracy of the measurement. This is the central dilemma of an inquiry into the education and training of Americans for overseas service.

Some consultants suggested that we have each of our interviewees rated by their colleagues; others proposed that we judge performance on the basis of remarks and observations by the local people— the Americans' "opposite numbers." Perhaps a better measurement of performance would hinge upon the marks given to an individual by his American and foreign associates. Nevertheless, there are pitfalls in the use of multiple ratings, averaged in some rigid arithmetic fashion. If one associate rated the interviewee "high" in performance and another associate rated him "low," does this mean he was a moderately effective performer on his overseas assignment? To get candid evaluations of an interviewee from either fellow Americans or foreign nationals, moreover, raised many analytical difficulties that both exceeded our resources and went far beyond the span of our research.

But in a world of pay raises and promotions there is one person, the job supervisor, who as a practical matter is compelled to evaluate the performance of an American at work abroad. Rightly or wrongly,

TABLE 5. ANALYSIS OF EFFECTIVE PERFORMANCE *Americans at Work Abroad*

Ratings by Supervisors on Job Performance		Ratings by Interviewers on Five Elements of Job Performance [1]									
		TECHNICAL SKILL		BELIEF IN MISSION		SENSE FOR POLITICS		CULTURAL EMPATHY		ORGANIZATION ABILITY	
		High	Low	High	Low	High	Low	High	Low	High	Low
HIGH	75	57	0	45	2	42	6	41	6	34	1
MEDIUM HIGH	99	47	3	44	4	36	18	33	13	37	26
MEDIUM LOW	30	9	3	10	2	10	6	9	7	8	7
LOW	15	4	2	3	5	3	7	1	4	4	8
NOT RATED BY SUPERVISORS [2]	25										
TOTAL	244										

[1] Only high and low ratings appear under this heading. Intermediate categories have been omitted. Essentially the table indicates that out of 75 men rated "high" by their supervisors, 57 were rated "high" on technical skill by independent interviewers, 45 were rated "high" on belief in mission, and so forth.
[2] Individuals not rated had no supervisors in the countries where they were interviewed.

the job supervisor has to make decisions about the general effectiveness of his subordinates, and he translates such decisions into tangible rewards or penalties. The supervisors of the overseas organizations, therefore, were asked to evaluate the performance of those of
their subordinates who had been interviewed. The whole profile of
the individual was stressed. Ratings were intended to encompass
not merely a narrow judgment about technical proficiency, but a
full appraisal of the person's general worth to the overseas operation
and its mission. Twenty-five Americans of this group of 244 could
not be rated on job performance because their supervisors were not
located in the foreign country, or, in the case of a few independent
businessmen, they had no "immediate supervisors." The ratings given
by the supervisors of the remaining 219 Americans at work abroad
were then compared with the ratings given by the Harris Associates
on each of the five elements of overseas performance. Table 5 indicates the results.

2

People who engage in social-science research generally describe
their conclusions modestly as "hypotheses which suggest further
lines of inquiry," and we do not intend to neglect this useful phrase.
Strikingly high correlations are not to be found between each of the
hypothesized elements and the supervisors' ratings on over-all
job performance. But as Table 5 reveals, there is a pattern of relevance that can hardly be ignored. Three-quarters of the Americans
abroad who were rated "high" on job performance by their supervisors were also rated "high" on *technical skill* by independent interviewers and none of them was rated "low" on this element. Between 45 and 60 per cent of those highly esteemed by their supervisors were also rated "high" by the interviewers on *belief in mission,
cultural empathy, a sense for politics,* and *organization ability;* only
six of these Americans were scored "low" on a sense for politics and
cultural empathy; only two were marked "low" on belief in mission,
and only one on cultural empathy.

As a consequence we believe that an understanding of these five
elements of effective overseas performance is a constructive approach to an analysis of "success" and "failure" abroad. We also be-

lieve that it can provide guidelines to recruitment and training for overseas service.

We cannot from these data conclude anything significant as to how different categories of overseas workers "rate" on each of our five elements. It is perfectly clear, for example, that among the individuals included in our selection the religious workers were the most empathic and evidenced the greatest awareness of the need to build durable institutions. Embassy people rank well on a sense for politics and belief in mission, but not on empathy and organization ability. USIS people seem to rank well on empathy and political sense, but not on belief in mission. Business people rank moderately well on belief in mission, well on technical skill, but medium to poor on empathy. ICA people are relatively high on technical skill and empathy, but not so high on organization ability, and fairly low on a sense for politics. We usually interviewed between 25 and 50 per cent of the professional staff in a given mission, but these are still accidental comparisons and apply only to the groups we surveyed. The conclusions might be somewhat different if another group of 244 Americans were taken from the same kinds of field missions in different countries.

No one would deny that our five elements of effective overseas performance are also related to "success" at jobs in the United States that have no connection with foreign countries; but they are especially relevant to work abroad. The ratings of 219 Americans abroad on these elements do reveal a correspondence with the general performance ratings given to them by their work supervisors. Technical skill, belief in mission, cultural empathy, a sense for politics, and organization ability may not be the only categories for measuring overseas performance, but we are not aware of major reasons for success or failure that are not taken into account in this analysis.

9 · Technical Skill and Belief in Mission

1

Personnel officers of government, business, and nonprofit organizations are deluged with applications from eager men and starry-eyed women who "want to work overseas." Many of these hopefuls, who may have studied a foreign language or vaguely followed international relations, cannot build roads, or fix radio transmitters, or analyze soil, or heal the sick, or perform any of the hundreds of specialized tasks required for overseas placement, nor are they specialists in political analysis or reporting or administration. The will to work overseas is extremely important in the calculation of an individual's potential performance, but the first consideration must necessarily be his ability to do the kind of job that somebody wants done abroad. In case after case of the Americans we rated on over-all job performance abroad, technical skill loomed as a critical factor; the rating on this factor also showed the highest correlation with the job supervisor's rating.

This may seem obvious, but we are convinced on the basis of our investigation that too many Americans who are being sent abroad are not competent at their particular jobs. In many of our discussions with foreign nationals they frankly said that some of the American "specialists" did not know as much about their work as the local people. Privately some American job supervisors complain of misclassification of personnel with a loose use of the word "expert."

In discussing an individual with his co-workers, American or foreign, and his supervisor, we found a remarkable degree of consensus as to whether the man knew his job or not. Supervisors never failed to praise a man or woman who had high technical skill, even though such individuals were not always judged to be top-ranking overseas performers. Undoubtedly more than technical skill is required for effective overseas performance, but without proficiency in the fundamental requirements of the job itself—whether it be typing, or fiscal management, or animal husbandry—the chances of success at a job abroad are minimal.

In a decade when there has been an increasing stress on "adjustment" and "understanding" in human relations, too often the hard disciplines of job training have been overlooked: namely, a formidable knowledge of facts and techniques. In training for overseas work, there is frequently a parallel view that knowledge of a foreign area should outweigh the specific skills required for an assignment abroad. The men who manage U.S. overseas operations do not agree. "Don't send me a specialist on West Africa who is curious about the oil business," said the manager of a large American marketing firm in Dakar. "Send me an oil man who is curious about West Africa."

In many ways the expert has to be better at his job overseas than in the United States. At home the specialist is likely to be more specialized; he has the support of rapid communications, accessible tools and supplies, and the consultation services of other experts. If a management expert in the United States runs across a special problem in budgeting, or an engineer is baffled by an unexpected layer of gravel on a drilling job, he can readily turn to a companion-expert. Overseas, the engineer or management expert is on his own. His expertness must include not only a sound grounding in his own specialty, but the imagination and adaptability of the general practitioner in a much wider field of professional activity. He must constantly adapt his skill to new and challenging situations—not just situations that he has never encountered before, but situations that may never have arisen before.

One trouble with an American when he comes over here at first and has never had experience in this type of construction which is mainly just mud, he doesn't know what

> *to do. The reaction is "Why not build something more*
> *permanent?" But you soon find out that they just cannot*
> *afford anything else. It's remarkable what they can do*
> *with what they have got.*

Thus spoke a construction engineer working for the Near East
Foundation in Iran.

A neurosurgeon, just back from a year in Greece on a Fulbright
fellowship, phrased it this way:

> *When I tried to operate, they didn't even have a proper*
> *instrument for drilling through bone. Many instruments*
> *they did have were old and broken and taped together.*
> *They have a different philosophy about doing things from*
> *the American idea. When things break, they don't get fixed*
> *immediately . . . and yet, with their handicaps, they do very*
> *good surgery. I was impressed. You know, they don't have*
> *blood plasma to the extent we have here, and so the sur-*
> *geons have to learn to operate without losing so much*
> *blood. They have to become more skilled, learn to work*
> *faster. . . .*

The point is that the overseas worker should be able to do his job
so well that he can find ways of doing it under the difficulties of a
foreign environment, such as the lack of trained personnel, modern
tools, and so forth. He will normally get a more varied experience
than his domestic counterpart, but he must be prepared to stand
alone more often than his colleague at home. Too often, however,
the men and women sent abroad have not more, but less job competence than would be tolerated in the United States. Because the
demand is great and the supply small, second-rate economists, agricultural specialists, religious ministers, or businessmen may be sent
into overseas operations. The deficiencies of such persons are quickly
recognized in a foreign post. Individual faults cannot be concealed
as well as they might be in New York, Washington, or Los Angeles,
by the organization.

Typical of the biographic data of Americans in the groups which
we studied who were rated "high" on job performance overseas and
"high" on technical skill were the following: an American Public
Health officer who assists the planning of the national health services
of an African state had a Doctor of Medicine and Master of Public

Health degrees, a short business career, some general practice in medicine, and fourteen years with a state sanatorium and a disease control division; an ICA educational consultant who had done graduate work in science, then obtained a doctorate in education, followed by 26 years of high school and college teaching.

In overseas posts, it would thus be foolish to imagine that technical skill requires the narrowest specialization. On the contrary, the people who often seemed to know their jobs best were those who had a variety of experiences to relate or compare to their special disciplines. The highest technical skill for overseas service is based on a breadth of education and experience that will allow an adaptable general practitioner to play a versatile role.

2

Some Americans are overseas by choice, and others, especially the military, are fulfilling a required assignment. Some Americans abroad have volunteered for two- or four-year jobs with a government, business, or nonprofit organization; others, like those in the U.S. Foreign Service or the religious missionaries, have deliberately selected a lifelong career abroad. Among the Americans we studied there was a mixture of "career" and "noncareer" personnel. Often it was difficult to differentiate between them, for many of the noncareer personnel were on their second, third, or fourth assignments overseas, reflecting a genuine commitment to overseas life and labor. While one would hardly expect to find the same enthusiasm for overseas assignments in each of these groups, an active desire to be there is highly relevant to effective performance in all lines of work abroad.

A belief in mission, however, is something more than a willingness to work in foreign countries for a long period of time. Among both career and the noncareer personnel some are enthusiastic about their jobs, some have a sense of purpose and achievement, and some regularly carry their work far beyond the call of duty. Others lack dedication to their work, think of their assignment as a form of tourism, or are merely enjoying splendid prerogatives while marking time on the job.

A belief in mission does not require heroic suffering in silence, but a wholesome understanding of the purpose of the foreign operation, a frank recognition of its frustrations, and the ability to overcome inherent difficulties without losing either organizational efficiency or self-respect. More than one American abroad is unchallenged by his work, and incapable of formulating the goals of his overseas organization in ways that induce a zestful response in himself. A personnel-fiscal officer with a string of government jobs behind him (scored "low" on job performance) moaned, "On the administrative side it's just administration, of course, and not very challenging. The relations with the people are all pleasant enough, but at the moment I'm pretty much bored with the whole business. My difficulty is that I don't think I should have gone into the Foreign Service at all."

Another respondent who was scored "low," a program-planning officer for ICA, after a number of probes about his career and future intentions, answered aimlessly, "The question goes back to that age-old problem of what do I want to do. I don't have any intense interest in anything, that is, there's no specific area that I want to study. I've thought of taking a job, for instance, with a nongovernmental agency, although there aren't many of those types of jobs here. Actually, I live very well out here. . . ."

An individual's dedication to the job at hand, whether spreading the word of Christ, improving the sales of crude rubber, or running an information program, is closely observed abroad. Comments by supervisors and colleagues are sharp about those men and women who are just "going through the motions." The humdrum worker rarely escapes criticism; an overseas post offers little camouflage for apathetic performance. Moreover, the nationals of a foreign country naturally view American experts somewhat differently from the way we might view the very same people in the United States. The standards they apply, the things that impress them, are quite different. Feelings of inferiority in the face of American technical prowess cause the nationals of most countries to appraise very critically the American's *attitude toward his job*.

How the American feels toward his job may not be related to the fact that he is overseas; it may just be a question of how (for example) the engineer feels about building bridges anywhere in the world. If he has decided in his heart that he really is not interested in building bridges, that attitude will inevitably show. Similarly, if the people with whom he is working sense that the American expert lacks confidence in their ability to do their part of the job they may bitterly resent it. Suppose that the engineer feels that the bridges he is building are not particularly good and that he does not care anyhow because they are in some sense not *his* bridges. Suppose he does not insist on preserving standards in small technical matters because he feels standards to be inadequate in larger things. His work will inevitably show that he feels his contribution to be unimportant, that he takes no particular pride in the supervision or advice he gives. His own attitudes will breed adverse attitudes on the part of others, which in turn will be reflected in the rating he receives on over-all job performance.

> *You've got to be able to supervise yourself here* [said an ICA executive officer]. *At home a goldbricker can get on pretty well in an assembly-line type of operation. But here he's forced to do things himself. Over here, no one is going to drive you. You've got to figure out what to do and drive yourself to get it done. I don't know how to measure this quality. A fellow may do pretty well in the States, then get out here where he has to supervise himself and then flop. This is quite apart from having to adjust to living conditions. A guy has to have the desire to do something and get it done and say to himself, "I did it."*

There is a sense in which all religious missionary workers have a belief in mission; their small cash incomes and the natural frustrations of their work require the highest conviction of purpose to keep the individual on the job at all. Not all missionaries, however, run the same risks or suffer the same economic deprivations. Many of the seemingly dedicated people in fact cannot meet the realities of overseas assignments. But, generally speaking, this element of effective overseas performance is strongly manifest in religious workers. Such semisecular groups as the American Friends Service Committee or the YMCA may be placed in almost the same category. As the scale of personal security and economic return rises among the educational foundation personnel, businessmen, and government officials, the measure of "dedication" is harder to assess. There are too many other reasons to explain the individual's presence abroad.

Yet neither the desire for high living standards nor the ambition for personal advancement, in themselves, preclude the kind of interest and enthusiasm in a job that is implied in the term "belief in mission." The man in Rio de Janeiro who loved the import-export business, was fascinated by the international exchange of commodities, had a belief in mission far greater than his economic rewards. He had much in common with the American information officer who shone with pride over the three small libraries he had laboriously established in the southern provinces of Italy. The involvement of a well-paid ICA officer shows through when he talks about his work:

I was the administrative officer in a provincial capital. This was really a tremendous job. It was two jobs. It was a general service officer job also, plus the administration. We had a fairly big budget of about $3,000,000 a year. I had a staff of 60 nationals under me. It was a very challenging and interesting job. I also had responsibility for the school-building program. They lacked a technician for that job, so I took it over too. I also worked with the health and agriculture people. We had pretty close contact with the local people.

Establishing a Christian hospital or selling sewing machines or helping reform public administration in an alien land can be projected with thoughtful purpose and pride by an American—or it can be just a job. Undoubtedly some overseas assignments are more challenging than others. Some of them lack a coherent organizational policy, through no fault of the individual abroad, or again, some reflect the failure to translate the salient purposes of the overseas enterprise from headquarters to the field. As a minimum, then, a belief in mission means making the most of a bad situation with grace and cheerfulness while attempting constructive remedies in the job itself.

Every individual in his overseas assignment encounters dozens of difficulties and he is irritated from time to time like anyone else; the antidote is faith in himself and the work he is doing. In a routine role he captures the larger purpose of his career and of the organization in which he finds himself; in a more demanding task he rises to the challenge and exploits his assignment.

In sum, a belief in mission is no monopoly of those who have contracted for a lifetime of overseas assignments. Instead, it is a spirit given to work that proceeds from an understanding of organizational purpose and a willingness to lend personal talent to the enterprise. Frustrations are weighed against opportunities; disappointments are balanced by achievements. Doing a good job on an overseas assignment is not wholly dependent upon a belief in mission, but without this spirit an American abroad is not likely to find in overseas work either challenge or satisfaction.

10 · Cultural Empathy

A veteran of many years in Africa told us that his fellow Americans often "come out with ready-made opinions. It is important," he added, "that they manufacture their opinions partly out of local materials." An American working in a foreign country must learn to dilute his "American" outlook, not merely in his attitudes and conversations, but in his own thinking as well. His training should include enough exposure to alien ways to ease his culture shock when he first goes abroad to live and work, to show him in easy stages how relative are the American values with which he grew up. For in overseas work he will be exposed early and often to tests of his cultural empathy.

Cultural empathy is the skill to understand the inner logic and coherence of other ways of life, plus the restraint not to judge them as bad because they are different from one's own ways. A certain involvement in alien ways—well short of going native—may become the most effective device for building a bridge from one culture to another. "You teach baseball by learning soccer," a Brazilian told us.

In the spring of 1957, on the island of Taiwan, the United States Army was tested and found wanting on the score of cultural empathy. It provided an object lesson for many a future overseas-training program. An American sergeant named Reynolds had killed a Chinese prowler, was court-martialed and acquitted by an American military tribunal. Local Chinese opinion was outraged, and it was not difficult for those most incensed to collect a mob on the street in front of the American Embassy and provoke it into wrecking the embassy and the U.S. Information Service building next door. What was the issue? Under Chinese law, if it is established that a person has killed, he must be adjudged guilty of the killing; only then does the question arise whether he should be penalized heavily for his guilt or whether there are reasons that would persuade the court to award some light damages. Our system is the reverse: if a man kills and sufficiently good reasons are advanced in extenuation, an American court will in effect judge him innocent of the killing. This latter view seems logical to us. It is part of our culture. But it looked upside down to the Chinese and they said so with sticks, stones, and vandalism. A more astute prediction of Chinese reaction, together with a special campaign in cooperation with the Chinese Nationalist Government to explain the differences in the law, might have staved off a very ugly situation.

Cultural empathy is not merely a matter of "liking people" or "getting along with the locals" in some superficial sense of these over-worked phrases. It has to do with perceptiveness and receptiveness. "I would say of Americans," mused Jawaharlal Nehru, when we discussed these matters with him, "that they are friendly—and this is very good. But the fact that they are friendly does not mean that they are *receptive*. When an American comes to India on a tech-nical job, he is a kind of teacher. The relation between teacher and pupil is a two-way street—or, at least, it must look that way to the student. A teacher's task is not simply to tell his pupils what is in his mind, but to find out what is in their minds."

Within broad limits of personality there is reason to believe that the cross-cultural understanding required by Americans working overseas can be learned. A wise Chinese named Liu Shao, more than 1,700 years ago, wrote in *The Study of Human Abilities* that a man can recognize in others only the qualities he himself pos-sesses. This simple observation may be the key to the teaching of cultural empathy. For none of the characteristics that we have at-tributed in this book to foreign societies is totally absent in Ameri-can culture; if an American has come to understand his own culture, he may have developed more empathy than he realizes for other people's ways. By the same token, a culturebound American (and we are all more or less culturebound, even those who have bound themselves to an alien culture by "going native") can be expected to perceive in another culture only those characteristics which he has already learned to recognize in his own.

In seeking to understand other peoples' concepts of time, for example, we can usefully scan our own culture. In Japan, Americans find it difficult to adjust to the fact that it might take three weeks, say, to consummate a business arrangement that might be accomplished in a single day in the United States or Germany, three days in France, a week in Southern Italy or Greece, and two weeks in Egypt. But do we always come *right* to the point in our own culture? When we call somebody on the telephone, we seldom if ever start with the subject of the call. First we say "Hello," then perhaps ask "How are you?" And we may extend the preliminaries to include a question about the wife and children. This may all be rather *pro forma*, we may not really care how the friend feels, and may not even be able to remember his wife's name. But these are the amenities and we follow them faithfully for fifteen or twenty seconds at the minimum. We know that if we ignore them, we will jeopardize the atmosphere of cordiality we desire. Even if it is only fifteen seconds, the warmup must be there, it must be taken seriously, and its absence would be noted with a sense of shock at the other end of the line. Once an American understands the function performed by a fifteen-second "How do you do" routine, he should understand easily the three-week round of geisha parties and weekends in the country that may precede the conduct of business in "modern" Japan.

Similarly in seeking to understand a society of indirection like Indonesia, we can usefully dwell on the vestigial tendencies to beat around the bush in our own culture. Even we Americans, who pride ourselves on our directness, do not usually speak up in a group of strange people without first putting out antennae to gauge the receptiveness of the group.

It seems, therefore, that the educational antidote for culture shock starts with making sure that American overseasmen have taken a sharp look at their own culture.

Another lesson to be drawn from our observations on culture shock may also be useful in finding ways to teach cultural empathy to Americans heading for overseas service. It concerns the *direction* of adjustments required by Americans abroad. It is easy to say, as the many authorities have said, that an American intending to work abroad must understand that culture is relative. But the reactions of the overseas Americans we interviewed suggest that we can go further than this. It may be possible to develop some useful generalizations about cross-cultural understanding that would be valid for all Americans at work abroad.

The first generalization is this: in the United States the processes of pursuing ends—legal process, economic process, political process, even the processes of intrafamily relations—have been gradually *depersonalized*. Unlike most of our neighbors in the world, the United States and other Western nations have tried to develop standards, measures, procedures, and so forth that minimize human judgment and personal prejudice in the making of decisions.

Our insistence that everybody is or ought to be equal tends to eliminate most forms of deference which are common in hierarchical societies; we started this in our Constitution, which outlaws the titles of nobility. Our government is rooted in a system of "objective" checks and balances. By building a governmental service with systematic salary arrangements we try to eliminate from the public service most of the personal preferment and spoils system so characteristic of some other societies and, indeed, of most of our own short history. The specialization of labor required for rising productivity in a highly industrialized society encourages an interdependence in our society that tends to eliminate the old discriminations between individuals and families based on birth or race or church or region of origin. The egalitarian view of man applied to the economy through the welfare state tends to level everybody into one class, limit extreme poverty and extreme affluence to tiny minorities, and thus attenuate the struggle between economic classes.

All of these trends in the United States reflect a way of thinking that is quite different from most other cultures. Americans tend to be pragmatic about next steps, to concentrate on the solving of problems (being sure that any problem is soluble if properly analyzed and tackled with sufficient vigor), and to be optimistic about human progress, a faith justified by their own history. Given this national tradition, it is natural that the pragmatic and practical Americans should find it hard to understand societies that still cling to highly personalized systems of human relations; hierarchical social arrangements which require a great many overt forms of deference; governments that live in a different ethical climate of honesty, justice, and mercy; caste and class systems which are regarded as necessary rather than (as with our race problem) embarrassingly alien to professed ideals; extremes of rich and poor justified by economic necessity and sometimes by religious or political sanction; emotionalism not only in politics but in the development of industry and in research; and the fatalism of acceptance or the desperation of revolution, instead of the orderly progress we read retroactively into the short but turbulent history of our own nation.

From the point of view of understanding the direction of the cultural adjustment that Americans must make when they go abroad, our society may therefore be in a favored position. Because the United States is the most "Western" nation of the West, the most highly industrialized segment of the industrialized fifth of the world and the world's most "open society," its environment may represent a cultural frontier, extended beyond the limits of most other societies. If it were possible, for example, to arrange all the world's cultures along a spectrum of attitudes toward time, the United States with its glorification of promptness and dispatch would be near one end of the spectrum while the attitudes of some Oriental societies (and perhaps some of our own Indian tribes) would be near the other end, with the rest of the world's cultures ranged between them. The same would evidently be true of a spectrum in which "objectivity" in human relations is at one end and "subjectivity" (*i.e.*, highly personalized human relations) at the other.

A conversation between two Americans in the United States tends to be primarily occupied with the object of discussion, and the two participants tend to make adjustments to morale, status, and ceremony by slight and highly subtle cues. By contrast, a conversation between two Javanese would be heavy with cues easily recognized by both participants, and the objective content of the conversation would tend to be subordinated to many subjective considerations of mood and face. In both cases, of course, objective and subjective considerations are present, but the proportions are very different.

Similar spectra could perhaps be drawn for other types of adjustment that loom large as the overseas Americans discuss their experience with culture shock. A spectrum could be laid out on a line between extreme directness and extreme indirection; between that clarity which tries to resolve contradictions and that fuzziness which thrives on them; between extreme egalitarianism and extreme verticalness of social relations; between easygoing informality and rigid adherence to traditional formality; and so on without limit.

If this analysis is correct, it means that an American's cultural adjustment overseas would almost always be *in the same general direction*. His attitude toward time will not have to become more rigid if he goes to one country and more flexible if he goes to another; it will always be moving in the direction of flexibility, to a greater or a less degree depending on the foreign country in which he finds himself. His native attitudes will not require as much adjustment in Italy as in Burma; but the *kind* of adjustment is common to both. Similarly, in sensitizing Americans to the more significant role of human relations abroad and the consequent need for patience and indirection in conducting business, the degree to which this lesson need be applied may vary between Italy and Burma but the core is applicable in either case.

If we were concerned with the training of Italians for overseas service, we could not confidently point the trainees in one cultural direction and say, "No matter where you go, your adjustment will likely be along the following line." An Italian going to Burma might have to adjust the direction of more flexible concepts of time, more sensitivity to human relations, more deliberate ambiguity of expression, more attention to questions of social hierarchy, more respect for traditional formalities. But if the Italian were to be sent on a mission to the United States, he would have to make his adjustment in the opposite direction: he would have to get to dinner earlier, come to the point more rapidly in conversation, present his views with more of a show of logic and clarity; he could treat all Americans as his equals and adopt a more informal style of doing business.

An American trainee, by contrast, could be safely pointed in one direction, since his own culture is in so many respects at the "end of the line." He would come to realize, so to speak, what cultural railway line he should take to go abroad; later, when he knows where in the world he is going, he will hopefully have developed the understanding and skill to get off the train at the right stop.

11 · A Sense for Politics

1

The American abroad is perforce more of a political animal than
he needs to be at home. The most conspicuous thing about him—the
fact that he, an American, lives and works in a foreign country—
is the result of specific political acts by two or more governments:
the issuance of a passport under certain conditions by Washington,
and the issuance of a visa by another nation that constitutes his permission to enter its territory and live under its government.

These official acts are only the beginnings of his political involvement; yet many Americans fail to grasp even this fundamental
relationship. A noisy minority behave as though their passports and
visas were grants of extra-territorial rights in a foreign country, prescribing the same laws and regulations for them in Asia or Latin
America as in Washington, D.C. Nearly everyone who has traveled
abroad has heard evidence of political obtuseness, sometimes in
embarrassingly American accents—"I'm an American citizen, you
can't do this to me." ... "I'll call the American embassy." A dowager
from Massachusetts, it is said, arriving by ship one summer in South-
ampton, England, indignantly refused to join the admission line
marked "aliens." Whether or not this oft-told story ever really happened, it is similar to a thousand real incidents each year in which
some Americans betray their lack of a sense for politics in less naïve
ways.

It is not only his little green identity-book that sets an American apart from his fellow men. He is also conspicuous in several other ways. In most of the countries he visits, the American is taller, lighter-skinned, better-dressed (according to his own Western style), and richer than the people about him. Automatically catapulted into the upper strata of the societies they visit, Americans are likely to find themselves classified as *ex officio* celebrities.

Most Americans are not used to being so noticeable, wherever they go and whatever they do. A Foreign Service officer, trying to describe the difference between working abroad and working at home, said his Washington assignments felt like "jungle warfare"—he could stick his head up when he wanted to but most of the time he was under the protective if treacherous cover of anonymity. But work overseas he compared to "desert warfare": "You're right up there on the horizon, for everybody to see—and to shoot at if they choose."

It is, of course, self-evident that the overseas soldiers and civilians employed by the United States have already a "political" mission—to promote by military, economic, or educational means the security and welfare of the American people. But businessmen, educational experts, or churchmen on ecumenical missions also find themselves, without choice, involved in the politics of the foreign nation in which they work, for they are foreigners, with all the political implications of that status, and their object is change—in marketing channels or purchasing habits, in techniques, in deep-seated cultural values.

"The job has political overtones. I call it a kind of ecclesiastical ICA," said a mission secretary in Indonesia. From the treaty of Nanking in 1842, and the subsequent imperial edicts of 1844 and 1846, granting Christians the right to build churches and worship freely in five ports, foreign missionaries were an issue of Chinese politics. For almost one hundred years American representatives of the Christian churches were backed by treaties and government power to carry on their work: they could never have been and are not now "nonpolitical" about China. Moreover, the thousands of missionaries in India today cannot offer their skills in healing, their education, and their Christian example of right-living without political caution in respect to the proud and nationalistic spirit at New Delhi. The missionaries in every country we visited spoke of the terrible dilemma resulting from the new policy of cooperating with nationalism: they must accept the relativity of their American values (which are rather difficult to untangle from their Christian values), yet they cannot abandon their claim to possess religious truth— even though it is Western. The overseas American who is trying to spread a foreign doctrine in self-consciously nationalistic societies without being ejected as a dangerous subversive had better have a high order of political skill—and keep a wary eye on the distribution of political power.

In the same way, secular philanthropic agencies cannot avoid the push and tug of political forces. During 1958, in a turmoil of political suspicions, the Asia Foundation was asked to leave Indonesia. Even the simplest act of charity can become fraught with political complications. A member of a relief organization told this story about his attempt to relieve suffering in Hungary:

> *In November and December, though, we did go in and distribute food packages. We had hoped that this would develop into a continuing program. We were able to send in some coal and textiles, and some food. But the negotiations with the Hungarian Government finally fell down. . . . After our first shipment of food, the Hungarian Government notified us that the packages couldn't have markings indicating that they came from the United States. Since this was about the only precondition we'd set—we had modified most of our other requirements—we decided that it wouldn't be wise to continue it. The Hungarians were obviously making the thing a political issue. It became evident by May that they just didn't want to accept things from the West. So we haven't been in there since.*

The businessmen abroad, the first to disclaim any connection with local politics, make very sure they are kept fully informed about the politics of the countries in which they have major interests. On their judgment about the movement of political forces may depend their staying in business. A new government can mean the reopening of a cherished concession, a stiffening of policy on currency convertibility, or a new ministerial appointment that dries up a useful source of inside information. Yet in a changing world no major business can afford to bet irrevocably on any ruling regime for fear of sharing

its fate if its time runs out. As a result, the most successful businesses
—such as Sears, Roebuck in Mexico, United Fruit in Costa Rica,
Creole Petroleum in Venezuela, Stanvac in Indonesia, and the rest—
touch the political pulse of their foreign hosts every day. They also
spend an extraordinary amount of time and money making sure
that their "philanthropy with a profit motive" is known to all the
primary political groups.

What is really meant by the principle of nonintervention in
politics, then, is an effective program of general public relations that
identifies the company with widely shared aspirations for progress
and modernization, but does not link it to any particular governmental administration or political party.

Turning to the government agencies, it hardly needs saying that
they deeply affect the "internal affairs" of other countries. It has become increasingly important for the official American representatives
to distinguish between leaders who are "comers" and those whose
future is mostly behind them. Even at the diplomatic level, as Dr.
Milton Eisenhower suggested in February, 1959, U.S. Government officials can make clear distinctions between "an *abrazo* for democratic
leaders and a formal handshake for dictators." At the informal level,
there are even greater opportunities for profitable political liaison
on a specialist-to-specialist, if not a people-to-people, basis:

> *I have two calling cards when I go out on these trips*
> [said a labor adviser in Japan]. *One is my formal one—like
> everyone carries here in Japan. The other is my union book.
> ... They have similar union books here in Japan and they
> know what it is. I show it to them wherever I go and show
> them that I am a paid-up union member even though I
> work for the government. Often when one meets Japanese,
> there is a certain coldness at first. But then when I have
> taken my union book out, we're soon buddies. ...*

While it is doubtful if any American achieves buddy status with
a Japanese "soon," if ever, the insight is there—Americans have
loyalties other than their nationality, loyalties which help bind them
to particular groups in other countries rather than dividing them
from others along nationality lines.

2

If the overseas Americans have been slow in developing political awareness, it is in part because the organizations for which they work do not want their field people to be accused of "interfering," and therefore do not encourage them to talk or even think in political terms. Nevertheless, the correlation that exists between supervisors' ratings and perceptiveness about political trends suggests that successful performance of an overseas assignment requires a sense for politics even if organizations have yet to develop an articulated concept of their own political role abroad.

The skill to sense the trends of which you are a part is vital both at home and abroad, but the overseas American's role as a representative makes this skill indispensable. A labor adviser said:

> *Ignorance about the country, arrogance, insensitivity, these are really disastrous for anyone working abroad. And the only difference about their being disastrous abroad and being disastrous at home is that abroad they are looked upon as national qualities. The difference is important, for while the man will fail whether home or abroad, the significance is heightened when he is a representative of our country, whether he works for the government or a private institution.*

Treading upon vested interests abroad can bring swifter, more direct reprisals than would generally occur in the United States. Hypersensitive symbols of national independence require special forms of obeisance. A foreign leader, for example, is no less a leader because his ideas or personal habits are unpalatable to the U.S. Government mission there, and an underestimate of his strength might seriously injure the mission's work.

But political symbols and forces are not alike in Indonesia, Ethiopia, and Mexico. Fundamental concepts about the purpose and power of government vary from state to state. "Here political allegiances are to personalities, not principles," said a U.S. Public Affairs officer with years of experience in Southeast Asia. "Many an American turns into a nervous wreck unless he grasps this fundamental fact about the whole government." Words and phrases, he went on to say, have to be interpreted within the whole context of a society—"just as

an American comes to understand the real meaning of the Constitution or a national party platform."

Culture patterns like the indirection of the Javanese are by no
means only matters of academic interest to cultural anthropologists;
they have very practical political overtones as well. In Indonesia the
whole system of government is deeply permeated by the tradition
that decision must be taken by mutual agreement. Village leaders in
Java are (at least in theory) selected by consensus of the villagers—
and when they say "by consensus," the Indonesians really mean that
the group talks itself out until everybody has had his say and until
the dissidents are brought around to the majority point of view. There
are analogies in our culture: a jury proceeds in this way, as does a
Quaker meeting, and there is at least one Anglican order in which
every living brother must agree to even a minor change in the rules.
But such organizations are not the dominant element in our culture,
affecting the thinking of the nation's political leadership on major
issues of the day. At the political level in Indonesia, President Sukarno has interpreted the *kotang royang*, or mutual-agreement, principle as meaning that all parties must be in the government; in the
resulting atmosphere of unanimous-consent administration any party
can hold up important decisions indefinitely. This fact, of course,
gives the Communist Party a kind of veto over national policy, and
an unexampled opportunity to wreck any kind of effective government. When asked two years ago why it would not be possible for
the other three major parties to rule without the participation of the
Communists, Sukarno replied with the kind of logic that drives
strong men to drink—if they are Americans. "Have you ever seen a
three-legged horse?" he asked. Yet Americans in Indonesia will ignore at their peril the deep-rooted attachment to *kotang royang*
among some of Indonesia's most powerful political leaders.

In the course of our research in Mexico we learned of two contrasting programs that illustrated the value of a sense for politics
and the dangers of its absence. A group from a Texan institution
came into Mexico under contract, got into trouble with the Mexican
Government, and was summarily sent home. Some basic personality
problems were contributing factors to its failure; but the consensus
around Mexico City at the time of our interviews was that the Texans
simply lacked an elementary sense for politics.

The fiasco was partly due to some Texas professors think-ing they could come down across the border and "help their little brown-skinned brothers" [said one close observer of the incident]. *It was also due to involved negotiations within Mexico which crossed state and national lines, po-litical and jurisdictional disputes, and a whole series of involved political deals within the Mexican Government. The point of it, however, is that finally a student strike took place, and picketing went on where the U.S. professors were, and after the settlement of the strike, out went the Texas boys.*

Of course [added another American observer, himself from a midwestern state] *sending in Texans to teach Mexi-cans is risky business anyway.*

A group from a midwest university, on the other hand, was able to set up and maintain a program for training Mexicans in the use of agricultural equipment. In view of the unfavorable political com-plexion of the Ministry of Agriculture, however, arrangements were made to call it training of mechanics and not an agricultural program. In a related program, the trainees were carefully named "appren-tices" rather than "students," and the course in English was offered under the term "Technical English"—to make sure that an unsym-pathetic Ministry of Education would not get its hands on the pro-gram and ensure that it would be considered a part of the Com-munications Ministry instead.

3

"I think perhaps the important thing is what I would call 'in-tuitive imagination,'" said a Jesuit missionary in the Far East. "This allows certain people to see beneath the surface and calculate all factors in a given situation. Any great military commander has that, or in a way it's the same as playing a game of bridge—you can read and count all the other guy's cards. Or chess."

Do Americans have this skill? An ability to read the barometer of events is certainly not built into the average American youngster. The top-ranking adviser on foreign policy to the government of one

African state—an American with exceptional legal training and international experience—says that in his observation "with very rare exceptions Americans abroad are politically naïve."

One way this naïveté comes out is the assumption that freedom must be measured with the measuring sticks we happen to have developed in North America. "In my home town they think everybody's ready for the vote ... they think you have to have free elections everywhere," said a USIS man in the Middle East.

To attune an American to the internal politics of a strange country requires radical shifting of his habits and attitudes. Most Americans are not deeply immersed even in domestic politics. We may express our preference for party or personality once every couple of years, but the United States election statistics suggest that fewer than 60 per cent of us even do that.

A highly-rated Foreign Service officer, assigned to commercial reporting and trade adjustment in Latin America, minced no words about the expectation that overseas Americans can achieve a political awareness that they do not have at home:

> *Back home you go and work like hell all day, go home at night, play with the children, have a drink, dinner, and go to bed. How much time do you spend understanding your neighbor, the next town, or the next state? I think the political campaigns of the past show how little Americans know about their own country. So what's the magic that will enable them to do it here?*

The "magic," of course, is awareness—the American's modest recognition of his alien status, his willingness to take account of dynamic political forces that mold whatever he has been sent to do, and his responsibility as representative of the United States and of his organization. This kind of astuteness goes well beyond simple courtesy. It goes beyond cultural empathy, to a consciousness of one's self as a political man who possesses the skill to analyze the power structure of which the visiting American is a part and the alertness to the political consequences of everyday behavior at work and play.

12 · Organization Ability

A talent for combining personnel and resources into dynamic, self-sustaining enterprises, an ability to utilize skills and forces to make the desired happen—these standard traits of the effective administrator, public or private, are as applicable to overseas work as they are to management of government, business, voluntary, and church organizations in the United States.

In two respects, however, overseas organization ability goes beyond managerial or administrative skills as these are normally defined in the American schools of business and public administration. First, the knotty problems of any headquarters-field relationships are multiplied by distance and compounded by cross-cultural misunderstanding. As a program planner in Addis Ababa exclaimed, "You have to meet the high-pressure demands of headquarters on the one hand and try to adapt these to a culture that's just at the other end of the scale." Second, there is an essential difference in the criterion of success for a responsible job at home and an equally responsible job abroad. In oversimplified form, the difference is this: in the United States, you are likely to succeed in a job by working yourself into it; abroad, you may not be successful unless you can work yourself out of the job by inventing the self-sustaining institutions and training the personnel to manage them.

1

The overseas American is typically sent abroad by a big American enterprise that employs a good many local people as well as Americans. It is therefore generally true that an American in an overseas operation needs more supervisory skill than he would need at a comparable stage in his career in the same line of work at home.

In government missions the ratio of local national personnel to United States citizens is almost 3 to 1; in business operations, as we have seen, the ratio is 15 to 1 or even higher. Representatives of philanthropic-educational organizations abroad usually have more subordinate personnel at their command than they would in their home offices—and the same is true of religious missionaries, although the assistants may not be paid for their services. The degree of importance of managerial skills, of course, depends upon the job itself.

A civilian personnel pamphlet published by the Department of the Army in the summer of 1958 comes close to a valid generalization: "Although managerial or supervisory duties may not always be indicated in the job description, most jobs in foreign areas filled from assignment from the United States require some supervisory ability."

The heavier supervisory duties are, moreover, assumed by executives with a relatively narrow plane of staff support; each specialist abroad has to do more of the administrative work which in a domestic United States operation would usually be handled by professional management people. Consequently no interview with an overseas American proceeds very far before the talk gravitates to questions of public administration—matters of organization and process both in the American bureaucracies (public and private) and in the foreign bureaucracies with which they interact.

A lanky, pleasant oil man in the Middle East explained that "to run a company out here takes a great deal of advance planning—more than in the States." Even professional administrators are sometimes appalled by the demands of overseas administration: "It often takes me three weeks just to see the Minister of Education for a ten-minute interview," said an American personnel-training official in Africa.

Even where the local difficulties are impressively great, they are at least local. Less easily tolerated in the field are the difficulties in

Washington or New York, Wilmington or Detroit, or wherever the ultimate decisions are made on budgets and staffing policies. Over and over again the overseas Americans complained of a lack of understanding by the top echelons of their own organizations in the United States.

The word bureaucracy, with its connotation of policy confusion and administrative delay, clings to government bureaus, but in overseas programs, the private groups, including business firms and churches, share with the government missions the characteristic frustrations of the headquarters-field relationship in a large organization. "The feeling in the home office is stronger than ever of bureaucracy.... Things are governed solely by what somebody who has never been here thinks should be done." Thus spoke one overseas business executive. A Public Health officer in Mexico maintained that the best training he had had for his field job was an assignment in Washington where he experienced the problems of dealing with policymakers. Few assignments overseas are without bureaucratic frustrations.

The reasons for these frustrations, galling to the spirit and morale-reducing for the mission, stem in part from the uncertainty of objectives in overseas operations, in part from the sheer length of the line of communications which increases administrative delays, and in part from the vast differences in the cultural frameworks within which the headquarters and the local office must operate. Rare is the individual in the field who can adjust easily to each policy change as it reaches him belatedly thousands of miles from home and who can be relaxed as he contemplates his unanswered requests for personnel, the inexplicable cuts made in his budget, and the burdensome demands for reports, in quadruplicate or worse, that seem to disappear into the endless rows of forgotten files in the United States.

Our interviews are replete with pungent comments symptomatic of acute "fielditis." A representative of a large American company in a Latin American country spoke bitterly:

> There is something ... bad in this recent trend.... We have five local men from management on our board and three from the home office. We meet three times a year here, when some VP flies down from the States, and we

*meet once up there, when the full Board is present. We
are supposed to have local autonomy, but the five of us
down here just argue till we're blue in the face. There is
a trend toward letting us debate but having all the decisions
made for us back in the home office. There are too many
bosses who feel they must justify their existence.... This
is management by conference, and it doesn't work....*

A certain tension between a headquarters and its field stations, of
course, is not only inevitable but highly desirable. Utter peace is unthinkable between two parts of an organization deliberately placed
so that each can see the organization work from a different point of
view, can pick up information unavailable to the other, and can deal
with a different constituency. A field organization is a consciously
created system of tensions within which each geographical unit is
expected to practice workways, make policy recommendations, and
cultivate outside relationships that are special to its location. The
function of over-all management is to draw from these disparate
forces the elements of wise action from day to day, consistent with
the purpose of the organization as a whole. Each unit's management
has to understand that it is a part in a larger enterprise, and that the
way the unit's executives see things is not necessarily the way they
should look to the organization as a whole. This is not to say that
vigorous advocacy of the unit's point of view is not in order; but each
unit and, indeed, every individual specialist within it needs a lively
understanding of the process by which his expert judgments are
stirred into the general administrative stew.

The problem is that administrative tension is often increased to
a pathological degree by two factors peculiar to most overseas posts.
One is the abnormally long lines of communication; messages are
often slow, sometimes garbled, and always expensive. The other factor
is that the operation is cross-cultural—because of this the geographical distance between headquarters and field is multiplied by a mutual
ignorance of the environment in which the other fellow is working.
In the government agencies, Washington is full of people who are
backstopping overseas missions in countries they have never even
visited; and the missions in turn are full of people who have only
the vaguest idea what actually happens to a request for action when
it enters the mysterious jungle of Washington's interdepartmental

clearance system—our very own cultural adaptation of *kotang royang*.

A certain bureaucratic tolerance, a high boiling point, and the kind of experience that teaches which techniques work for you and which against you in getting action inside a large organization—these, then, are requisites of effective performance on an overseas job. One typically healthy attitude was expressed by an ICA man in Yugoslavia: "Our relations between the mission here and Washington are excellent in my opinion. We're pretty tolerant of each other. Of course, there are differences. They probably think we're crazy on some of our requests, but the differences aren't insurmountable." The ingredients are clear: an expectation of tension, plus the ability to win at least some of the resulting fights. It is the people who must win *every* engagement who never last long enough to win the war.

2

Unless an American can get along with his peers and supervisors in his own organization, his technical proficiency and cultural empathy may go unused as he puts all his political skill into a relentless struggle to survive on his job. Because he is far from home he is unusually vulnerable to the rumors about his effectiveness or ineffectiveness that float around among his colleagues, and to vindictive or spiteful action by superiors who dislike him or disagree with him on points of policy. If he works for the Government he is also vulnerable to the administrators and security officials who control what gets into his permanent personnel record and his security file to haunt him for life every time he comes up for promotion.

It is clear from our interviews that getting along with one's American peers and superiors is usually far more important to the individual's morale than getting along with the nationals. The high-minded man who is bright with ambition for the local population, but who cannot bear the machinery of a complex United States operation or suffer the controls of detailed auditing in his expenditure of American money may very likely quit—or be fired. His self-esteem may remain high, but his actual performance abroad may be close to zero.

Even in the case of the Foreign Service officer whose job is basically one of representation of the United States and negotiation with foreign nationals, the officer's appraisal of his own success is likely to be closely related to the effectiveness with which he gets through to the upper levels of his own embassy and to the relevant officials of the State Department back in Washington. This is a more serious problem for the individual in a larger post than in a smaller one. But it is in the nature of things that such an officer's most useful work—his influence on the foreign officials with whom he deals, the hints he drops, the advice he gives by indirection, the general impression about Americans he creates—cannot be reported in formal dispatches. He can report what he learns, but it is rather difficult for him, without inflating himself unduly, to report what he teaches to those from whom he is learning.

Sometimes the overseas Americans sense a direct conflict between their obligations to be empathic with the local population and their need to get along with their fellow workers. Americans who too obviously relish contact with the native people are, indeed, subjected to a certain amount of pressure from their more culturebound colleagues to conform to more American ways. A machinery sales supervisor in the Far East, for example, complained that one of the men with whom he worked, had "completely transplanted himself":

> *His kids go to a Japanese school, not that that's bad or anything. As a matter of fact it would be a good idea if more Americans went to Japanese schools. But he has his kids sleeping on the floor. Now even the Japanese don't do that.*

But are these tendencies "good" or "bad"? Much depends on the point of view. Our purpose here is not to judge them, but to point out the resentment caused among other Americans by those few who do successfully cross the cultural barrier.

The conflict between crossing the cultural line and living with your own organization is probably felt in some degree by every American working abroad. Even without the social pressure to conform to the expectations of other Americans about the way Americans should act, there is the daily competition in each person's schedule between getting out among the people and doing the things necessary for survival in one's own organization. After describing the impressive range of his contacts with members of the Iranian Government, an embassy political officer in Teheran said he wished he had even more time for such contacts:

> *In my own opinion, I still think that I would serve the embassy best if I did nothing but go out and talk to local politicians and such, and write up reports about it. You can't just do this. You have to sit at your desk a good deal of the time and do an incredible lot of bureaucratic things, like working out travel orders for people coming through town.*

The problem is even more serious where an agency has built up elaborate project-review procedures like ICA's famous "Operation Blueprint," involving paperwork by the ream and very long lead times in planning ahead. Moreover, a Gresham's law of administration decrees that housekeeping matters always tend to take priority over the substance of program. One member of the ICA mission in Laos complained that the focus of attention was almost entirely on internal matters of administration. He spoke of:

> *... the constant stream of mimeographed notices issued for the information of all personnel* [dealing with] *such matters as personnel policies, commissary hours, recreational activities for Americans, requisitioning of supplies and administrative procedures. During 1957 there was not one notice on procedures for dealing with the Laotians.*

Businessmen in large companies perceive similar conflicts of interest and attention between their own bureaucracy and the necessary outside contacts with clients, customers, suppliers, and government agencies.

The combination of cross-cultural administration plus the frustrations of the headquarters-field relationship within the United States bureaucracy thus constitutes a primary condition of work abroad. No wonder that when the overseas Americans are asked what special preparation they would recommend to United States citizens about to take a foreign job, they so frequently reply with phrases such as "study administration," "learn how to write reports," "work in a big organization."

3

The American technician or professional man or woman overseas is nearly always an adviser on organization and procedures and on personnel and financing—which is to say, on public administration —in addition to his primary role as substantive specialist in his own field.

The Making of Moo, a play by Nigel Dennis recently staged in London, shows a British engineer successfully building a dam in a backward country, only to see all sorts of antisocial behavior break loose—for he has killed the local river god by damming the river. Since there was no longer any authority to restrain the people's baser instincts, the engineer and his wife set about the creation of a new (and hilariously dreadful) religion. Most of the overseas Americans are not called upon to perform a similar feat of social invention. But an essential feature of their work is often the creation of social institutions.

The engineer does not build a bridge, he helps construct an organization to build bridges. The educator abandons his departmental field to energize the building of schools and the training of teachers. The agronomist forsakes his seedbed and chemical laboratory to advise on building an agricultural extension service. The salesman finds himself busy helping future clients organize their businesses so that they can afford to buy what he has to sell next year or the year after. They are all essentially engaged in *institution-building*.

One of the Middle East's most successful politicians, speaking of the Americans in his country, said it very clearly: "You can't just go ahead and do something, you have to understand that first it is often necessary to create an organization." As a consequence, the American who arrives abroad finds more of a premium attached to an understanding of "public administration" than would normally be the case in the home environment.

In the United States a professor can be successful without understanding the elements of academic administration; a doctor can operate successfully without appreciating the problems faced by the hospital administrator. As Paul H. Appleby has remarked, we all successfully use the post office, but fail to understand the postal system; we handle currency and write checks with confidence without comprehending the monetary flow or the banking system. But the task abroad is something else. Helping to create a well-functioning organization gets an American deep into such mysteries as employment practices, budget procedures, records and accounting systems, channels of administrative communication—and beyond these into the intangibles of organizational cohesion and morale.

In every major type of American civilian enterprise abroad, one important measure of success is this: If tomorrow you suddenly remove the American from the scene, what is left behind? Just a memory? Or an institutional legacy? If the institution-building functions of American overseas establishments are to be fulfilled, the local people must ultimately cultivate some sense of identification with the new institution and take over its leadership. The first condition of effective institution-building is, therefore, to build from within.

Within an hour's drive from Teheran, for example, one finds abundant evidence that people will adopt only what they think is truly theirs. A pump that was pressed into service by the Point Four program in a village called Khatoonabad stood there for four years before the local village council took the responsibility for maintaining it and financing its use, and in its fifth year the famous pump was still not working. In the nearby village of Palashat, by contrast, a similar pump is working full time, for at Palashat, the villagers themselves had the idea of acquiring a pump for irrigation—after government agents from the village development program had adroitly planted the idea that Palashat should not be left behind Khatoonabad just because the Americans had selected Khatoonabad for assistance.

In Khatoonabad, as in the United States, improvements are not valued unless they are part of a process in which the beneficiaries themselves participate. The philosophy is familiar to us: Most of our own Federal programs of matching grants to the states are based on this principle; philanthropic foundations often require that part of the cost of a project must be raised locally by its sponsors. And, human nature what it is, any plan will work better if the man responsible for carrying it out thinks it was his idea in the first place. So we are not surprised to find that other countries and other peoples also resist ideas that seem alien and strange. A young Iranian emphasized that change, even if it is for Iran's own good, will be resisted if it seems to be imposed on Iran from without.

> *How can I tell the man who sells cheese that he ought to cover up the cheese with a piece of cloth so that the flies will not get on it? He will resist the idea at first, then he may adopt it as his own by saying, "As a matter of fact I was just about to buy a piece of cloth and put it over the cheese when you mentioned the idea." Let the cheese man think it was his own idea; you will get results faster that way.*

The American overseas institution-builder, working in highly nationalistic countries, must not only plant ideas by indirection, but he also needs the patience to await their growth and the restraint not to take credit for them when they eventually appear, even in altered form.

> *Let me give you an example* [said an ICA supervisor]. *Here we've got five men in city planning ... but only two of them are really accepted by their counterparts. The others aren't accepted at all. One of the governors-general of a province where one of these men was working came in to me not long ago and said, "You know I think terribly highly of G——; he concurs with and supports all my ideas." Actually a great many of his ideas were coming from G——, but G—— was able to get the idea across and that's exactly what he wanted to do; he didn't care about any credit for it. By contrast another one of our men came in here not long ago and was complaining about his governor-general. He said, in effect, that he was always taking his ideas and giving him no credit. Needless to say the governor-general doesn't have any confidence in him....*

Institution-building in a foreign country is not just a matter of avoiding pride of authorship, important as this is. It requires a creative act of applied anthropology, a fitting together of elements of two (or sometimes more) cultures that cannot be accomplished except by an American who has taken the trouble to understand both his own values and techniques and the new environment to which he presumes to bring them.

In the year 601 A.D., Pope Gregory I showed an understanding of this process when he wrote a letter of advice to his priests in Britain. The priests were encountering cultural obstacles in their attempt to convert the heathen Britons and their instructions from headquarters gave them a more flexible directive with which to work:

> *We must refrain from destroying the temples of the idols. It is necessary only to destroy the idols, and to sprinkle holy water in these same temples, to build ourselves altars and place holy relics therein. If the construction of these temples is solid, good, and useful, they will pass from the cult of demons to the service of the true God; because it will come to pass that the nation, seeing the continued existence of its old places of devotion, will be disposed, by a sort of habit, to go there to adore the true God.*
>
> *It is said that the men of this nation are accustomed to sacrificing oxen. It is necessary that this custom be converted into a Christian rite. On the day of the dedication of the temples thus changed into churches, and similarly for the festivals of the saints, whose relics will be placed there, you should allow them, as in the past, to build structures of foliage around these same churches. They shall bring to the churches their animals, and kill them, no longer as offerings to the devil, but for Christian banquets in name and honor of God, to whom, after satiating themselves, they will give thanks. Only thus, by preserving for men some of the worldly joys, will you lead them more easily to relish the joys of the spirit.*

Of all the peoples engaged in international relations, perhaps it is hardest for Americans to coordinate their ideas about institutions with the ideas of others. Our confidence in our own American institutions, plus the extravagant if uninformed admiration of American material progress on the part of so many other nations, tempts us to export to the benighted peoples across the seas the institutions we believe to be essential to such progress. As Walter J. Ong puts it, "Seeing others moving toward the same goal as himself, but somewhat behind him, the American is likely to believe that they have their eyes on him rather than on the goal." * But what Paul

* Ong, *op. cit.*

Hoffman once said of technical assistance—that it "cannot be exported, it can only be imported"—is emphatically true of social institutions. The world is full enough of charming examples:

• In Japan, the postwar democratic constitution, which was drafted in English and imposed by General Douglas MacArthur when he was Supreme Commander, still has not lived down its nickname, "The Translation." If, as appears likely, much of the doctrine it contains survived the revision process, it will be in spite of telltale phrases like "We, the people of Japan" and "to secure the blessings of liberty" which betray its origin as a transplanted and not an indigenous product.

• From an interview in the Middle East:

> *The villagers are good Moslems.... We had an engineer here who designed houses. Of course, he put latrines in them. He didn't consult the local people at all on this point. When they finally went up for occupancy, nobody would take them. He couldn't figure out why, so we had an investigation. The whole thing turned out to be because the latrines faced the wrong way. People had their fannies facing Mecca. So we had to tear out the latrines and turn them around.*

• As John Fayerweather has remarked, Americans in Latin America are struck by the attitude toward planning which is summed up in the term *proyectismo*. Latin Americans sometimes seem to feel that the making of a plan is an adequate substitute for carrying it out; the idea that planning is merely a prelude to action is both unfamiliar and uncongenial to many. The American view that the beautiful plan should be sullied by the compromises required to put it into effect is often a source of annoyance to our neighbors to the south; and their ability to derive satisfaction from having made a beginning rather than from finishing a project is equally a shock to the impatient North Americans.

• The administrative complexities involved in building a company town across cultural lines was illustrated by a story from the NPA report on the Firestone rubber plantation in Liberia. When the company hospital opened, strict sanitation requirements forbade the entry of husbands into the delivery rooms with their wives. Very few wives seemed to be using the modern hospital, and the hospital staff heard that they were ordered by their husbands to stay away. Checking further, the company found that "according to tribal belief and custom, the wife was thought always to cry for help to the child's actual father during the pangs of birth, and if the name uttered was different from that of the husband the latter could collect a substantial fine from the former. As soon as husbands were permitted in the delivery room, the number of wives allowed to come to the hospital increased significantly."

With good reason did an ICA office in Baghdad popularize a slogan to remind its employees of the limited transferability of institutions: "Adapt, Not Adopt."

4

Each bureaucracy is indigenous to its own culture. The American institution-builder must therefore come to understand not only the political environment but the administrative procedures and approved methods of communication. He learns the hard way, by shock and adaptation, that the so-called American businesslike approach to government does not flourish in all the countries of the world. He learns, too, that in many societies the government is not automatically regarded as the people's servant. He learns to act on his understanding of how things are, or else suffers the frustration of the man who declines to understand his surroundings.

Outside of northwestern Europe, governments appear to many Americans as politically unstable, highly centralized, badly overstaffed, and corrupt. With few exceptions there is little or no appreciation of the kinds of administrative practices we regard as indispensable concepts like merit as a basis for advancement, central budgeting, and adversary proceedings at law. Even in Europe, the descendants of our ancestors look with ill-concealed skepticism at the application of modern management methods to public administration in the United States. During a recent discussion of international technical assistance in the field of public administration, a British expert who works for the United Nations spoke up in genuine perplexity. "I always worry when I see an American personnel classification expert going out as a technical adviser," he said. "After all, the British civil service has been going on in one form or another for close to a thousand years, and it hasn't yet got around to having personnel classification experts!"

This kind of criticism is evoked by the attempt in many places to transplant directly the techniques of management that seem to work well for us in the United States, without adequate study of the soil and climate in which they are supposed to grow. Throughout Asia, Africa and Latin America, it is common observation that in the process of modernization only the gadgetry of modern office management has proved highly transferable. Bells, buzzers, and girl secretaries are everywhere to be found, but concepts are harder to transfer. "They don't even have a word for administration," said a distracted management adviser in the Middle East, "let alone for the rest of our public-administration jargon. We have had to create a new language. We struggled with glossaries and so forth." The underlying public understanding, the ethical base on which Western management practices ultimately rests, is the least transferable element of all. We know this from our own American experience in trying to build in the Philippines a replica of American political institutions, only to see governmental corruption become a desperate problem within a decade after the Filipinos got their independence. A staff member of the *Philippine Free Press,* visiting the United States recently, made a perceptive comment about the reason why:

> *There was not much graft in the government, we are told. The Americans kept corruption at a minimum. Dishonest officials went to jail. The government was good; it could not help it. But this American supervision of official morals did not prepare Filipinos to cope with the corruption that set in when the government was run entirely by them. There is graft in the American government today, but Americans prove themselves quite capable of dealing with it; they have had a lot of experience. They have developed the proper technique, the necessary attitude. It is just one more democratic problem. There is graft in the Philippine government and Filipinos find themselves helpless before it; it is new to them.*

The trouble here is not with systems of organization and management; the trouble lies deep in the inexperience of a whole people.

Similarly in Iran a couple of years ago, some of the American experts on administration were tackling the problem of surplus employees as an exercise in management methods rather than in social analysis. In Teheran every government agency has literally hundreds of employees who draw pay but do not work in the government. Instead, they may work at one or two other jobs in the community. If another government agency wants to hire someone in this category, it is very difficult to do so because if an employee moves to another government agency he must give up his position, his favored status as a surplus worker in his present agency. Viewed from an American standpoint, this is an inefficient and costly aspect of public administration in Iran. "The Iranians have a tremendous number of loafers on the government payroll," a United States embassy official told us in a shocked tone of voice. "Some of them work only on payday. As a matter of fact [the Iranians] freely admit themselves that if every one came to work they probably would not have enough office space for them."

From the Iranian point of view, on the other hand, the surplus employee practice was not at all regarded as a problem. Payments to workers who do not work is the normal and economic equivalent, in underdeveloped Iran, for the more complex forms of transfer payments which are common in the more developed societies—old-age and survivors' insurance, unemployment compensation, veterans' payments, agricultural price supports, and many, many others. It is true that the recipients of some of these more sophisticated payments usually have a past record of having performed services for the government—bearing arms in a foreign war, for example, or plowing under a specified acreage of surplus cotton. But the same could probably be said for many of Iran's surplus employees, even if it was only parading in the streets of Teheran, shouting loyalty to the Shah in moments of crisis. Until Iran develops a social security system and an economic development program that puts more of its trained people to work at useful jobs, it seems doubtful that any amount of administrative advice will solve the surplus-employee practice.

Adaptation of American institutions to the needs of an alien culture is especially difficult for Americans because they are accustomed to rather decentralized administrative arrangements. In the United

States, education is in the hands of local school boards and college and university boards of trustees. Agricultural extension and demonstration work is carried on by state and county officials and state agricultural colleges. Public health and welfare programs are managed by state and local agencies. Outside the government, churches are often loose federations of local parishes, large firms sell their products through contractual arrangements with more or less independent dealers. Even the search for oil, which is almost wholly a function of large companies overseas, is often carried on by semi-independent wildcatters in the United States.

In most other countries, by contrast, centralized national ministries take direct responsibility for functions which in our federal system are reserved to the States; the function of entrepreneurship is often assumed, in the absence of other realistic alternatives, by the government; in some societies there is even a Ministry to deal with religious problems. Americans are generally sure that the process of modernization in which they serve as the cultural midwives requires a large measure of decentralization both of initiative and of effective control. But they are less certain as to how, starting with a centralized power structure, one goes about diffusing that power to subordinate units of government or private entrepreneurs. Until recent years Americans have never faced the problem in this form. Our development has been in the opposite direction; modernization has required the central government to take over more and more power from localities and states and from private individuals and businesses. It is only very recently, in such fields as agriculture and public health and urban renewal, that American central government agencies have faced the question how to drum up some initiative on the part of local units so that power and resources available to the central government can be effectively utilized under local control.

5

Institution-builders are made, not born. It is no accident that some of the most enduring contributions to American foreign relations in the postwar period—the community development programs in India, Iran, and elsewhere; the land reform program of the Joint Commission on Rural Reconstruction in Taiwan; the near-miraculous efforts to eradicate the ancient scourges like malaria, yaws and trachoma; and the extraordinary improvement in public sanitation in many corners of the world—have been made by men and women trained in agricultural extension and state public health work in the United States. The agricultural people know from experience the difficulty of educating conservative rural folk to the use of modern scientific methods. The Public Health officers know that first of all, as an overseas malaria expert said, we "have a job of persuasion on our hands. . . . Some problems you settle by blasting, others by digging with a spoon."

One of the most persistent illusions about institution-building in the less-developed areas is the notion that Americans can do their most effective work at the village level. Americans do sometimes operate effectively in remote places; but for most types of United States overseas operations, the reward is the development of social institutions that provide a conduit for tangible benefits from a government to its people, and for participation by people in their own government. Not only government agencies but also the business firms and voluntary and religious agencies find they have a stake in the endeavor of their foreign hosts to fashion nations out of societies that have previously been merely tribal federations, feudal satrapies, or European colonies. Again and again the overseas Americans cited examples of the truth that even an effective village-level institution (a pump project, a clinic, a school) may not serve the purpose of its sponsors if it is insufficiently related to a larger plan of institutional action.

In Iran, for example, the American aid program has put a good deal of effort into establishing vocational secondary schools. But after a young Iranian spends three or four years at a boarding school that is clean and well-managed, learning enough about the world to realize how much he does not have, he is often sent back to his village rather than on into a national agricultural-development program. Returning home, the young man is disgusted at the ignorance of his parents and the squalor of their condition; the inevitable reaction sets in and he goes off to a big city, there to join the army of unemployed or underemployed white-collar workers—for even by serving as the lowliest government clerk he can make more than he could earn by staying on his parents' land. The absence of an adequate program of agricultural development makes excellent local schools less relevant to the national welfare than their sponsors intended.

Working yourself out of a job is far from an easy assignment. The temptation is great to get things done by doing them yourself, rather than training others to do them. It is all too easy, and dangerously soul-satisfying, to become the indispensable man. But in overseas service, organization ability means the vision and force of character that enables a man to see his work in this perspective: his task is to make people grow—to build a government agency or a money-making firm or a school or a church that does not depend for its survival on a single personality. American government personnel, businessmen, missionaries, or other "ambassadors" can go abroad with such dedication and inner conviction that they will seem at first to sweep aside all obstacles and achieve their immediate goals with popular acclaim. But if they are unable to institutionalize their mission severe disappointments may follow the wake of their leadership. Viewed in these terms, the self-sustaining growth of institutions may prove to be the best available measure of effective performance by the overseas Americans.

13 · The Recruitment Sieve

1

Those who have been responsible for an overseas operation can describe at length and with relish the American who should *not* be sent overseas. A wide literature exists filled with scandalous cases of alcoholic men, neurotic women, and boorish citizens who have arrived abroad to blur America's image. Such cases make smug table-talk, provocative headlines, and readable novelettes. Clearly there is little excuse for not eliminating disturbed personalities or obvious misfits who, lacking simple competence or elementary courtesy, will undoubtedly fail in a foreign assignment.

Apart from the obvious and much-publicized threat to our national prestige, unsuitable personnel in foreign installations also pose a serious economic problem to the organization employing them. The misfit or failure thus represents a large item of administrative cost in the budget of a mission board, corporation, or government program. The salary has often been abnormally high as an inducement for overseas service; the allowances push the salary cost higher; and the employee and his family must be moved great distances in both directions, usually on first-class accommodations by air or sea.

Few reliable figures exist showing how many of the overseas Americans "don't work out" and have to be sent home, but the indications are that the proportion is very high. One guess by the foreign-aid agency, the International Cooperation Administration, is that 25 per cent of the people sent to its mission to Iran did not make the grade. In that same mission, consisting of 295 persons at the time of our survey, about twenty-five families a year, or about two a month, were being sent home for reasons ranging from the wife's morale to the husband's morals, from the health of a child to the frustration of his father in trying to "get things done" in an unfamiliar environment. Some business and missionary enterprises report rates of attrition even higher than this. Among short-term consultants and contractors, the attrition rates are obscured by the tendency of employers to withdraw the misfits quietly, preferably at the end of an assigned tour of duty, rather than firing them or sending them home (as occasionally proves to be necessary) in a strait-jacket.

Keeping misfits out of overseas service is of course only a small part of the whole problem. The recruiting officer is trying not only to block those poorly suited to work abroad but positively to attract men and women who seem likely to be highly competent on foreign assignments. In recruiting for comparable jobs in the United States, he would have two essential aids: a generally accepted theory about what kinds of people fit best into particular kinds of jobs, and decades of efforts by the whole American educational system to prepare people for them. But the experiences of Americans abroad, remaining largely unanalyzed, have yielded little guidance to the recruiting or training officer on whose judgment so much depends. Nor is the American educational system providing, as yet, a pool of Americans who, in addition to their vocational skills, are known in advance to have the understanding and the attitudes necessary to survival in overseas service.

As a consequence, the present arrangement in all the major types of overseas service is for the hiring agency to select people for their vocational skills and to provide training for overseas work, if at all, after the employee is already on the payroll. Personnel men who would not dream of hiring a lawyer who had not been to law school, or a minister who had not studied the Bible, cheerfully engage and send out into an unsuspecting world men (and their families) who have neither been abroad before nor have ever given any particular attention to matters outside of the United States. In spite of the cost of failure, there has been little systematic effort even to define the elements of success in overseas service. With some noteworthy exceptions, recruiters have been flying blind.

The lack of general theory about overseas service has delayed a serious attack on the demanding task of prescribing the proper education, training and orientation for foreign assignments. The United States today contains an impressive variety of curricula and special programs designed in one way or another to prepare Americans for international life. Some of them seem to have been born out of hearsay or intuition, while others are more reasonably based upon the wisdom of individuals who have traveled widely or who themselves have worked abroad.

Most training and orientation programs therefore limit themselves to teaching the new employee about the purposes and practices of the American agency with which he will be associated overseas. Some programs stress the study of the language of the country to which the employee may be sent. There is no generally accepted "doctrine" about what the recruiter should be looking for, or what the training programs should try to instill, or what the colleges and universities should be teaching that is relevant to overseas service. It is, therefore, fair to say that most of the weeding out of misfits and most of the relevant training for service abroad now takes place after the American has arrived at his foreign post.

No one will deny that it is difficult to identify those elusive qualities of mind and spirit that warrant the prediction of sterling performance by an individual about to be sent abroad. But what *should* the recruiting or training officer be looking for? The rub is here. The carefully constructed psychological tests are not highly regarded because they are not solidly based on agreed assumptions about what background, experience, training, and personality characteristics are relevant to success on an overseas assignment. Recruiting interviews often fail to draw out the relevant information because the recruiting officer is vague about what he is seeking.

A surprising number of intuitive judgments already exist: one educator suggested that if you take a Quaker or a Mormon you cannot go wrong in picking overseas personnel. "Just send me a graduate of Amherst, Williams, Wesleyan, or Bowdoin," said the Deputy Chief of a U.S. Mission in one country.

But surely we can do better than this. Our analysis of the elements which make for effective overseas performance can serve as a guidepost to those who select people for overseas assignments.

Virtually every major organization that maintains people overseas has joined in the search for the ideal pre-selection test to eliminate the misfits and assure a congenial and effective team in the field. The results have been far from impressive. The Civil Service Commission selective procedures, developed after studies costing several hundred thousand dollars, have not been widely used by the Federal agencies for which they were developed. The Creole Petroleum Corporation has had second thoughts about a whole battery of psychological tests on the ground that there did not seem to be any discernible connection between what the tests indicated and how the employees later performed in Venezuela. The mission boards have also been distressed by the prognostic uncertainties of social psychology. Everybody seems to feel that with all our modern scientific lore about man and society, it should be possible for a simple test to be devised that would separate the potentially successful from the potentially unsuccessful *before* their wives, children, and furniture are moved across the seas at great trouble and expense. But nobody has yet devised that formula.

The difficulties are two. First, the testmakers have usually failed to study carefully the elements of effective overseas performance. Since they often do not know exactly what it is they are looking for, it is difficult for them to prepare valid tests. Second, despite the recent progress in measuring human skills, abilities, aptitudes, perceptions, and attitudes, psychological testing is generally overrated as a method of picking people for jobs in organizations, whether abroad or in the United States.

The intelligence and armed services have developed certain stress tests to try an individual under exasperating or frightening situations. Management consultants have devised ingenious gimmicks for rating executive-administrative skills. More than one religious organization puts its neophytes into a cramped community house to evaluate their tolerance of other human beings. (The Koininea Foundation used to instruct the Negro cook at its New Jersey training camp to be deliberately nasty to the newcomers, to simulate the shock of dealing with nonwhite peoples elsewhere in the world. This gimmick has now been abandoned. The training officers concluded that the strains of living together in close quarters were quite adequate to bring out the worst in people, without creating artificial ones.)

But simulation has its limits. Even with the best disguise it cannot be prolonged. Such tests of human behavior, by definition, must always lack much of what differentiates reality from contrivance.

Screening personnel for overseas service, then, is still more art than science. But art is not without its canons of order, balance, and perspective. Where specific abilities or qualities are required, specific tests may prove quite useful. But where an indefinable range of human attitudes and behavior must be explored, the instrument for appraisal must be highly flexible. Application forms, letters of recommendation, psychological tests, even photographs—all have merit when skillfully used. But when it comes to recruiting for overseas service, nothing is likely to replace an interview—except a longer interview or multiple interviews by different interviewers. Face-to-face discussion makes it possible to judge an individual's manner or attitude far more accurately than any other method; the good interviewer can probe with questions, uniquely relevant to the respondent, in a way that no pre-arranged test can do.

Whatever the technique used, the person making the selection should have some idea what he is looking for. If the universals of effective performance are the five we have described—technical skill, a belief in mission, cultural empathy, a sense for politics, and organization ability—what tests or trials can a recruiting officer use to screen out the riskiest cases and place the others in jobs where they are most likely to succeed?

In considering any job applicant, one would look for facts about personality, background, education and experience. Our study suggests concrete factors to look for under each of these four major headings:

> • In assessing personality, give preference to the person who seems more than usually resourceful and buoyant, whose emotional gyroscope enables him to snap back rapidly from discouragement and frustration.
> • In examining a person's background, look for environ-

mental mobility, for the information that early in life he has been exposed to many kinds of people at different levels of society.

• In a person's education, look for evidence of intellectual curiosity beyond minimum requirements of academic duty.

• In a person's work experience, look for signs of a talent for building institutions.

2

The strains placed on individuals in overseas service by their living conditions, the need to collaborate with representatives of other cultures, and the hindrances to their work make emotional balance even more important than it is at home. Tensions created by personalities that cannot tolerate such repetition, intimacy, and mutual adjustment of values and traditions can wound the individual and hold the organization back from its appointed task. The emotional instability of a United States citizen, kept in check by a familiar pattern of society, may flare up quickly when he is assigned to a foreign country where isolation, tedium, excess money, or different moral standards can easily unbalance a tenuous self-control. Married couples who have not solved their marital difficulties present special problems that would be personal matters so long as they remained in the United States but quickly become the organization's concern when they work abroad.

Nearly everybody these days is enough of an amateur psychologist to look for sources of deep maladjustment in the searing experiences of childhood. On several occasions in the interviews with the 244 overseas Americans, early psychic difficulties showed up vividly. One man employed in Latin America bitterly recounted the escapades of his father, married four times, and of his mother, married twice, who moved him like a pawn from place to place. Another man told of being rejected in his boyhood, for religious reasons, by neighborhood children and college classmates in a fraternity. Some of those interviewed had suffered blows in their love life and marriages; others had felt the shock of losing their jobs or being rejected for promotion.

Not all the victims of past emotional difficulties, however, were rated low on job performance by their supervisors. Many had recovered their equilibrium, bandaged their psychic wounds, and moved ahead positively in both their work and their human relations. But others had not.

The recruitment officer must be alert to the possibility that certain life forces may have harmful effects that no training program except individual therapy could reach. He must assume responsibility for sorting out those men and women who have already gone through the psychiatrist's sieve without showing any major personality aberration, and yet would probably fail in the subtle adjustments to living and working in a foreign milieu. Layers of formal education superimposed upon middle-aged Americans with emotional instability will not help much in the preparation of personnel for overseas service; nor will the best films, lectures, or seminars eradicate social attitudes that have been patterned in childhood.

In our research we asked each American interviewed to take an adjective check list and a Guilford-Zimmerman temperament test. The results, analyzed by a consulting psychologist, were not notably revealing. The only hard conclusion to be drawn is that those Americans abroad who regarded themselves as "cheerful," "enthusiastic," "self-confident," "courageous," and "generous"—in other words, with positive and buoyant attitudes—were generally rated higher on their performance by their supervisors than other Americans. The respondents could readily be classified into five personality types:

- anxious-defensive ("wary," "tense," "worrying")
- passive-conformist ("conservative," "restrained")
- narcissistic-indulgent ("charming," "good-looking," "impulsive")
- constricted ("formal," "painstaking," "awkward")
- positive-buoyant-overt-resourceful-active

Only the last type appeared to be highly esteemed by overseas supervisors.

Generalizations about an ideal personality at home or abroad, however, may carry more peril than profit, for in a world of infinite kinds of people and infinite types of employment the task of the organization is to fit the right personality to the right job: the actor who thrills millions on a cultural exchange between nations may need to be narcissistic-indulgent, while the chief accountant of a firm in Brazil may perform his job the better for being conservative.

Every one of us has a "personality problem." In American life conventional praise falls upon the good-hearted, self-confident, friendly, cooperative person, more crudely recognized in the hearty handshake, the direct gaze, the easy use of first names, and generally affirmative and enthusiastic observations. Reality belies this stereotype of ideal behavior, for society has need of the individualists, the scoffers, the cynics, the perennially restless souls who stir and shake and disrupt the complacency of an organization. Some people are most happy when they complain and, contrary to popular notions, they are often among the hardest-working personnel in a firm or agency. Both rascals and saints have gained pinnacles of public admiration. Any search for a single personality type as being especially likely to succeed in overseas work will probably prove a fruitless enterprise.

The recruitment-training officer is thus compelled to do something more subtle and more relevant: establish criteria for selection appropriate to the particular demands of the overseas job. Our interviews would suggest that in overseas work, the demand for the "buoyant type" is probably somewhat higher than it would be in domestic employment in the comparable lines of work. This outgoing kind of personality, moreover, fits most of the elements of effective performance heretofore discussed—the strength to absorb and learn from culture shock, the ability to empathize with all kinds of people, the sensitivity to act as a "political man," the drive to build institutions in unfamiliar surroundings. But the variety of functions the overseas Americans perform would make it risky to elevate buoyant optimism into a "principle" of overseas recruitment.

No training program of one month or one year's duration is likely to revamp the most rigid elements of an individual's makeup. But man is malleable; and some are more malleable than others. The major elements of effective overseas performance are not something you are born with; they can be the product of education and experience.

The versatility of the general practitioner is learned from wide reading and broad exposure in professional school and on the first few jobs. A deep belief in his mission results from a matured understanding of the positive character of the overseas operation in which the American finds himself. The ability to analyze power structure and see oneself as a political man is a carefully cultivated competence, like playing the piano. Knowledge of American civilization, a foreign area, or a foreign language is usually acquired in college or after, not in early youth. The maturity to tolerate the exasperations of large-scale organization and the taste for institution-building are not innate gifts but the result of executive training and leadership experience.

Cultural empathy, too, is partly the child of intellectualized experience—but it also implies a positive emotional attitude toward differences in people. The feel of empathy thus seems to be built into (or left out of) a person in early youth. Judging from the limited group of overseas Americans we interviewed, cultural empathy is more natural to those men and women who have had to get along with a variety of people from their tenderest years on. Of all the factors in a person's family background, this one stands out most clearly as relevant to cultural empathy, and therefore to effective performance in an overseas job. We have called it *environmental mobility*.

3

By environmental mobility we mean the vertical circulation of an American through different strata of society and his early exposure to several kinds of cultural experience. Some Americans we interviewed were never really introduced to a way of thinking and living radically different from that of their own family until they arrived in a foreign country. Others had a record of childhood, formal education, and work assignments rich in that diversity of experience that helps a person develop versatile skills and flexible social attitudes.

In the group as a whole, there was a striking correlation between the individuals' records of environmental mobility and the interviewers' ratings on cultural empathy. Almost three-quarters of those whose records showed little movement between different economic and social classes prior to the overseas assignment were scored "low" or "moderate" on cultural empathy. By contrast all those Americans whose records indicated a high degree of environmental mobility were scored "high" or "moderate" on cultural empathy—and none was scored "low." It did not seem to matter much what exposure the person had had in an orientation program just before departure; a week or two of instruction about cultural differences can hardly be expected to broaden and deepen the narrow attitudes or predispositions that result from years of protected living in a limited cultural province.

The United States with its tide of immigrant population and its frontier civilization is supposed to stand as the ideal land of opportunity for the individual to advance in education, economic rewards, and social status. The success of an American in forging ahead of his parents yields some clues to environmental mobility, but it also represents a danger: often a second-generation American rejects the ways of his parents, deliberately closes his mind and tastes to his own foreign heritage, and becomes more intolerant of his former social group than those who have never been members of it. The test of environmental mobility, perhaps, should be not only the number of different social exposures that an individual has known, but his rounded assessment of them and the ease with which he can move up, or down, or sidewise among them.

In recruiting personnel for overseas service the administrator will therefore want to know a great deal about the individual's childhood, educational pattern, travel experiences, and work challenges. Some of these background elements are normally assessed by recruitment officers only as preparation for a specific job rather than as indices of work adaptability and cultural empathy. One plant pathologist we interviewed was rated "high" on both his technical competence and his attitudes toward foreign nationals. It turned out that as a boy he had heard many stories from his mother about her two brothers who lived and worked abroad. He had gone to a private, all-scholarship school that combined practical farming with intensive academic studies, and at 17 years of age, with $200 saved, he simply took off for Europe, eventually landing in Leningrad, unable to speak a word of Russian. Making his way to Moscow, he visited an agricultural trade show, met an English-speaking geneticist, and accepted an offer to operate a tractor in the Ukraine for the summer. At the end of the summer he decided to continue his education in Moscow for a year; he enrolled in an academy, lived with Russian students, learned Russian, and shared with his friends both their rigid studies and their off-time visits to concerts, ballets, and the countryside. The United States contains many plant pathologists, but few whose records of environmental mobility prepared them so well as this one was for service abroad.

Another American presents a contrasting case. He has been working for the government overseas for almost a dozen years; now employed in his specialty by the ICA, he deals with local officials at the highest level. He says with complete candor:

> *The only reason I got into government was because, after college, a guy came up and offered me a job in Europe. . . . If a young man getting out of college asked me for advice, I would tell him, first, don't get into government and, second, don't go overseas. If he wants to get ahead financially, he shouldn't do either of these things. . . . If I were single, I would quit the government immediately. . . . My wife would like to go back to the United States. . . . She was quite unhappy out here, mainly worrying over the children, their health, and other dangers to their general welfare. Most American families in this neighborhood have been robbed. . . . We're not interested in running around very much. Life, for us, is pretty much a matter of home and family and the children. We don't have much contact with the local nationals. . . . It's so much better to sit down at home and have a beer and read the paper. As far as language is concerned, I don't myself feel that in two years, even if I knock myself out, which would hurt my job, that I would end up knowing it very well. Then I would leave and in the future it would never be of any benefit. So why should I do it? I've been able to get along without the language.*

This case only typifies hundreds of others in which the individual, empty of goals and incentives, concentrates upon the inconveniences and the discomforts, the bother of getting about in a strange milieu, the nuisance of learning a foreign language. Why do people feel this way? In this case, at least, family background and limited environmental mobility seem to have set the stage for an unimpressive and joyless overseas performance. "We lived a normal sort of suburban life," he said, "except we had a lot of financial trouble." From caddying at a golf club (which he detested) to the selection of courses at college the whole focus was on "the idea of making a lot of money and getting out of the bind I was in." He worked hard and studied hard, subjects like banking, finance, and accounting, always with an eye toward success, and even his several extracurricular activities were calculated with the cold eye of ambition rather than the joy of the activity. He ruefully admitted, "I knocked myself out because I thought I had to be successful."

Our files contain a great many other illustrations of environmental mobility as a contributory factor in the development of cultural empathy—and its lack as a warning of limited empathy. Environmental mobility is impossible to measure, but it is not too hard to discern if one learns enough about the early experience of an applicant before he is hired. It is clearly risky for an overseas organization to select personnel who have had too little prior exposure to different societies within the United States, too few opportunities in a sheltered life to learn the value of cultural difference.

To the unperceptive recruiting officer, a person with high environmental mobility may look "unstable" or "escapist," if he reveals a great deal of moving about, a number of different kinds of jobs in different places, an "inability to settle down." But our evidence suggests a second look at the rooted prejudice most large organizations have against mavericks. Special consideration for a foreign assignment should be given to those Americans who have demonstrated a spirit of adventure, an eye to far-off vistas, and the capacity to weather without physical or psychic discomfort a series of experiences different from those of their family or home-town pattern.

The evidence to look for is not mere residence near people of different religions, skin color, or economic status; propinquity does not necessarily generate a sensitivity to other outlooks on life. Nor does a high score on environmental mobility depend mainly on frequent geographic dislocation. Travel is an attitude, not just an exercise of the senses. Environmental mobility is not a transference of the body, but an index to an American's capacity to let his mind run up and down the scale of human understanding without stumbling over his own prejudices.

It may be argued that books, motion pictures, television, and other media of modern communications can provide an individual with vicarious changes in environment. Classroom instruction can provide formal insights to other ways of life and study materials about personality, environmental determinism, and culture patterns. Wise and tolerant men who have demonstrated a sympathetic comprehension of human nature without ever traveling far beyond their home town light up many pages of history. One does not have to be poor in order to appreciate the importance of welfare; one does not have to be oppressed in order to appreciate freedom.

Nevertheless, for most Americans who will find themselves overseas there can be no substitute for personal experiences with other ways of life. Culture shock abroad is an emotional disturbance as well as an intellectual puzzle. The American who, before he takes an overseas job, has lived with folkways that once jarred his habitual sense of time, safety, decorum, cleanliness, or probity, will have *felt* a difference (which he may or may not understand) that no intellectual presentation by a book, picture, or the most dramatic lecturer can duplicate.

Environmental mobility is only one determinant of cultural empathy, and empathy in turn is only one of the five elements of effective performance in overseas service. But evidence of such mobility (or its absence) should be probed for in every interview with an applicant for an overseas job.

4

The administrator in search of the "best" man for an overseas assignment will nearly always have access to one source of supposedly hard facts about each prospect. The record of his formal education can readily be inspected: so many courses in such-and-such fields, so many hours of credit, these grades, this diploma or that degree. But he will have to get behind the formal transcript if he is going to try to find out which applicants have what it takes to work and live abroad. With the depreciation of the American academic coinage at the undergraduate level, a bachelor's degree may mean much or little: it usually denotes some inoculation of knowledge but may have been that and no more. Most graduate degrees have not been planned with overseas service in view, so their relevance to effective performance abroad is usually difficult to assess. Even the recommendations of teachers and professors, on which recruiting officers often rely heavily, leave much to be desired. Where classes are very large the teacher may have a grade based upon a few tests—sometimes marked by an assistant, not the teacher himself—with but a blurred memory of the individual. Many professors take little interest in a student beyond his required class performance. Others write notes about character that they have scarcely had an opportunity to test in forty class hours spread over fourteen weeks. And the judgment of university administrative officers about the significance of the individual's formal education may be even less reliable than that of the faculty.

In spite of these deficiencies in the system, it is possible to make a rough judgment about the breadth of a person's education. This is important because breadth is demonstrably relevant to both technical skill and cultural empathy.

We have seen that for an American abroad, technical skill includes the skill to adapt: the overseasman has to be more of a general practitioner in his craft than would be indicated if he remained in the United States. In judging the promise of an applicant for overseas service, therefore, the recruiter should never fail to beware of too-rigid specialization. The question is whether, given a pair of competent engineers or dieticians or theologians, one has indicated during his formal education the possession of an intellectual curiosity.

The hiring agency can also learn something about an individual's cultural empathy from an inspection of his formal education. Those individuals in the group whom we interviewed with college or postgraduate degrees were rated higher on cultural empathy than those with more limited exposure to formal education. Among those with more formal education in their records, moreover, the individuals rated "high" on cultural empathy again tended to show more breadth of coverage.

Among the 244 Americans we interviewed abroad, nearly half had

had little or no formal exposure to the behavioral sciences in college or afterward. If cultural, political, and institutional factors are as important as our study would indicate, this is indeed a sorry reflection of the lag in helping through education to prepare Americans better for international responsibilities. Even where an individual has taken a course called anthropology or sociology or psychology or economics or government, the net result for overseas performance is uncertain. But a strong case could be made for the proposition that no American should be sent abroad in a responsible assignment without some exposure to the comparative study of culture, politics, and administration.

5

Since most Americans in responsible overseas jobs are institution-builders it follows that in considering a person for such a job, special weight should be given to any indications of talent for creating and sustaining group action.

When we asked the overseas Americans for advice about the "right" people to send abroad, the adjective that cropped up most frequently was "creative." To most of the men and women who used the word, creative seemed to imply more than the imagination of the artist or the brainstorming ability of the idea man. It nearly always suggested a capacity to translate ideas into enduring group processes and social institutions.

A talent for institution-building must of course be judged in relation to the age and opportunity of an applicant for overseas service. A recent college graduate can hardly have shown experience in creating and managing a giant enterprise. The importance of such a talent also varies according to the kind of job to be filled. Less consideration of the institution-building talent need be given to the applicant who will be a bursar or an overseas analyst than to the doctor, engineer, or agronomist who will be advising foreign peoples on the development of health, public works, or soil conservation programs. Yet some experience with institution-building among all Americans selected for foreign assignments would probably raise the standards of overseas performance. "Regardless of what appears on the job specification," wrote a handicraft expert who has worked in Italy, India, and Nepal, "almost every task has hidden in it and, organically interlocked, some planning, some executive work, some learning and teaching, some diplomacy and public relations, all this focused on a moving target."

Anyone who has had experience with starting ideas through the mill of group approbation and group support will at least have encountered, if not mastered, the intricacies of organization of people: the uses of myths and symbols, the importance of empathy, the relative value of exhortation and incentive, the distinction between intimidation and consent. Whoever has held the top post even in a very small organization has some experience with responsibility, some taste of the moral complexity of cooperative endeavor, and (most important) some idea whether or not he enjoys the role of leadership.

In conducting our interviews with the overseas Americans, therefore, we started with the hunch that an American cannot be expected to display outstanding organization ability overseas if he has shown no talent for institution-building in the United States. The hunch was certainly shared by the most experienced of the overseas Americans. Their analysis of their own backgrounds stressed again and again the relevance to overseas success of some prior experience in building an organization.

In our kind of society nearly everybody gets some opportunity to be a civic leader if he has the talent and the taste for it. Students in high school and college are literally bombarded with chances to participate in a variety of pseudo-civic activities, and it is almost impossible for a young adult to avoid some role in church, veterans', business, charitable, or other local brand of committee work and small-time fund-raising. There is consequently some record of the organization potential of nearly every American who has not made deliberate efforts to be a hermit. In analyzing the record of civic activity in campus or community, the important consideration is not whether the person has participated—it is practically impossible not to do so. The crucial question is: What was the applicant's role in the organizations?

The answers we received from men and women in the field suggested three kinds of experience to which the recruiting officer might look for evidence of a talent for institution-building. One is in the applicant's school and college record, especially his extra-curricular activities. Did he manage a school magazine? Did he take over a one-year chairmanship of an international club or a science club—and leave it stronger than he found it? Was he one of the upperclassmen in college who managed the football team (a much more valuable preparation for the real world than playing football)?

The second place to look for indications of organization ability is in early work experience. Here again, in our highly organized civilization a job is frequently in some form of group effort; in performance there the recruiting officer can find evidence of interest in and talent for group leadership. One industrial consultant told of his activity on an early job that surely could have predicted he would be successful in building a business overseas:

> *... A magazine-selling crew came by our house in Elmira, N.Y. one day, and before I knew it, I was selling magazines. I had never done anything like that before ... soon I was in charge of a crew. I made two trips coast-to-coast selling magazines and kept it up during three years at college. I learned to be a pretty good salesman and made money at it.*
>
> *I learned how to get around objections—how to find another way to do it. For instance, now I often have to get approval for a consultant contract from three or four different places in Washington, no one of which has the sole power to say yes or no. I know how to get around in a bureaucracy. If one way won't work, try another. And I learned how not to waste time on trying to sell something that can't be sold.*

A third clue to institution-building talent is of course to be found in previous service abroad. The test of such service is not only "Did he get along with the local people?" or even "Did he get promoted?" An equally important question is whether he tackled with relish the institution-building aspects of whatever task he was sent to perform, and whether he effectively built himself out of rather than into the foreign situation. Consider this story of an American, highly rated by his business supervisor, who had learned a thing

or two about organization ability during a wartime assignment in
Central America:

> *We decided one of the things we would do was a survey
> in one country on the possibilities of growing fruit and
> produce there ... the Caribbean was a war area and we
> had 80,000 troops to feed in the area. Shipping was getting
> sunk from the States. I made my decision in August. I
> begged a representative of [private company] to head up
> the produce program. He refused. I begged a representative
> of [another private company] and he also refused. So there
> I was, without any experience in produce-growing or in
> Latin America, and I volunteered to take on the job. Boy,
> did I ever confuse Washington. Every day I took action
> without authorization, and every night I would send a cable
> back saying that I had exercised the power of the United
> States this day in such and such a way. I even borrowed
> $5,000 to plant some seed. I persuaded the National Bank
> to underwrite more expenses. I had only a portable type-
> writer and no staff at all.... By January we had our first
> harvest to send to the Army. Then we really took hold. I got
> a staff and an Army officer.... The whole program was a
> gigantic success. We ended up with a $30,000 overapplied
> overhead item, which I would never have dreamed calling
> profit. The whole operation became self-sufficient finan-
> cially, including my salary and the staff's. It gave that
> country the first stable export market in its history.*

Not all organization experience is so obviously relevant to another job abroad, but the search for relevant prior experience is one
of the recruiter's clearest mandates. The evidence is that the most
successful overseas personnel are likely to be individuals who
started young as organizers, who had institution-building both in
their blood and in their training.

6

Even the many advantages of working abroad do not guarantee that
the people interested in serving abroad will be those with the
highest aptitude or the best preparation for the experience. Some of

the Americans with the most buoyant personalities, the most environmental mobility, the broadest education and the most evident talent for building institutions simply do not want to pull up stakes and work in a foreign country—or their wives resist the idea. By the same token, many Americans whose nature, background, training, and experience should warn an overseas agency against hiring them are eager for one reason or another to accept a foreign assignment. Hence the need for a recruitment sieve—to prevent the misfits from going and to persuade the naturals to take on an overseas job.

If the sieve is to work more effectually, there will have to be three kinds of changes in the recruitment practices. First, the people who select overseas personnel must be better prepared for their important function. Second, more time and money will have to be invested by the government agencies, business firms, mission boards, and foundations in the process of identifying and preparing those Americans who seem best suited for particular foreign assignments. And third, the selection of overseas staff will have to become the primary responsibility of the educational system itself.

In some agencies with overseas responsibilities—public and private—the recruiting officers have had little overseas experience themselves. Often the personnel officer has made only a flying trip abroad and has never actually had to face the experience of living and working in a transcultural operation. In many organizations the task of recruitment does not command the high prestige that it should, and the selection of personnel is sometimes foisted upon untrained part-time subordinates. In the past, recruitment and training officers from government, industry, and philanthropic agencies have made little effort to meet, to examine their mutual problems, and to educate themselves on methods and criteria for selecting personnel for overseas operations.

The great lament of the agencies themselves is that they have no time to make a careful study of an applicant by putting him through the interviews, tests, and training programs required to judge adequately whether his future performance abroad may be successful. As a midwestern business leader told us, "Listen, when we have a vacancy abroad we have a hard time finding one of our staff willing to go, let alone spending weeks to decide whether he'll be successful or not." It is now generally agreed that the adjustment of the wife in a foreign country may be just as important as that of the husband; nevertheless most organizations feel fortunate if they can interview the applicant at any length and very few make any provisions for seeing the wife before overseas departure.

But what is most wrong with the selection of Americans for overseas service is neither amateurish recruiters nor lack of time for processing applicants. It is the simple and extraordinary fact that selection and training are regarded as two different actions. Except for some of the missionary organizations, agencies and business firms first select an individual for a job abroad, then (time and funds permitting) give him some training for his new work.

Training for overseas service is thus generally regarded as specific preparation for the overseas job, rather than as part of the recruitment process too—the aspect in which attitudes are tested and observed while skills are taught. A brief orientation program cannot significantly change attitudes; it is, as a matter of fact, a rather long interview and should be treated as such. By close observation and continuous testing for the elements that would predict high-level overseas performance, the instructors in even a short training institute should at least be able to screen out the weakest prospects. But this can be done only if the decision to hire is made *after* the training period.

Some of the hiring agencies would say in rebuttal that, by and large, they know their people well before they send them out. The mission boards have often become acquainted with prospective missionaries through church sponsorship of the small colleges that produce so many of the overseas religious workers—or they are known by the clergy. Many business firms that do not require much special training for work abroad beyond in-service training at the overseas post itself nevertheless protect themselves by selecting for overseas assignment only men who have already proved themselves in company assignments in the United States. Some government agencies do the same. The Army, for example, selects for civilian work abroad its own regular civil-service employees and will only go outside this pool in the few cases when technically qualified personnel are not available. Moreover, the Army consciously discourages a repeat or extended overseas assignment, wishing to distribute its foreign posts to domestic employees and arguing that overseas employees need repatriation to keep up with technological advances. (There may be other unvoiced reasons, such as avoiding the possibility that Army people will build themselves permanently into comfortable, lucrative foreign posts.)

All such recruiting systems are firmly based on the good-man-at-home-is-a-good-man-abroad theory. It is true that a man's supervisor knows him fairly well after working with him for a year or two, and that this acquaintance is adequate enough when the man's advancement within the company structure at home is being considered. But unless the supervisor has himself served overseas, and has clearly in mind a set of criteria which are demonstrably relevant to fine accomplishment in overseas work, his judgment that Joe is a good man may actually be misleading to the overseas company or field station to which he is transferred.

The best selection method for overseas Americans, therefore, is an extended educational experience that stresses how work and life abroad differ from the work and life in the United States. The American educational system, with its opportunity to take people in their formative years and expose them to a long, purposeful program, has a prime responsibility in preparing United States citizens for work abroad. Only the liberal arts colleges, technical schools, and graduate faculties can fashion imaginative programs that will adequately test and develop the potential of students on the five elements of effective overseas performance.

The effort to improve the foreign services of the United States will reach deep into our system of higher education. Just how deep is the subject of the chapters that follow.

Part Four
THE MEANING
FOR EDUCATION

14· The Internationalization of College

1

Some years ago in Washington the administrator of a government program in the Far East was visited by a Public Health officer on his way to Burma. The health man had been selected because he was a doctor who had had some experience with preventive medicine in the field. His security clearance was final and he had been "oriented" for two weeks; he was, in fact, on his way to the airport.

"There's one question I'd like to ask you," said the doctor, looking at his watch and lowering his voice. "I've only got five minutes before I catch the airport limousine. But can you tell me—just what *is* Buddhism?"

Virtually every overseas American worth his salt wishes he had been exposed to a different or broader education. With one accord, Americans abroad seem to be searching, as the doctor was searching, for last-minute answers to questions that somehow should have come up before. Yet, although their numbers grow, the provisions for the education and training of future overseas Americans lag far behind the need they all vaguely feel.

The worst aspects of the situation lie far beyond the scope of this study. A thorough inquiry into the intellectual limitations of many of our college students would clearly extend back into secondary and even elementary education. In the broader cultural sense that would include informal experience, a psychologist might say that the processes vital to education really start with prenatal care or, at least, at a mother's knee. But because the elements of effective overseas performance seem to be predominantly the kinds of skill and understanding that come from higher education and experience with real-world complexity, our story is limited to college and post-graduate education.

For our purposes, then, we may think of the preparation of people for overseas service as a four-part educational sequence. The first step is a liberal arts education adequate to the needs of a world in which the dividing line between "domestic" and "foreign" affairs has been permanently blurred; the study of foreign cultures and foreign languages should therefore be the rule rather than the exception. The second step is professional training in a subject-matter field—medicine or law, engineering or agriculture, journalism or military science, economics or public administration. Step number three is exposure to the special linguistic skills, area knowledge, and other kinds of understanding that are relevant to the first overseas assignment. The final step is the immediate orientation to the particular job to be done abroad.

If the United States is serious about making sure of first-rate representation abroad, in private as well as public enterprises, there must be a conscious effort to build into the educational system *at each of these steps* the kinds of education and experience that develop the qualities of mind and spirit that make for success in work abroad.

2

It is the exception rather than the rule for a college to think of itself as engaged in training for overseas service. There are, to be sure, a number of special concentrations offered to the undergraduate who expresses an interest in overseas work, including some special preparation for the Foreign Service exams and in foreign trade or the history of missionary work. Often such programs are made up with greater or less ingenuity from the regular course offerings in the college catalogues, and represent an effort to utilize present facilities for overseas training rather than an attempt to rethink the basic curriculum with the overseas Americans in view.

There is, of course, the chronic danger that the new enthusiasm about overseas service will damage the quality of liberal arts programs by introducing too much vocational education into them. But there are numerous examples of colleges that do combine an acceptable liberal arts curriculum with vocational training for overseas service. The oldest and most famous program of this type is the School of Foreign Service at Georgetown University, which prepares undergraduates directly for the Foreign Service examinations, with emphasis on such subjects as diplomatic history, world affairs, and modern languages. Tufts University, the home of the Fletcher School of Law and Diplomacy with its distinguished graduate program, also offers an undergraduate liberal arts degree, with a concentration of special interest to persons going into overseas service.

A newer and more ambitious venture of the same general nature is the School of International Service at American University, financed in part by a special grant from the Methodist Church. American University now offers B.A.s and advanced-degree programs for six types of international service: the Foreign Service, overseas business, church missions, overseas representation, international administration, and international relations.

More significant than the few special courses of study for overseas service is the slow shift in what a liberal arts education means—the gradual internationalization of the American college.

The reasons for the big change are clear enough. In the 1940s and 1950s, tens of millions of Americans became personally aware of the reality of international interdependence. This reality was impressed on the public mind by soldiers, sailors, airmen, and Marines, returning from World War II and the Korean conflict after seeing corners of the world which to their fathers (who fought, if at all, in France and Belgium) were merely colored shapes in a geography book. The unprecedented tourist travel after World War II and the rapid turnover of the Americans living and working abroad have been educational not only for the travelers but for their sisters and their cousins and their aunts who received post cards from faraway places or listened to the wanderers tell of strange lands and dubiously friendly peoples. The foreign intellectuals, many of them fleeing from distant dictatorships, have had a particular impact on the many American colleges and universities that grasped the opportunity to enhance their academic standing by attaching distinguished émigrés to their faculties.

The foreign experiences of American college professors once were almost exclusively European and for the most part limited either to touristic sabbaticals or to research projects for the relatively few specialists in foreign culture. Thousands of faculty members each year now have the opportunity to study or teach in foreign universities throughout the non-Communist world. Many more act as advisers or consultants to the governments of these nations.

The export of United States power and wealth has drawn into foreign affairs a host of academic institutions that, through government contracts, have been enabled, without having to pay for research leaves out of endowment money or alumni gifts, to permit their staff to get some foreign experience. During the 1957–1958 academic year, 184 universities in the United States conducted 382 international programs, and of these, 234 programs involved sending United States faculty members abroad.* The thousands of American college students who manage to get a foreign experience of some kind each year (12,845 of them in 1958) have likewise had a wide impact on their home campuses and communities when they returned.

Since World War II an extraordinary number of foreign students have flocked to United States campuses; American economic growth and military power had brought world-wide prestige to American education. Their number exceeded 40,000 by 1956; in 1958–59, there were 47,245 foreign students from 145 nations and other political subdivisions of the world registered in American colleges and universities. Of the total, 24,349 were undergraduates; the rest were in graduate or professional schools, or studying under that conveniently undemanding designation of "special students." More and more of these students come from the world's less-developed areas; it is no longer possible to glance out at the main quadrangle of any major American college without seeing a turban, an Indian sari, or a high-collar Oriental frock—and a mixture of skin colors that even internationalizes the issue of racial integration in American higher education.

* *The International Programs of American Universities,* Institute of Research on Overseas Programs, Michigan State University, East Lansing, 1958, pp. 14, 33.

It is hard to measure the total impact of all these factors on the liberal arts colleges, professional colleges, and graduate schools. In an attempt to gain some general impression of this impact we have examined the educational offerings of all accredited institutions of higher education in the United States for which current information could be secured to see how many of them announce programs or concentrations that represent an internationalization of the classical content of undergraduate colleges' curricula. Such an exercise can give only an approximate indication of a trend, since there is normally a wide discrepancy between statements in the college catalogue and reality in the college classroom. The excessive boasting of Podunk, however, is partly offset by the reticence and understatement of the Harvard catalogues. Furthermore, a statement in a college catalogue, quite independently of the value or even existence of the reality it seems to advertise, is an earnest of a desire, a symbol of an attitude or aspiration, and therefore is significant.

With these reservations in mind, let us see what result is obtained by taking as a measure of internationalization the presence in a college or university of one or more of the following:

- a graduate area program
- an undergraduate area concentration
- an international-relations concentration
- fifteen or more semester-hours in a foreign language other than French, Spanish, German or Italian
- a special program for foreign-service training
- a foreign study program
- a foreign business concentration

As Tables 6 and 7 indicate, about 35 per cent of the 965 accredited colleges claim to have taken at least one of these steps; these awakening institutions, however, include 63 per cent of the students. The non-sectarian private colleges have the "best" internationalization record, the women's colleges the poorest. If the institutions are divided regionally according to their accrediting bodies, the Middle States Association (comprising Delaware, the District of Columbia, New Jersey, New York, Pennsylvania, and Puerto Rico) led the field, and the Southern Association (comprising 14 Southern states) lagged the farthest behind. Taken all in all, the better American college classrooms are becoming a window on the world. In

TABLE 6. THE INTERNATIONALIZATION OF COLLEGE (1958 Survey)

	Total of accredited colleges in the U.S.A.[1]		Colleges in which "international" programs are formally established		Colleges in which "international" programs have not been formally established	
	Number of colleges	Number of students	Number of colleges	Number of students	Number of colleges	Number of students
1. TOTALS	965	2,136,534	315	1,254,300	552	731,838
2.a. Men's colleges	104	166,869	31	86,334	63	75,776
b. Women's colleges	154	91,338	51	33,359	89	44,985
c. Coed colleges	707	1,878,327	233	1,134,607	400	611,077
3.a. Public colleges	329	1,169,555	91	699,498	189	366,530
b. Private colleges	636	966,979	224	554,802	363	365,308
4.a. Non-sectarian private colleges	173	485,291	84	342,024	74	125,278
b. Sectarian private colleges	463	481,688	140	212,778	289	240,030

[1] A total of 98 colleges accounting for 150,396 students did not respond to inquiries.

TABLE 7. COLLEGES WHICH DO AND DO NOT HAVE PROGRAMS PERTINENT TO INTERNATIONAL WORK

States	Pertinent Programs		No Pertinent Programs	
	Colleges	*Students*	*Colleges*	*Students*
New England	27	85,324	41	64,052
Middle	69	296,858	97	132,206
Southern	67	229,976	173	206,666
North Central	117	480,887	186	245,947
Northwest	18	62,118	28	31,027
Western	17	99,137	27	51,940
Total	315	1,254,300	552	731,838

315 colleges and universities, including virtually all of the major ones, one and a quarter million college students have some opportunity to participate in "international education" as we have defined it. This exposure, available from year to year to a growing student population, will in time be an important factor in determining whether the overseas Americans are wise or otherwise.

3

Two of the changes associated with the internationalization of college are especially important in building a pool of young Americans who have both the motivation to serve abroad and the beginnings of wisdom about other societies and cultures. One change is the sudden growth of courses for undergraduates which treat of non-Western cultures; the other is the enlarged opportunity for a present-day undergraduate to take part of his college course outside of the United States.

Both "non-Western" courses and the Study Abroad movement are essentially designed to immerse the student in cultures alien to his own, to teach him the relativity of the American Way and help him sharpen some tools for learning about the ways of others. Neither technique is ideal for the purpose: in the first case the immersion is vicarious since it is limited to reading and class discussion in the United States; and in the second the experience, while foreign, is

usually in a European country with close historical and cultural
ties with our own. Yet even under the attenuated conditions the
new programs can be basic testing and training grounds for cultural
empathy and political sensitivity.

The case for non-Western studies as a new but necessary feature
of the liberal arts has been persuasively stated by Robert F. Byrnes
and John M. Thompson in a recent article:

> *American colleges must recognize that traditional educa-*
> *tion requirements fall short of meeting the needs of the*
> *twentieth-century world, that knowledge of Western cul-*
> *ture alone will not suffice for the citizen of tomorrow and*
> *that liberal education must be universal in outlook, draw-*
> *ing on the values, experience and aspirations of all peoples*
> *and cultures. It is not far-fetched to imagine the day when*
> *the study of non-Western societies will be regarded, not*
> *as something unusual and exotic, requiring special interests*
> *and extraordinary resources, but as part of the normal*
> *activity of the social science and humanities departments*
> *of every college and university in the country. The time*
> *may also come when some knowledge of non-Western*
> *peoples and civilizations will be accepted as part of the*
> *customary intellectual baggage accompanying every Ameri-*
> *can undergraduate as he leaves the campus.**

This baggage has generally been smuggled into the college curriculum either as an undergraduate offering by a graduate area
studies program or through a course on a foreign civilization devised
especially for college students.

Undergraduate area programs may be quite modest affairs: some
are one-man shows (Japan at Amherst, Latin America at Fresno
State); others are primarily interdepartmental majors. In the former
case, their degree of excellence will depend primarily on the qualities of the single professor; in the latter case, on the fortuitous
availability of interested and able teachers in several departments
of the college faculty. While most of the programs aim at acquainting the student with a culture he would normally consider exotic, a

---

* Robert F. Byrnes and John M. Thompson, "Undergraduate Study of Russia and the Non-Western World," *Liberal Education* XLV, No. 2 (May, 1959),
pp. 277–278.

few attempt to teach him an appreciation of the culture of his immigrant ancestors (France at Assumption College, Germany at Marquette, Poland at Alliance, Sweden at Augustana). In such cases the purpose is often to foster a religious tradition as well as to enrich the student's knowledge of a foreign culture.

There is danger in divorcing the undergraduate program from a strong area program, in that it may not be firmly based in a continuous current relationship with the countries in the area. But the contrary danger is perhaps more serious: that of contaminating the undergraduate program with a strongly vocational approach.

A director of the American Council of Learned Societies is authority for the opinion that "by far the largest proportion of Americans who graduate from the institutions of higher learning do so without ever meeting a civilization differently patterned from their own." * The undergraduate foreign-civilization courses are designed to repair the omission.

Such survey courses are typically less elaborate, less professional, and less costly than undergraduate area programs. They also reach a far greater number of students. It is therefore worth pausing a moment to consider the variety of forms of attack which American colleges have invented to demonstrate to liberal arts students that the world is indeed round. The non-Western survey courses are most often concerned with Asia. They may take Asia as a unit for a year's study, as at California, Michigan, and Pennsylvania Universities; they may divide Asia into the Near East, Middle Asia, and the Far East, as at Chicago; or they may divide the subject among the traditional academic disciplines as at Columbia.

California's Asian civilization course is a sweeping study of Asian history and geography and the interaction of one upon the other. In the first semester the course is divided into five sections according to geographical area: Near East, India, Southern Asia, China, and Japan. In the second semester a topical sequence is followed within three broad historical periods: the Asiatic Empires (Ottomans, Safavids, Moguls, Tokugawa, Ming and Ch'ing dynasties), the period of Europeanization, and World War I to date.

* Quoted by Ward Morehouse, "Asian Studies in Undergraduate Education," *Journal of General Education* XI (1958), p. 125. Copyright 1958 by the University of Chicago.

The California course assumes no previous knowledge of Asia. The material studied is substantially limited to history and the social sciences. No special effort is made to acquaint the students with the languages or the arts of Asia, although readings in translation of Asian literature are encouraged.

In some places, as at Michigan, this kind of survey course is taught by a panel of experts, each teaching the period or geographical area he knows best. But the director of the California program, Woodbridge Bingham, argues that the students benefit by the greater integration his course achieves through the use of a single teacher. No man can be an expert on all Asia, he cheerfully concedes. But the course does not pretend to create experts. If it is too broad a subject for a college professor to teach, then it is much too broad a subject for undergraduates to learn.

The University of Chicago follows a quite different educational philosophy in planning its elementary work in Asian civilization. Three separate one-year courses are offered in Islamic civilization, India, and China. Each of these is structured differently.

The course on Islamic civilization deals with the art, history, literature, philosophy, and religion of the Islamic world from the time of Mohammed to the present. No attempt is made to teach Arabic and all required reading is in English; about 20 per cent of the supplementary reading, however, is in French and about 5 per cent of it is in German.

Chicago's "Introduction to the Civilization of India" starts with anthropology: the first assigned reading is Robert Redfield's *The Characterization of Civilization*. Only in the winter quarter, when the course is taken over by a new squad of professors, is the history of India taught. This section stresses intellectual and social history over political and military history, and stresses the philosophic and religious development of India. In the spring quarter Chicago returns to a social-science approach, employs six faculty members, and deals with the conflicts between the Indian traditions and the modern world.

The Chinese Culture course resembles the Islamic course more than it does the India one. The fall quarter, except for the two opening lectures on geography and the three closing ones on art, deals primarily with early Chinese intellectual and cultural history (up to 200 B.C.). The winter quarter covers the period 200 B.C. to 1249 A.D., and the spring quarter takes the students the rest of the way.

Although the Chicago program is described by its former chief as a group of "culture courses" rather than "area courses," they are directed to somewhat more sophisticated students than the comparable programs at most of the large universities. In practice their membership consists mostly of upper-class and graduate students.

Columbia University divides the subject matter of its Oriental survey courses by disciplines rather than by geography. Two one-year courses are offered as electives in Columbia's general-education program: one is called "Oriental Humanities" and the other "Oriental Civilizations." The latter is a compromise between the California All-Asia survey and the Chicago concentration on a single civilization. It consists of an intellectual and cultural history of Japan, China, and India, with a rapid jump from the description of the ancient tradition to a review of the modern period. Thus Part IV of the Chinese section is called "The Confucian Revival" and Part V "China and the New World," while Part V of the India section is "Sikhism" and Part VI "Modern India and Pakistan."

The "Oriental Humanities" course at Columbia might be called the Great Books of Asia. It deals with the philosophical, religious, and literary masterpieces of Japanese, Sinitic, Indian, Islamic, and Persian cultures and stresses those with an appeal that transcends their time and place of origin. The Near East and India are studied during the first term, China and Japan during the second.

The weakness of this kind of program is of course the students' lack of background for what they are asked to do. In traditional classical studies it is not unusual for a student to spend a semester reading and studying a single masterpiece of Western culture such as Dante's *Commedia*. Some universities devote a whole course to the exegesis of a single book of the Bible. With these examples in mind, scholars might well gasp at the thought that Columbia expects undergraduates to read intelligently, for a single three-semester-hour course, the *Koran*, the *Avesta*, the *Rig-Veda*, the thirteen principal *Upanishads*, the *Mahabharata*, the *Ramayana*, the *Bhagavad-Gita*, the *Shankemtola*, as well as selections from the *Vedanta Sutra* and the *Ramakhrisna*, not to speak of parts of the autobiographies of Gandhi and Nehru, the *Arabian Nights,* and some fifteen other required items. Frustration and disillusionment might be the reactions of a tolerably intelligent student to such a diet; complacency or sense of achievement would mark the insensitive student.

From the viewpoint of providing background for possible overseas life and work, the classicists here have the better of the argument. Racing through the underbrush of half a dozen cultures at breakneck speed is a dubious approach to learning how to learn about culture. Digging deeper into one or two of them might be of greater intellectual profit.

The area study program at Colgate appears typical of what can be done (but generally is not) by a small college. The Colgate program consists of a group of one-semester courses, one of which is required of all students during their junior year. The areas offered are East Asia, France, Russia, Mexico, Brazil, Germany, the British Commonwealth, and the Mediterranean; an area study of Africa will be added in 1960–1961. The French program is offered in French and in English. The purpose of the course is to give the student "a vocabulary of basic data about the specific area . . . the area's mainstream of ideas, a weighing of the professed ideals against the contemporary policy and performance, a sympathetic objectivity regarding motivation and performance, . . . a *whole view* and not limited by the terms of any specific discipline."

The Colgate area study is followed in the senior year by another one-semester required course, entitled "America and the World Community." Essentially a survey of American foreign policy, it is able to tackle directly the manner in which the United States is involved in other nations' internal affairs by building on the students' vicarious immersion in one area during the previous year.

At Rochester the introductory survey sweeps through Asia, Africa, Latin America and Russia in a single year; about one Rochester undergraduate in six takes this program. In St. Paul, Minnesota, a consortium of colleges known as the Hill Center of Area Studies has put together an eight-semester interdisciplinary course of study on one culture area, open to ten students of each of the four colleges; the area rotates annually among the Far East, the Near East, and Russia. At Syracuse it is possible to major in Russian studies or

Latin American studies—and in American studies as well. Earlham and Antioch are jointly planning a Japan-and-China program, which unlike the Chicago pattern will stress social sciences rather than the humanities. The Western College for Women requires an area course of all students, and rotates the offering among four areas—Far East, Near East, Latin America, and Europe and Colonial Africa. The extreme example among the wide-angle survey courses seems to be the program at New Paltz State Teachers College, which requires as part of its general education sequence a series of one-semester courses on American Institutions, Western Civilization, Asia, Africa, and the Middle East.

4

In all these programs and many more, the educational dilemma is the familiar one: depth at the expense of breadth or breadth at the expense of depth? Viewed as education for eventual overseas service, the Chicago type of program has important advantages. It concentrates on studying the great Eastern traditions in their own terms, and stresses the humanities in so doing. To be sure, something is lost thereby: the direct comparison of cultures. But on balance, while the wide-angle surveys can be justified as part of a minimum preparation in world affairs for liberal arts majors, they cannot be expected to give the basic understanding of a foreign culture that is such an important element in the training of the overseas Americans.

As John Dewey has said, "shared experience" is the essential ingredient in social organization. Unless the students become truly involved with at least one of the alien cultures to which they are exposed in college, the all-Asia survey may be as unsatisfactory for breaking the culture barrier as a single year of college French would be for breaking a language barrier. As for the students who are expected to become acquainted with the whole world in the New Paltz program, they might consider how little they could learn about American civilization in a semester course and judge by this humiliating scale their understanding of the foreign cultures to which they are fleetingly exposed.

It is true that a main purpose of education is to help the student develop the ability to generalize, and the broad surveys are often defended by saying that useful generalizations can be drawn from a sweeping comparative study of the whole Asian continent. However, the educational value of a valid generalization lies not in passively accepting it but in learning to pave the approach to it with stones of hard fact cemented together with rigorous logic. Students, particularly undergraduates, are seldom prepared to make valid generalizations over a wide range of subject matter, and a university course that consists in the main of accepting the instructor's generalizations smacks more of indoctrination than education. Can one imagine a geometry course in which the QEDs were memorized and the method of arriving at them cast aside?

An emphasis on the humanities, history, and geography in a survey course gives the student a basic knowledge of the essential facts of a culture upon which he can later build his own theories, or criticize those of others. An emphasis on the social sciences other than history and geography is likely to mean an emphasis on interpretation (by the teacher) based on facts with which the student is familiar only at second or third hand.

From the point of view of education for overseas service, then, the most important thing a liberal arts college can do is teach its students how to understand a foreign culture. The best way to start is by learning about one culture alien to our own. With whatever deference may be due to Emile Gobineau, the racist, or Ellsworth Huntington, the physical geographer, the barriers between men today are mainly intellectual. To break the culture barrier one must learn to think differently—one must become aware of the ideologies and the patterns of thought that have developed over the centuries in another cultural tradition. For this understanding, art, literature, philosophy, and history are the core disciplines, at the expense of the other social sciences. Neither the politics of a country nor indeed its language can be understood by the foreigner who does not have some acquaintance with its intellectual traditions.

The particular political, social, economic and administrative problems of his area are obviously going to be of great importance to the overseas American. But the facts about these are constantly changing and are relatively easy to learn. Their acquisition can therefore safely be postponed until shortly before the overseas experience itself, when the incentive to learn them is at its peak. In his undergraduate or early graduate education, it is important that the American learn how to think about whole cultures through such devices as the Chicago program's Islamic and Chinese civilization courses, or the popular undergraduate offerings on China and Japan offered by historians John Fairbank and Edwin Reischauer at Harvard. In a course built around Moslem culture, for example, the student may gain a knowledge of the basic cultural heritage of another world. To communicate successfully with a cultured Arab it is just as essential to know something of the *Koran* and of Arab history as it is to know Arabic—though each of these accomplishments complements the other.

That it would be just fine if many more American college students knew much more about alien (including non-Western) cultures is now a virtually undebatable assumption. But there is a limit to what a college student can absorb in that fraction of his four years that remains after time for vacations, campus activities, athletics, and an active social life has been deducted. The introduction of a whole new body of material into the undergraduate curriculum raises an alarming specter: we may have to pay for our additions by costly amputations of subjects already being taught and (worse) of the people who are teaching them. The coming struggle for the student's time may be more intense than ever.

Yet it is possible in education to kill more than one bird with one stone. If the teaching profession accepts the premise that liberal arts education is designed to train the mind rather than impart specific facts, something more than a gray compromise may result from the debates about internationalization which have already begun in faculty meetings across the nation. The enthusiasm about Russia's teaching methods in mathematics, for example, has carefully obscured the fact that the problems worked by Russian students may be permeated with Marxist doctrine. This does not prevent Soviet youngsters from learning about numbers theory; but it does expose them at the same time to their government's political and economic prejudices. In a similar fashion (though for liberating rather than narrowing purposes) non-Western and Latin American material can find its way into many of our present courses without replacing anything essential that is presently taught—if the people doing the teaching make the effort to revise with this objective in mind.

The habit of adding new courses, rather than analyzing how the old could be altered to accomplish a new purpose, is deeply ingrained in nearly every academic community. At Michigan State University, where Glen Taggart became in 1957 the nation's first Dean of International Programs, the philosophy of infiltrating rather than competing with other aspects of education was clearly established in a university policy:

> *It appears vital for the future growth of ... higher education generally that practical means be developed to incorporate the cross-cultural dimension into the professional activities of each college and the various bureaus, institutes and programs that compose the total University. Disciplines which have not thus far taken into account the international aspects of their field might well be enriched by doing so.*

Dean Taggart has selected a difficult row to hoe, but it is probably the most sensible approach—as well, of course, as the most complicated.

5

Beyond taking new course offerings on the home campus, a student's major opportunity to learn about a foreign culture is to get abroad —during the summer if necessary, during the school year if possible. The Study Abroad movement, still a relatively tiny part of American education, seems due for a big expansion as part of the internationalization of the liberal arts.*

We estimate that about 3,500 American undergraduates a year receive credit in their home colleges for academic work they complete in foreign countries. Some 2,000 of these take summer courses abroad; of the remaining 1,500, rather more than half study in formal programs of the Junior Year Abroad type; the others go over for

---

* For an excellent account of the foreign study movement, see John A. Garrity and Walter Adams, *From Main Street to the Left Bank*, East Lansing, Michigan State University Press, 1959.

independent study approved by their own colleges. There is also a sizable graduate population among American students abroad: Fulbright, Ford, Rhodes, Henry, and many other kinds of scholars and fellows, plus the thousands of students abroad on trips unrelated to academic credit though not unrelated to their education as citizens of the world.

While the annual increase in these figures is substantial, the totals are still very small in terms of total undergraduate enrollments in United States colleges (3,402,297 in the fall of 1959). We may, however, be at the beginning of a sharply rising curve of expanded Study Abroad programs. Certainly from the point of view of building a pool of young Americans with some prior exposure to foreign cultures, it would be desirable for every college student to have the opportunity of taking at least a semester of his four-year college course in a foreign area. The time is probably not far distant when the chance to study overseas will be an optional part of every liberal arts curriculum.

There are few limits in theory to the places where American students might go abroad to study, but in practice Europe has so far remained the focal point of interest in the Study Abroad movement. There are one or more organized programs in Austria, Belgium, Denmark, France, Germany, Great Britain, Italy, the Netherlands, Norway, Spain, Sweden, and Switzerland. The list of cities is even more impressive: Vienna, Louvain, Copenhagen, Besançon, Caen, Dijon, Grenoble, Paris, Göttingen, Heidelberg, Munich, Stuttgart, Tübingen, Florence, Pisa, Rome, Leiden, Madrid, Salamanca, Fribourg, Geneva, Trogen, and most of the university cities of Great Britain, Norway, and Sweden. Independent study is possible almost anywhere else, provided satisfactory arrangements for credit can be made with the home college. The few American students in Yugoslavia, Poland and the U.S.S.R. during 1959 may even presage the raising of the Iron Curtain for this purpose.

The Western Hemisphere has less appeal. Smith has given up its Mexican program. Spanish majors at the Lake Erie College for Women prefer Spain to Mexico despite the fact that Mexico is probably better equipped to handle foreign students than is Spain. Earlham College, however, sends students to Mexico, Antioch to Cuba, Colgate to Argentina, and Swarthmore to South America

TABLE 8.

	Program Started	Students 1957–58	Sexes	Students from Sponsoring Coll.	Language Requirements	Live in Families
CLOSED PROGRAMS						
Antioch	1957	59	m.f.		varied	Yes
Earlham	1956	15	m.f.		1 sem. Spanish 2 yrs. French	
Georgetown	1954	21	m.			
Hollins	1955	31	f.		none	Yes
Lake Erie	1952	87	f.		2 yrs.	Yes
Marymount	1924	18	f.		2 yrs.	
Newcomb-Tulane	1954	36	m.f.		2 yrs.	Yes
Stanford	1958	63 [1]	m.f.		none	No
OPEN PROGRAMS						
Smith	1925	102	m.f.	72	2 yrs. [9]	Yes
Sweet Briar	1948	84	m.f.	2	4 yrs.	Yes
Rosary	c. 1925	22	f.	11		No
Wayne	1953	43	m.f.	4	2 yrs.	Yes
Hamilton	1957	32	m.f.	5	4 yrs.	Yes
Fordham	1950	9	m.	7		Yes
New York	1958	11	m.f.		2 yrs.	Yes
Heidelberg	1958	8 [12]	m.f.		2 yrs.	Yes
Syracuse	1959	90 [13]	m.f.	75	none	Yes

(1) 1958–59 figures for first semester.
(2) Alternate years.
(3) Includes tuition, board, lodging and travel to and from port only.
(4) Mexico.
(5) France.
(6) Including 3 months summer travel.
(7) Lake Erie junior quarter abroad costs are part of the regular tuition.
(8) Only for students going to France.

STUDY ABROAD (*1958 Survey*)

Live in Dormitories	Students from How Many Colleges?	Program in France	Program in Germany	Program in Italy	Program in Spain	Program in Switzerland	Other Programs	Approx. Cost [3]	No. of Months	Honor Students Only	Initial Period of Lang. Study Abroad
X		X	X			X	Austria Mexico Scandinavia	$1300 to $2200		No	
		X [2]					Mexico [2]	$1175 [4] $1575 [5]	7	No	Yes
					X	X		$2600		Yes	
No		X						$3000 [6]	12	No	Yes
No		X	X	X	X	X	Holland Denmark	[7]	3	No	Yes
Yes		X		X			England	$2500	10		
Yes		X	X		X		England	$2000	9½	Yes	[8]
Yes				X	X			$1250	6	Yes	No
[10]		X		X	X	X		$2700	10	Yes	Yes
	44	X						$2300	9½	Yes	Yes
Yes						X		$1900			
	30		X					$2050	10	Yes	Yes
	20	X						$2200	9		Yes
	3	X			X		Belgium		14		
						X		$1800	9		Yes
Yes			X					$1620	10		Yes
No	12			X				$1400 (Sem.)	4		

(9) Smith requires 4 years of French or equivalent for Paris, 2 years of language for other countries.
(10) Smith students live in dormitories part of the year in Geneva.
(11) No program in 1957–58.
(12) Figures for 1958–59.
(13) Figures for 1959–60.

(usually Peru). Independent students also go to Mexico and Guatemala in substantial numbers. No one, it seems, prefers to perfect his French in Quebec rather than in Paris.

Interest in Africa and Asia is still very limited. Three Afro-Asian programs are virtually inoperative. These are Brandeis University's Israeli program, New Mexico State's Pakistan program, and Lincoln's Ghana program. The Presbyterian Church, however, does get students to go to the various Protestant colleges in Asia, and the Hebrew teachers' colleges have a cooperative program for Israel.

A quick inventory of the major Study Abroad programs can be seen in Table 8. With a few exceptions, most are of recent origin. All send their students to Western countries for periods ranging from a quarter to a full year; the cost to the student for tuition, board, lodging, and travel within Europe ranges from around $1,200 to $3,000 a year. They can be classified in many ways; for our purposes four major kinds of foreign study stand out:

> • Restricted programs that usually take only honor students and require some knowledge of the relevant language;
> • General programs that take students of average academic standing and do not require proficiency in a language;
> • Programs with modest academic pretensions;
> • Independent study arrangements.

The first of these categories includes most of the classic Junior Year Abroad programs, notably those of Smith College and Sweet Briar College. Their philosophy is that in order to be a significant experience for the student, the foreign experience should be the culmination of a substantial process of selection and training. They are not trying to serve all students; their market is an élite which can meet rather stiff prerequisites—honor standing (typically a B average or better), proficiency in the language of the country, and the inclination and funds to spend an entire year abroad. All restricted programs are set to serve the needs of the language majors who often are prospective language teachers. The best of them are also eager to attract the second type of students and are ready to offer them the broadening experience of studying their fields of specialization in a foreign language and under foreign professors.

The case for a year's foreign study, as against a shorter period, rests on the theory that the benefits of cultural immersion do not derive just from the initial culture shock but are by-products of the later adjustment process. A child does not benefit from being thrown into the lake unless he has some previous instruction in swimming and is given enough time to learn to swim after he hits the water. In most of the restricted programs it is possible for the student to live with families; where this is done, it often turns out to be one of the most rewarding elements of the program, especially if it is continued beyond the point where the foreign family feels it has to be unnaturally polite to a short-term visitor. A family home stay seems to build into the program more kinds of cultural adjustment— notably the little adjustments which come the hardest—than any other type of experience reasonably available to an American student abroad.

A major advantage of the restricted programs has been the readiness of virtually all the best colleges and universities to give a full year's academic credit for the successful completion of a year's foreign study, as attested by the institution sponsoring the program.

Restricted programs, like the other foreign study enterprises, can be designated either as "open" or "closed." Students from all accredited colleges or universities may be admitted to the open programs; closed programs are reserved for the students of the sponsoring institution. There are advantages and disadvantages either way. An open program can draw its applicants from a far wider student population and can therefore maintain higher academic standards for admission. Advocates of open programs also stress the importance of avoiding too much homogeneity in the groups. By the same token, however, many of the students in an open program are not known to each other before departure, and it is more difficult to fit the overseas experience into the students' college program, since so many different patterns of undergraduate work may be represented in a single group.

In the 1950s a number of American and European colleges and universities, realizing the value of a foreign experience for a wider group of American students, including the great majority who lack proficiency in a foreign language, set up programs designed partic-

ularly for this new clientele. Until this time there was no way for
these students to include an immersion in a foreign culture as an
integral part of their liberal arts education except through some
special arrangement, usually for independent study abroad. Even
when the students were successful in making such arrangements, the
foreign experience itself was often disappointing from an academic
point of view and not infrequently the foreign experience, through
poor planning and lack of supervision, was also of extremely limited
value.

The new programs designed for this purpose generally differ from
the élite programs in that students with less than superior academic
standing are admitted; there is no language prerequisite; all courses
studied abroad, except language training, are taken in English; and
the duration of the program is often less than a year.

The case for slightly lower academic standards in these programs
rests on the somewhat different purpose to be served. Since the academic work of these students performed abroad is in an environment essentially similar to that of an American university, and the
majority of courses are taught in English by American professors,
the problems of adjustment on the academic level will be easier
than for the participants in the restricted programs. It is therefore
considered safe to accept students with a high C average.

Although these programs require no previous language experience, they all make intensive language instruction a mandatory part
of the foreign experience. This lack of a language prerequisite for
admission is one of the controversial elements in these programs.
The experience of Hollins Abroad, however, is that of all of its
participants who had no previous knowledge of French before departure, none failed to make satisfactory progress in French and
to be able to take courses taught in the French language after a
semester's concentration on the language in France. Those who
failed in French were found to have been taught or mistaught
French in America prior to their departure.

These programs generally have a duration of from four to six
months (though Hollins Abroad, the first of them, is still a year's
program). There are practical reasons for a shorter period. These
programs attract students of widely varying backgrounds, majors in
all the liberal arts departments as well as students in schools of

speech, journalism, education, home economics, business administration, art, and music. In order to give all these students one-fourth of their undergraduate education abroad and in English, it would be necessary to set up so large an American center as to make an immersion in a foreign culture a virtual impossibility for the participants. In the second place, the most appropriate courses to offer students who are studying in Europe are those that deal with European culture, and most of the participants in these programs cannot work more than a semester of such courses into their programs. Not to be overlooked is the fact that the program of shorter duration makes the overseas sequence financially possible for more students.

The major "general programs," although they are quite dissimilar in other ways, are those instituted by Stanford (in Stuttgart, Germany) and by Syracuse (in Florence, Italy). Both are designed for sophomores as well as juniors and seniors. The Stanford program is limited to Stanford students, whom it houses in a dormitory. The Syracuse program is open to students from all accredited colleges, and encourages rapid language learning by lodging its students with Italian families.

Various European universities and institutes also offer programs of this general type; the most notable examples are the University of Stockholm, the Institute of European Studies in Vienna, and the Institute for American Universities at Aix-en-Provence in France. Other respected European universities may follow Stockholm in establishing programs in English for American students. Under present conditions, institutes such as those now operating in Vienna and Aix-en-Provence face an uncertain future; it is difficult for them to maintain accreditation standards without substantial financial backing, which in time would make it possible to recruit a distinguished faculty. At present students who attend any of these programs face serious problems of transferring credits and will continue to do so until a generally recognized system of accreditation for such institutions is established.

Unlike the situation encountered by the élite programs, where the demand is easily met by the existing programs, this new type of program dips into a market in which the demand is steadily increasing and is probably already far ahead of present capacity.

Unless political and economic conditions change seriously for the worse, many new programs of this kind are likely to be born in the 1960s.

A third category of Study Abroad programs are those with modest academic pretensions, generally sponsored by the smaller liberal arts colleges and normally catering to female students. These programs must be judged against the standard of education offered at the sponsoring colleges, and in that light they often seem to have considerable merit.

The proponents of the less academically oriented programs point out that the real value to a student of a year abroad is not to be measured by the academic credits he may amass. From this point of view, the most valid experience is often that of the student who "wastes" a year going abroad on his own and absorbs by himself what he is capable of absorbing. This is the view taken at Swarthmore College and until recently at DePauw. Swarthmore encourages its students to take a year out to study abroad without credit, and DePauw has assisted a significant number of its students to pursue independent study abroad for credit; DePauw, however, is now planning its own foreign program. The Antioch foreign program, with its typical work period, and the Lake Erie program with its required independent research, also offer the students a considerably less supervised foreign experience than is permitted under the better programs in the other categories.

At the other extreme from these loosely supervised programs are those operated by the Roman Catholic female colleges, which transplant a girl from an American convent atmosphere to a French, Italian, Spanish, or Swiss one. Relative to other foreign study programs they appear to offer a quite attenuated cultural immersion; but if the only valid measuring rod is the program offered by these colleges in the United States, even a hemmed-in experience abroad may have much to recommend it.

There remain to be considered the activities of the four-hundred-odd students a year who receive credit for independent study. The program pursued by these students is often independent only in the sense that the student must obtain special permission from his college for his plan of study. Actually the dividing line between the independent study programs and the programs discussed above is sometimes little more than the classification of the sponsoring institution or the size of the program. When the sponsoring institution is an American college or university and students from other universities are accepted, the program is open; when the sponsoring institution is a foreign university or an American institution other than a university the program is classed as independent study.

A major problem that arises in independent study programs is the question of credit. The equating of grades in an equitable manner is a task that either thoroughly perplexes an American registrar or is often beyond his capacity—or that of anyone else. The truth of the matter is that independent study abroad at the undergraduate level is rarely rewarding if the achievement is measured by strictly academic standards. For this reason the best colleges either frown on this kind of foreign study or, like Swarthmore, encourage it as a fifth undergraduate year.

If we face the fact, however, that perhaps half of our 965 accredited universities and colleges offer little higher education in the sense of a rigorous mental discipline but serve principally as finishing schools, or "cultures" in which adolescents are encouraged to mature, the academic argument against even independent study turns specious. As a maturing experience a year abroad, or even a quarter abroad, may be more worthwhile than the same period spent in the home institution.

6

Never before have there been opportunities for so many Americans to get abroad so early in life. Student interest in foreign study is a national asset, since it can help create that pool of Americans who have already taken the first steps toward training for overseas service—or toward education in international understanding even if they never again stir from a home in the United States.

Foreign undergraduate study also serves some other important purposes. It can be expected to encourage proficiency in foreign languages and to increase interest in and offer a very valid motivation for their study. The prestige of professional training abroad is high in some fields other than language, particularly in the arts.

The proliferation of employment opportunities abroad, for many of which prior foreign experience is regarded by the hiring agencies as prerequisite, gives the student who wishes to study abroad a vocational as well as an intellectual or emotional incentive.

But the new importance of study abroad, and the widened student interest in it, requires a sharp look at some of the demerits of foreign study for undergraduates.

Some question whether a college undergraduate is mature enough to benefit greatly from such an experience and whether it is fair to expect him to compete with European students who are naturally better prepared for their own universities than the Americans. Others hold that while the experience is generally pleasurable and probably broadening, it adds little to the student's intellectual training and is hardly more valid as a source of college credit than such valuable extracurricular experiences as working, listening to music, or falling in love. Others claim the experience, if successful, is so emotionally upsetting that the value of the remaining period of study on return to the American campus is seriously jeopardized. A final major complaint is the relatively high cost of the experience, which bars a large number of otherwise qualified students from study abroad.

None of these criticisms is unanswerable. The maturity of undergraduate students naturally varies, and many of them would doubtless be well advised to postpone their trip until after graduation. The undergraduate years may indeed not be the optimum time for the experience. For most students, however, it is the only feasible time. The question is not whether they could gain more from postponing foreign study, but whether they can get enough out of it during college to justify going.

Most adverse criticism of the intellectual validity of foreign study at the undergraduate level is valid only if the work taken overseas compares unfavorably with whatever the individual student would be doing if he or she had stayed in the United States. The foreign study program that does not meet the standards of Harvard or Bryn Mawr may nevertheless show up favorably when compared with the cultural and intellectual stimulation of courses offered in many of the nation's institutions of higher learning. If studying abroad helps awaken a student to the excitement of using his mind, it may be far more valuable than an equal number of additional hours of work in many an accredited American college. From this point of view a year of Podunk in Peru may be a better educational gamble than a year of Podunk in Podunk.

Foreign study is not inexpensive; its cost is undoubtedly a deterrent to many able students. While this factor is extraneous to a consideration of the educational value of the experience, it does limit the supply of students who can be exposed to it. The financing of undergraduate study abroad must be realistically faced.

The problem is not that United States colleges and universities are losing money on foreign study. Once they get well established, the economics of a foreign study program are perfectly reasonable from the point of view of the sponsoring institutions; indeed, one of the factors in creating new programs has been the hope of university administrators that they could be managed at a modest profit. Nor is the absolute cost of the experience so high. Normally the managers of a foreign study enterprise can save something on cost of food and lodging, compared to what these items would cost on the home campus; in the Syracuse calculations, these savings offset about half of the round-trip travel (by off-season steamship) across the Atlantic. Where the students are placed in a foreign university, the tuition is generally a fraction of what it would be in a private college or university in the United States; if the student pays the regular tuition to his home institution for the year, the institution can count part of that payment as a contribution toward other costs of the enterprise, such as the travel and maintenance of an American faculty adviser. College presidents and their financial advisers are also conscious of the fact that, if any substantial number of their students take part of the college course abroad, their absence will enable the college to increase its enrollment without a corresponding increase in dormitory rooms, eating facilities, athletic equipment, classroom space, or teaching staff. Finally, the economics of these enterprises will be favored by the general trend toward cheaper long-distance air travel.

But from the standpoint of the student and his parents, the economics of the matter hardly seem so favorable. The fact that a semester abroad may cost only a couple of hundred dollars more than a semester at a private United States college may not be persuasive to a family which was counting on the student living at home, paying little or no tuition at a state university or community college, and earning all or part of his keep at part-time jobs. It seems clear that foreign study will tend to be reserved for the more affluent students (and continue to attract more girls than boys) until more scholarship money is funneled into the American educational system to compensate for the modest but unavoidable additional cost of foreign study. The favorable prospect is that the more students study abroad, the cheaper the experience can be; economies are not as impressive here as they are in the mass production of automobiles, but guaranteed volume can significantly reduce travel prices, cost of living abroad, and cost of instruction and supervision provided by the sponsoring college.

Foreign study programs are as easy to announce as they are difficult to set up and administer effectively. The troubles a program may encounter between its first mention and its ultimate success are many and will normally take several years to work out. The peculiar problems of guidance and discipline can, if not foreseen and forestalled, rapidly bring the program into disrepute. The organizers need intimate first-hand knowledge of the country in which the program is to operate, and should possess the elements for effective overseas performance. They must be able to think through the academic problems that arise, student by student, in the effort to make the overseas experience a part of a systematic plan of intellectual training in the student's own college. They must be institution-builders of special skill to graft new growth on an institution governed as much by collective consent procedures as a college or university will typically be. They must be unusually tolerant of the lapses in administrative efficiency created by cross-cultural wire-pulling and intercontinental communications.

Yet in spite of the massive obstacles, student demand and the national interest will probably combine in the new atmosphere of internationalism to produce a mighty growth in Study Abroad programs. Few developments in education will be so relevant to preparing Americans for effective overseas service. The best way to learn how to live and work abroad is still to live and work abroad.

15 · The Internationalization
of Graduate Work

1

At the graduate level in American education, the mushrooming
interest in non-Western civilizations has produced a tropic growth
of area programs. The latest government count of these special
study centers—a 1959 inventory of their usefulness to the State
Department—listed 96 area programs at 45 universities.* Twenty-
three institutions had only one program, 8 maintained two programs
each, 4 supported three, and 10 major universities boasted more
than 3 reputable facilities for graduate area study. (See Table 9.)

The concentrated study of a major culture area is, of course, no
new technique in education, whether in Europe or the United
States. Classical education was a kind of area study, using the
Greek and Roman world to illuminate the universal tendencies of
man as a social animal. Some of the better American universities
have long and distinguished traditions of Semitic, Indic, and Sinitic
studies; it is, indeed, from these nuclei of scholars, books, and
scholarly research that some of our best graduate area programs
have recently developed.

* U.S. Department of State, Bureau of Intelligence and Research, External Research Division, *Area Study Programs in American Universities*, Washington,
D.C. 1959.

TABLE 9. GEOGRAPHICAL DISTRIBUTION OF MAJOR

	Asia	Africa	Near East	West Europe	Russia and East Europe	Latin America
AREAS OFFERED						
STATE, CITY, AND UNIVERSITY						
ARIZONA						
Tucson, Univ. of Arizona	•					•
CALIFORNIA						
Berkeley, Univ. of California	•		•		•	•
Claremont Graduate School	•					
Los Angeles, Univ. of Calif.			•			•
Univ. of Southern Calif.	•				•	•
Palo Alto, Stanford Univ.						•
San Francisco, Amer. Academy of Asian Studies	•					
CONNECTICUT						
Hartford Seminary Foundation		•	•			•
New Haven, Yale Univ.	•	•			•	
DISTRICT OF COLUMBIA						
Washington, George Washington U.						•
Howard Univ.			•			
FLORIDA						
Gainesville, Univ. of Florida						•
HAWAII						
Honolulu, Univ. of Hawaii	•					
ILLINOIS						
Chicago, University of	•		•			
Evanston, Northwestern Univ.		•				•
INDIANA						
Bloomington, Univ. of Indiana	•		•		•	•
South Bend, Univ. of Notre Dame					•	
IOWA						
Iowa City, State Univ. of Iowa	•					
LOUISIANA						
New Orleans, Tulane Univ.						•
MASSACHUSETTS						
Boston University		•				
Cambridge, Harvard University	•		•		•	

GRADUATE AREA-STUDY PROGRAMS

	Asia	Africa	Near East	West Europe	Russia and East Europe	Latin America
MICHIGAN						
Ann Arbor, Univ. of Mich.	●		●		●	
Detroit, Wayne State Univ.					●	
MINNESOTA						
Minneapolis, U. of Minnesota	●			●	●	●
MISSOURI						
St. Louis, Washington Univ.	●					
NEW JERSEY						
Princeton University			●			
South Orange, Seton Hall Univ.	●					
NEW MEXICO						
Albuquerque, Univ. of New Mex.						●
NEW YORK						
Ithaca, Cornell Univ.	●					
New York, Columbia Univ.	●		●	●	●	
Fordham Univ.					●	
New York Univ.	●	●	●	●	●	
Syracuse University					●	●
NORTH CAROLINA						
Chapel Hill, Univ. of N.C.						●
Durham, Duke University				●		
PENNSYLVANIA						
Philadelphia, Dropsie College			●			
U. of Penna.	●		●		●	●
TENNESSEE						
Nashville, Vanderbilt Univ.						●
TEXAS						
Austin, Univ. of Texas					○	
WASHINGTON						
Seattle, Univ. of Washington	●				●	
WISCONSIN						
Madison, Univ. of Wisconsin	●			●		●

General interest in the area expert and in the cultural region as a contemporary field of study came to life during World War II, partly because of the sudden American concern with the more remote regions of the world and partly because the Washington agencies dealing with foreign affairs (the State Department, the military departments and the intelligence organizations, the foreign economic programs, and the information agencies) had to develop strong area desks and began to look around for experts to man them. First the Carnegie Corporation, then the Ford Foundation and other philanthropic foundations, sensing a major development in United States graduate education, responded by investing a great deal of money in area programs. Universities converted or invented programs to take advantage of the new demand for experts and the new sources of budgetary support. The resulting picture suggests an intriguing theory of comparative geographic advantage: area programs tend to develop in those parts of the United States nearest the foreign areas to be studied. The best and the greatest number of Latin American programs are to be found on the South and West Coasts; there are outstanding East Asia programs in the western part of the United States; and the outstanding Middle East and African programs are located almost exclusively east of the Mississippi and north of the Mason-Dixon line. Federal largesse under the National Defense Education Act, with its built-in bias in favor of even geographical distribution of its grants, may in time change this "natural" pattern.

The term "area program" refers to an interdisciplinary concentration for the study and understanding of a particular culture region of the world—"interdisciplinary" in the sense that the job of understanding the area is tackled by several people, expert in various fields of knowledge and different kinds of research methods. The first essential of any superior graduate program is a comprehensive research library and a number of first-rate faculty members whose primary dedication is to the study of one region. It must be a center of scholarly research, and should ideally have sufficient faculty so that all the relevant phases of a culture can be included in the program.

While language training is normally part of a graduate area pro-

TABLE 10. THE ACADEMIC VARIETY OF GRADUATE AREA PROGRAMS (*1958 Survey*)

	Africa	Far East	Latin America	Near East	US.S.R.	Southeast Asia	South Asia	Western Europe
Anthropology and Sociology	●●●	●	●	●	—	●●	●	—
Art	●	●	—	—		—	●	●
Economics	●●	●	●●	●	●●	●	●	●●
Geography	●●	●	●	●	●	●	●	—
History	●	●●●	●●	●●	●	●●	●●	●●
Literature	—	●			●		●	●
Political Science	●	●	●	●	●●	●	—	●●
Religion	—	●	—	●	—		●	—
Spoken Native Language	—	—	●●	—	●	—	—	●
Written Native Language	—	●●	●●●	●●	●●●	—	●	●●
French and German	●	●	—	●	●	●	●	

●●● Generally regarded as of prime importance.
●● Generally regarded as of secondary importance.
● Generally regarded as of lesser importance.
— Generally regarded nonessential.

gram, it is sometimes not regarded as essential to associate language instruction directly with the program. The teaching of exotic languages is a difficult and expensive process, and since it can be done successfully in a concentrated form, at least with respect to the nonliterary languages, graduate students are often sent to a special language institute such as the Division of Languages at Cornell or the Yale program in Chinese for a summer, a semester, or longer periods. The language requirements for area programs differ widely. Knowledge of a foreign language, for instance, is essential for a Latin America program or a Russian program; it has less value in an African program. Students in South Asia and Middle East programs may have greater immediate need of European languages (notably French) than of Asiatic languages—though the best area programs operate on the assumption that some exposure to the native language is advisable because of its contribution to cultural understanding even when it is not a means of communication among scholars and gentlemen.

Language skill is, of course, not the only academic variable among graduate area programs. Table 10 suggests the relative importance of the major academic disciplines for the study of the different regions of the world, judging from our survey of what the graduate area programs actually offer their students and produce in the way of scholarly research. Historians are evidently welcome in all the major graduate area programs, and so are economists, but the study of religion is deemed vital only in some of the Asian programs, while the study of regional art is generally ignored in Latin American, Middle East, and Southeast Asia programs. Anthropology, which is the core of an African program and is prized in most Latin American concentrations, normally rates as a luxury in the field of Russian studies. Sociology is even more frequently lacking; of the seventeen Russian area programs only two (Harvard and Indiana) include sociology; three of the strongest of these (California, Columbia, and Washington) openly lament this gap in their offerings. Only India seems to be a major exception to the principle that sociologists have not been anxious to venture into foreign areas.

Another variable from area to area is whether the student can reasonably expect to get some field experience in the area while he is studying it. Our proximity to Latin America almost assures the student that he will have a chance to get there, while the Communist countries, at the other extreme, present the would-be visitor with travel and visa problems ranging from expensive and difficult to insurmountable.

2

The justification for an area studies program is that each culture area is in crucial respects different from all the others. The differences are certainly impressive, and they are faithfully reflected in the kinds of programs set up at American universities to study them. Asian programs take on some of the aura of classical serenity and esoteric scholarship that befits the study of the centers of ancient wisdom. The Russian studies, with their strong interest in training government experts, mirror America's political concern with its powerful nuclear rival. Middle Eastern programs reflect the diversity of cultures and traditions that have fought and lived together in the crossroads of world history. The African programs, like the continent they study, are still poor relations by comparison with the others, with little tradition but a promising future.

The Latin American programs, as might be expected, take on some of the vitality, optimism, and expansiveness of the New World that is the focal point of their interest. They constitute the largest part of the area studies movement, whether measured by the number of undergraduate and graduate students they educate or by the number of colleges and universities (28) which have solid claim to a special interest in Latin America. This area also includes the brashest examples of academic advertising and (because of their size) the strongest tendency to develop program administrators who are not themselves productive scholars in an academic field. They also offer the readiest job opportunities, particularly in business. A list of the strongest Latin American institutes—at Florida, Tulane, Texas, New Mexico, UCLA and Stanford—shows the correlation between geographical propinquity and program success to which we have already referred.

The emphasis on vocational training in useful subjects like business administration, animal husbandry, and civil engineering, which characterizes some of the larger programs, makes them peculiarly vulnerable to the ebb and flow of job opportunities in the field. There is some evidence that the Latin American field as a whole is somewhat overextended; a good many of the fringe programs are in difficulties, and some of them may wither away through lack of money, lack of students, lack of leadership, or some combination of the three.

The job opportunities that result from a successful completion of a graduate Russian area program are quite different from those open to a graduate of a Latin American program. Although in each case the academic profession will absorb a certain number of graduates, a large number of the Latin American experts will find employment overseas in business, in missionary work, or via the government, while the Russian expert still has a limited opportunity to reside behind the Iron Curtain and even a visit there cannot be undertaken with the spontaneous informality of a trip to Rio or Mexico City. The Russian expert who does not become a teacher is most likely to be employed by the government, but on this side of the Curtain. The talents, techniques, and personality traits desired for this type of government employee are not so noticeably different from those suitable to prospective teachers and scholars as they are from those appropriate to prospective Latin American business representatives. To satisfy the Central Intelligence Agency a university has to have a more solid academic basis for its Russian program than Casa Grace or Pan American Airways yet require for the Latin American training of their junior executives.

The importance of Russia to the Western World and to the United States, the interest in and concern about Russia generally felt in the United States, and the many academic disciplines to which Russia has made and continues to make significant contributions have all conspired to hold high the number and prestige of Russian area programs in the United States. In the general field of Russian and East European area programs, the State Department in 1959 described 18 programs, 7 of which operate in both the Russian and East European areas.

Although more than a decade has now passed since the Communist take-over of China, it is not yet the pattern for universities to establish communist bloc programs that would combine Soviet Russia with Communist China. Traditional differences in history and culture, rather than current similarities in political ideology, still seem to be the organizing principle of graduate area studies.

In the field of Asian studies the American universities tend to concentrate their attention on the Far East and the Middle East: the

Indian subcontinent and the mixture of peoples and cultures in Southeast Asia are neglected by comparison. For the Far East, 15 universities offer 17 area programs, and 6 other institutions offer general Asian studies that include East Asia.

The supply of good programs for this region reflects, of course, the long history of American missionary and business relationships with China and Japan, the special importance the area assumed with American involvement in the Korean and Indo-Chinese wars of the 1950s, and the prestige which Sinitic (and more recently Japanese) culture has traditionally enjoyed in the United States. There are consequently more scholars superbly equipped to teach area studies on the Far East than any other area outside of Western Europe, and some of the programs in this field have had long periods of gestation. The leisurely history of California's Institute of East Asiatic Studies, for example, is truly Oriental. In 1872 a chair in Oriental languages was set up, in 1898 the chair was filled for the first time. Courses on East Asia were gradually added in other departments, and in 1949 this activity culminated in the establishment of the Institute. Other strong programs in this area are located at Michigan (mostly for Japan), Yale (with emphasis on languages), Cornell (which limits its East Asia work to China, but also has the nation's strongest Southeast Asia program), Harvard (which is strong in history), Chicago, and Columbia. With these institutions devoting major attention to the Far East, it can hardly be regarded as a neglected field of study.

The same cannot be said for South and Southeast Asia. We find there are only 4 major Southeast Asia programs in the United States: California, Chicago, Cornell, and Yale. South Asia likewise can claim only 4 academic homes of real distinction: California and Cornell again, together with Pennsylvania and Michigan. Johns Hopkins' School of Advanced International Studies has a center in Rangoon, Burma, which represents a significant effort to give on-the-spot training in area studies. But whereas it is generally agreed that languages are best learned where they are spoken, it does not seem to follow that area studies are best pursued in the field. It is often desirable to go to the field for thesis research or other special studies; but by and large the best library facilities and the most knowledgeable scholars are still those in the American and Euro-

pean universities. Just as the best documentation on Ethiopian
history is still in the British Museum, so the best fund of scholarly
research on Indonesia outside of Holland is now in Ithaca, New
York. As long as this condition persists, the major portion of graduate area training is best obtained in Europe or the United States.

The distinguishing feature of the Middle East as an area for concentrated study is its historic and linguistic variety, which is a trial
for archeologists and historians of its past as well as for economists
and political scientists who study its turbulent present. The past
itself is divided into many separate histories; Egyptologists, Hebrew
scholars, Christian scholars, Islamic scholars, scholars of ancient
Greece and Rome are all concerned with the history of the Middle
East. The area's languages, ancient and modern, are so many and
varied that it is difficult to decide what languages to teach in a
Middle East area program, and by what method. At least seven
varieties of Arabic are found in American college catalogues (Classical, Egyptian, Iraqi, Lebanese, Moroccan, Palestinian, and
Syrian) as well as Hebrew, Kurdish, Persian and Turkish, and the
numerous dead languages of the area.

The major Middle East area programs are located at Chicago,
Columbia, Dropsie, Harvard, Johns Hopkins, Michigan, and Princeton. Of these, two have little interest in the training of contemporary area experts. The Oriental Institute at Chicago is an arche-
ological institute and the Dropsie program is almost exclusively
concerned with training Hebrew scholars. The well-known Princeton program, built up by Philip Hitti, has survived its founder, but
it has now lost some ground to Harvard where Sir Hamilton Gibb
is in charge of Near Eastern studies. Competition for the few
available students is keen among competing programs, and in area
programs as in other graduate enterprises, big names attract good
students.

African studies in the United States are subject to a further dis-
ability: they were latecomers in the area studies movement. The
stimulus the war created for the Russian, Asian, and Latin American programs did not immediately spark interest in Africa, and
the early foundation bounties that nurtured other area programs

were therefore not available to the Africa field. By the time Africa bowed its way into American education, foundation support for area programs had passed from the stage of youthful exuberance to that of measured skepticism.

The Africa area is essentially a geographic region, normally delimited on the north by the Sahara desert. Some critics object to thus decapitating the continent, on the practical political ground that the North African Arabs should be encouraged to see their future as Africans rather than as part of a modern Arab empire. Even excluding the Arabs, however, the area is a study in cultural, linguistic, economic, and political disunity.

The area has no indigenous *lingua franca,* and it has little recorded history, philosophy, literature, art, or developed musical forms—in spite of the interest aroused in Western culture by Africa's primitive art, musical rhythm, and legal theory. As with Southeast Asia, therefore, the study of African affairs has to lean heavily on the social sciences.

Until recently, there have been only four significant university programs on Africa—at Northwestern, Boston University, Howard, and the School for Advanced International Studies at Johns Hopkins. Northwestern's excellent program, led by anthropologist Melville Herskovits, is well built into the university's academic structure and has an outstanding library; Boston's prestige is based primarily on its highly respected faculty; SAIS at Johns Hopkins is able to use part-time government experts for much of its teaching (but this system does not of course yield much sustained research). Howard's program is more modest but it does try to teach an African language, either Swahili or Yoruba, to most of its students. Since Africa is the largest missionary field for American churches, it is natural that the Hartford Theological Seminary should house the nation's oldest Africa program. Other programs, gleams in the eye at this writing, are getting under way at New York University, Duquesne, UCLA, and the Stanford Research Institute. Yale, which has long said that it had no Africa "area program," illustrates the problem of deciding what an area program really is. In one department or another, Yale offers 56 hours of work on Africa; a student could learn a good deal more about the area by taking the courses

Yale offers than he could by getting a degree in many area programs. A somewhat similar situation with respect to African studies is found at Columbia.

When it comes to Western Europe, the foreign area on which Americans have the greatest fund of knowledge, there are the fewest area programs of all. Columbia and New York University have general European programs; Minnesota and Wisconsin maintain the special Scandinavian studies that are appropriate to the ancestry of some of their constituents. SAIS maintains a branch of Johns Hopkins in Bologna, Italy, concentrating on international law and the political economy of France, Germany, Italy, and Austria, while Duke's British Commonwealth Studies Center is concerned with a European culture which (except for Gibraltar) is absent from geographical Europe.

The curiously undeveloped state of Western Europe area programs raises questions about the future of area programs in general. If it is sound to organize academic research and graduate training on the basis of culture areas, why has there been so little interest in establishing area programs for the study of that region of the world about which we know the most, with which we have the most in common, and in which we have the greatest interest?

As an approach to knowledge the area concentration seems to be valid in inverse ratio to the amount of knowledge we have about an area or at least to its degree of general dissemination. There is no glaring need for Western European area programs because there is no dearth of knowledge about Western Europe. The information is readily available to the scholar who seeks it. Only in the case of Scandinavia and Eastern Europe does one find units sufficiently separated from the general stream of European culture and history and sufficiently unknown to the educated American to provide the focus for area studies. Area programs, then, serve their most useful purpose when there is need to create, assemble, and purvey knowledge that is little disseminated and hard to come by. When the knowledge is accessible and easily available, the organization of an area program might be a superfluous act.

3

Area knowledge, like language skill, is easily confused with cultural empathy. Understanding of a country's political history is likewise confused with political sensitivity. Empathy may produce a curiosity about area knowledge and political sensitivity can spur one to study of political trends—but the logic does not necessarily work the other way around. The student trained as an area expert will have acquired during his training some of the skills that seem relevant to overseas success, such as a background in the languages and culture of the area, and he may already have done overseas research. But his training has made him an area expert, not necessarily an effective overseas worker. The rating "area expert" is thus a professional rating, like "physician" or "engineer"—and the area expert is as likely as the physician or engineer to be in need of guidance for overseas work.

The area programs attract two quite different kinds of graduate students. Some expect to be lifetime scholars. Others are seeking vocational training for work in government, missionary effort, or overseas business, and have no special intention to contribute to the sum of academic knowledge about the region; they simply want to be brought up to date on what the scholars already know. Normally the two types of students seek different degrees. The scholar works for a Ph.D. in a discipline—economics, anthropology, history, geography, literature, political science, or whatever; in some programs he can get his doctorate in area studies, but this deviation from the academic norm is frowned on by some of the best programs on the ground that an area is not a discipline and has no distinctive research methodology and advanced theory of the types normally required for advanced degrees. However, the advanced student in an area program will typically build into his doctoral work a dissertation on a subject related to his major discipline as well as to his area, thus adding to the sum of lore about the area as well as contributing to the advance of the frontiers of knowledge in his discipline.

The person training for a nonacademic vocation is usually content with a master's degree, often taken in area studies as such. If he is already employed, he may come for training not leading to a degree; but the prestige of advanced academic degrees and their relevance to advancement in the more intellectual corners of the government service cause most students to want to work toward a degree even if that was not why they first came to take university work.

From the point of view of the directors of many of the best programs, the primary functions of a graduate area program are to train scholars who are area specialists and to produce research. They serve only incidentally as vehicles for vocational training of diplomats, intelligence officers, missionaries, and business executives. But since many area programs have more enthusiasm than students and are financially precarious enterprises, the student who seeks area *expertise* as a working tool rather than a way of life is nevertheless welcomed with open arms.

There is another function of area programs that is hardly yet present in their planners' dreams—and by some would be regarded as nightmare if it were. It is to use a program's facilities and expertness to set up a course of study on one country with the *primary emphasis on the transferability to other countries of what is learned and of the method used to learn it*. In this third role, for example, a program specializing in Latin America might teach the trainee about Brazil in such a way that he is thereafter somewhat prepared (as far as universals go) for life and work in Indonesia, Turkey, or the Congo.

Shifting their educational gears to meet this last need will be a monumental effort for the sponsors of most area programs. Yet unless they do add this purpose to their traditional interest in training lifetime area experts, they will miss the opportunity of affecting during their formal education most of the Americans who may become the nation's overseas representatives. Many students in professional and graduate programs have a yen for overseas work but few are clear where they would like to go—and practically none can be sure when they are studying where they can eventually find overseas jobs in their own fields. Even the student who knows where his first job will be can predict with reasonable certainty that he will live in several different countries if he remains for many years in overseas service. Under these conditions the most relevant goal for an engineer or nurse would be to learn enough about one area and language to guide them in understanding the essentials of whatever alien environment they may encounter later. At minimum, such an experience should teach them the relativity of the American Way, which is the beginning of wisdom in cross-cultural operations.

The internationalization of the university cannot, of course, stop with the liberal arts college and the graduate area programs. Every professional school, and every graduate program in the social sciences, must in time reflect in its curriculum the recognition that some of its students will practice their profession abroad, by building into its technical field of study an awareness of world-wide developments in that field, an interest in the experience that members of its own profession are having abroad, and an emphasis on the breadth and adaptability that constitute the "plus" of transplanted technical skill. With overseas assignments in mind, it may have to plan to turn out more general practitioners than ever before.

Thus, for example, students in an engineering school should be faced early and often with questions like this: "Looking at the whole process of building a bridge [which is a social as well as a physical process], can you distinguish between what is universally applicable, and what is merely American practice?" Or a graduate student in economics should be exposed (as indeed should sophomores in the elementary college course) to models of underdeveloped and overinflated economies, not merely to Marshallian and Keynesian models based on judgments about industrial societies. If the social work profession is going to bid for participation in community-development programs around the world, students in schools of social work should learn about foreign rural villages as well as American urban slums. Agriculture and public health schools will need to carry further an already noticeable tendency to introduce their students to the tropics as well as to the temperate zones. Students of administration should study the transferability of institutional theory and practice, not just assume that because we are "advanced" our thinking about organization and management is universally valid.

Most professional schools, of course, already have a hard enough time trying to give a superior vocational training in the limited time available to them; the explosion of knowledge in every field makes it more difficult to fit into a given number of years the facts and techniques essential to the trade. When overseas training is included in their curriculum, therefore, it is either in the form of a *post* postgraduate course, as is usual in law, medicine, and agriculture; or a direct attempt to introduce international subject matter into the regular courses, as in a few programs of business administration and even fewer of engineering. Some examples, drawn from the field of business administration, may help illustrate some of the approaches now being tried.

On the whole the graduate schools of business administration have developed more elaborate devices for training persons planning a foreign career than have most other types of professional schools. Many of the better business schools are attempting to broaden the background of their students by requiring more courses in the humanities and the social sciences, and some have developed programs specifically for the purpose of preparing their graduates for overseas assignments. Among these latter are the business schools at Columbia University and San Francisco State College.

Columbia's Business School offers a special graduate program in international business that is particularly well equipped to meet the training needs of tax and finance men for American concerns with extensive foreign interests. Eighteen of the sixty hours of this two-year course are in "International Business," and twenty additional hours may be taken in foreign aspects of economics and geography. There are no language or area study requirements in the present Columbia M.A. program. The program director, Roy Blough, a former member of the President's Council of Economic Advisers, believes that in the future there will be some language requirement and that area study may become a required part of a Ph.D. program. These changes would quite revolutionize the present program, converting it from a foreign trade program into a general training program for overseas business operations.

San Francisco State College began in 1949 an elaborate training program for overseas business through its School of World Business and International Development. In this program, A.B.s, B.S.s, M.A.s and M.S.s in world business are offered in an accredited college. In addition to regular work in economics and business administration, the student of world business may choose from more than two dozen specialized courses such as "Export-Import Procedures and Documentation," "Marine Insurance," "Area Studies in Business in the Far East," and "Pacific Coast and International Trade."

These courses are designed to meet the needs both of the un-affiliated student who seeks overseas employment and of the company that wishes to train its employees for overseas work, but most of the students seem to be on their own.

The San Francisco State program does not minimize the importance of foreign languages, but language is not stressed since most of the students do not know where they are going. The School prefers that the students take a concentrated language course shortly before departure or on arrival in the field. Part of the undergraduate program is an optional half-year of independent study abroad. This is open to honor students and is preceded by preparatory courses in the area and field of study and followed by rigorous written and oral examinations.

The Harvard Business School offers no special degree in "world business," but it does offer two optional courses in the specific problems faced by businessmen abroad: "International Economic Relations" and "Management of Foreign Operations." These courses are taken by about 10 per cent of the students in the Business School.

In all, perhaps 40 colleges and business schools offer concentrations in foreign trade. These programs are usually basically similar to, but considerably less elaborate than, the program at Columbia.

Outside the universities, the most notable academic program for overseas business is the American Institute for Foreign Trade, established after World War II on the site of the Air Force's Thunderbird Field near Phoenix, Arizona. Sponsored by a number of business firms, it does an impressive job of teaching Spanish and Portuguese in a hurry, both to one-year students seeking a second bachelor's degree in foreign trade, and to key men who are taught languages intensively in six weeks by heavy stress on the modern aural-oral techniques. Area studies are also taught at Thunderbird Field, but with little emphasis on research by students and no opportunities for student field work. The "business administration" part of the curriculum suffers from the extreme vocational slant that plagues many of the university business schools.

4

By and large the special graduate programs in the professional schools attempt no more than to widen the definition of "technical skill" by internationalizing its content. Where the graduate program includes a period of residence and study abroad (usually in connection with research for a thesis) there may be important by-products in cultural empathy, political awareness, and the understanding that institutions cannot be transplanted but must be fashioned of local cultural raw materials. But American graduate education has been lacking in direct efforts to prepare Americans for overseas service.

The historic programs for this purpose were aimed at what is now a relatively thin market: the Foreign Service of the United States, which, even in its expanded form, now constitutes only about 3 per cent of the civilian posts for Americans abroad. Georgetown University long maintained a successful cram course for the Foreign Service examinations. The Fletcher School of Law and Diplomacy (at Tufts), repository of the nation's best League of Nations library, has managed a successful graduate program based on the study of history and international politics, with international trade and finance as a later addition. The students at the Fletcher School live together and develop a notable *esprit de corps;* the School's alumni can be found in impressive numbers today in the upper reaches of the Foreign Service, as well as in overseas business and university teaching of international relations.

The "modern" approach to international relations, stressing the people-to-people interpenetration of whole societies, has not only affected the programs of the established schools of diplomacy, but has also brought into being a number of experimental graduate programs more explicitly oriented to the study of cultures, the development of the student's personal philosophy, and the ability to understand the power structure and administrative process in foreign lands. The most substantial of these are: the School of International Service at American University, the School of Public and International Affairs at the University of Pittsburgh, and the Overseas Training Program at the Maxwell Graduate School of Citizenship and Public Affairs of Syracuse University. International institutes of various kinds have also been established at Montana State College, the University of Oregon, and elsewhere.

The American University enterprise, headed by Dean Ernest Griffith, builds on top of its undergraduate program a variety of graduate programs normally leading to a degree of Master of International Service, but oriented strongly toward particular overseas vocations: the Foreign Service, foreign economic operations, business administration, voluntary-agency operations, or missionary work. The graduate degree can be achieved in a year by graduates of the School's undergraduate program and in two years by others. For some kinds of specialists the School recommends taking the undergraduate degree at the School and going on to graduate training in the appropriate professional school at the University—the School of Business Administration, for example, or Wesleyan Theological Seminary. Overseas training is thus treated as an academic discipline, to be added to a vocational specialty.

The Pittsburgh School, established in 1958 under a dean (Donald C. Stone) whose career has been in public administration, treats international service as part of a larger graduate program in public affairs that also includes specialties in urban administration and community leadership. It offers a one-year master's degree in the administration of international affairs, which is in effect a Master of Public Administration degree with strong international overtones.

At the graduate and professional level, the idea that educational institutions should supervise the first shock of work experience is already settled doctrine—physicians must interne in teaching hospitals, teachers do practice teaching, ministers are apprenticed as assistants or curates. Public administration is perhaps the newest field to use similar techniques successfully, through the "internships" in Washington agencies sponsored by the Rockefeller Foundation during the 1930s and 1940s, and the many similar programs that have now blossomed at every level of government.

Following this distinguished trail, the Carnegie Corporation has already sponsored two experiments, at Syracuse and Montana State, with a supervised experience overseas as part of a regular university graduate overseas-training program. If the feasibility of this kind of program is demonstrated, many other institutions will doubtless move in this direction. It may therefore be worth pausing a moment to examine one species of the new genus.

At Syracuse, groups of ten students are selected from nationwide applications; they are deliberately drawn from a variety of professional fields, and the students must already have completed the equivalent of a master's degree in their specialties. The overseas experience is preceded by ten weeks of intensive course work in the Maxwell Graduate School, stressing the analysis of foreign cultures, the analysis of the process of economic growth, the development of political leadership, comparative study of public administration and the building of social structures, and the relevance of American values and institutions abroad.

Four weeks of intensive aural-oral language study at Syracuse follow, and then the trip together to a foreign country, accompanied by a professor whose area *expertise* includes both language skill and a broad understanding of that foreign culture and society; this faculty member is selected for his ability to relate the seminar to the particular country in which each group's overseas experience is planned. If an overseas experience is planned for Brazil, the guiding hand for the group from start to finish is a man especially qualified by experience and scholarship to take the seminar to Brazil for a period of supervised study of Brazilian society and of American operations in Brazil. He works with the students through all the course work, though the primary responsibility for instruction lies with anthropologists, economists, political scientists, geographers, teachers of American civilization, and language teachers.

Once abroad, each student stays in the home of a non-English-speaking family and continues his intensive work on the language for another month. Thereafter each is assigned to work with an American overseas operation, public or private, there to pursue an individual research project which relates his major professional field to the special problems of overseas service.

This summary of the graduate overseas program at the Maxwell School in Syracuse is not intended as a pattern that any other institution can or should follow in detail. The program is merely an experiment to determine how an academically feasible graduate program can best be built around a substantial overseas experience. Many more such experiments are needed.

16 · The Use and Abuse of Foreign Languages

1

There is a new awareness in the United States of the importance of foreign languages, a discontent with the way languages have been taught in the past, and a desire to find and adopt new ways of teaching them. Today a popular majority would probably support the proposition that the national interest requires a reversal of the trend against the study of foreign languages that marked American education after World War I.

It is not easy to assess the relative weight of the reasons for the apathy, even the antagonism, toward foreign languages that has long been a prominent feature of American culture. A major reason, however, is that most Americans simply have not perceived a need for more than one language. A frontier civilization, preoccupied with its internal growth, could readily assume that the language barriers it encountered ought to be breached by imposing the dominant English tongue upon such Indians, Spaniards, Frenchmen, or Mexicans as stood in the path of American expansion. The main centers of American population are still so far from lands that speak a different language that there is no immediate incentive for people to try to possess another tongue.

Knowledge of a foreign language has historically been associated with two groups in the United States: the upper classes, who learned French or German early in life in private schools, from European governesses, and through grand tours or university residence on "the Continent"; and, at the other end of the social scale, common laborers who immigrated to the United States through New York or California and brought with them their own languages —German, Swedish, Yiddish, Polish, Russian, Spanish, Italian, Greek, Chinese, and Japanese. In America until recent times the native ability to speak a second language lacked the prestige value associated with it in Europe because it smacked of the recent immigrant who was, generally speaking, poor, uneducated, and of a peasant-laboring class. The conformist spirit of our nation in this respect can still be seen in the resistance by the children of recent immigrants to their parents' efforts to raise them in a bilingual tradition.

Apart from the lack of immediate incentives by virtue of America's geographical position and native prejudices, American students by the millions were disillusioned by the experience of passing traditional foreign-language courses while failing to acquire a usable foreign-language skill. An extraordinarily small proportion of the Americans who spend two or three years on French or German or Spanish succeed in acquiring even a reading (as opposed to a deciphering) proficiency in the language studied. The explanation lies partly in the methods used and partly in the kinds of teachers who used them.

The traditional teaching methods based on grammar and meticulous translation appear to have been devised for and first applied to the teaching of classical languages—which are highly inflected, and are mainly valuable for their literature, their effectiveness in enriching the student's English, and the mental discipline their study involves, rather than as tools for communication among living persons. When a similar emphasis on grammar and translation is applied to a modern language, it turns the living language into a code and language lessons into exercises in cryptanalysis. Latin composition and Greek grammar, however, have supplied mental discipline, which is part of education, and if this drilling resulted in the acquisition of a reading knowledge of these languages, the student so skilled was *ipso facto* admitted into the company of gentlemen scholars. Girls, for whom pretensions to scholarship were considered in bad taste, became ladies by enduring over a prescribed period the *où est la plume de ma tante* method of French language instruction.

Language teachers themselves today concede that some of their colleagues must share the blame for the apathy and antagonism of students toward foreign languages. The teacher who cannot speak or think in a foreign language is not likely to be able to impart to his students what he lacks himself. Many a perceptive student has witnessed with distaste a pathetic encounter between a language instructor and a native speaker of the language.

2

Among the principal causes for the new awareness of our need for greater linguistic proficiency are the Russian scare, the one-world concept, and the specific needs of our overseas personnel.

The Russian influence is easier to state than to explain. There is a hair's-breadth distinction, which defies the logician and may even puzzle the psychologist, that determines when Americans reject or when they seek to emulate the aims and achievements of Soviet Russia. It is now widely known in the United States that Russians are rigorously trained in language before they are sent abroad to live and work and that in some special schools language studies are begun in elementary school. This time the American reaction, instead of total rejection, has been expressed at least verbally in terms of frenetic emulation.

In addition to the Russian threat to the United States there is reawakened appreciation of the usefulness of studying alien cultures in general education. The case for language instruction as a route to cultural empathy is an important factor in the rapid expansion of the Study Abroad movement. It has led to the growing popularity of summer homestays abroad, as advocated by The Experiment in International Living, the American Field Service, and some smaller organizations in the student travel field.

What has really created a sense of national crisis in the language field is the discovery that most overseas Americans are not able to deal with foreigners in the local languages. For the first time in our history, language proficiency has indeed become a valid professional qualification for hundreds of thousands of Americans. As we shall see, this new motive changes not only the clientele for language instruction but also changes the languages to be studied, the skills sought, and the methods used.

There is little need to belabor the point that many of our overseas representatives are seriously handicapped by a lack of language facility. The lamentations from the field are overwhelming proof that not enough linguists are available to be sent overseas and that too few Americans learn foreign languages even when they work abroad.

In interviews done as part of this study we heard many extraordinary rationalizations and a few good reasons for lack of effort to learn the local language. People on short-term assignments of two years or less typically feel that no purpose will be served by learning a second language unless it is widely used; some Americans in Ethiopia, convinced that they should be learning some foreign language, concentrate on French rather than Amharic. For the most part, however, the matter is hardly approached with logic and reason. Those with lively curiosity or an ear for language, or both, often spend much of their spare time studying it; those without these natural gifts usually reason that their particular jobs do not require them to know anything but English.

In a surprising number of cases, the wife puts in more time on language study than the husband. At the office or in the field, a man may deal with local people who have got their technical training in England or the United States. But if his wife wants to try crossing the culture line in her social life, she must at least be making an obvious effort to learn the language of her hostesses.

The interviews confirmed the popular image of the linguistic shortcomings of Americans abroad. Magazine writers have coined an impressive series of picturesque phrases—"language curtain," "our silent spokesmen abroad," "our tongue-tied Foreign Service." James Reston's statement in *The New York Times* of March 18, 1958, that "50 per cent of the entire Foreign Service officer corps do not have a speaking knowledge of any foreign language" and that "70 per cent of the new men coming into the Foreign Service are in the same state," did not tell the Foreign Service anything it did not already know, but it did provide ammunition for the attempt to get some Congressional support for correcting the condition.* The popular press has repeatedly regaled the nation with the information that American ambassadors to most of the major countries have to work through interpreters. Statesmen, politicians, and novelists (secure in the knowledge that nobody expects them to speak Urdu or Swahili or even an acceptable French) have been beating the drum hard and effectively for action. Congressmen who are opposed to large overseas operations of the United States have used the atmosphere of crisis as an argument for not doing anything else until we have "solved" the language problem.

All this excitement has naturally produced some action. The resurrection of the Foreign Service Institute is a case in point. The Congressional hoppers have been full of bills seeking to improve language training; Senator Leverett Saltonstall of Massachusetts and Senator Mike Mansfield of Montana have co-sponsored a bill to enable the State Department to devote more time and money to making linguists out of its overseas representatives, and provide money incentives, comparable to flight pay in the Air Force, for language proficiency. (The Central Intelligence Agency, whose funds are buried in the general defense appropriation and do not have to be separately justified, already does the same thing without an Act of Congress.) And in the National Defense Education Act of 1958, Congress placed language training on a federally supported pedestal alongside mathematics and the natural sciences. The Act's statement of policy says the nation

> ... requires programs that ... will correct as rapidly as possible the existing imbalances in our educational programs which have led to an insufficient proportion of our population educated in science, mathematics, and modern foreign languages and trained in technology.

The Act provides for massive support to language centers and institutes. The study of cultures and societies, of which languages are the expression, is relegated to satellite status in the language centers. The Act also excludes the possibility that there may be elements of

* In a subsequent article, *The New York Times* of November 19, 1959, Mr. Reston reported that Foreign Service officers are considerably improved in their mastery of foreign languages.

effective overseas performance that have very little to do with language studies.

In short, language has all at once been promoted to a position as a primary element of overseas success. We believe that a knowledge of the language of the country in which the overseas American works is, in the long run, indispensable. But we also believe that the knowledge of any foreign language should be regarded as an *index* to an individual's quality of mind and spirit, not as a proof of his cultural empathy. An exclusive emphasis on learning foreign languages will undoubtedly produce "results," but they too are likely to be out of perspective. We need to worry less about the behavior of an overseasman who is *simpático* but tongue-tied than about that of the American who is fluently arrogant in a foreign language.

Linguistic skill, moreover, does not seem to be closely correlated with other intellectual abilities. A good linguist, like a good chess player, is not necessarily good at anything else. In picking a good linguist for an assignment, therefore, one does not always pick the person who is best qualified for the job.

3

The ferment about America's "language gap" has popularized three kinds of innovations—new techniques of language training, new times and places for language study, and a new emphasis on exotic languages. The new techniques are usually some variant of the aural-oral method. Prominent among the new times and places are: in childhood in the elementary school, at maturity in the graduate school, and after assignment in the native habitat. Among the exotic languages, Russian leads in student interest, but Chinese, Japanese, Arabic and Hebrew, among many others, are winning an unwonted attention.

The "new" aural-oral method based on constant repetition is actually as old as mothers. Its code, with its emphasis on accent, word order, and repetition of simple sentence structure, is the essential feature of the Berlitz method that has been successfully practiced for some eighty years. In the Berlitz method, all teachers must be native speakers of the language, and no English may be used in class.

Variations on the same general idea have been practiced on a limited scale for decades. Professor James Taft Hatfield, head of the German Department at Northwestern University, for virtually the first third of the century experimented successfully with a similar method.

Aural-oral teaching received a new impetus from the Armed Forces' language-training practices during World War II. The services had to train men quickly to communicate in a foreign language. Since the servicemen often lacked the time or the intellect, or both, to learn languages in the classical manner, and since they more frequently needed proficiency in the spoken rather than the written language, the whole training program was focused on oral communication. The teaching function was divided between a professor of linguistics, a "teacher" (also called a leader) and a "native informant" (also called a guide).

In order to meet the mass requirements of wartime, the Army and Navy programs altered the Berlitz method in two ways. First, they replaced the trained native teachers employed by Berlitz with untrained, or partially trained, native informants. They then supplemented (and overshadowed) the native informant with mechanical teaching devices, instruction in linguistics, and teachers. The Armed Forces' method also relaxed the stringent Berlitz rule against use of the students' native language, for the accommodation of the professors of linguistics as well as for that of the students.

A War Department education manual of 1944 describes the division of labor as follows: The linguistics expert prepares the exercises suitable for training English-speaking people to speak the language, bearing in mind the similarities and differences the two languages display in syntax and phonetics. The teacher directs the class. The native speaker "does not need to know any English. ... He is a model for you to imitate, and as a check on your pronunciation; it is *not* his business to be a teacher or to 'explain' the language to you. ... He should neither be overeducated nor too uncultured. ... [The] native speaker ... is always right." The student must always "imitate the pronunciation of [his not too uncultured] guide, rather than that of the phonograph records or of the Aids to Listening" found in the text.

Apart from the resistance to "mechanization of teaching" the critics of aural-oral technique find repellent the manner in which the Armed Forces use their native informants. The charge is that a category of the overeducated is created, and conformity to the uncultured is mandatory. The student who aspires to speak a foreign language well is guilty of insubordination if he attempts to carry out his wish; his goal must be mediocrity. And even if he resigns himself to setting his sights on this mean achievement, he has before him the native informant as a constant reminder that he can never succeed because a native speaker is by definition the only good source of first-hand knowledge of the pronunciation and usage of any language.

Since World War II, many language teachers have been experimenting with some of the techniques used by the Army and Navy. As a result, several systematic programs designed to improve language study are now under way. Among the most significant are projects now being conducted at Middlebury College, the Georgetown Institute of Language and Linguistics, and Cornell University.

Another innovation in language teaching—the language laboratory, consisting of booths, tape recorders, earphones, and other mechanical equipment—has come into widespread use. The equipment permits a student to read a book and hear it read at the same time, and gives him a chance to hear many different native speakers, some of whom may be more cultured than others. Electronic devices can also be used to expose a student to the highly educational experience of listening to his pronunciation alongside that of a native speaker, thus enabling the student with a ready ear to perceive and correct his own errors in tone, rhythm, and phonetics.

Admittedly the language laboratories are important new teaching aids, but words of caution about their use are frequently heard from some of the more thoughtful scholars in the field. Language is essentially a means of communication between people, and the right people are better language teachers than machines. Some proponents of the modern techniques of language teaching warn against the exaggerated and inappropriate use of mechanical teaching devices. "There is serious danger," says Ronald Hilton of Stanford, "that they will become just another educational gimmick. We already have the language teacher who is an expert at running a language laboratory, but himself cannot speak the language of his tapes with any accuracy or facility." Albert Menut of Syracuse observes that an important aspect of language learning is the asking of questions and that, for better or worse, machines do not answer questions. European students, who are generally regarded as superior to American students as linguists, have the advantage of a considerable amount of aural-oral practice, but they are also required to make a thorough study of grammar.

The wisdom of wholesale adoption of aural-oral methods by schools and colleges is still in question. But when it comes to training for overseasmanship, there is an important role to be played by the "crash" program, in which some facility in the language is achieved in a relatively short period of intensive study.

The most concentrated program that we have come across is that offered by the Jehovah's Witnesses, where the student studies language for 300 hours the first month, and for 150 the next. The Berlitz school claims that 100 hours of study in a six-week term is sufficient to break the language barrier in a European language. The American Institute of Foreign Trade successfully trains executives to speak Spanish and Portuguese in an intensive six-week course, and claims that the best of its students can thereafter conduct sales conferences and make extemporaneous speeches using a solid business and general vocabulary that runs to 2,000 words or more.

Most academicians are inclined to consider such claims exaggerated, and to insist on a minimum of six to ten months of six-hour-a-day work. At Syracuse the six-month full-time course in Russian for Air Force personnel was found to be too short for satisfactory results, and the normal span of the course was set at close to a year. There is merit in the psychologists' suggestion that concentration is no longer productive beyond a certain point, that it takes time as well as hard work to learn a foreign language. Also some experts frown on the idea of using crash programs in teaching the more difficult languages. The wartime experience with intensive year-long courses in Japanese and Chinese, however, does argue that a minimum proficiency in just about any spoken language can be acquired in a year or less of full-time intensive study under proper supervision.

The crash program leads to the acquisition of a technique that, unfortunately, is soon forgotten unless there is continued opportunity to employ it. Therefore the study of a language in this way must not precede the overseas assignment by too great a period of time. The government once considered a "linguistic stockpile plan," according to which people would be trained in various strategic languages and then held in reserve for possible future use. The idea was soon abandoned; now the government attempts to train only the persons for whom it has an immediate need.

Concentrated programs thus find their most important clientele among people whose need at the moment is the rapid acquisition of a particular language skill. The aural-oral method of language teaching may not be, as its most enthusiastic devotees would seem to imply, the greatest invention since the wheel. But for overseasmen in a hurry, it can be an indispensable aid to effective performance on the job abroad.

The dispute between the supporters of traditional and modern language teachings has led to internal struggles and mutual recriminations among language teachers. The basic dispute concerns the nature of language itself. Milton Cowan, the Director of the Division of Languages at Cornell, one of the most dynamic and distinguished of the "modern" modern language teachers, states the position of his school in a positive fashion when he says "The fastest way to learn a language is to speak it. The written is simply a derivative of the spoken language. Language is pseudobiological, passed on from parents to children by word of mouth. There is no argument about the best method of learning a language." The protagonists of the aural-oral method tend to define language differently from the traditionally minded grammarians. The latter want to teach English or French (or any other language) as it ought to be spoken; for them language is a system that has been developed in part unconsciously, and in part through the conscious efforts of educated people, for the purpose of accurately (prose) and suggestively (poetry) conveying ideas, and as a normative discipline, the growth, discovery, and formulation of which occur through processes similar to those observable in the statement of the common law. The aural-oral school, on the other hand, wants to teach English or French "as she is spoke." For them language is empirical, and the task of the scholar is to codify rather than to purify. Proponents of the aural-oral school thus speak of the ease of language learning and state categorically that all normal children succeed in learning a language. They would say that almost all children living in the United States are proficient in English by the sixth year, while, according to the proponents of the normative theory, many Americans have failed to master English even by the time they have graduated from college. The conclusion reached by each group is correct, provided we accept the definition each gives to language. Fair-minded persons on both sides will admit that under certain circumstances one is justified in studying only the literary language and in others only the spoken.

4

A vast subject peripheral to our study concerns the practicability of teaching foreign languages to all or part of our elementary school children. Stephen Freeman, Vice President of Middlebury College, is one who lends his prestige to the proposition that we start training in a foreign language for all students from the first grade, primarily as a device for breaking the culture barriers.

It is possible for the interested student in many high schools and colleges to study French, Spanish, or German, and, to a lesser extent Italian, Russian, or Portuguese. His opportunities for learning Chinese, Japanese, Arabic, or Hindi, however, are quite inadequate, and his chances of finding other exotic languages in a school curriculum are practically nil.

In addition to a great deal of new effort in the schools, there has also been much activity directed toward the building up of language training in postgraduate and professional education. Here, however, the several trends appear somewhat contradictory. The traditional Ph.D. language requirement is everywhere under attack, yet at the same time new specialized language programs are blossoming at the graduate level all over the country. Reasons for the apparent paradox are to be found in the changing needs that American graduate schools are trying to meet.

Most graduate schools have long insisted that aspirants for advanced degrees should pass "tool examinations" in one or two languages before the faculty formally admits them to candidacy.

TABLE 11. TIME REQUIREMENTS

Levels of

I *Sufficient proficiency in speaking a foreign language to satisfy routine travel requirements.*

Language Categories		Class Hours *	Training Required for People with *High Aptitude/Average Aptitude*	
A				
Italian	German	1	4 months	6 months
French	Swedish			
Spanish	Norwegian	2	2 months	3 months
Portuguese	Danish			
Rumanian	Dutch	3	1½ months	2 months
B				
Russian	Esthonian			
Byelorussian	Finnish	1	6 months	8 months
Georgian	Polish			
Ukrainian	Hungarian			
Lithuanian	Czech	2	3 months	4 months
Bulgarian	Greek			
Persian	Turkish			
Indonesian	Hindustani	3	2 months	3 months
	Serbo-Croatian			
C				
(*With the Chinese Writing*		1	6 months	9 months
System) •••	Chinese	2	4 months	6 months
Korean	Japanese	3	3 months	4 months
D				
Arabic	Cambodian	1	6 months	9 months
Vietnamese	Burmese	2	4 months	6 months
	Thai	3	3 months	4 months

The estimates in this chart are based on the assumption that students possess no less than average aptitude and positive motivation. It is further assumed that the structure of the language is learned through the spoken language, and that the necessary drill is obtained through proper laboratory facilities, with the aid of fluent speakers of the language and an instructor trained in linguistics.

* Class Hours of Instruction per Day
   1 1 hour per day (plus 2–3 hours drill and study).

FOR FOREIGN LANGUAGE ACHIEVEMENT

Language Proficiency

II *Basic familiarity with the structure of a language with sufficient proficiency in speaking to conduct routine business within a particular field. Sufficient familiarity with the writing system to read simple material with the aid of a dictionary.*		III *Fluency and accuracy in speaking with sufficient vocabulary to meet any ordinary requirements which do not involve the speaker in a technical subject outside his own specialty. Ability to read newspapers and documents with limited reference to a dictionary.*	
Training Required for People with *High Aptitude / Average Aptitude*		Training Required for People with *High Aptitude / Average Aptitude*	
●	●	●	●
4 months	6 months	9 months ●●	12 months ●●
3 months	5 months	6 months ●●	9 months ●●
		●	●
●	●		
9 months	12 months	15 months ●●	18 months ●●
6 months	9 months	12 months ●●	15 months ●●
●	●	●	●
15 months	18 months	24 months ●●	30 months ●●
12 months	15 months	18 months ●●	24 months ●●
●	●	●	●
12 months	15 months	18 months ●●	24 months ●●
9 months	12 months	15 months ●●	18 months ●●

2 2–3 hours per day (plus 4–6 hours drill and study).
3 4–6 hours per day (plus 4–6 hours drill and study).

● Not practical to achieve on an hour-a-day basis.
●● Plus 3 months in part-time training and using the language, preferably in an area abroad where the language is widely used.
●●● This group of languages requires a substantial increase in time in Categories II and III because of the difficulty of the writing system.

Whether the student was training to be a chemist, an economist, or a literary critic, the principle was the same: "scholars" should have the language facility that would make foreign publications, especially in their own fields, available to them.

The principle is noble, but it is widely applied with a large dose of hypocrisy. Even in the best universities, the graduate language examinations often insult the intelligence of their students and compromise the announced standards of the institution.

The problem is that the world of scholarship has changed since the language requirement became fixed in graduate school curricula. Once a large proportion of the new work in science was being published first in German; now the mysteries of physics, chemistry, and biology are more likely to be available first in English—or, in some subfields, in Russian. In the social sciences it is now the exceptional graduate student who explores anything but English-language sources in his research. For the humanists, the cultural vigor of the English-speaking world, and the speed with which major foreign works of literature and criticism are translated into English, have changed the relative need for a reading knowledge of the European languages; France is no longer the main repository of Western culture and French is no longer the universal language of educated men. Moreover, the rapid increase of knowledge in every specialized field has tended to preempt the student time formerly available for the study of foreign languages.

The response to these trends is now evident in many of the nation's university catalogues. One common practice has been to set up special language courses for graduate students, where special professional vocabulary and little grammar are taught. This device is most often used for German, but similar courses are occasionally available in French as well. Some graduate schools have discarded the requirement altogether; others have modified it to one foreign language rather than two. These solutions are honest in that they face frankly the average student's lack of language preparation, but ignoble and academically embarrassing in that they retreat from an important traditional element of "quality control" in graduate work: that scholars should not be ignorant of languages. Often these schools substitute statistics, accounting, cartography, or some other methodology for the formal language requirement, on the tenable theory that these, too, may constitute a new "language" from the student's point of view.

A contrary trend is evident in the several direct attempts of the colleges and universities to offer superior language training particularly, but not exclusively, at the graduate level and in the more esoteric languages.

The work in Chinese may stand as an example of this tendency. Yale's East Asia program works exclusively on the spoken language. One of the main reasons for its success has been a guaranteed clientele: the attendance of over 1,500 United States airmen in the past years. In addition to the Air Force personnel the school has been attended by missionaries, people desiring to serve overseas, Foreign Service appointees who have had some language training at the FSI, and persons sent by foreign governments. Subsidies from the government have enabled Yale to develop excellent library and recording resources and to bring together an outstanding staff of American and foreign national teachers; there are 20 Chinese instructors for the Air Force men alone.

Each separate language course has a basic core of six months taken by all students, no matter what their interest is. After the basic course the curriculum is tailored to meet specific needs. Missionaries, for instance, study the Bible and vocabulary necessary for preaching sermons, teaching Sunday School, and spiritual counseling.

Most students remain in the program from one to two years. Little research is done; "it would take at least two years' training for a student even to dabble," one professor explained. Since the program is for the spoken language, the written characters are not taught in the early stages of the classes. The program's director, Henry C. Fenn, says that while undergraduate Asian language courses stimulate interest in Chinese and Japanese, over three-fourths of the time in these courses is spent reading, and they are often not highly useful as preparation for other schools, such as Cornell and the University of Washington, which stress the spoken Asian languages.

Among the Western languages, the primary changes have been those of relative emphasis: because they are important qualifications for some kinds of jobs in business and government, Spanish has been gaining on French, the traditional leader, and German is being displaced in student interest by Russian. But it is in the non-Western languages that our most extreme linguistic deficiencies are found.

The new interest in the non-Western languages is a direct result of our involvement in the world at large, which has created a need and a demand for more and better linguists. The initial appeal may be a vocational one, but the cross-cultural understanding to be derived from acquaintance with non-Western languages is increasingly patent.

Any program for the large-scale production of Americans skilled in spoken and written Arabic, Chinese, or Japanese must, however, face the sobering reality of the extreme difficulty of these languages for English-speaking Americans, the high cost of teaching and learning them, and the limited vocational value of this proficiency for various types of employment as compared to other skills that could be developed at the same cost of time and money. University efforts to train Americans in what the Government now officially calls the "hard" languages cannot operate without massive subsidies, either from philanthropic foundations or from government agencies. We have seen this already in the case of Chinese language programs; it is also true, for example, of the notable program in Russian and Eastern European languages at Syracuse University.

Like the Yale Chinese program, the Syracuse enterprise was made possible by Air Force funds and a guarantee of Air Force personnel as students. The Air Force thus farms out to universities the language-training functions performed for the Army by its own language school at Monterey, California. The advantage of this farm system is that the government funds permit the establishment and maintenance of a language-training program which the contracting university can then make available also to civilian graduate students aspiring to work with civilian agencies of government (State Department, CIA, USIA) or private firms and agencies. This is the trend now at Syracuse. On the basis of the present market for "hard language" skills, no university could maintain on tuition income alone a large aural-oral program even in Russian or Arabic, let alone in Chinese, Japanese, or some of the less popular languages.

Another advantage of using universities as a base for language teaching is that the student can more readily be exposed to related instruction in foreign cultures, national and international politics, and comparative institutions. Neither the government contracts nor the "language money" in the National Defense Education Act make adequate provision for such a tie-in; the foundation grants in this field have been made with a more farsighted perception of the wholeness of culture and society than is yet evident in the Department of Defense or even the United States Office of Education.

One other type of graduate language program, the product of new vocational needs, is training in practical linguistics—designed not so much to train future teachers of linguistics as to prepare men to use and to transcribe exotic languages in the field. This type of training is particularly interesting to the kind of missionary who is preparing to bring the Bible to preliterate people.

Best known for this type of training is the Summer Institute of Linguistics at the University of Oklahoma, which is associated with the Wycliffe Bible Translators and several other mission boards as well. This Institute, which operates branches in England, Australia, Canada and North Dakota, is an apparently successful example of an organization set up for the purpose of supplying a very specific training to a limited number of overseas workers. Over 3,000 students have been exposed to its courses, many of them interested in recording preliterate languages and in translating the Bible into them. The Institute has been single-mindedly pursuing this limited but important aim for a quarter of a century.

Four courses only are taught at the Oklahoma summer sessions: Phonetics and Phonemes, Advanced Phonetics, Morphology and Syntax, and Advanced Morphology and Syntax. The Institute boasts that "the qualified graduate is prepared to face any language he may meet, whether or not there is any literature in it or written about it."

5

A final important innovation in language teaching is the practice of sending Americans abroad for their training. Just as some of our forefathers sent their sons to France, Germany, and Italy to pick up the graceful language proficiency that added another dimension to their classical education, so in the contemporary era of the language speed-up the tendency is increasingly to establish training schools overseas. The reason is not only that it costs less, but that the students get along faster with their studies than they would at home.

Language schools run for, and often by, Americans are now operating in the habitats of most of the world's important languages. Mission boards control or cooperate with language schools in Belgium, France, Portugal, the Belgian Congo, Brazil, Costa Rica, Taiwan, Japan, and India. The United States Government maintains schools in France, Germany, Mexico, Taiwan, Japan, and Lebanon. The Berlitz schools are practically everywhere. Many foreign governments, particularly the European ones, maintain elaborate programs for teaching the native language to foreigners. Switzerland has developed a particularly successful program of this type; and France and Italy are active also.

Harold Hoskins, director of the State Department's Foreign Service Institute, says that students at the FSI language schools at Nice, Frankfurt and Mexico City learn languages faster and better than in Washington. Not only does the student hear and live the language day after day around the clock, but he is also relieved from the many personal and professional entanglements he finds if he takes his training in the Washington area. Mr. Hoskins' opinion that languages are studied more effectively abroad is shared by most government agencies, and is making headway in Congress, especially in the Senate. Any substantial program to improve the language proficiency of the overseas Americans will have to take into account the parallel need to educate the people's representatives and their constituents as well.

Language training overseas has also come to be settled doctrine among the missionary societies; almost all of them give most of their language training in the field. The proponents of this method stress the advantage of cultural immersion and the extraordinary effect of overseas residence on the motivation of the students. Where it is not naturally and spontaneously spoken, a language seems unreal and nonessential; in its native environment it becomes in fact a living language. On the other hand, those who place the greatest emphasis on the use of mechanical equipment in aural-oral teaching are inclined to favor starting language training in America, where the language laboratory is most highly developed.

Language study abroad is generally post-entry training throughout the Foreign Service officer's career, both at its foreign schools and in Washington. Since career government employees are typically transferred from post to post every few years, they have a special need, not only for refresher courses, but to learn new languages in mid-career.

There are, however, problems connected with giving language training abroad that, although they are not intrinsic in the method, are likely to be endemic in the environment. Where the training is conducted by nationals of the country concerned, their tendency to be polite may overbalance the importance of maintaining educational standards. A language school in the Orient, used by a large number of American missionaries, has been cited as a case in point. The founder of this school, a cultured Japanese, allegedly believed that Americans could never learn Japanese anyway, and that although it would be courteous (and perhaps profitable) to offer them an opportunity to study Japanese, it would be discourteous (and perhaps unprofitable) to expect them to make much progress. It is probably unfair to pick out one school as the example, as anyone familiar with foreign schools set up to teach the native tongue to Americans is likely to be able to think of a similar case elsewhere; we could as well have cited, for example, the *Corsi per stranieri* at the University of Florence.

The language "problem" will not be solved by attempting to teach foreign languages to all students. Instead, the study of foreign languages will continue to be, at best, an occupation for selected segments of the American student body. Those who wish languages taught only to some people are, however, not agreed as to how to choose the students for whom this privilege or duty is to be reserved.

One criterion for foreign languages in the elementary and secondary schools would limit language instruction to "gifted" students. This category, however, is a difficult one to isolate. If by "gifted" is meant students with high I.Q.s, the category appears arbitrary, as languages can be taught successfully to mentally retarded children. If, on the other hand, "gifted" is taken to mean high language aptitude, there is no sure way to isolate the category except through exposure to a foreign language.

Attempts have been made to test language aptitude, one of the most "scientific" being that of Professor John Carroll of Harvard. This test appears to be useful to the United States Army as a way of eliminating the least apt, but its accuracy seems to vary with the language to be studied. It is said to be better for European than for Asiatic languages. A simple rule of thumb is to test for tone deafness and eliminate those who suffer from this aural deficiency. As in music, so in language, however, one must distinguish the comparatively rare tone-deaf person from the person with a badly trained ear. The former is hopeless; the latter, if properly motivated, can go far. The third method is probably the most reliable, but it is impractical when a large number of persons is involved. This is to give each prospective student a series of five to ten private lessons in the language and let his tutor determine his language aptitude. This method is used by many private corporations, for whom the Berlitz school often provides the tutors.

There is, then, no sound method by which to eliminate the students who should not receive further language training, except that of exposing everyone to a foreign language. Thus, since the language profession finds it difficult to decide who should learn languages, the decision is remanded, as in a democratic educational system it would be anyway, to the ultimate consumers, the students themselves.

Some of the categories of students who will actively want or need either language proficiency or a certificate thereof can be readily predicted from past experience. Persons with social pretensions will continue to want French. Certain ethnic groups will continue to urge on their children the language of their ancestors. The liberal arts major who aspires to the epithet of scholar and gentleman will still need to have a reading knowledge of the major languages in which his culture has been expressed. But for the rest, a new motivation will be required if the pool of language skills is to meet the growing demands of the nation upon it.

The shortage of Americans trained in the hard languages, and indeed in the "non-hard" ones, cannot be traced entirely to shortages of time, money, or teachers, in or out of the universities. One part of the problem is a lack of motivation by the potential students. Where courses in non-Western languages already exist, students must either be "delivered" by military orders or induced by handsome fellowships to devote their efforts to learning tongues whose cash value in the vocational marketplace has yet to be demonstrated.

In the case of Chinese, the student has to take the calculated risk that the United States relations with Communist China will open up sufficiently early in his lifetime to make the long and arduous study of that difficult language more than an academic exercise. In general, the career offerings to experts in the hard languages are still limited, and they also require the successful completion of a program much more difficult than that of the ordinary professional or graduate degree. Fellowships that encouraged students to study exotic languages as a career would be funds well spent.

A further basis for a new motivation is likewise at hand. It is provided by foreign-language study undertaken as part of a foreign-study program. In these programs language proficiency is often a by-product rather than the principal goal of the program. The programs, however, serve the cause of language in a dual fashion. They do not only teach languages and give students the opportunity to learn languages; what is perhaps more important, they give students a new appreciation of the significance of language and a new incentive to master at least one language besides English.

One can hardly exaggerate the importance of this second by-product of an overseas experience. A fundamental cause for the poor showing of Americans as language students is their lack of motivation. Although it sometimes happens that an American college student, as an essay in self-discipline, will voluntarily take and pass a course that is difficult for him, that he does not like, and in which he sees no purpose, by and large people do not easily learn or long retain skills that do not interest them and to which they attach little importance. An immersion in a foreign culture is a likely way to change a student's attitude toward a foreign language and to give him the incentive to study and to perfect his knowledge of it. If most members of the incoming freshman class knew that a semester abroad was in their horoscope, language professors would have a new pool of highly motivated students and every department of a university would profit from the broadening of cultural interest.

6

The reaction of the American public to its new awareness of our language deficiencies has been an equal mixture of hysteria and complacency. In one phase, we try to solve something called the language problem without relating it usefully to a dozen other problems that affect its solution. In the matter of language deficiencies, we are on the verge of deciding that something should be done, and prepared to will that it be done by appropriating large sums of Federal money for doing it. The danger is that then having set up some institutes to train some teachers and provide scholarships to coax students into deciding to be taught, we will have as our second phase the illusion that the language problem is as good as solved, and any expression of doubt as to whether the goal has been achieved will be taken as an act of *lèse majesté*.

That the linguistic unpreparedness of many Americans constitutes a serious problem for American education is beyond doubt; that a series of attacks on it will improve the situation is highly probable. But the United States will not develop an adequate language policy by working on the supply of teachers and equipment alone. The need for overseas experience as a major spur to students to tackle them must also be in the picture.

Many of the overseas Americans will have to be taught foreign languages before they go abroad or after they get there. It is easy to say that all overseas representatives should be experts in the languages of the countries in which they are located. The sober fact is that we have neither the time nor the manpower necessary to prepare all our overseas representatives with high language skills. For that matter, it would be hard to demonstrate that such a policy would pay off in improved achievement. To a person going out on a temporary assignment, language training, if he needs more than a refresher course, often cannot in practice be made available. In such a case it is necessary either to appoint only persons who already know the language or to plan the job for persons who do not know the language. Fortunately, although language fluency is normally a positive attribute for the overseasman, it is no *sine qua non* of success, and its relative importance varies with the post, the position, and the aptitude of the individual American abroad.

A realistic overseas training program must ascribe a relative, rather than an absolute, value to language training. The price of languages, particularly the difficult ones, is high in time, money, and effort. This cost must in each case be assessed against the specific assignment in order to reach a sensible decision.

The practicality of mastering a native language varies from locality to locality. In many parts of the world a *lingua franca* is more immediately necessary for communication than the native language —though it may not help much in comprehending the underlying traditional culture. For some assignments in Lebanon or Iran, French is more useful than Arabic or Persian. Similarly, Swahili in Eastern Africa, Italian in Eritrea, Somaliland, and the city of Tripoli, and pidgin English in New Guinea are more useful than are the native languages. In some countries, such as India, English itself is the *lingua franca;* and because of this, fluency in any other language is relatively less important for Americans on short-term technical assignments in such countries.

The kind of language facility that is needed also varies with the type of job on which it is to be used. In some cases the spoken language is more important; in others the written language is given preference. As far as many overseas Americans are concerned, however, the current popular emphasis on the spoken language is somewhat exaggerated. Often, the greatest language need of the overseasman is the ability to read the native language. Next in importance, in many situations, is an understanding of the spoken language; third is speaking it; and last, writing it. Although this progression—the eye, the ear, the throat, and the hand—is not the "natural" order that is dear to the aural-oral people, it has the merit, beyond its practical value, of ranking the four skills in the order of their increasing difficulty.

This does not mean that the spoken language is unimportant. In some countries it is of the highest importance. The point is that the overseas American often requires an extensive reading vocabulary so he can quickly get information and understanding about the foreign environment. On the other hand, the American who must work in the field with semiliterate people will normally seek first to establish command over the spoken language. Persons employed in localities where the native language is not generally written will obviously prefer aural-oral competence to a visual proficiency.

The value of language is therefore a variant that depends on two major factors: the assignment and the country. The salesman and the preacher, for instance, must speak the native language. If the language is written, the missionary must know its literature. On the other hand, the clerical workers in the American embassies in Taiwan, India, or Iraq do not need fluency in either the written or the spoken forms of Chinese, Hindi, or Arabic; to require them to attain it would be extravagant. A third-rate engineer sent to India with fluent Hindi will not build as good bridges or as durable social institutions as a first-rate engineer with no Hindi.

The Foreign Service, a habitual whipping boy, operates in a field where language proficiency obviously deserves high priority in vocational training; yet even with the expanded program of the Foreign Service Institute, no attempt is being made to demand proficiency in the difficult languages like Arabic, Chinese, and Japanese of all or even the majority of the personnel stationed in countries where these languages are widely spoken. In the missionary field, where the importance of language facility was first recognized, the experts do not intransigently demand language proficiency of all their overseas workers. Short-term missionaries are not expected to learn the hard languages; and teachers for missionary schools where classes are conducted in English are often selected even though they lack proficiency in the relevant foreign language, and are sometimes not even expected to learn the language in the field.

In every category of overseas service, however, there is a decidedly new emphasis on language skill. Berlitz, Linguaphone, and the other specialists in quick-learning techniques are doing a thriving business. A dying race are the "old China hands" and "old Japan hands" who could spend thirty or forty years doing business in the Far East without picking up more than the local vernacular for "bottoms up" and "go away." More modern—though not yet typical—was the serious effort of the Champion Paper Company to teach Portuguese (together with something about Brazilian culture and society) to all members of its staff who were erecting a new plant in

Brazil—even though they were not expected to stay there more than eighteen months. Not all the staff members achieved a high proficiency in Portuguese, but enough of them had the requisite aptitude and interest to make the whole organization highly successful in a situation where success depended crucially on the Americans' relations with their Brazilian co-workers.

Perhaps the best way to get language into perspective, after all, is to concentrate on the linguistic competence of the organization rather than just that of the individuals. An embassy must be able to read, understand, speak, and write with fluency every language relevant to its operations. So must an ICA mission, a military advisory group, a business firm, newspaper office, philanthropic foundation, religious mission, or American overseas school. Each of these organizations must also do other things just as important and just as difficult as communicating effectively in the local idiom. A good organization is a pool of wisely differentiated skills and attitudes; language competence is no more a universal skill than a comprehension of budgeting and accountancy. But the overseas organization cannot get along without it, either. In a plan of overseas operations, an adequate supply of first-rate linguists is one of the indispensable elements.

We are coming out of a long period in which foreign languages were ignored or relegated to secondary importance in American education. We are still woefully short of the trained linguists which our responsibility as a world power requires. The pendulum of popular opinion may now swing too suddenly and too far. Language ought to be viewed as an important subhead under cultural empathy and our linguistic renaissance should not preclude our giving adequate educational attention to other elements of effective overseas performance.

Whether the overseasman is able to master it or not, he should certainly be subjected to at least one foreign language as part of his training. He should come to realize that poor language skill is nearly always an obstacle to a successful career. The time and expense of such training would appear justified if the trainee learned only enough to realize his own weakness in communication across cultures, his own arrogance in forcing foreigners to speak English with him.

17 · The Limits of Training Programs

If you ask the overseas Americans to prescribe the educational antidote for overseas bumbling, you find them talking not about basic preparation but about how to use to best advantage the one or three or six weeks just before the American leaves for his foreign assignment. It is clear that fundamental attitude changes are not to be wrought in a few weeks of distracted study—the same weeks in which he is visiting the doctor for his shots, making arrangements for his aging parents and helping his wife pack. Yet most agencies do make some kind of effort to give the new overseas worker some last-minute training; many useful things are done, and many educational sins are committed, in the name of short-term "orientation."

Nearly all short-term training programs assume that a man should be hired first and then given a brief exposure to some knowledge of the particular country to which he will shortly be dispatched. The training provided ranges from a year spent in a university area program to a week or two spent at headquarters talking in unsystematic fashion to the people who will read the trainee's reports and answer his letters and cables when he gets into the field. The missionary organizations, which have been at it the longest, have some of the best training courses. Among the government agencies, only the efforts of the State Department's Foreign Service Institute and the Central Intelligence Agency can be rated as serious attacks on the training problem; the other agencies' efforts range from fair to very poor. Most overseas business firms are only now awakening to the fact that there is a problem at all: with few exceptions, most of them very recent in origin, the training programs for overseas businessmen are either inadequate or entirely absent.

1

The problem of training missionaries is evidently serious: a 1957 survey of Protestants who had quit foreign service for one reason or another indicated that 83 per cent lacked training in cultural orientation and 77 per cent were without training in a foreign language.* (Fewer than 1 per cent, indeed, had had any language instruction as undergraduates in college.) There seems, moreover, to be a positive correlation between the success of missionary selection and training and the rate of missionary turnover. Available statistics combined from various sources show that about 25 per cent of missionaries either do not complete their first tour of duty or do not return to the field after their first furlough. About half this loss is considered to be avoidable.

There are, of course, some basic differences between the training needed by the missionaries and that appropriate to other categories of overseas Americans.

• The missionary generally knows where he is going. Courses in general linguistics and general social anthropology thus have relatively less value to him and courses in the language and culture of a specific area mean more to him than to the typical overseas American.

• The missionary is normally expected to remain in the same culture area for the duration of his missionary activity. This fact further increases the relative value of specific language and area training over general linguistics and social anthropology.

• The missionary goes abroad as a Christian rather than as an American; as J. A. Robison of the Seventh-Day Adventists says, "One of the first things a successful missionary must do is to forget he is American and to identify himself with all he finds good in the local culture." Some of the boards, however, notably the Meth-

---

* Kenyon E. Moyer, "A Study of Missionary Motivation, Training, and Withdrawal, 1932–1952," Missionary Research Library, New York City, pp. 34–35. In this survey, 915 ex-missionaries answered out of 1,771 questioned.

odists, want their missionaries to act American, but in these cases the missionaries can and should be less chauvinistic, politically and culturally, than the government official or the business representative.

• The missionary has less than average need for training in international economics, and, among overseas Americans, he is singularly fortunate in that he need neither explain nor defend the vagaries of official foreign policy.

The trend in the missionary field is consequently toward more and broader training. This is reflected by the number of new training schools, both denominational and interdenominational, that have sprung up in this country and abroad since the close of World War II. The number of schools now in embryo gives promise that the trend is not losing momentum. No single pattern is followed in the new schools, except perhaps the new policy of preference for language study in the field.

Missionary training in the Roman Catholic Church is not centralized, but rather is carried out independently by the several missionary groups, the most important of which are the Jesuits, the Congregation of the Holy Redeemer, the Maryknoll Sisters, the Society of the Divine Word, the Franciscans, and the Marists. All of these orders have the advantage of dealing with personnel who have a lifetime commitment to their faith. There is consequently plenty of time in which to train them, weeding out those who do not seem to have the will or the intelligence to survive a rigorous program, the goal of which is a relatively erudite man. Some of the Catholic missionaries, notably the Jesuits, may be said to be in training for more than a decade, and it is not unusual for a priest to be in a foreign post for several years before he is assigned heavy duties that would interfere with his developing fluency in the local language.

Among the traditional missionary training programs the Roman Catholic system stands as something of a model, providing longer and more relevant study than the other major churches. Perhaps the reason is that the Roman Catholics have addressed themselves more explicitly to the problems that people in foreign service must resolve; for example, a papal encyclical of Benedict XV, issued in 1919, contains one of the earliest and clearest expositions of the principle that a person in overseas service must have a broader and deeper professional training than he needs to perform the same kind of work in his familiar home environment.

The United Presbyterians maintain more than 1,000 missionaries, more than any other board that cooperates with the National Council of Churches. In spite of its larger numbers, the Presbyterian Study Fellowship puts on a course of study lasting more than six months, part of which is language study in the field; moreover, the Presbyterians insist that wives should undergo the same training program required of their husbands. The directors of this course regard it as a very important part of the selection process itself; the candidates and their families are kept under constant scrutiny, outside of the classroom as well as inside.

The new training center of the United Lutheran Church takes a different tack, stressing theological training and skimping on other skills required for effective overseas service. Of the three main faculty members, one is a specialist on the history and theory of missions, a second is a Biblical theologian, and the third teaches missionary practice and evangelism. No language is taught; the missionary normally learns it in the field after his arrival. In Japan and India, for example, two years are devoted to the language, during the first of which language study is the missionary's sole responsibility.

The Seventh-Day Adventists carry out one of the largest missionary operations in the world, comprising 2,000 missionaries (including 1,272 Americans) in every main country except Saudi Arabia, Afghanistan, and Tibet. Their training is almost wholly homegrown; they recruit their missionaries primarily from their own schools, and train them in their own academic institutions (though foreign languages are normally taught either by Berlitz or in the field after the missionary gets on the job). The Seventh-Day Adventists maintain, on their own, ten universities which offer B.A. and B.S. degrees and one College of Medicine and Evangelism, where physicians, dentists, nurses, and physiotherapists are trained for medical centers abroad. As in many other denominations, the directors of the Seventh-Day Adventist training programs have recently become dissatisfied with the traditional emphasis on professional training combined with courses in theology and mission history, and now project a six-month course in Washington where linguistics, cultural anthropology, and area studies will be the primary diet.

The Jehovah's Witnesses, who claim every initiate as a minister, had 2,060 missionaries in 1957, of whom about one-third were Americans. They appear to have no educational requirements for candidates; fewer than 2 per cent are estimated to have college degrees and large numbers have not finished high school. The main criteria for selection are high motivation and excellent physical condition. Training sessions stress theology; during his course each trainee must read the whole Bible. An effort is made to teach the language of the candidate's destination, but no area studies are offered.

Taken as a whole, the training programs of missionary churches span a wide range from excellence to failure. The traditional stress on professional skill (as theologian or doctor or whatever) at the expense of other qualities is giving way now to greater-than-ever efforts to teach language and the beginnings of systematic study of culture and linguistics. But as yet none of the training programs expose the prospective overseas minister or teacher to the study of political power or the analysis of the process by which institutions are built in foreign societies. Little is being done along the lines suggested by the National Council of Churches: "It is becoming increasingly important for a foreign missionary candidate to have considerable knowledge of international politics." Even the Kennedy School of Missions at Hartford is oriented toward culture and language and gives short shrift to economic, political and administrative studies. Moreover, the emphasis on area studies in missionary training courses, just as at the universities, still neglects the possibility that work in one area may be excellent training for work in another. This neglect is, indeed, a settled policy with many of the mission boards, and is reflected in their assignment policy: "once a China missionary, always a China missionary."

Hardly any of the mission boards yet see much value in mixing their personnel with trainees from business firms and government agencies in courses designed to explore the common factors in overseas employment. This is natural enough; after all, such courses have not been offered by the universities for very long, and are not offered by very many universities even today. But the exclusiveness of missionary training is also the result of two other deeply rooted prejudices: one is the feeling on the part of each denomination that a training course must, in order to develop the necessary motivation, stress its own brand of theology. The other is the widespread but questionable assumption that the task of a missionary is almost wholly different from that of other overseas Americans.

In spite of the impressive strength of some of the missionary training establishments, most of them are remarkable for a lack of scholarly research on what should, after all, be the most important subject: the nature of cross-cultural operations. The mountains of lore about the history and theological presuppositions of missionary work contrast strangely with the paucity of hard facts and solid professional analysis about how religious missions actually operate in the face of the secular revolution all around them.

2

Until World War II no systematic overseas training existed for even the professional Foreign Service officers of the United States. Many diplomats and consuls studied French, German, or Spanish for a few years, but in the majority of cases their proficiency was not outstanding, and in-service training other than language was negligible. The assumption was that a broadly educated "generalist" could climb the career ladder of diplomacy without special training for particular jobs and different cultures. Since the war, the new tasks of the Foreign Service, together with the new agencies operating alongside the Foreign Service in the field, have forced attention to the problem of special training for government service abroad. Although the Rogers Act of 1924 had made the Foreign Service a merit system, it was not until the passage of the Foreign Service Act of 1946 that problems of recruitment and training for the Foreign Service were attacked head on.

Among other things, the Act of 1946 established the Foreign Service Institute, based upon the Division of Training Service that had been set up in the State Department in 1945. The intention was to provide a system of overseas representation that would serve the interests of the United States abroad by providing adequate incentives for recruitment of able personnel. It also provided for economists and other academically trained professionals to work with the diplomats, who sometimes regarded themselves more as political or administrative specialists than as old-time generalists.

For the ensuing decade, the Foreign Service Act was the vehicle for a considerable expansion of the career corps, though sometimes at the expense of quality. As time went on, the earlier insistence that an entering candidate for the Service should have had some language training in college was dropped, and the Foreign Service Examinations, once famous as a tough series of essay questions, became a mass-production exercise in which the candidate for a lifetime career as overseas report-writer marked his multiple-choice squares with a graphite pencil and did hardly any original writing at all. Nor were the lower educational standards for entering the Service offset by first-rate training in the State Department. Courses at the Foreign Service Institute often consisted of a series of individual lectures, each by a different person, making almost no demands on the individual student for creative independent research. The low state of language learning, especially the non-Western tongues that were becoming more and more relevant to American foreign relations, was a national scandal; it became widely known, for example, that of the 285 officers entering the Service in 1956 only about 25 per cent had a useful-to-the-service proficiency in any foreign language.

A few Foreign Service officers were sent off to the universities for extended area studies or graduate work in economics or international relations; only for them could the government's training programs be described as a serious effort to meet the postwar challenge of world-wide United States involvement in the affairs of other nations.

If the Foreign Service was slow to develop relevant training programs, the new operating agencies were even slower. The USIA and the several agencies of the foreign-aid program have had a brief series of orientation lectures for new employees almost since they began to hire people; but at first they were all heavy with information about the agencies' own internal procedures and advice (often badly out of date) about living conditions in the field. An inspirational lecture or two had to serve as training for political sense and the building of institutions; visits with experts recently returned from a foreign area were the substitute for the systematic study of foreign cultures; and language training was generally left to the new employee's own energy and initiative. The teaching materials were even more primitive than the teaching; case studies and general theory about cross-cultural operations were (and, indeed, still are) in conspicuously short supply. The training of military-aid administrators could not even be described as primitive; until the late 1950s, officers assigned to the Military Assistance Advisory Groups, responsible for administering two or three billion dollars worth of military aid a year, received no special training at all.

This sorry state of affairs, dramatized in the public mind by the lack of language officers in the Foreign Service, produced during the 1950s a series of major reforms. The milestone in this process was the Secretary of State's Public Committee on Personnel, headed by President Henry M. Wriston of Brown University, which not only expanded the Service by transferring many of the State Department's Washington employees into it, but also called for an expanded system of recruitment and a major overhauling of the training of Foreign Service officers throughout their careers. Spurred by widespread public and Congressional interest in the subject, the Foreign Service Institute was reorganized, with a new director, Harold Hoskins. The newer agencies started to use the FSI courses to supplement their own explanations of agency policy; and, as they gradually came to realize that United States foreign operations were not a temporary aberration but a permanent addition to the functions of the Federal Government, long-range training policies began to be born.

The Foreign Service Institute is an in-service training organization within the Department of State. According to its catalogue the "primary responsibility of the Institute is to furnish training and instruction at the graduate level . . ." However, the Institute is not a graduate school in the traditional sense of the term; rather it is a vocational in-service training school.

The FSI offers five major types of programs, including orientation and language and area studies. Although established primarily as a Foreign Service training school, other government agencies, notably the USIA and the ICA, use its services while the Institute itself utilizes the services of other government institutions as well as universities, particularly for language and area training.

The orientation programs are given to personnel being sent abroad for the first time, to personnel in Washington between assignments, and to wives and adult dependents of officers. Typical orientation programs are of three weeks' duration for employees and of two weeks' duration for wives. Most of the curriculum for the three groups is identical but there are some differences. The wives, for instance, do not attend the lectures on security and cryptography. The lectures shared by the three groups deal with the structure and the functions of U.S. Government agencies concerned with foreign relations, intercultural communications, and Americana.

The best-known service of FSI is the general career training program. All officers entering the service take a twelve-week course in the duties and functions of Foreign Service officers. Highly competent specialists are brought in, primarily from universities, to give lectures and conduct discussions.

Recently a nine-month course for senior officers was formally instituted by the Secretary of State. Its function is to prepare them "for the exercise of high level executive responsibilities, policy recommendation and implementation, and coordination in the field of all aspects of the government's policies and programs."

In the language program of the Foreign Service Institute the aural-oral method is employed; language laboratories and native speakers are utilized, and with impressive results. Any government employee can take one of these courses if his supervisory officer certifies that knowledge of language is essential to the performance of his duties. The instruction is designed to equip employees with at least a rudimentary knowledge of the language of the country of assignment. The intensive language classes run from four to six hours daily for from six to twelve months, depending upon the language. Some of the courses are given in conjunction with area specialization. Two dozen languages are taught. Field schools have been established in Frankfurt, Mexico City, Nice, Beirut, and Taiwan.

Some specialized training in area study is given. These programs run from nine to thirty months and are generally conducted at the Institute's field schools overseas, while some officers are sent to universities with special area programs.

Another phase of the FSI program involves management courses such as "Administrative Operations and Disbursing" and "Budget and Fiscal Operations" for overseas administrators. Assignment to universities is not limited to area studies. Some officers are encouraged to pursue regular graduate work at universities in such specialties as economics and public administration; others are sent to the Defense Colleges to learn something about military strategy.

Most of the field jobs in the United States Information Agency are held by civil service people who are transferred into overseas assignments, and junior officer trainees recruited from outside the Government, usually men between twenty-five and thirty years of age who have their military service and some graduate work behind them. Neither of these groups can be presumed to have been in training for overseas life and work. As the USIA shook off the paralysis induced by Senator McCarthy's vendetta and came to realize that, with or without Congressional sanction, it would have to start treating its overseas staff as a permanent career service, it began to require major segments of time to be devoted to in-service training.

For the junior officers, the Agency has adopted two of the principles that would be indicated by our own research: that training is an important selection device, and overseas training should include an overseas experience. Thus the incoming trainee, after training and internship experience in the Washington office, is sent to the field for nine months of practical work which is considered to be still a part of his "training program." If the trainee does not measure up in the opinion of his field supervisors, he is dropped from the service before being given a regular assignment.

A second course is for the "specialists," who are usually older people, now drawn almost entirely from the government service. In some ways these specialists are comparable to the Foreign Service Reserve Officers who have been recruited in mid-career for specific positions in the Foreign Service. The major difficulty encountered with these professionals has been their lack of overseas experience, for they often feel that their professional competence alone can assure them successful overseas performance. In the past, persons from this group without overseas experience were made mission heads and the results were sometimes unfortunate. Now all new mission heads must have at least one tour of foreign duty behind them. Performance has improved considerably as a result of this new policy.

The USIA also operates refresher courses, but finds it difficult to get officers to attend, and when they do, their work is frequently inferior. According to the men interviewed at USIA there is a prevalent belief that training is simply a way to mark time before assignments, or between posts, and that top-notch people cannot be spared long for training.

The information agency's courses include four main subjects: the theory and practice of communications; the study of American civilization, especially history, art, drama, and religion; the theory and practice of communism, and methods of meeting the Communist challenge; and "area studies" in which the trainees are taken to meet the people at USIA headquarters who have had experience in an area, and sometimes to the State Department's area deskmen as well.

The USIA is particularly proud of its *Meet the Critics* sessions in which experienced USIA officers, pretending to be obnoxious and informed natives of the country to which the trainee is to be sent, discuss American foreign policy and related subjects with him— he is judged according to the urbanity, wit, and accuracy of his *ripostes.*

At the USIA, as in other corners of Washington, there is a good deal of talk about training wives, but no funds have yet been provided for this specific purpose. Wives are encouraged to attend the training courses, but not very many do this with any consistency. In all the operating agencies the effective training of wives must still be described as a pious hope rather than a going program.

In the earlier period of the United States foreign-information program, the acquisition of language skills was considered as primarily the officer's own responsibility; some, but not most, took advantage of the Foreign Service Institute's language instruction. That a voluntary system was hardly adequate for Americans who were going abroad as professional communicators was amply illustrated by a devastating survey, dated January 31, 1957, of the language proficiency of USIA personnel in the field.

At that time there were 197 officers serving in an area comprising the Near and Middle East and those parts of Africa where neither English nor French is considered the principal language. None of these men was granted a top rating in the principal language of the country or region to which he was assigned, and only one had a "fluent" rating in the language—in this instance Turkish. Of the 59 officers assigned to India only one had a "useful" rating in a modern Indian language. Of the 187 officers stationed in the Far East, excluding Japan, only one officer was rated fluent in the principal language of the country, Vietnamese. Although Indonesian is considered a relatively easy language, none of our 18 USIA officers in Indonesia then had a useful-to-the-service knowledge of the language.

As a result, the USIA training program shares with the State Department's Foreign Service Institute the kind of passionate interest in language instruction which is to be expected of the newly converted. By November, 1958, more than 100 USIA officers were being trained in 26 languages, including Japanese, Chinese, Malay, Vietnamese, Korean, Thai, Burmese, Indonesian, and Cambodian. These languages were being studied in Washington and abroad at government schools, notably those of the FSI, at universities here and abroad, and in commercial language schools.

The training program of the International Cooperation Administration is the third major governmental effort to prepare its own people for service abroad. Its history reflects the agency's continuing status as a temporary institution, dependent for its life on a yearly Congressional decision to stay in the business of economic and technical assistance. ICA is now establishing a career service by executive action. As part of the plan, the agency has laid out for the first time some concrete plans for in-service training and long-range career development.

The "regular" orientation of new ICA employees has been a far from successful enterprise, in the opinion of many field men who went through it on the way to their overseas assignments. New employees are brought to Washington for two and a half weeks, just before they leave for their overseas assignments, and exposed through lectures and discussion to an extraordinary variety of subject matter ranging from travel and health hints, problems of adjustment to overseas living, the procedures for review of technical assistance projects, the place of foreign aid in United States foreign relations, and the theoretical aspects of communism. A variety of techniques is employed for teaching, including roundtables, individual conferences, buzz sessions, contrived demonstrations, role playing, and other products of the postwar enthusiasm for the manipulation of small groups. A reading list of books is circulated, but no claim is made that much reading is done. Greater reliance is placed upon shorter mimeographed articles that are circulated at most of the lectures.

Wives are invited to attend most of the sessions, but the number who do so is not large. There is also a special session for technicians' wives on family adjustment to life abroad. In addition there are special lectures for clerical and secretarial women.

The main criticism of this program is that far too much is attempted in too brief a period. In this brief period when last-minute details of a move abroad must be dealt with, the orientation schedule tells the employee, "You will learn about your new assignment from its broad over-all relationship to American foreign policy down to its specific aspects." It is a noble aspiration, but a doubtful prediction of what will really happen in two weeks and a half.

For the past two years, however, a career-conscious ICA administrative staff has created an impressive number of opportunities for "mid-career" training of officials who have not yet been told by Congress that they can think of their ICA employment as a career. At the conclusion of each overseas tour of duty, it is possible for an ICA officer to apply for "refresher study" for up to forty-five days, to broaden his knowledge of methods and techniques in his own field; a rotation assignment outside the ICA for a year or two, to enable, for example, a public health nurse to bring her knowledge of American nursing practice up to date; "developmental training," for nine to twelve months, to enable people who lack the necessary formal training in their own specialty to spend some time working in a university, research station, hospital, or other training facility;

or area and language study, usually in a university graduate program. None of these opportunities can in the nature of things be available to very many people, but the fact that they are available at all is evidence of how far ICA has already moved away from the assumption that whatever its employees lack in education or training can be made up by a couple of weeks of lectures in Washington, followed by practical experience in an operating job abroad.

ICA's most ambitious educational venture is a contract with the School for Advanced International Studies of Johns Hopkins University, to put on a twenty-one week Institute on ICA Development Planning for a couple of dozen mid-career officers at a time. This enterprise, which involves hard work and a certain amount of independent research, is organized more like an academic program than is typical of in-service training schools. The program includes, for example, three lecture-discussion periods a week on the economics of development planning; two lecture-discussion periods a week on the culture and politics of economic development; workshops two afternoons a week where teams study specific problems and present their recommendations to the group; guided reading; and an individual report dealing with a country in which the officer has had no previous experience.

The Defense Department employs the largest number of United States civilian citizens abroad. The Army uses about 12,000; the Navy 2,000; and the Air Force 7,500, for a total of over 21,000. The recruitment of civilians in numbers for overseas assignments by the Armed Forces is a postwar development resulting from the policy of trying to maintain overseas more installations than can be staffed with the reduced manpower of a peacetime draft.

The basic personnel policies for overseas employment adopted by the Armed Forces stress selection techniques and short tours of duty. These policies interact, for elaborate training programs become prohibitively expensive when contracts are normally for only one or two years. As in the case of most government personnel employed abroad, with the notable exception of the Foreign Service, there is no formal provision for career service as a civilian employed abroad by the Armed Forces; as a result, of course, there is no provision for training other than the briefest briefing.

The recruitment process followed by the three armed services is much the same. The number recruited annually is high and runs to about 2,500 for the Army alone, and to 500 for the Navy. The positions fall conveniently into four categories: (1) technicians; (2) teachers for elementary and secondary schools; (3) recreation specialists; and (4) stenographers. The range of specialties required of civilian technicians is broad; it embraces journalists, prison administrators, firemen, interpreters, translators, funeral directors, chaplains, as well as experts in personnel classification and fingerprint identification.

The sources from which the Armed Forces recruit their overseas civilian personnel are two. Technicians, and to a lesser extent, stenographers, are generally recruited either from demobilized military personnel or from career civilian personnel within the department. It is believed that these people can be best relied on to fit into an Armed Forces installation abroad. As the Armed Forces do not normally employ teachers and recreation specialists, these are generally recruited from outside the Government. A factor in the high turnover of the overseas civilian personnel is the necessity of accepting teachers on a one-year basis so that they may be on a leave of absence from their permanent teaching position and maintain tenure there.

In the absence of systematic training, the quality of Defense Department civilians depends mostly on the recruiting policies of the three services. Army, Navy and Air Force are at one in regarding overseas performance as very similar to performance in the comparable job in the United States.

The Army's description of these qualities is remarkable for its lack of analysis of the elements of effective overseas performance. The search for cultural empathy is rendered simply as "consideration for others" and "cooperation": "The capacity to understand, work with, and lead other types and nationalities of people is important in any foreign situation." No attention is directed to the qualities we have described as a sense for politics and a talent for building institutions, and there is no published evidence that the Army has devoted to the subject of overseas success or failure the deep and careful study which the number of overseas Army civilians, not to speak of military personnel, obviously deserves.

The Navy selection procedure is basically the same for overseas as for domestic assignments, but it will send no one overseas if there is a history of alcoholism or of marital discord. An agency memorandum says, "Where possible preference is given applicants who have been overseas, who have not led sheltered lives, and who have experienced group living. . . ." About 85 per cent of the naval civilian personnel abroad are said to be former Navy men; this figure probably does not include teachers. No special training for overseas work is provided, but courses at some overseas posts in such languages as Japanese, Arabic, and Italian are open to the civilian employees.

The overseas civilian employees of the Air Force are recruited to the extent of about 70 per cent from the Air Force and of about 15 per cent from other government agencies (these figures also presumably exclude teachers). Its selection policy is similar to the Navy's. As in the case of the Navy, the major emphasis is the negative one of screening out the potential troublemaker. The Air Force, for instance, makes a fifteen-year police check on all applicants.

Little attention, however, seems to be given by any of the major units in the Department of Defense to an applicant's interest in the language of the area to which he is to be sent, or to either his possession of the inherent qualities or the possibility of his acquisition of the acquired qualities that promote successful work with foreigners. A partial explanation of this situation may be found in the policy of insulating personnel from all but the most superficial contacts with foreigners. It is simple to criticize the restrictiveness and the frustrations of the isolated encampment or "compound" and to decry its use. Given the lack of preparation of Armed Service personnel for intimate contact with a foreign culture, the compound is not without its merits in that it saves the American personnel and the native population from misunderstanding and friction. At its best, however, the compound is a quarantine rendered necessary by the inability on the part of the Armed Forces to prepare their personnel for fruitful personal contact with the foreign culture.

As late as 1958 there was no systematic training of Military Advisory and Assistance Group officers for overseas service. Today the MAAGs account for about 5,000 men and officers working in more than 35 countries. They are close to the military leaders of many foreign governments, advising them in training their security forces, and administering military equipment and supplies provided by the United States Government as "assistance." In many countries MAAG's are closer to the center of political influence than any other American agency and in every country they have close contact with their native opposite-numbers in the military command. Yet more than half of the new Military Assistance Institute's program, which trains more than 100 MAAG officers with a staff of six full-time instructors and six part-time instructors, deals with the structure and procedures of the military-aid program narrowly conceived.

The training of government workers for overseas service is a rapidly developing field. One of the most successful programs is the one most difficult for other agencies to copy, since it goes on beyond the opaque security screen of the Central Intelligence Agency. But even among the other agencies, there is a growing awareness of the limits of short-term "orientation," and the consequent broadening of the kinds of educational experience to which Washington top administrators are willing to expose their subordinates. In summary form, these findings about government training for work abroad stand out:

    • Overseas training by government is new and still in a highly experimental stage; in some agencies it is just beginning to win acceptance.

    • Considerable confusion still exists about the purposes of overseas training, and the curricula reflect an emphasis upon the particular work of the agency rather than elements of effective overseas performance.

    • The potentialities of training as a screening device for overseas personnel have not yet been fully recognized.

    • The majority of the programs are short-term, sometimes cram courses, frequently on a voluntary (and unattended) basis, most often given in that hectic period between appointment and embarkation when the mind is befogged and the nervous system jittery.

    • Although some joint use of facilities at the Foreign Service Institute is made by government agencies, there is still need for a greater coordination of training programs and resources by the State Department, the International Cooperation Administration, the United States Information Agency, and the Department of Defense.

• There is surprisingly little systematic self-evaluation of overseas operations that reaches down into the elements of individual effective performance and provides illustration or training principles for the selection of overseas personnel.

3

Despite the fact that the American business representative abroad needs special skills for overseas operations just as much as any other worker abroad, he is the least likely to have been offered systematic training.

Several factors contribute to this state of affairs. Perhaps the most important is that American business is not likely to consider foreign representation a career in itself; overseas assignments are normally thought of as temporary. When personnel are specifically hired for foreign representation work, preference is frequently given to persons who have already had some foreign experience and some training in the language of the country to which they are to be sent.

In order to accomplish his mission the business representative abroad must either have received some extensive training in a wide variety of fields or rely on whatever capabilities he may possess for felicitous improvisation. Besides the technical competence in his field, which must be broader than that necessary for success in the United States, he needs a familiarity with political and economic analysis, a feel for alien cultures, and some fluency in the appropriate native language. It is partly economy and partly the lack of these latter attributes on the part of many Americans that make some American companies prefer the European or the European-trained representative.

On the basis of the answers we received to letters sent to all American business firms known to employ 100 or more American representatives abroad, it is apparent that many personnel officers are not convinced of the need for overseas training at all. Most of the answers showed an awareness of the advantages of recruiting people with foreign experience and with language proficiency, but only 12 out of 34 answers came up with special recruitment policies for overseas representatives. Some of these were special forms of discrimination (*e.g.*, Aramco does not take Jews because they are unwelcome in Saudi Arabia), and the majority showed little more than an awareness of the problem (*e.g.*, Goodyear prefers people who have studied international trade; Bechtel and Caterpillar look for "adaptability"). Several gave more rigorous physical examinations for overseas employment. None required any specific additional training over and above that demanded of a domestic employee.

Only 5 of the 34 companies described any special training (other than language) for overseas representation. Atlantic Refining, Creole Petroleum, Aramco, and Bechtel offered "historical and cultural orientation." United Fruit has an internship program for agricultural workers on arrival in Honduras. Two of the companies offer furlough training. For this purpose Grace uses the Harvard Business School, and Atlantic Refining uses the American Management Association, whose courses generally last only three days.

The most obvious form of overseas training is language instruction, and Berlitz schools are much used by business firms to train their people before and during foreign assignments. Although the general courses at the Berlitz schools are open to the public (and anyone who wishes may arrange for private lessons), most of their work for business firms is carried on in special classes, which often meet on the firm's business premises.

Berlitz has done its most extensive work in New York with Stanvac and Caltex in teaching Indonesian. This training begins in New York and continues in Indonesia, and special books and charts have been prepared in order to teach the peculiar vocabulary relating to the oil industry. Other firms such as General Motors use Berlitz for evaluation of language aptitude. Within a period varying from four to ten hours of private tutoring Berlitz claims to be able to give an accurate estimate of a man's language aptitude. The firms that employ Berlitz for this purpose appear to feel that this method is more accurate than the "scientific" tests of language aptitude now available, at least when the number of persons to be tested remains small. Berlitz is also ready to test language proficiency. They perform this service for such concerns as Pan American and TWA, which, it is understood, do not employ personnel in positions requiring language proficiency without Berlitz approval. The Language Guild, a smaller language institute in New York City, and the Linguaphone Institute are also used by a limited number of corporations.

Occasionally business firms have hired private consultant firms. Their primary function, and the one they are presumably best fitted to fulfill, is that of research consultants, but they also offer their services for preparing business personnel for overseas assignments. The social anthropology-cultural empathy-human relations angle is usually taught by members of the organization with perhaps the help of a native informant. The language teacher is often forthcoming from the copious foreign-student populations of Cambridge, Massachusetts, and Washington, D.C.

Apart from language instruction the training programs of major business concerns are of two kinds: programs designed to teach new employees about the company, and programs designed to orient the company's foreign employees, expressly imported for this purpose, in the company's policies and procedures. We have found no permanent training program operated by a business corporation within the United States for its American representatives abroad.

Standard Oil of New Jersey is a partial exception to these rather negative observations. It has inaugurated an interesting program for training future executives through an international experience. The Americans work for European subsidiaries of Standard at local salaries. After three or six years' experience they return to the home office, are credited with seniority for the period spent abroad, and receive their full American scale salary for the period. Socony-Vacuum has a similar but less elaborate program.

A few nonacademic organizations, as well as business schools, have conducted some educational experiments in training overseas-bound businessmen. The American Management Association, which already had a big program of executive development for United States business at large, began in 1956 a special set of conferences and seminars where executives who have something to do with

United States business operations abroad could exchange experience and hear talks by experts on overseas administration. By 1959 more than 4,000 executives had participated in these seminars, and 2,100 had enrolled as members. The plan for 1959–60 called for more than sixty seminars of three to five days on such subjects as "Market Research in Foreign Operations," "Antitrust Laws and Foreign Operations," "The European Common Market," and "Investment in Argentina." The approach is frankly pragmatic, with little attempt to build systematic theory on the subject of overseas business as a whole. The focus is on management problems *per se;* yet wherever the troubles arising from cultural differences are pertinent, as in the several seminars on "Investing in Brazil," these problems are given full and frank treatment by qualified experts.

A second phase of the AMA program is just getting under way through a new affiliate, the International Management Association. IMA was formed to set up Management Centers in various parts of the world; at these centers, it is proposed not only to run AMA-type seminars for American overseasmen, but to enlist the qualified executives of U.S. companies as instructors of the executives of national companies. The first of these centers is scheduled to open during 1960 in São Paulo, Brazil.

About sixty United States companies are clients of the Business International Executive Service, a private enterprise that promotes special meetings of executives of the client firms and publishes a weekly newsletter. Apart from its seminars, it operates as a consulting firm, publishing special research studies done by its own staff, maintaining an extensive library and research files, and doing research on the problems of individual client firms.

The Executive Roundtable in many respects is the most interesting of the BIES services. Heads (or their alternates) of international divisions of client companies meet ten times each year for informal off-the-record discussions of common problems. Annually, one of these conferences is held in a foreign country with the leaders of the foreign government and representative businessmen. One meeting each year is held in Washington with administrative and legislative leaders. The theme of this conference is: "What government can do to cooperate with U.S. business abroad, and vice versa." As in the meetings in foreign nations, high-ranking people have generally taken a personal interest in these Washington sessions—including members of the President's Cabinet, the head of ICA, and the chairman of the Senate Foreign Relations Committee.

Despite many obstacles some businessmen are beginning to sense the importance of stable, long-range overseas operations and the necessity of training their American personnel in something besides the legal, fiscal, and administrative details of their own organization. In 1959 some of the most important and progressive firms combined their interest in preparing personnel for foreign assignments by encouraging the establishment of the Business Council for International Understanding. Under contract with The American University in Washington, D.C., the Council now plans to train businessmen in four-week courses that will run throughout the year; the first session was held in the fall of 1959.

The object of the new program is to "provide the ability to quickly, skillfully, and affirmatively understand the people of the host country" and will include lectures in cultural anthropology, American civilization, and "the beginnings of a speaking knowledge of the country of assignment." It is also planned to give some knowledge of "the concrete situation—business, social, domestic— which will be encountered in the country of assignment, as well as an orientation of the executive's wife." The success with which the "practical" business executive is to be introduced at a mature age to cultural anthropology, American civilization, and foreign-language training (of brief duration in the United States) needs further demonstration, and the BCIU experiment will be an interesting one to watch.

The reasons why business is so far behind the mission board and government agencies are easy to summarize. The corporation's officers are often unaware of the need; they are not equipped to meet it; the number of Americans that most firms would want to train is too small to make the establishment of a training institution feasible; the trend in any case favors the employment of foreign nationals in place of Americans; and there is usually believed to be not enough time for formal training between the date of appointment and the deadline for getting on with the job overseas.

4

The foregoing survey of the major types of specialized training for the preparation of Americans entering overseas service gives, we believe, a fair impression of the considerable attention to this activity in the United States today. It also indicates the measure of ignorance, improvisation, and instability to be found in training for overseas assignments. The field is a new one, and the experimental stage in the field's development has yet to run its course. It is only natural that at this stage of development there be wasted efforts, duplication, false starts, monstrous growths, and above all contending schools of thought apparently working at cross-purposes. It is wasteful to continue the haphazard "selection" of overseas personnel —the forced resignations of Americans after they are already on the job, sometimes even for two or three years. It is foolish not to recognize that living and working abroad is different from living and working at home, that training programs must go far beyond the establishment of technical competence and some indoctrination in agency procedures. It is dangerous, in short, for any operating agency to learn only from its own experience, and not from that of others which face similar problems of personnel adjustment abroad.

There are two general policies which would greatly extend the limits of what can be done in a few weeks of "orientation."

The first would be a wider recognition that *the best recruiting system is a training program.* Ideally, the candidate for an overseas job should have applied to, been accepted by, and completed successfully a program of special training in overseas operations. During such a program the instructors would be able to develop a mature judgment as to how good a risk each trainee is for work and life overseas, and come to know his wife and his family situation well. The hiring agency would then be in a position to select from a pool of qualified people who have already had some exposure to learning about and being tested in the elements of effective overseas performance—instead of being hired beforehand and tested on the job.

Secondly, *the orientation of Americans to overseas service should be done in most cases by the colleges and universities.* Whether the

United States educational system will rise to the new challenge is still in question; but the arguments for its doing so are strong:

• Each agency is in the best position to teach its own people about the agency's own policies and procedures. But if the common factors form, as we have suggested, a core of overseas training, their universality can be stressed by deliberately blending several different kinds of people in a common program. The universities can readily develop mixed sessions for instruction in the avoidance of cultural, political, and administrative shock. It is true that sending their employees by twos and threes to several different university-training programs will make life more complicated for the training officers in those government agencies, business firms, mission boards and other organizations that have enough overseas staff to put on their own orientation programs. But the price of excellence is often an increase of administrative complexity.

• Whenever the trainee knows to what country he will be assigned, relevant area and language study is important in addition to an exposure to the "common factors." Language instruction can be successfully handled by government agencies, as the Foreign Service Institute and the Army Language School at Monterey have amply demonstrated, or by universities, as the many distinguished intensive language programs at major universities will attest. But area study programs are a different matter: they require basic research, a tradition of scholarship, academic specialists, and the kind of library resources that are built up only by dedicated scholars over long periods of time. The employing agencies will get a better bargain if they build up university area programs than if they try to duplicate them—as the Federal Government has begun to recognize in the National Defense Education Act. In the process they will do well to insist that the university language programs be brought into the closest possible association with the corresponding area programs.

• Even in agencies which spend a good deal of time and effort teaching their own people about agency policy and procedures, there is remarkably little research about their own operations, little systematic effort to understand, evaluate, and codify for teaching purposes the lessons about cross-cultural operation to be learned from years of engaging in them. In the case of the government agencies, such research as is done is generally hidden from view by SECRET and CONFIDENTIAL stamps; this is true, for example, of Foreign Service inspection reports and the evaluation studies that ICA did for several years. Whether in government or private operations, there remains a striking disproportion between the acknowledged importance of American overseas operations and the amount of constructive thinking and writing that has been done on the subject.

If the nation is to step up to the challenge of educating Americans for work and life abroad, therefore, a first essential is that the relevant academic faculties—the economists, the political scientists, the sociologists and anthropologists, the historians, the geographers, the professors of language and literature, the natural scientists, and the teachers in the many professional specialties—be induced to do research about cross-cultural operations and to rethink their own contribution to the task of training the operators. Day-to-day contact with the operating agencies through joint arrangements for training their personnel will spark ideas for new and more relevant undergraduate courses and new kinds of graduate research, thus helping to speed the internationalization of higher education in the United States.

Part Five
CONCLUSION

18 · Agenda for Action

1

The shortfall in the education, selection and training of Americans for work abroad has not been exaggerated. As a nation we can ignore only at our peril the international impact of any "misrepresentation" abroad. We feel, however, that the findings of our research point the way to a program of action—by government, by business, by philanthropic organizations, by churches, and particularly by universities—that over a period of years can greatly improve the caliber of the overseas American.

In summary form, those findings are two:

First, the international relations of the United States are increasingly concerned with the "internal affairs" of other nations. Most Americans in responsible overseas jobs must therefore be seen as deeply affecting foreign societies from the inside, rather than as dealing with them from the outside.

The still-incomplete response to the challenge of overseasmanship is partly due to the speed with which Americans have been injected into the internal affairs of other societies, and is partly the result of our national reluctance to believe that we are so deeply involved. But since we are, we need more than ever to be equipped with foreign languages and other tools for cross-cultural understanding, and to try to avoid the charges of superiority that stem from color consciousness, segregated housing, and other signs of discrimination.

Second, certain qualities of mind and spirit are particularly associated with effective performance in an overseas assignment. These elements of success are generally applicable to the American in a responsible position abroad regardless of the kind of work he is doing or in what foreign country he is doing it.

Our research has pointed to five elements of effective overseas performance: technical skill, belief in mission, cultural empathy, a sense for politics, and organization ability.

No one individual can be expected to possess all the ingredients of effective overseas performance. But every American *organization* that operates abroad can be guided by awareness of these qualifications in trying to recruit the proper people to mix together in carrying out its mission.

2

Those who would press for a broad effort to educate Americans for overseas service will not be disheartened by the opposition or incredulity of the overseas Americans or of most of the agencies that send them forth. Even among opinion-leaders at large, fictional bestsellers and a certain amount of semifictional reportage about United States failures and frustrations abroad have begun to develop a sense of urgency in the matter. The receptive atmosphere has in fact already produced some action: Once the new problem was identified (and long before it was systematically analyzed) many churches, voluntary agencies, government agencies and educational administrators, together with a few of the larger business firms, began to set in motion a remarkable assortment of action programs designed in one way or another to prepare Americans better for international life.

There is danger, however, in backing into the problem the way the nation is now doing: the danger that the most popular "solutions" to the problem will be of the dragnet variety. Already certain easy assumptions and fallacious premises have come to be widely accepted. These fallacies, often hidden behind generalized exhortations, are likely to hold back a serious national effort to give an American, before he goes abroad, the kind of education and training most relevant to overseas work.

Fallacy number one is that knowing a foreign language is all-important.

The ability to use and understand the local language of a foreign country is of unquestionable value to the overseas American. But, like other skills, its value for any given individual is not absolute, it is relative to other types of skill and understanding required for the particular assignment. Knowledge of a second tongue (or a third or fourth) is *by itself* no indication of an American's aptitude for effective overseas performance. It is a tool, not a quality of mind or spirit; skill in communication is no substitute for having something to say.

The ability to handle a foreign language is certainly a component, usually an essential component, of cultural empathy. The enthusiasm for a foreign tongue, the willingness to work hard at learning it, is perhaps the most reliable and certainly the most measurable index to empathy. Learning a language contributes crucially to an understanding of the culture with which it is associated—but only if its learning is associated with the study of culture and society.

For an American *organization* operating abroad, there is an absolute need for foreign-language skill. Every overseas organization must equip itself for understanding its environment by having in the field an adequate number of Americans who are truly fluent in the language of the people with whom the organization deals.

Fallacy number two is that training for one foreign area is completely different from training for another foreign area. The biggest postwar development in international education is the growth of area study programs. The very existence of these programs may lead the unwary to infer that the differences between countries and regions are more significant than the similarities. For the profound study of another society *in its own terms,* this is no doubt a valid premise. But when one studies the experience of Americans whose overseas careers have moved them from area to area—as is normally true of government people and some classes of businessmen—it is the factors of general applicability that leap to the eye.

The specific facts about one place may not be directly useful in another, but the process of learning them seems to be sufficiently transferable to facilitate greatly an American's orientation to a second post abroad. Just as learning a second language is (the language experts agree) immensely helpful in picking up a third, so study and experience in one country help a person understand the culture and analyze the power structure of another. As Rowland Egger suggested early in our research, "The primary benefit conferred by area specialization is the skill in its acquisition." If area studies are considered in this light, they may be enormously useful in training large numbers of Americans for overseas service.

Fallacy number three is that orientation for overseas service should be rigidly compartmentalized according to the kind of work the trainees are going to do abroad. The normal pattern is that all Presbyterians are trained in one clump, Stanvac oil men are trained in another cluster, ICA employees are put through an orientation program all their own, and so on down the long list. The implicit assumption here is that being an oil man is so different from being a missionary, and being an ICA technician is so different from either, that no advantage accrues from mixing the specialists in a common training program.

The conclusion of our investigation is just the reverse. In consequence the elements of success—the appreciation of foreign cultures, the sense for politics, the institution-building capacity—are common to responsible overseas workers in all professional categories in all countries.

The new realization that there are, after all, some universals in overseas service now threatens to produce *fallacy number four— the premature conclusion that overseas service is a new profession and (in university organization) a new academic discipline.* There are already several graduate programs and three major undergraduate programs which treat overseas service in this way. But our review of what American civilians are actually doing abroad does not suggest the presence of new vocation; the picture is rather of familiar vocations being pursued in strange surroundings. Education overseas service is not a new food; it is more like a new recipe for combining ingredients which already have an honored place in the academic cupboard.

3

The study of Americans at work abroad has led us not only to question several widely held ideas about education for international responsibility, but also to suggest that certain lines of educational policy need immediate attention. Five of these are of special importance.

1. *Immersion in an alien culture is central to an overseas-training program, and should also be an important element in the internationalization of higher education in the United States.*

"Nearly all our mistakes at this post are made by people on their first tour of duty outside the United States. If we could only make sure that every person sent here were on his *second* tour of duty, having made his mistakes somewhere else!" This wishful thought, uttered by an American diplomat in Teheran, is echoed in different ways by many an experienced executive abroad. Cultural empathy can be learned *about*, but it has to be practiced by trial and error before it comes naturally. The conviction that there are logical and valid alternatives to familiar American ways of thinking is not merely an unfelt intellectual conceit; it is also the product of experience.

A first, if vicarious, taste of this experience can be exposure to a good undergraduate course that digs deep into the history of some one culture very different from our own. But by all odds the best way to learn the feel of empathy is for the student to live among people whose ways are truly alien and discover for himself that he can deal with them on their own terms without compromising his own standards—just as he can use a foreign language without giving up his own.

The "immersion" that accomplishes this psychological transformation is not just any foreign travel experience, nor is it a matter of the amount of time spent abroad. The Experiment in International Living, a student travel organization which over the past twenty-five years has placed 8,000 American students in foreign homes, has demonstrated that a significantly deep cultural immersion can be carried out in ten weeks of a busy adolescent's summer. One important result of a successful contact with a foreign culture is a break-through of the language barrier. Well-supervised experiences abroad can do more to motivate young Americans to learn foreign languages than the most persuasive exhortations by their monolingual elders.

If the matter were left to the students to decide, overseas study would become a major feature of every campus, and with astonishing speed. If it is left to their parents and faculty advisers, the inevitable will take a little longer.

If the first overseas experience is so influential in shaking prejudices and molding attitudes, its meaning for education is obvious. Education is "hastened living"; if the educational system offers a supervised experience abroad, will it not bring back into the educational framework those beneficent things that happen to a person during that critical first year or two abroad? This implies a gigantic expansion of the Study Abroad movement as part of an internationalized college curriculum. *It should be a live option for every student at a reputable American college to study abroad for at least one semester under competent supervision and conditions that immerse him in an alien culture.*

Immersion in a foreign culture should also be a component of graduate and professional training for Americans heading toward overseas service. The nation needs a variety of experiments with working and living experiences abroad, including internships in both American and foreign governments, business firms, and voluntary organizations. The fact that more and more American graduate students are married before they complete their advanced degrees also makes it increasingly possible to test and train American wives for their exacting role in life and work abroad.

2. *University area programs should be expanded to serve the three "markets" for regional studies:*

• The first of these is *the scholar who plans to make a career as an "area expert."* His scholarly research will be the basis for our understanding of the history, culture, and current developments in the area; his needs will make the building of good regional libraries both necessary and possible; his policy research will provide an important part of the raw material for decision-makers in the United States agencies, public and private, which maintain field operations in the area. But his central position in the scheme of things does not mean that he is the be-all and end-all of area study programs.

• *The professional in a subject-matter field who expects to work in the area* needs an academic haven to which he can repair for intensive language training associated with the study of cultural history and contemporary social and economic trends, geographic and military facts, and the personalities and relationships that constitute the "power structure" in which the American will be an influential factor whether he likes it (and knows it) or not. The problem here is not to create a junior-grade area expert, a pale image of the lifetime scholar; nor does the educational problem involved require an academic degree, even though many of the participants will want to earn one. What the area program can do is help the student develop an intellectual framework on which he can hang what he learns in the field about the culture and society in which he will be doing his work—and to help him face frankly, before he goes abroad, the nature of his role in speeding and influencing rapid social change.

• Area programs should also "tool up" to organize *for regular undergraduate and graduate students a brief but intensive exposure in one country,* its culture, its language, and its contemporary social and political life. The strong reasons already cited for an overseas immersion in college or graduate school hide the danger that these experiences will not be carefully organized by people who know something about the areas concerned, but will be regarded as merely another profit-making enterprise external to the university's educational purposes. Ideally every overseas study program outside of Europe should be closely tied to a strong area-and-language program, so that the students can be adequately prepared for the experience ahead of time and supervised while abroad by teachers who know the area intimately from first-hand study and experience.

The purpose of this kind of immersion is not to recruit students for lifetime work as area scholars, though a few of them will undoubtedly develop such an interest as a by-product of their overseas experience. The purpose is to illustrate, in one alien society, the truths about all societies. From this point of view, learning all about Brazil may be an excellent first stage in training an American to live and work in Egypt or Japan.

3. *Every professional school, and graduate program in the social sciences, should reflect in its curriculum the certainty that some of its students will practice their profession abroad.* In each profession the new international dimension can readily be defined by those of its members who have worked overseas. The need is for a broadened range of subject matter, a deeper interest in technical developments in the underdeveloped world, a lively awareness that every overseas program seems to involve the specialist in that "generalist" form of activity we have called the building of institutions. There is plenty of room for study and work experiences abroad, for internships in American overseas operations, for the development of opportunities to study and work *inside* the institutions (the hospitals, the schools, the factories, the agricultural experiment stations) of a foreign society.

Here again, the emphasis should be on the creation of opportunities to learn that the American way of doing things is neither the only way nor the standard by which other ways should be judged. In every American professional and graduate school the next revision of the curriculum should give a prominent place to that disturbing and useful question: "What is universal about the rules and standards of our profession and what is merely American practice?"

4. *An overseas training program should stress the comparative study of political and administrative process.* This requirement stems, of course, from the importance of a sense for politics and of organization ability in most of the responsible positions in American overseas operations.

It is a great advantage to overseas worker and observer alike to be accepted as an insider, as one who knows the ropes. He must be familiar with the formal and informal political and administrative processes as well as the eccentricities, foibles and special prejudices of the principal manipulators of these processes—the power structure of the community in which the American has elected to live and work.

Here, as in the case of cultural empathy, the educational task is not so much one of instruction about facts as the search for values and encouragement of attitudes. And what needs most of all to be encouraged is a positive attitude toward social and governmental complexity. At home or abroad, the people who are successful in politics and administration—which is to say the leaders—are those men and women who are challenged rather than repelled by the complications to which a highly organized society naturally gives rise.

The crucial element in the teaching of comparative institutions is the study of process, not merely of structure. Much of what passes as comparative study is no more than a colorless comparison of alternative structures erected in various countries to perform the same political or administrative task. The comparison of constitutions, army regulations, economic controls, or legislatures has a certain tidy interest as an academic exercise; but for Americans who are going to operate abroad, the key question is not "How is it set up?" but "How does it actually work?"

From this point of view, an American on his way overseas might learn more of what he needs from studying the writings of a great reporter like Lincoln Steffens than from a series of standard lectures on comparative social and political systems. The case studies in public administration developed during the past decade in the United States are a more contemporary step in the desired direction; what is needed now is a great deal more comparable case material from various societies on similar governmental processes, always stressing how institutions actually work and what the people associated with them actually do and say when important decisions are in the making.

5. *Every American planning to work abroad should know America first,* learn to take delight in its pluralism and savor the contradictions in its heritage.

The very fact that every American who spends some time abroad can and perhaps should be an effective "goodwill ambassador" does not necessarily require that he have an encyclopedic knowledge of the United States, but it does place a premium on the kinds of knowledge that enable him to interpret to others, when the occasion presents itself, the special flavor of American civilization.

"Know America first" can easily sound like the shallowest kind of jingoism; but in our thinking American studies occupy a central position in an overseas-training program precisely because an understanding of one's own culture and institutions is a prerequisite to cultural empathy and a sense for politics abroad. Some sense of our literary and artistic life helps us relate ourselves to people in other lands who have been exposed only to the more strident voices of America. Without some prior exposure to the philosophic bases of American life, the American abroad is awkward in explaining his overseas role to others or even to himself.

For all these reasons the overseas American needs to study the several versions of the American dream, and the stories of those who have striven to make it reality. He may thereby learn to refrain from the quite unsporting and unproductive pastime so commonly indulged in by Americans abroad of comparing the American dream to the foreign reality.

4

The education and training of Americans for overseas service is clearly an important item on the U.S. national agenda. The task before us is new in its dimensions and partly strange in content, but a vigorous effort to tackle it is quite consistent with the traditional American belief that education should be relevant to the nation's as well as the individual's needs. The rate at which our great decentralized system of schools, colleges and universities rises to the new challenge depends on who prods it, with how sharp a stick, and in what direction.

The most immediate interest to be served is that of the employing agencies; it is to them that we should look first for prodding action. The organizations that operate abroad, whether governmental, business, religious or philanthropic, can:

> • enable universities to become training stations for overseas service as well as for vocations in the United States—by insisting that applicants for overseas jobs be tested first in a university training program.
>
> • recognize the advantages of mixing overseas personnel from different agencies or organizations in a common overseas training program and overcome the administrative complications of sending individuals to train at a number of schools.
>
> • make it possible for some universities to build and

maintain distinguished area programs with good libraries and scholarly research by providing such programs with a steady flow of students and generally insisting on area knowledge and language competence as prerequisites for the jobs that require them.

• assist some universities to "specialize" in the common factors (the study of foreign cultures, the internal politics of other nations, comparative administration, American civilization, foreign policy and foreign operations); and facilitate their continuous basic research on overseas administration and thus the development and publication of usable theory about the elements of "success" in work and life abroad.

• conduct (or farm out) policy research about their own agency operations in the field, in order to provide case material for teaching, to check general theory against daily practice, and to enable each agency to pass along to its own new staff members some systematic idea of what the organization has learned through field experience in cross-cultural operations.

There is, however, a limit to what the employing agencies, even the largest of them, can do in reaching deep into American education to reorient whole college and university programs. A few weeks or even months of orientation cannot compensate for a prior lack of genuine exposure. In the longer run, the way to improve the performance of the overseas Americans is to catch them young, while they are still subject to the processes of formal education.

The problem is certainly too big for the employing agencies and too urgent for the normal process of curriculum change in academic institutions. The private educational foundations have already done much, but they can do more. Indeed, it seems likely that the foundations will find in the internationalization of higher education an opportunity to perform a major service in strengthening the programs of overseas training and research and in experimenting with new techniques in this field. But the problem goes even beyond the resources of the philanthropic foundations. A new kind of coordinating agency, focused on education for international responsibility, may have to be built into the American educational system by the Federal Government, as an expression of the national interest in a marked improvement in American overseas behavior.

The need for such a coordinating device at government level is amply demonstrated by the anarchy of present arrangements. Several different Federal agencies have different policies about whether to use universities to educate their recruits for overseas service. Some agencies are trying to construct their own programs. Others are experimenting with various kinds of contracts, most of which do create a facility for the government's use but fail to build enduring programs solidly based on scholarly research.

In so far as there is a government policy on the subject of overseas training, it is contained in the National Defense Education Act of 1958, which provided generous financial aid for university programs in a limited number of foreign languages. As we have seen, however, the Act treats area studies merely as a by-product of the study of rare languages, and ignores the other main elements of the overseas-training problem. Moreover, the Congressional history of this legislation made it mandatory for the Department of Health, Education and Welfare to favor grants to those colleges and universities which discovered the language shortage *after* Congress did; many institutions that had foreseen the problem and already had made a strong start in developing teachers, libraries, and language laboratories were bypassed in the first grants under the Act.

In the absence of a serious attack on the whole problem of education for overseas service, a frustrated sense of urgency inevitably produces a good deal of enthusiasm for specialized panaceas. One of the narrowest is also the most frequently advocated: a Foreign Service Academy, modeled on West Point or Annapolis. Such an approach would abandon as hopeless the entire United States system of higher education and establish from scratch a school under bureaucratic control to train a few career diplomats for a Foreign Service that is no longer an élite corps of diplomatic specialists but a large body of Americans, encompassing many different specialties, which will increasingly have to assume the coordinating role in all governmental operations abroad. A proposal less relevant to the size and character of the real overseas-training problem would be hard to imagine. It is to the credit of the Executive Branch and the Congressional leadership that this hardy perennial, the proposal for a Foreign Service Academy, has been given the "Yes, but" treatment whenever it has showed its head.

But if it is not going to solve the overseas-training problem with a cure-all, the Federal Government must face up to the broader task of inducing the changes required in American education to serve the nation's interest by providing a pool of young Americans who will be adequately prepared for living and working abroad. That the Government can do this without slipping into Federal control of education has already been amply demonstrated in government-sponsored research, in the use of the government's contracting power to pull private as well as public universities into the overseas technical-assistance program, in Federal support of public school construction, and more recently in the carefully permissive administration of the National Defense Education Act. The tradition of Federal support to education without Federal dictation of content is in fact a long and honorable one, dating back to the first authorization of land-grant colleges in every state under the Morrill Act of 1862. More recently, the national need for more scientific research and more specialists trained in the application of science and mathematics impelled Congress to create a National Science Foundation to prod the educational system and induce more of the nation's gifted youngsters to seek both financial rewards and a personally satisfying career in fundamental or applied science. The national need for more organized medical research likewise persuaded Congress to build up and support with substantial appropriations the National Institutes of Health.

Following these distinguished precedents, the United States Congress might usefully establish in the Executive Branch a National Foundation for Overseas Operations, with a Board of Trustees drawn from the Federal agencies concerned and from private business, educational, and philanthropic organizations. The National Foundation would not conduct research and training activities itself, but would exist to pull together activities of government and spur the actions of non-governmental organizations as they relate to the education of Americans for overseas assignments. Specifically the National Foundation might:

> • act as a coordinating research center and assist scholarly publications in the field;

> • develop and dramatize a nationwide attack on the problem of educating and training Americans for more effective overseas performance; and
>
> • distribute government financial assistance in such a way as to encourage programs useful for the preparation of Americans for overseas life and work.

Optimum performance by Americans in work abroad will evidently require pervasive changes in American education. The changes will not happen by themselves; changes in settled institutions never do. They will be brought to pass by educational and political leadership, blended in about equal quantities. Government and other employing agencies cannot greatly improve the personnel on whom their effectiveness depends, without deep thought and vigorous action by American educational leaders. The United States educational system, on the other hand, will change very slowly unless there is vigorous prodding by the Government acting for an aroused citizenry.

5

The overseas Americans are an important new element in American foreign policy. The soldiers and civil servants, businessmen and missionaries, scholars and students share with the diplomats the power to affect international relations and the responsibility of representing the United States. Because they are conspicuous, their behavior has become a national concern, and there is some tendency to blame them for everything that seems to be wrong with United States foreign policy. But while they may think of themselves as surrogates for the Secretary of State, they do not in fact make the crucial decisions about policies and attitudes which determine how the rest of the world will treat them.

If we have not yet built into our foreign policy an assumption of revolutionary change in the rest of the world; if we are mesmerised by our Russian rival and pay too little attention to the dramatic happenings in the rest of the world; if we still practise bigotry or tolerate demagogues in public office; if we react with heightened tariffs and tightened quotas to signs of business competition from Europe and Japan; if we are not yet as a nation particularly excited about the task of building free and workable institutions in the newly developing countries where the Declaration of Independence is still a thrilling statement of faith; if we have so multiplied the instruments through which we deal with other countries that they do not really know who speaks officially for the United States anyway—the overseas American must live with the reactions that these national actions and attitudes create abroad.

No matter how effective the individual performance of Americans in overseas work, no matter how well they exercise their technical skill in new surroundings, appreciate the need for cultural empathy, and act as political men and builders of social institutions, their success will be deeply affected by the foreign policies chosen by the United States. Individual performance can be much improved, but the collective performance of the overseas Americans is unlikely to be better than Main Street and Pennsylvania Avenue permit.

INDEX

for success and achievement, partly instilled by its parents, can easily lead to a conflict of interests between familial obligations and personal desires. It may lead to movement away from home, changed ideas and way of life and so forth, that make family relations difficult. The familial problems and barriers created by social mobility through education are well described by Jackson and Marsden (1962).

Again the studies of pathological families often describe the conflict of interests between family and self. The Danzigs' especial concern was for their family reputation and they expected that their children should put this first. Any activity that they thought might breach this reputation was especially threatening. Their daughter's behaviour was seen as just such a threat: 'It was the danger to their family reputation they found so sickening about her "sickness"' (1972, p. 33).

The idea that the ideology of the working class is collectivist, whereas that of the middle class is individualist, is familiar, and the terms tend to be used here primarily to contrast the self as opposed to the collective orientation of the two groups (Goldthorpe and Lockwood, 1963).[11] This ideological distinction between the two social classes does not vitiate my assertion that the ideology of non-familial relations is individualist, since it is the middle-class ideology that is institutionalized and dominant within the society, and so influences what is expected by those who represent those institutions. What it does mean is that we must here distinguish between the ideas and values of both partners to a relationship. So far I have assumed a reciprocity of ideas and expectations. If, however, the working class bring a collective orientation to non-family relations as well as to family ones, then in non-familial interactions there will be a conflict of ideas and values, as has often been observed. One consequence of this is that the locus of conflict is different for the two social classes as the balance of values is different. For the middle class it is family relations that are especially difficult since they are incongruent; for the working class conflict arises in non-familial social relations: it is in dealing with teachers, employers, and so forth that contradictory ideas and values are encountered. This of course has repercussions on family interaction. I have already commented on how social mobility creates and exacerbates conflicts within the family. For the working-class person this is doubly so, for success involves not only acceptance of values unfamiliar to the child – a re-socialization that is not necessary for a middle-class child – but also the adoption of values that do not match with those that govern familial relations.

11. The individualism of the middle class means that they hardly constitute a *class* at all by Marx's standards.

This too has important implications for the study of family pathology. For it suggests that middle-class family relations are currently more difficult than working-class ones. On the other hand the working class are more likely to encounter contradictions in social expectations in non-familial encounters. There has, however, been no attempt to consider whether the degree of conflict in familial relations varies by social class. Although such differences would have no simple or straightforward implications for the incidence or prevalence of mental illness by social class they are surely worth some attention.

A third aspect of our ideas about family relations is that we expect them to be based on feeling and concern, whereas we do not assume non-familial relations have such a basis. In particular we expect family members to show love, affection and support, and whilst these feelings (and their behavioural consequences) may be shown elsewhere they are not expected to match them in strength. The ideology of family relations is that of support, provision and help through familial love and sacrifice; the philosophy of each man for himself does not operate here.

The norms of family love, support and solidarity are manifested in numerous ways. Not only do parents give considerable help to their children even when they might be self-supporting (Bell, 1968) but they frequently talk of providing opportunities for their children and giving them things they never had. Since parents also have values of self-interest and reciprocation this creates numerous contradictions and conflicts. Although they talk of providing opportunities for their children and suggest that provision is a one-way phenomenon, they inevitably expect some sort of return from their children. For the Danzigs this return took the form of maintaining and enhancing the family's reputation. Whilst talking of what they did for their children they nevertheless explicitly viewed their children as an investment and expected a definite return. 'Let's have something back in return for my effort on their behalf, on my wife's behalf' (Esterson, 1972, p. 49).

Children who do not make use of the opportunities provided by their parents, who do not 'make good' in their parents' eyes, tend inevitably to be seen as failures by them, to be criticized and so forth. Even if the sacrifices are on a smaller scale, like subsidized living at home, whilst earning, or the provision of various domestic services when these could well be carried out by the child, there still tends to be the expectation of return, often in the form of physical presence (Barker, 1972). For many parents a child's continued residence at home, or return for visits, once they are starting to gain more independence, is the salient reward. A child's presence is vital in two ways. On the one hand it literally makes the family; on the other hand it is a symbol of the sentiment and affection that is deemed an essential component of familial relations. A child's willingness to spend time at home becomes then a sign that the family is a successful functioning unit. Presence is, of course, not only a symbol of the strength of family feeling, it is also necessary to the companionship and emotional support that family members expect of each other.

The extent to which love, support and affection are ideologically restricted to family members differs to some extent between social classes. In the working class personal relations are more obviously restricted to family members. Working-class men and women commonly think of other family members, such as their mothers or sisters, as their best friends. In contrast in the middle class the term friend usually refers only to persons who are not family members. This means that for the middle class there is a category of non-family persons, friends, with whom (by definition) they are also involved in affective relationships. The social relations involved in the notion of friendship are especially interesting here since they provide an apparent anomaly. On the one hand friendship relations are often juxtaposed to family relations and are thereby attributed different characteristics; on the other hand they involve the notion of an emotional and supportive bond that is supposed to be the key feature of family relations. One marked difference is that friendship relations are explicitly individualistic in that they are individually chosen. In some ways they are the counterpart to familial relations in an individualistic society. Family relations in such societies tend to act as some sort of ideal model for friendship relations. Friendship ties are not expected to be as strong and longlasting as family ties and where friends do display the degree of emotion and concern expected of familial relations they tend to be described in familial terms: 'he's just like a brother to me', or 'like a sister', or 'he's the father I never had'.

One consequence of both the collective orientation of family relations and their emotional, supportive emphasis is the idea that family members should be given preferential treatment. According to Parsons (1956) it is the contrast between particularistic and universalistic values that is the main conflict between familial and economic values in America. Certainly it is one aspect of the contrast in expectations of family and non-family relations that is salient here. Within a family it is generally accepted that family members will be given better treatment than anyone else. Nepotism illustrates this ideology realized in practice. Concern for providing opportunities for one's children and doing one's best for them also reflects particularist values. So too does the norm of family inheritance, a convention which provides a vital mechanism in the maintenance of social differentials. In contrast in non-familial institutions the assumption is that each individual is to be treated on criteria that are applied more universally.

Finally there is the contrast between familiarity and privacy. As the common origin of the words suggests, we expect familiarity between family members: we expect openness and trust, whereas non-family relations assume more privacy. The ideology of family relations is antithetical to individual privacy: privacy becomes *secrecy*. Yet this is crucial, for personal privacy is deemed important to the development and maintenance of the autonomy and independence of the individual, as it allows the necessary control over information that they both demand. In Goffman's (1972) analysis of the individual, privacy is essential to the impression management that self-presentation requires.

This contrast in ideas about family relations and other social relations creates conflicts and confusions in expectations both about how much personal privacy family members should have and how much privacy the family as a whole should maintain vis-à-vis 'outsiders'. Both areas of difficulty emerge very vividly in the Danzig family. The following passage illustrates how Sarah's (the daughter) attempt to retain some personal privacy and her father's desire to know what she is doing leads to a situation of great contradiction.

However, Sarah found out about their watching and was resentful. But when she accused her father of prying, he indignantly denied it. And his wife and son backed him. He did not feel he was being contradictory, for he knew he was concerned only for her welfare. Her reputation demanded he should properly fulfil his familial role as guardian, while her happiness required she should not feel she was being watched. So they continued watching her while denying they were doing so (Esterson, 1972, p. 180).

But privacy of the family to the outside world is just as important in an individualistic society. Here Esterson comments on Mrs Danzig's concern to 'manage' impressions:

On the 'public' appearance of domestic clockwork familial cooperation and order depended her reputation as a successful, conscientious housewife and parental trainer. So important was it to maintain this 'public' appearance that after her daughter had failed to cooperate 'publicly', she tried to hide the fact, so ashamed did she feel before 'the others', and such failure (1972, p. 115).

IV

What I hope emerges from this discussion is the special value placed on family relations within the culture. They are subject to a set of ideas, values and beliefs that do not readily correspond with those that dominate other social relations. It is because of this that they are of such especial interest. The family tends to be espoused by traditionalists who see in it the Christian virtues of love, altruism, trust and sacrifice, and to be attacked by radicals either because it is held to maintain social differentials or because it is seen as a threat to the autonomy and freedom of the individual. All tend to ignore the fact that family relations are one of the few bastions of values that are antithetical to capitalism. The epithet 'bourgeois' when applied to all families in contemporary society is surely mistaken. This is the contradiction; the family is essentially conservative, it is an 'ideological conditioning device' (Cooper, 1971, p. 3) and yet it is almost the last defence against the commercialization and individualization of society. Thus it both attracts and repels.

Family relations in our society are not an easy matter for anyone. They involve a balancing and reconciliation of many conflicting social pressures. Work on family 'pathology' needs to be set against such a background.

References

ARIÈS, P. (1962), *Centuries of Childhood*, Cape; Penguin, 1973.

AUSUBEL, D. P. (1961), 'Personality disorder is disease', *Amer. Psychol.*, vol. 16, pp. 69–74.

BARKER, D. (1972), 'Young people and their home: spoiling and "keeping close" in a South Wales town', *Sociol. Rev.*, vol. 20, pp. 569–90.

BATESON, G., JACKSON, D. D., HALEY, J., and WEAKLAND, J. (1956), 'Towards a theory of schizophrenia', *Behavioural Sci.*, vol. 1, pp. 251–64.

BEGELMAN, D. A. (1971), 'Misnaming, metaphors, the medical model and some muddles', *Psychiatry*, vol. 34, pp. 38–58.

BELL, C. (1968), *Middle-Class Families*, Routledge & Kegan Paul.

BERENT, J. (1954), 'Social mobility and marriage: a study of trends in England and Wales', in D. Glass (ed.), *Social Mobility in Britain*, Routledge & Kegan Paul.

BROWN, G. W. (1967), 'The family of the schizophrenic patient', in A. Coppen and A. Walk (eds.), *Recent Developments in Schizophrenia*, Royal Medico Psychological Association.

BUSFIELD, J. (1974), 'Ideologies and reproduction', in M. Richards (ed.),' *The Integration of a Child into a Social World*, Cambridge University Press.

COOPER, D. (1971), *The Death of the Family*, Allen Lane The Penguin Press; Penguin, 1973.

DUMONT, L. (1965), 'The modern conception of the individual: notes on its genesis and that of concomitant institutions', *Contributions to Indian Sociology*, vol. 8, pp. 13–61.

ESTERSON, A. (1972), *The Leaves of Spring*, Penguin.

FONTANA, A. F. (1966), 'Familial etiology of schizophrenia: is a scientific methodology possible?', *Psychol. Bull.*, vol. 66, pp. 214–27.

GOFFMAN, E. (1972), *The Presentation of Self in Everyday Life*, Penguin.

GOLDTHORPE, J., and LOCKWOOD, D. (1963), 'Affluence and the British class structure', *Sociol. Rev.*, vol. 11, pp. 150–55.

HARRIS, C. C. (1969), *The Family*, Allen & Unwin.

JACKSON, B., and MARSDEN, D. (1962), *Education and the Working Class*, Routledge & Kegan Paul; Penguin, 1966.

LAING, R. D. (1967), 'The schizophrenic experience', in *The Politics of Experience and The Bird of Paradise*, Penguin.

LAING, R. D. (1965), *The Divided Self*, Penguin.

LAING, R. D., and ESTERSON, A. (1971), *Sanity, Madness and the Family*, Penguin.

LANE, M. (1974), *Money Maketh Man: The Economic Ideology of Everyday Life*, Cape.

LUKES, S. (1973), *Individualism*, Macmillan.

MITCHELL, J. (1971), *Woman's Estate*, Penguin.

PARSONS, T. (1956), *Family, Socialization and Interaction Process*,
 Routledge & Kegan Paul.
SEDGWICK, P. (1972), 'R. D. Laing: self, symptom and society', in R. Boyers and
 R. Orrill (eds.), *Laing and Anti-Psychiatry*, Penguin.
SINGER, M. T., and WYNNE, L. C. (1965), 'Thought disorder and family
 relations of schizophrenics: four, results and implications', *Arch. Gen. Psych.*,
 vol. 12, pp. 201–12.
STONE, L. (1967), *The Crisis of the Aristocracy, 1558–1641*,
 Oxford University Press.
SZASZ, T. S. (1960), 'The myth of mental illness', *Amer. Psychol.*, vol. 15,
 pp. 113–18.

10 Alienated Children:
The Psychologies of School Phobia and their Social and Political Implications
Tim Lang

This article is intended to substantiate, in the case of one human problem, a major theme of this book, namely that much of the uneasiness of many contemporary psychologists is due to a grossly inadequate understanding of the complexity of the social nature of the human world. The psychologist acts as a prescriber of a world-view, and whether he likes it or not is an actor in and a proponent of a complete social–political system and ideology (which he often believes to be nothing to do with him). Psychology, then, is like all other 'disciplines' concerned with humanity. It contains internally contradicting and contrasting images of what people are like. What we are given as 'psychology' is important for what it tells us about the writers' social theory, what they think human life is all about; secondly, for how their views contribute to our perception of the social world, how far they mystify or clarify our understanding, and hence our actions; and thirdly, for how they reflect the actual composition of the social world.

It is due to the importance of these issues that it is worth bothering about the pathetic state of social psychology which claims or seeks to explain the individual's position in society. The very lack of understanding of the social meaning of life which we are offered by social psychology merely shows up the shortcomings of psychology as a whole. Both deny the full substance of social existence. In view of this, there is no point in believing those psychologists who opt for more professionalism or a more 'scientific' approach as ways of coping with the hearteningly growing dissatisfaction with psychology. It is not just that old methods are now seen to be deficient or that psychologists lack good equipment; it is, simply, that they are asking the wrong questions. Once we realize what is involved in the social world (it is there in front of us after all!), different, and I think more important, issues are raised: whom do psychologists serve? what can be done? do we want psychologists or psychology at all? To consider these issues takes us out of the realm of psychology as we presently know it. In this article, I want to make clear the thinking which prompted me to accept that these are the central issues for the present day. Far from wishing to dispel the confusion and dissatisfactions in psychology, I believe we ought to clarify their existence and maximize rather than minimize the conflicts. Specifically, I want to show that it is impossible fully to understand even a comparatively everyday human problem without juxtaposing psychological and socio-political (and hence, historical) realities. I want to show this for the so-called school phobic. The psychologies of school phobia have succeeded in cutting the children from the very social world they inhabit.

The set explanation and variations

One of the conventional ways of describing psychology is to contrast psychoanalysis with behaviourism. Despite its appeal this strategy fails to come to grips with the deficiencies both schools display, as we see in the case of school phobia whose commonest model is a bastardization of Freud's explanation of phobias and which goes as follows:[1]

The child will not go to school. Something is preventing him from doing so. Both mother and child are highly emotional. On inspection by experts, the mother is observed to have a 'close' relationship with her offspring, characterized by mutual dependence and maternal overprotection. It is suggested that it is their inability to separate that is inhibiting school attendance. Hence, somehow – either through psychotherapy or through putting the child in hospital or child-care unit – the expert believes that if he separates mother and child, and encourages the recalcitrant to be sufficiently independent to go to school, all will be well. Some say that the child must be immediately returned to school and then psychotherapy can work on creating psychological independence unfettered by the non-attendance which is symbolic of 'deeper' ills.

This separation–dependency model is a straight example of psychologistic explanation. The action is explained in terms of the pathologies of individuals and families (see papers by Pearson and Busfield, this volume) whose interpretations of what happened are treated somewhat disparagingly by caseworkers. At this point I will briefly outline some variations on this general explanatory model.

In the first, the child is said to be suffering from a conflict between his reliance upon his mother and his 'natural' drives for independence. In turn his mother is said to be still suffering from mutual overdependence which existed between herself and her own mother. She is also often regarded as having an inadequate relationship with her husband. More-

1. I have refrained from giving full references to works on school phobia partly because the literature is so absurdly extensive. Should readers want to check my criticisms, let them inspect Kahn and Nursten (1968), which has a lengthy bibliography. For a strict psychoanalytic explanation see Klein (1945).

over, her child is characteristically seen as being rather precious and weak-willed, having a tendency to cling to the mother. It is further alleged that the mother and child frequently manipulate each other for their own ends.

The second variation, still within the psychoanalytic camp, reflects the growth in the 1940s and 1950s of 'ego' psychology (Erikson, Melanie Klein, Fenichel, etc.). Its advocates accepted the separation–dependency model, but modified it for adolescent school phobias. In these cases they identified a 'character weakness', a deficient ego which had been fixed at a prepubertal mental level. They suggested that in the course of the phobia's emergence the adolescent regressed until he was back in a symbiotic tie, a mutual attachment with mother. School refusal reflects individual in-adequacy.

A third view adopts the Adlerian belief that all children (like adults) strive after 'omnipotence': the will for power. The school phobic, according to this perspective, is wilful and self-asserting. The act of non-attendance is one of defiance, rather than the 'cowardly' withdrawal, that the character-weakness image implies. It follows that the child 'needs' containment or discipline.

For all their trumpet blowing, the learning theorists, who provide a fourth variation, have not added much to our general understanding of the causes of school phobia. They focus upon what happens *after* the phobia is under way. In a sense they specify that learning is involved in deviancy amplification. Retreat from school, the feared object, lessens the inhibiting influence of fear upon actions and therefore reinforces the fear-generated retreat or avoidance behaviour pattern. Thus a vicious circle is set up which prevents the conditioned fear response from being eradicated (that, then, is the therapist's job). Eysenck and Rachman (1965) propose that the traumatic or phobic experience (the unconditioned stimulus, appearing apparently from nowhere) is transferred in conditioning onto 'a neutral or logically irrelevant stimulus'. We might expect, then, that when these eminent psychologists outline the paradigm, they conceive the school as being neutral or logically irrelevant. But not so. For they, alone among psychological writers, claim to take the school's part in the causal chain seriously. Somehow school is both irrelevant or neutral *and* involved in the refusal's origins.

This rather muddled account of the relationship of the child's experience in school to the act of refusal is important. However confused it is, despite it, the writers (along with all other perspectives) still insist on the child's return to that situation they recognize as being involved in the avoidance behaviour. In view of the fact that learning theorists contend that they are clear and rigorous in contrast to the woolliness they ascribe to psycho-analysis, it is amusing to observe that not only are they self-contradictory, but that they even borrow the original causal hypothesis from the Freudians (separation–dependency anxiety). Moreover, the behaviour therapists suggest forms of treatment that the analysts have already used, such as immediate return to school (is this implosion?) or gradually phased return to school (desensitization).

The Freudian explanation for all its 'deep' assumptions at least accepts that adequacy of explanation is partially dependent upon the meaning of the act's origins for the actor. On the other hand, the naked ideology of the neo-behaviourist account heightens our awareness of the existence of social-control philosophies within the school-phobic world. It is remarkable that all therapies, claiming different kinds of theoretical justifications manifesting different conceptions of social reality, get the high 'success' rates of return to school that they all claim. Are they all right? How (in what sense) can they be all right? In order to assess these questions and realize the common thread to all accounts, we must put school phobia and attendance as a whole into the context from which the psychologies have robbed it.

Childhood and the school as historical and cultural artifacts

Psychologists have failed to understand the fullness of the social forces at work on the child in both home and school and hence have failed to grasp the tension that exists between individual and society, and, clearly, within the school-refusing child. Either, the child is visualized as a plaything of forces internal or external, and as having little agency. Or, when autonomous motivation is ascribed to the child, it is depicted as of a reprehensible nature (manipulation, wilfulness, etc.). To surpass both these accounts, then, I suggest that the refuser's act can only be understood as a clash of a child's private and particular experience with wider social mores and forces. By focusing upon individuals, paradoxically, psychologists surrender themselves to an arbitrary societal consensus, and sacrifice both themselves and their subjects to an overarching but subtle repression for the 'good of society'.

The individual–society tension is particularly noticeable in the status accorded to children's accounts. The child's experience is noted as being of confusion, conflict, depression and anxiety, yet the source of these feelings is left inadequately explained or more often no investigation of the child's account is made. They often say they are bored by or dislike school, yet such is the confidence in the set explanation that this is dismissed as the child's rationalization for internal inadequacy, or as fantasy. 'Inflated' self-images have to be made 'more realistic'.

Children have not always been considered objects to be controlled. In earlier centuries they were disregarded until they reached seven or four-teen, when they were recognized as having become 'human', i.e. adults. Before then, their status was suspended, undefined between birth and adulthood.[2] Once childhood was 'discovered' in the sixteenth and seven-teenth centuries, it seems to have been synthesized into the idea that *children need training for life*. With the spread of the new conception, schools (previously institutions for training the professions or colleges of humanist scholarship) developed into places where order and the training for living were to be instilled. Although the middle and upper classes crea-ted different forms of education to fit into their own needs, of interest to us here is the idea that training for life gradually replaced the notion of a *natural induction into life*. By the eighteenth century the debate in Europe concerned the means for that training, hence the enormous interest in Rousseau's *Emile or Education*. At this time, of course, interest in educa-tion and the developments in images of childhood were restricted to the nobility and bourgeoisie. Amongst the literate classes, who began to be in-fluential and voluble on this issue, opinion crystallized into different and sometimes even polarized positions which are still with us today and which psychology (see the models of school phobia) has inherited. We have the notion that children were born innocent and were only tainted by the foul-ness of the world, and therefore they need protection from it. Life, accord-ing to this view, could only be learned through the accumulated experience of others. The contrary position, finding its roots in Christianity, held that children, like all humanity, suffer from Original Sin, but being children are pure Original Sin, and thus need chastisement and control to minimize its effects. It was feared that failure to enforce such sanctions would lead to the breakdown of the social order. A third position suggested that the child was essentially rational: responsible, capable, unemotional, clear-thinking and honest; in short, an ideal being. (As may be expected, this view has lent itself to many ideological perspectives, at different historical stages!)

These preoccupations became important to more than just the leisured and merchant classes with the introduction of mass compulsory education (in Britain) at the end of the nineteenth century. It is worth remembering that this step grew out of an enormous conflict of economic and ideological interest concerning both its advisability and format. For years there was considerable resistance among the lower paid. Children could supplement the family income (see Rubinstein, 1969; Pallister, 1969). School now is so much a part of growing up that it is hard to conceive the years of youth spent otherwise. School is not a god-given institution, but an outcome of men creating social reality for others. School refusers are not separate

2. See Ariès (1962); Pinchbeck and Hewitt (1969); Ruskin History Workshop (1974); Coveney (1967).

from but part of this social setting. In that they have attempted such a separation, the psychologies of school phobia are frauds.[3] Since social reality is in permanent movement through history, the meaning of non-attendance is relative to its historical location. The development and variations in the psychologies of non-attendance from 1930 to 1970 underline this point. What does bind the experience of the non-attender of 1890 to that of the school phobic of 1974 is the common experience of restriction and compulsion. The political prescriptions of 1870 are now the internalized 'common-sense'. What then was an ideological conflict now appears as a psychological, private ailment in the child.

Compulsion and the anti-school child

School is not just a matter of ideas or social theory, its importance is also, perhaps fundamentally, economic.[4] Education is an industry responsive to industrial forces. As such, school channels energies, learning and desires in particular directions; it segments the population by structuring and legitimizing inequality. Since it (along with other forces) dominates a child's life, reaction to any aspect of that life is liable to appear in or against school. As far as the young are concerned, school is a major component of living, and it brings certain demands; the foremost, obviously, is attendance, but also the subjugation of self to pre-existent structure (however liberal). Thus those psychologists of school phobia who 'treat' the school refuser, in order to make him return, reinforce an image of the child in an over-powering social structure. Thus they turn science into the pragmatics of control.

Compulsion to attend, then, is worthy of more than the passing reference previous writers have given it. It is central to our analysis. To the psychologist, compulsion is the boundary rule of his therapeutic game. To the child, it is, to put it crudely, one half of the conflict: he knows he ought to go, but he does not want to. Compulsion restricts not only the possibility of working out the dilemma in other ways, but brings conscious focus onto attendance for its own sake, rather than, say, placing emphasis upon happiness.

There is and always has been an anti-school culture in Britain. All we are seeing are new forms of it: school phobia, lesson refusal, resistance (being in school but not in class) and, most pernicious of all, psychological ab-

3. Littman (1961) offers an all-too-rare overt expression of the view that psychology should exclude the social.
4. Rowntree and Rowntree (1968) relate youth and education to the USA economy. In a less clear way so does the Conservative Party in Great Britain (see Department of Education and Science, 1972), but they deny its true political meaning.

sence (being mentally but not physically absent from school)![5] This culture no longer derives from the adult demand for cheap labour and from the poor's reciprocal acute financial need. (Though there are cases of financially induced early withdrawal.) Many, however, cannot see the point of staying on at school beyond the legal minimum when there is money to be made which may supplement the family income, and which as far as the young are concerned symbolizes the end of childhood and the entry into consuming adulthood. It is for this reason that the experience of thousands of fifteen-year-olds has been sharpened by the raising of the school-leaving age. The recent rise in truancy figures causing so much concern to 'authorities' must be set into this context to be understood; it has not very much to do with free school milk being abolished as someone in the House of Lords recently suggested! Anti-school values go beyond the strictly school situation in meaning. In society as a whole satisfaction can increasingly be achieved only by material consumption (which further surrenders labour to the cash-nexus) and by family life. Thus the new material spending power of the young is part of a narrowed range for the search for life meaning, from which one can only react; hence the search for kicks, the vital meaning of fashions, music. These highlight the boredom of school, and by being available make school tedious. The youth culture is about symbols, images and values (rarely different from the parent society's) which crystallize the place of the young and accentuate the tension between what they want and what they have to accept. I do not mean to depict a politically conscious and sophisticated counter-culture. One of the problems for youth today, for me, is their failure to see the political nature of their peculiar situations and experiences. The school refuser thus epitomizes the weakness of all the young, locked as they are in a cycle of bewilderment, before which they can only retreat.

I do not accept then that the adoption of anti-school values is always a reaction to failure in school, as Lacey's work (1970) may be taken to imply.[6] Undoubtedly, though, one psychological mechanism at work is often expectation. Grammar-school failures fail in relation to high parental pressure or the experience of success at primary school. These as Lacey shows are the inevitable outcome of a school structure founded upon narrow criteria of success; it is impossible for everyone to be the 'ideal pupil' (top). The consequent reconstruction of self-images (some may become anti-school, or take up outside interests, e.g. hobbies), is a compensa-

5. See *New Society* (1973); Talbot and Henson (1954).
6. Interestingly, he explains school phobia as the outcome of disconfirmed high expectations. Like the psychologies of school phobia, Lacey's sociology accepts the immutability of the social structure.

tion not just for the school structure but for the meritocratic social dream, and our unequal form of competition (capital-based) as a whole. The majority of young have to compensate for denigration and denial (which is why the home can provide a cushion). The film *Kes* made this point admirably clear. Strategies and interests are the only way to make sense of an insensible world.

The school refuser, then, acts in accordance with a *realistic* rather than fantastic or rationalized assessment of his social position. Inability to negotiate the school years in our society *is* a sentence to living death and self-stagnation or decomposition: failure drastically reduces life chances outside school. Absence of strategy removes the only possibility of making sense of his own repression. It is in this sense that the phobic differs from the anti-school and the pro-school young. The intensity of emotion he shows at this discovery signifies the extent to which others rationalize the tension of the psychological and the social world. Mental equanimity is most commonly retained by the acceptance of specific values. (Yet to accept a superior power, as religious experience shows us, is to betray the breadth of humanly created happiness.)

Why do some children crumble and others not before this massive pressure? We can only understand this when we contrast the phobic's with others' strategies. The pro-school child is secure in the harmony between the dominant culture and his personal orientation; he is well socialized, content until his world-values militate against him (when 'success' criteria rule him a failure). The anti-school child, on the other hand, rejects certain attributes of school (e.g. boredom) and acts accordingly: he may find meaning in becoming a classroom comic, truanting, taking up hobbies, switching off, etc. Those whom psychology has passed off as school phobic are neither of these types. They are in a kind of value vacuum, neither positively for or against school, with no security of policy and hence no shred of psychological unity. To understand this we have to observe the child's immediate world.

It is a commonplace of both clinics and written reports that the school phobic and both or either of the parents are weak and ineffectual people. Superficially, this may be true, but just as the full import of the whole category of school phobia has been veiled, so has the individual's experience. First, weakness is relative to others'; it is not a private characteristic. Secondly, what the psychologists have depicted as a total character-ailment in certain cases, to my knowledge, is the outcome of the parental weakness before particular demands of their children. In short, the attribute is situation–person specific. Thirdly, as far as many of these children are concerned, their parents do not give strong positive evaluation for *any* courses of action. The parents are distant and accommodating, even laissez-faire, all of which, to an authoritarian, is weakness. Thus when the child takes a strong exception to something at school, or when the child feels swamped by the new and large comprehensive after a small, cosy primary school, or whatever, the home atmosphere and the parental ambivalence do not encourage a return to school. Nor do they prevent the initial withdrawal. The child who has made this unexpectedly positive act (in view of the internalized acceptance of school noted above) surprises the parents who react anxiously, or in a fashion the child does not expect. The spiral thus begins, which may end with them or teachers turning to 'experts' with the misleading question: what is wrong with this child? The home's early cushioning or ambivalence can only be said to cause the refusal if all is seen from a psychologistic standpoint. For us, however, the act symbolizes and is made intelligible by an awareness of the separation of the individual child from 'society'. The refuser faces the social wall (rules), experiences anomie (where am I?) and is frightened (not necessarily in that order). Thus the behaviourist view of school refusal as a failure to learn correctly is near the mark, but an inversion of the truth. This failure can only be understood in the light of the assumption of the *moral* correctness of obedience to norms (even presuming we could agree on what those norms are, which depends upon political philosophy and who you are, etc.). Hence, intentionality and its absence are central to my account. The so-called school phobic unlike the partially intentional non-attender (the 'truant') has received no positive direction from his early experiences (such as anti-school parents) with which to wrench his being from the abyss which a structuring social order imposes. For this reason, socialization is a socially relative experience, and can only be described structurally. We can now understand why all therapies have a high success rate (and why some resist therapy). A 'cure' is the reimposition of psychological order to correspond with the social order defined by the dominant culture. I have myself observed at one clinic that the refuser who is 'really' cured is the one who comes to believe that return to school is unavoidable (the lesser of two evils), or better still actually *desirable*. The recurrent 'phobic' (for psychologists) is he or she who sees little point in going but has not adopted a strong position either way; the unhappiness (which psychologists use as a justification for intrusion) is an expression of the tottering between unhappy rebellion and miserable subjection. It is to capture this experience, the key to the child as far as I can see, that I describe it as a state of existential (and value) vacuum.

Obviously, this is my account of those that I have witnessed. I can only claim that it makes more sense of more of the social world of the school young than previous accounts have. By 'de-contextualizing' the experience of the refuser, other writers, I suggest, have frozen it. They thus freeze the fluidity of real life. The meaning of the episode in question thus eludes them. They can do no more than reimpose the ordinances which have thrown up the child before them, and impose a false correspondence between private and public worlds. School phobics stand stripped of the totality of their social world, and thus the relationship between the psychological (in particular experience) and the social forces has been radically misrepresented.

Ramifications: child status, independence, individual cases, the psychologist

All the set explanations, as we saw, place considerable emphasis upon the idea of independence, yet both practically and ideally it is socially and historically relative. Mead and Calas (1955) nicely describe how official Russian prescriptions for the ideal child character and behaviour in the family suited what the governmental élite wanted the social system to be. The interrelationship of ideology, practice, social conditions and power structure is not restricted to the case of the blatant control of the Soviet system. In our society it is more subtly done. It can be shown for example that experts (the people technocrats of an anti-human culture) give different advice on child-rearing within even comparatively short spaces of time, and that these reflect shifts within the social world as a whole (Bronfenbrenner, 1958; Newsom and Newsom, 1974). Such developments underline in what way culture presides over nature. (Remember how the culture–nature and man–society dichotomies are themselves cultural/social constructs.) It is not possible, then, to accept the view of childhood as being a 'natural' period of 'natural' innocence or striving for independence. Socialization, the entry and passage into socially constituted rules and meanings, is what defines the characteristics a person has after birth. Potentialities (powers) are open to control by others. Infants cannot fend for themselves. But at what point does care stop being biologically necessary and in what direction are control and dependency to face? School is not biologically necessary at five years, but a socially rationalized necessity. I have pointed out some of the sideshoots of its present construction.

The status of the young in crucial respects is inferior to that of others in our society. The child is in a sense *owned* by others. Power, the concomitant of ownership, resides with parents, schools, churches, the therapist, and is celebrated and enshrined in law by the *in loco parentis* principle (Berger, 1972). The common view that children these days have more freedom than previous generations obscures the fact that they are still dependent upon others. Control and training for life are shared with the family, by others, notably the school. Peers, as group manipulators know and use only too often, are influential. The dependency–independency im balance, then, has only been translated into contemporary terms, and i disguised as progress *per se*. We are all, as the psychologies of schoo phobia did not let on, over-dependent, protected and unable to separate Growing up does not bring freedom but subjugation. Independence as the therapies offer it, is nothing but enough to go to school, to mee other children (provided they are a 'healthy' influence) or to take up a steady job (a criterion of cure for those school phobics who become too old while under therapy to return to school). These psychological criteria are only meaningful insofar as they adopt a conservative view of life. My analysis has sought, therefore, to open up what the psychologies have as sumed and kept closed.

Clearly, children are not automata, and clearly there are those who benefit from the structure of school, the break from home, the company, the competition. I merely claim that factually these phenomena are by no means universal and that what vibrant culture childhood encompasses (such as the Opies (1959) have shown) is in reaction to and expresses their internalization of domination.

By reanalysing school phobia, my account goes further and questions the very term itself and its increasingly wide application. Many children so described are merely nascently anti-school who covertly see little point in going to school or hate a high-handed teacher. (Often criticisms by the young are dismissed which may in fact be substantiated; some staff *are* arrogant and nasty or pick on particular people.[7])

By stressing the historical and social relativity of meaningful acts I have emphasized the consistency of certain structural attributes of social and mental life. Situations and psychological representations change, and hence so do notions of actions' causes. We cannot assume, as the psychologists have, that what they see as the same behaviour events are psychologically or causally similar. When a child referred for refusal arrives at a clinic, clinging to the mother, showing emotional stress, this does not mean that the child is school phobic (as the set explanation means it). The behaviour may be an outcome of and reaction to concern shown by authorities about what in the child's mind was only an interim withdrawal. Many non-attenders get away undetected or, if they are 'trouble-makers', teachers are relieved at their absence and turn a blind eye. It would be reasonable, too, to expect investigators to ask themselves and the child why he refused to go at this point in time, when he had previously attended school.

7. See, as an example, Lazarus, Davison and Poltfka (1965).

From the psychologies of school phobia we receive no indication of the variety of personal experiences which may bring on the sense of direction-lessness: new school, contrast of styles of education, increased pressure, troubles at home, doubts about self-identity.... The list is potentially end-less and varies according to the child and especially age. Thus, the catch-phrase of school-phobia explanation – the child is 'not so much a school-phobic as a mother-phile' – seriously mistakes the child's preference for home (where else is there to go?) as an obsession about mother. Young people older than, say, twelve can and do, in such conditions, reject home and take to the road.

In restricting possibilities and freedom on paper, in the laboratory and in practice, the psychologies of school phobia mirror wider social realities. By pointing up the tenuous nature of their message, we see the tenuous nature of social cohesion. The psychologies fail not only in that they are bad depictions of what really happens, but in that they paper over the cracks; they see no other viable culture. Thus, by subverting a definition of the problem, in a small way we subvert the rationale for a whole way of life. The absurd obscurantism, false representation, professional self-congratulation and segmentation of the psychological, the social, the economic and the political (which creates the Great Mystery: how do they connect?) reflect and encourage the indefensible, the anti-human. To des-cribe psychological phenomena only psychologically is a strategy premis-ed upon non-psychological ideology. Common sense cannot dictate to us, for it too, as we have seen in the case of childhood and education (school), is an historical flux.

If we are not to be involved in disguised human control, then we must accept the lesson that unwitting 'testers' like the school refuser offer us. My own experience as their observer has led me to question not just other writers, but myself. What was I doing being another spy? Why ask 'Why do these children not go to school?' and why not ask 'Why do the vast majority of the population *go* to school?' (Only Pallister's article on the situation in 1850 has done this!) Why do not more children refuse? Why not investigate non-attendance among teachers (NCCL, 1972)? If the analysis points to the existence of subtle and overt domination, why inves-tigate the dominated at all? Is childhood the best time or school the best place to learn (what learning?) at all (Freire, 1972)? By considering the psychologist's assumption: from learning follows action, I have learned that the dialectic of thought and action can be reversed; the most important 'testing' is not conceptual, but active and beyond the lab or clinic. I no longer accept the view of culture as an inevitable matter of acquiescence (so clear to the school refuser), but substitute for it a political everyday con-

ception of culture as the struggle for heightened freedom and consciousness. I criticize the psychologies for denying and holding back this task.

The school phobic as previously constituted stands doubly alienated:
his alienated experience is reinforced by the psychologists (but not them
alone). When the interpenetration of psychological reality and contemporary social conditions is seen for what it is, the psychologies of school
phobia (like social psychology) disappear. The truth of this conflict between commonly accepted representation of human reality and its real
substance is a direct reflection of the conflict between the needs of individuals and those of society (whose society?); between *need* externally
imposed and internalized, and *desire* personally enacted with, towards or
against others. Practising psychologists (of all types) face a paradox: my
analysis generates (or substantiates) a call for the fermentation of unrest
and action against exploitation by the powerful, and the critical appraisal
and active questioning of authority; in the case of children in school this
means a demand for the end of compulsion in schools, particularly with
regard to attendance itself. In short, psychologists question themselves.
They bring out their self-doubt, rather than bury it in methodology or professionalism. It is my shame that I have seen this through the suffering of
others. A truly social psychology dissolves the myth of a 'pure' or self-
sufficient psychology.

References

ARIÈS, P. (1962), *Centuries of Childhood*, Cape; Penguin, 1973.

BERGER, N. (1972), 'The child, the law and the state', in L. Adams *et al.*, *Children's Rights*, Panther.

BRONFENBRENNER, U. (1958), 'Socialization and social class through time and space', in E. Maccoby *et al.*, *Readings in Social Psychology*, Holt, Rinehart and Winston.

COVENEY, P. (1967), *The Image of Childhood*, Penguin.

Department of Education and Science (1972), *Education: A Framework for Expansion*, HMSO.

EYSENCK, H., and RACHMAN, S. (1963), 'The application of learning theory to child psychiatry', in J. Howells (ed.), *Modern Perspectives in Child Psychiatry*, Oliver & Boyd.

FREIRE, P. (1972), *Cultural Action for Freedom*, Penguin.

KAHN, J., and NURSTEN, J. (1968), *Unwillingly to School*, Pergamon.

KLEIN, E. (1945), 'The reluctance to go to school', *Psychoanalytical Study of the Child*, vol. 1, pp. 263–80.

LACEY, C. (1970), *Hightown Grammar*, University of Manchester Press.

LAZARUS, A., DAVISON, G., and POLTFKA, D. (1965), 'Classical and operant factors in the treatment of a school phobic', *J. abnorm. Psychol.*, vol. 70, pp. 225–9.

LITTMAN, R. (1961), 'Psychology: the socially indifferent science', *Amer. Psychol.*, vol. 16, pp. 232–6.

MEAD, M., and CALAS, E. (1955), 'Child-training ideals in a post-revolutionary context: Soviet Russia', in M. Mead and M. Wolfenstein, *Childhood in Contemporary Cultures*, University of Chicago Press.

NCCL (1972), *Rights of Children*, Discussion Paper no. 6, National Council for Civil Liberties.

New Society (1973), 'Yes Sir, No Sir', 18 January.

NEWSOM, J., and NEWSOM, E. (1974), 'Cultural aspects of child-rearing in the English-speaking world', in M. Richards (ed.), *The Integration of a Child into a Social World*, Cambridge University Press.

OPIE, I., and OPIE, P. (1959), *The Language and Lore of Schoolchildren*, Oxford University Press.

PALLISTER, R. (1969), 'The determinants of elementary-school attendance about 1850', *Durham Research Rev.*, vol. 5, no. 23, pp. 384–98.

PINCHBECK, I., and HEWITT, M. (1969), *Childhood in English Society*, Routledge & Kegan Paul.

ROWNTREE, J., and ROWNTREE, M. (1968), 'Youth as a class', *Inter. Socialist J.*, vol. 25, pp. 25–58.

RUBINSTEIN, D. (1969), *School Attendance in London 1870–1904*, Papers in Economic and Social History, no. 1, University of Hull.

Ruskin History Workshop (1974), *Childhood*, Ruskin Essays in Social History, no. 20.

TALBOT, M., and HENSON, I. (1954), 'Pupils psychologically absent from school', *Amer. J. Orthopsych.*, vol. 24, pp. 381–90.

11 A Bias in the Social Psychology of Prejudice
Godfrey Harrison

Origin

Paul came over and, like many two-year-olds would, he began 'Mummy, . . .'. The woman on the other end of the park seat stood up and moved to another close by; it was just as sun lit. The brown child and his parents had the bench, a long one, all to themselves.

The incident reported above is not a scientifically acceptable observation. More than most data it is compatible with other hypotheses. My hypothesis here is that there is discrimination against mixed families. Again the hypothesis is, of course, *post hoc*. I have no control group to cite and the sample is small and biased.

We started our family, Ann and I, by adopting an ethnically Anglo-Indian boy born, in Britain, four months before. We had done so believing that in years to come some awkwardnesses might arise, but that nothing beyond the usual problems of developing children would trouble us, at least for a little while. Curiously enough this bland confidence had something of a beating by the time Paul was two. By the time he was six Paul had had something of a beating, more than once, and on similar grounds. One gets a shade despondent to hear a son remark of his brother, 'I wish I was pink like him. They wouldn't hit me then.' Perhaps that is enough unscientific observation.

I am pink-skinned, a man, of middle-class English origins, in a secure job with good pay and in a line that rarely involves overt social derision and tolerates, still, a few eccentricities. All of which has made me rather surprised on becoming an object of prejudice, usually by association but still as a recipient rather than as a mistakenly involved bystander. Naturally I went and read some books about prejudice – I still do. Some of the ones that seemed authoritative were precious little help. They told me about the likely personality characteristics of the people whose actions hurt us, but not how to dissuade them. I read, too, that anthropometric differences between groups of human beings generally did seem to be accompanied by psychological differences; when I looked in other works I found this denied. How authoritative were such books? There were some books and papers that did tell me something about the experience of prejudice as well as about its existence. It was welcome to know a little more than that there is Dettol on the shelf and that bruises will heal. Not many of the books that I found helpful were written by psychologists. This is remarkable because psychologists have written at length about prejudice. This piece is written because if I don't like an imbalance I had better try to redress it; because if I suspect that the main themes presented in courses in social psychology could stand additions from other fields I may as well indicate some of the other possibilities.

Theme

Mostly my intention is to point out some aspects of people and our lives that I think would help us in comprehending the social psychology of prejudice and in reducing discrimination. I am writing from the point of view that such comprehension and reduction are aspects of a single enterprise.

There is no claim here that success in that enterprise is guaranteed. The albino young of some animals may always be set upon by others of their own kind having a more normal colouring. It is not even beyond belief that in human societies with far fewer and smaller social and economic inequalities than any contemporary society there might still be occasional persons who will show a pervading and active antipathy to all those who share some actual or imagined characteristic – like being left-handed, or having a liking for yellow clothes. Should there be some refractory, obdurate and even immutable prejudices they would give no proof that all, or even most, prejudiced discrimination is inevitable and open to description but not to alteration.

We cannot sensibly even suspect that some prejudices may be ineradicable until we have tried to be rid of them and failed. As is often said in psychology 'That is an empirical problem.' Questions about such problems must be put before their particular answers can be seen to exist, let alone applied. Social psychologists have asked many questions about what characterizes those who are prejudiced and likely to discriminate irrationally and harshly against people in other groups simply on the basis of that group membership. The answers to those questions form part of current social psychology. Studies that compare and contrast the degree of particular abilities or traits possessed by those in different groups have often been attempted and been seen as germane to the psychology of prejudice. The interest in such studies is illustrated by recurrent controversies over differences in the scores on intelligence tests which are achieved by Black Americans and by Americans descended from Europeans. By comparison with the number of questions asked in the two areas just cited the number that have been asked by psychologists on what it is like to a victim of prejudice is small. Later in this essay I shall discuss some work that suggests that the relatively small number of studies of the victims of prejudice in their own terms is also a regrettably small number if the hope of ending discrimination is to be realized, and indeed if social psychology is to have a chance of being representative of its subject matter. (I take this matter to be: what it is to be one person living among others).

Before considering that work it is worth noting that particular topics, like the one of IQ scores cited above, do not always occur at any random time but may reflect both the state of knowledge within a discipline and central issue in the societies in which they are made. Recognizing that specific events have their unique or rare qualities as well as more general ones is important in studying prejudice.

There are numerous manifestations of prejudice and attendant discrimination. There is a need to look at the various situations in which prejudice is manifest. The explicit anti-semitism of the Roman Catholic Church of the Middle Ages had different roots from the even more explicit anti-semitism of the Third Reich. There is a distinction between, for example, an aversion to usury and the view that nationality can guarantee superiority in all things (or an inferiority just as encompassing). The responses of the victims of these two institutions and their experiences of anti-semitism were different – if all unsought in both cases. The differences between the Church and the Reich clearly are more than a history of over 1000 years and the intention to endure for that period and it would be stupid to pretend otherwise, even if some neat theory must be discarded to avoid the stupidity.

It seems likely that any full account of imperialism will pay close attention to the outrageous racism that it has both engendered and been sustained by. And yet it is difficult to equate imperialism with Nazism. The anti-semitism of countries that have, or have had, empires has commonly been more apparent within the country than outside.

The worst excesses of prejudice against black or brown people have been in their countries. The problems of such people when they have emigrated to imperialist, or allegedly post-imperialist, countries are grave but often less appalling than in their own(-ed) countries. Certainly the Metropolitan Police have shot dead non-European immigrants, and British police often seem to have failed to treat black or brown people with the same consideration they generally afford their horses. (There are reports from the NCCL (1971) which support this assessment.) These assaults are bad but they are less widespread than the comparable or worse ones by the police, for example, in colonial Kenya and Hong Kong. The point is not that injustices in metropolitan and colonial countries cannot be related to each other but that their relationship is not one of simple equality.

There are other varieties of prejudice and they can be found in numerous situations. The homosexual men who were murdered in 1936 by Spaniards, claiming of all things to be anarchists, were victims of a prejudice, legitimated there in the so-called, and far from explicit, Law of Nature. Walloons in Belgium have been attacked by Flemish-speakers, and Tamils in Ceylon and in Southern India have suffered on similar grounds, for they too speak a minority language.

It is even less easy to relate prejudices against the physically handicapped to any straightforwardly political theory of prejudice. To appreciate such prejudices notice how a blind person is addressed when in a group who are not well acquainted but do know that the blind member has a particular companion. A very common form of prejudice there shows itself in inquiries that are phrased, 'Does he . . . ?' or 'Does she . . . ?'. As many blind people hear perfectly well they tend to resent being addressed in the third person, especially when they hear others present being asked ' Do you . . . ?'. Jane Arden once asserted that prejudice took away the completeness of a person's humanity by concentrating on one aspect only as well developed and worth attention. She remarked on the great intellectual qualities ascribed to all Jews, the vigorous sexuality ascribed to all Negroes, and perhaps the enormous patience ascribed to the handicapped takes on a similarly double-edged universality.

Politics and sociology and kindred topics clearly need to be included in a thorough account of prejudice in its many forms but it seems improbable they they can individually provide such an account. The same limitation seems certain to apply to any single study.

Illustration

We are now, probably, at a point where the attack on the bias in the social psychology of prejudice can be made directly. In general, discussions of prejudice are little concerned with synthesis, or with a structure that attempts to inter-relate varieties of available evidence. Anybody who says that to try such a structuring would take one into the realms of grand theory and should be avoided because it becomes unreadable is not only a follower of C. Wright Mills, they are probably right – today. It may be that one basis for the correctness of the mentioned criticism is the reliance on a few kinds of evidence and a disinclination to develop sources of other kinds. For their part social psychologists have often declined to accept individuals as foci for their interests, rather they average over groups –

Illustration **193**

and this when they clearly stress that groups are more than individuals brought together. As indicated earlier social psychology can be about what it is like to be one person among others. A person integrates his, or her, experiences into a conceptual world and draws on that world to structure his, or her, experiences. If we turn to the survivors of prejudice there is a hope that their lives will distil for us what they have experienced. This simple hope is obviously full of holes because at best we can approach only the survivors. When Mary McCarthy reviewed John Hersey's stringently factual account of the bombing in *Hiroshima* (1946) she remarked that 'he should have interviewed the dead'. Thinking of the survivors of prejudice I do not want to commend or emulate inquiries exemplified by the cold-blooded science of Americans with medical training who examined the survivors of the atomic blasts in Japan and then retired simply to write their reports of the observable damage to people. (I know it is more common to term damage to people 'injury' but that use here sounds incongruous, for injury is what the medically trained usually treat and in these cases there was no treatment although there was damage to people.)

People in exploited and hostile situations that constitute their readily available world have not been entirely without voices and these inform those outside, and seem sometimes to help those in such situations. Some illustrations of such studies may indicate the strength of the approach. It is worth noting that some examples are almost incidentally revealing for psychology. The Trachtenberg System is a way of doing mental arithmetic that has attracted some attention recently. The system was apparently invented to help its author remain sane while a prisoner of the Nazis. There are studies much more directly on such survival. One is by a fairly well-known psychologist: Bruno Bettelheim. He described his experiences and observations in Dachau and Buchenwald in *The Informed Heart* (1970); more recently he has written a very different book, *Children of the Dream* (1971), which is about growing up on a kibbutz. I do not think the two books are equally successful but they each exemplify one method; presenting what people in some institution offer of themselves. This presentation is made in a context of facts and theoretical frameworks that the people may not know at all but which serves to make their experiences more understandable to others. There is a stress on unity in this approach, allowing loose ends perhaps, but not running off a list of observations sequentially and then concluding. The discussion in *The Informed Heart* of how to increase one's hope of survival, or unintentionally to reduce it, when encountering Gestapo corporals illustrates not only the possibility of adaptation in bleak circumstances but the need to admit new realities, however diabolical. It may seem absurd to think of some victim of concentration camps as ill-advised but Bettelheim's account of one prisoner makes it almost acceptable. This man was quite as unjustly imprisoned as any and he was unable to accept the implications of the differences in his life in the camp from his life outside it. Indeed he continued to believe he could still be a person of some influence. He offered to make things easier for a prison guard once the former state of society was re-established. This offer did him no good but the exchanges between some other prisoner and their guards did sometimes help them live longer. These more fortunate prisoners did not necessarily join themselves to the regime that terrorized them, but neither did they respond to Dachau as a transient nightmare from which they would certainly return to the light of day. Jehovah's Witnesses seemed to survive better than members of most groups that the Gestapo persecuted; an ability that Bettelheim tries to throw light on.

That concentration camps, and their like, are vile is quite obviously beyond denial and that some people did, and do, survive such horrors in any way at all is both remarkable and a tribute to those people. In one way it is easy to understand the response: these horrors are over now, forget them and let their survivors pick up what they can of their lives with what help they can get and we can afford. This kind of response would make even more sense if there were no more prisoners, especially political prisoners, but there are still people held arbitrarily, in brutal places, by vicious institutions and regimes. For as long as (or, perhaps, if) any of us are prepared to challenge, at whatever level, these inhumanities then we need to look at how people have managed to survive. And this, at the least, because we may need to try also.

The ordeals and experiences that Bettelheim discussed are ones with very small hope and do not affect a very large proportion of people, although one would be too many. There are other manifestations of prejudice which are very cruel and more widespread. Many of these rest on racism against people of African, or partly African, origin or descent. It is not because of any inclination to condone or forget the fascist regimes of Southern Africa that the studies considered below concentrate on people, situations and studies in the Americas.

The selection made here reflects rather the greater available number of American psychologists and works concerned with prejudice. Before turning to the kinds of work that I think could well be followed by far more psychologists, it is worth commenting that the bias I am opposing is very noticeable in English-language studies of prejudice. They deal with subjects through questionnaires or in laboratories and while certain socio-economic, or demographic, data may be included in these studies the development of particular people into exponents of racism, or to becoming its victims, is an uncommon approach. Even where it can be found a

Illustration **195**

psychoanalytic framework may have been invoked and this unfortunately will cut off the authors of such studies from a large readership. (The origin of this schism need not be gone into here.)

I have already dropped my own brick on the edifice of questionnaire studies; it was published in 1967. As it was made of paper like they all are the heap only grew more littery. My disenchantment with the predominance of these efforts crystallized in 1968 in thinking over a seminar I had attended. The seminar considered the application of signal-detection theory to accuracy in recognizing the Jewishness, or otherwise, of people whose faces were photographically presented to students. There are theoretical reasons why one might wish to distinguish whether people who recognize faces as typical of a particular group of humans are, in fact, objectively accurate, or simply over-inclusive in their use of a way of grouping people. A precise analysis of this kind of query can be made using something called the theory of signal detection. From the data that he obtained Adrian Simpson was able to show that the theory could be used without doing anything violating some mathematical rules that need to hold. Once the theory had been applied the measures it gave could be compared with those from questionnaire measures of anti-semitism. The outcome of the comparison was that the association of the results from the two kinds of measure was trivial. In discussing these results some other data were mentioned that also related to prejudice: the number of broken windows in Sheffield shops owned by Pakistanis, and the number of fires in Washington DC following the fatal shooting of Martin Luther King. Adrian Simpson acknowledged the huge gap and expressed his doubts about the likely usefulness of remote studies when urgent events were happening. This was rather welcomed by those of us who had extended the discussion because not everybody there seemed to think our comments could be other than negative. I mention this because if I am arguing against a bias it should be taken as clear that a balance is what I seek, not an alternative imbalance. It is not at all impossible that something that would strike many people as interesting could come from studies based on questionnaires and careful mathematical analyses. The differences in attitudes to the arrival of Ugandan Asians in various regions of the UK was assessed by questionnaire methods at various times after their coming and the decline in hostility to the immigrants interested many people. It may have encouraged them, too. To stop all such studies would arguably be to reduce freedom. Unhappily the freedom to pursue other approaches has either been little pursued or is absent. When this freedom has been taken up the results have been interesting, complementary to other findings, and sometimes even immediately useful.

There are certainly more than five books that invite explicit reference but that small selection will have to serve for present purposes. In Richard Wright's *Black Boy* (1970) he describes his life up to the time when, in his 'teens, he has left the rural American South for a northern city. The perspective that is thrown on being young among racists is one that admittedly has the weaknesses of an autobiographical account but it also has all the strengths. The responses to persecution and indignity that Wright describes extend to topics on which controlled or even quantitative work is not easily possible, if indeed undertaken at all. Sometimes we can see that a numerical statement might just be irrelevant to the situation in which it originated. This comes out in the description Wright gives of 'going forward' during a service in an Evangelical Revival, which is a key theme in his sixth chapter. To know that twenty-seven, or forty-one, or eighteen, people went forward would be to know a different part of what was happening at that fevered service. The social-psychology interest in his account is one that complements and informs other work on conformity and the achievement of conversions. It adds to laboratory studies like those of Asch (1955), and also to more physiologically based, if historically articulated, writings like Sargent's (1957). Beside this interest in such culturally independent terms as conversion or conformity – for that is what social science would lead us to accept these terms to be – there is another interest in Wright's book. It is the opportunity to know more about what it is like to be black and oppressed.

The other explicitly autobiographical book in the five cited here is *The Autobiography of Malcom X* (1970). It, too, spells out details about how to survive and it also presents one view of the roots of black people's movements that faced their state in America. It outlines the need for assertion that was a prime force in the development of the Black Muslims. This assertion was of a distinct world view, of an organization dependent on efforts from those who shared that view, and who were prepared to say to oppressed, exploited and miserable people that their plight was not of their making but their progress could be. The practical success of the Black Muslims in, for example, breaking people off a heroin addiction depended on therapists who were themselves former addicts and, like parallel efforts, it helped thousands of people.

In Bobby Seale's book *Seize the Time* (1970) there is a watchword: 'Check out the facts'. This stress is found in other books by militant black Americans. It would be interesting to know how much help studies by psychologists have been to groups of people who suffer serious discrimination. Most directly, have psychologists written so that the information they have can be used by people who need to set about solving their own problems? It is not that psychologists have been without concern to end

Illustration **197**

prejudice – at least some have had that aim. The problem is the style of reports which are aimed either at the world at large, as long as it reads learned journals, or are aimed at agencies of established power. Now this latter tactic sometimes helps to ameliorate the effects of racism: the evidence of psychologists to the Supreme Court of the United States did contribute to the ruling on the illegality of segregated education and that was the ruling that bodies like the National Association for the Advancement of Coloured People were seeking. (Geoffrey Pearson points out in another chapter in this volume that the evidence of experts from 'helping' professions has its curiosities. Fortunately, in my view, the 1953 decision on the illegality of segregated education is one that psychologists who oppose racism can cite without shame.) Perhaps the question is when not to go to agencies of established power but to groups of small power, instead.

It is difficult to believe that Fanon gave a complete answer to the reluctance of psychologists, and other social scientists, too, to join in efforts formulated by the oppressed rather than in those proposed by the agencies of established power. Fanon wrote, in *The Wretched of the Earth* (1967), of the small numbers of graduates from colonized countries who returned home with a clear commitment to deal with problems of national liberation in terms congruent with the lives that their compatriots lived. He remarked that these educated homecomers got up to tell the peasants the truth but that the peasants were the truth. What would it mean if graduates are reluctant to put their knowledge with the knowledge of the oppressed? Could it really be that those in either group know so little that is relevant to the struggle that the other group can ignore it? I do not believe it – even if I do say that the social psychology of prejudice has a bias. I suspect, too, that Fanon did not believe it, either. He learnt his psychiatry in Europe. His work had been in a French-administered hospital in Algeria. When he resigned from it and joined the insurrection against French colonial rule he did not forget his psychiatry: he put his knowledge to work in another context. He did something else, too: he included a collection of case studies as an appendix to one of his major books and thereby sought to show why he advocated the views of revolt that are developed in *The Wretched of the Earth*. You may dismiss the political thesis, but whether you do, or not, the case studies are startling and afford further illustrations of the lives of the oppressed.

Not all of us need to take up arms in the same way as Fanon. Kenneth Clark did not. He has pursued the studies summarized in *Dark Ghetto* (1965), and other writings, partly within an academic setting. Among his most striking work has been the investigation of identity in black children. In 1947, with his wife, he reported how these children preferred pink dolls to brown ones, a preference they shared with Caucasian children. In England, in 1971, Milner has reported somewhat comparable preferences among the children of black – or brown – immigrants. In taking his approach to the situation of blacks, Clark considered part of the lives of the oppressed, and not the description of the prejudiced, as his first interest. He took methods that reflected mainstream psychology in the 1940s and used them with other people who were like him in at least one important way. *Dark Ghetto* can be seen as a development of that theme. It is a book which in some of its approaches resembles Bettelheim's, as Clark acknowledges. If Clark's preparedness to relate his findings to the culture within which they were obtained is like Bettelheim's other things about the books differ. Even in New York there is still some chance of making life less desperate and a book may help realize that chance; Dachau, as an institution, had ended before anyone had any chance to write books on it. Clark had room to be dispassionate if interested; Bettelheim in a concentration camp, and Fanon in an insurrection, had, at best, far less room. The checking out of facts is one suitable application of the detailed, repetitive, quantitative and systematic procedures that are propounded in psychology departments. Facts alone rarely win struggles but in all battles information is worth having. Clark does more than find facts by methods that are scientifically acceptable. He puts his facts in a wider setting and analyses the value systems they both arise from and determine. Perhaps he is not without a bias (that the plight of ghetto dwellers is of first importance) but he is without the bias that I am arguing against and sometimes there is the hope that two imbalances can tend to equilibrium. ...

Clark took his knowledge into a ghetto of people who were like him. As a startling example of an own subject-control study (N = 1) we can cite John Howard Griffin's *Black Like Me* (1969). Griffin is pink-skinned normally. In his experiment he altered his pigmentation and shaved his hair. For weeks he was a black. His report of his experiences during those weeks is a check on what others report of being black. The success of his best-selling book has an irony. When a black/white man wrote about the changes he had experienced vast numbers of people, many pink-skinned, were impressed. It is not easy to believe that Richard Wright, say, knew less about being a Negro than Griffin did and Wright certainly has a claim to be a greater writer but his impact in the sixties was less widespread. That may be because he was not as topical, and smacked of bygone days. It is only if you believe that all people in any group are intrinsically incapable of accurately presenting evidence about themselves that you will be certain, in the case of American blacks, that Griffin's account must be superior to any from a black person.

Illustration **199**

A direct concern with the lives of people against whom prejudice acts an throw a cold light on contrastive studies which might otherwise seem very plausible. It is not difficult to divide people into two kinds: there are those who divide people into two kinds and those who do not. Many psychologists have made studies that distinguish people into two kinds: male and female, or monoglot and bilingual, or black and white, are the common dichotomies found in contrastive studies, and left-handed and right-handed seems to be another one that is often used. The implications of some of these labellings are considered elsewhere in this book. What is of interest here is a particular way that contrastive studies have been construed. An underlying argument seems to run like this: 'If group X really are poor at behaviour B when compared to group Y then to treat group X accordingly is unexceptionable.' The gravest problem with such a proposition is that it does not rule out any way of treating anybody, and yet there are some practices that are widely accepted as unacceptable ways of treating anybody. Of course, given some values for X and Y and B this conditional statement can be innocuous enough: 'If children who make lots of mistakes in copying from a blackboard are not well able to focus objects at a distance then to offer them the chance of acquiring appropriate contact lenses is unexceptionable.' Other versions with different values of X and Y and B seem more debatable: 'If the travellers cannot lie down fittingly in Procrustes's bed, and Procrustes can, then to ensure that the travellers fit is unexceptionable.' One point here is the lack of chance to decline to play the game if you are a traveller. If you are offered something, for example a pair of contact lenses, you may perhaps decline the offer. There is a version of the above general conditional statement that numerous – often American - psychologists have spent years getting baffled and vehement and less-than-convincing data about. In this version the chance of declining to play is not very great. It goes like this: 'If Negroes score differently on IQ tests from whites then to give them different education is unexceptionable.' Notice that the people using state education have over the years had to take IQ tests. That was a game that had to be played. A version of the conditional statement that little interests psychologists professionally goes: 'If women are less effective at acquiring money than men are, then to change the behaviour of employers is unexceptionable.' Quite clearly that version could be taken to have political implications, but, who knows, perhaps some of the other versions also have such implications.

I have done things to sentences, in these and later versions of what I am calling the conditional statement underlying contrastive studies, that are so various that the kinds of assumptions I am not stating surely must be obvious. This effort to force attention to assumptions that may underlie the contrastive studies will be worthwhile if it indicates how they may decline to examine each of the contrasted groups in its own terms and yet hold a promise of action if positive findings emerge. The promise may be implicit but it is often perceptible. The studies of Negro/white IQ scores show a certain one-sidedness because they decline to use available information about black Americans. There have been recent studies of language and its use by black Americans that show little-known and less-appreciated aspects of their lives. For example, so little was a complete oral tradition of Black folk poetry represented in print that the anthology *Deep Down in the Jungle* (1964) was the first collection of it, and that book was published in 1964 while black Americans had been around for 400 years. More directly germane to the IQ studies was the scant consideration given to the way many black Americans who lived in ghetto areas spoke. The idea that the way people spoke might make it awkward to know what they thought was not much in evidence in studies of IQ scores. (I am not talking about how people think but about the input to and output from their thinking). For some of the people concerned with the under-achievement of black Americans one can see why such omissions should arise. Some very striking targets for their concern were clearly to hand: for example, the horrendous school conditions that ghetto dwellers had to face. To have left the way respondents to tests speak out of discussions of the respondents' scores seems rather more surprising when thinking of psychometricians. One reason for this surprise is because they have considered another version of the conditional statement. It is a rather longer version and goes: 'If people who speak two languages, without first learning one at school, score differently on IQ tests from monoglot speakers, the less-common language should be considered potentially dangerous for children likely to acquire a similar bilingualism.' Psychologists have got pretty baffled and vehement about this longer version of the conditional statement, too. Cognitive development and IQ surely ought to be related and the early mastery of two languages is clearly a matter of cognitive development. This set of inter-relations makes it all the more improbable that the commonly observable differences between standard English (as spoken in America) and non-standard Negro English were not thought of as one possible determinant of IQ score differences. They could have been experimentally studied. Part of my surprise, at the omission mentioned, rests on the thoroughness that has been shown in looking at variables that can affect performance on material used in assessing IQ. For example, the effect of dental treatment on memory span was cited as long ago as 1938, by Blankenship.

One fortunate result of the publicity accorded Jensen's (1969) review

of the IQ scores of Negroes and Whites in the USA was that the socio-
linguist Labov (1972) came to appraise work on the topic and to express
his reservations about its treatment and to offer his views on the under-
achievement of black Americans at school. He was surprised that those
working on the cognitive growth of black children from ghettoes were
less than well-informed about how and when those children spoke.
Happily Labov's trenchant treatment of this kind of difficulty is now much
reprinted and need not be summarized here. What is germane now is to
point out how a contrastive study dealing in IQ scores could be criticized
cogently because the people in one of the contrasted groups were not
appreciated on their own terms. Contrasting people in groups seems an
especially difficult thing to do when you do not know much about their
characteristics which covary with the criterion by which they are assigned
to one group rather than the other. The co-variation of attributes has
had important, if unsought, results for some people. This had happened
on one occasion when the co-variation was so obvious that to ignore
it is easily seen as malevolent or stupid – which perhaps goes to show that
what is easily seen may not always be correct. . . .

A recent Californian court decision directed that any Spanish American
child, in the area of jurisdiction of the court, and assessed as educationally
subnormal (to use the term common in the UK *must* have been assessed
by a competent psychologist and that competent here denoted a command
of Spanish as well as of English and psychology. Following the directive,
the re-assessment of forty-two Spanish Americans from one group of
forty-five was sufficiently improved to allow them to be offered a more
usual education. It may not be clear what the co-variation in this example
is because it comes near to an equivalence: to be Spanish American is
usually to have a knowledge of Spanish as well as of a particular culture.
However, an equivalence of the language(s) and culture(s) of particular
citizens based on the nations of their forebears does not always appear.
There are many Irish Americans who maintain an interest in things Irish
but very few of them speak Irish; equally Afro-Americans rarely use any
language of Africa that was found there before the seventeenth century.
All of which goes to show how misleading labels can be.

Cessation

It is probably clear that I am not enraptured by contrastive studies.
They seem replete with moral and political ramifications alongside
empirical difficulties. Without solving the value or other problems just
indicated we may discern the hint of a summary, among the shadows
and also the squabbles, of contrastive studies on IQ. I make it out to

be this: that any effects of racial origin, or how many languages you speak from infancy, are small indeed compared with other influences that also operate statistically; for example, being a first born, having rich parents, living in a country which accepts that the culture in which you grew up is not without its own strengths.

Psychologists who wish to use their knowledge of psychology as a formal study commonly work for large agencies and develop specialist techniques concerned with circumscribed topics. In getting results that are helpful overall this strategy can be a sensible one. The success of the laws on driving vehicles after drinking alcoholic drinks illustrates that well enough. Very interestingly, on thinking of the virtually universal approval for reducing road accidents, we can still recall the opposition to the enactment of the laws on drinking and driving. There is, almost by definition, a far from universal approbation for the aim of advancing people who are the victims of prejudice. It could just be that taking up circumscribed topics that are important to minorities (other than the very rich) might help those minorities to defeat their oppressors.

I have tried to take up one notion: that the current social psychology of prejudice has a bias in predominantly studying the prejudiced, or how they compare with those whom they injure, and in far less considering the victims of prejudice. This theme is explored here, but no more. I have sought to indicate why we need to remove the bias in the social psychology of prejudice. In brief there are two bases for this suggestion. The lesser basis is in terms of the social psychology of prejudice as an abstracted discipline where the bias guarantees a gap between what we do know and what we might know. I hesitate to summarize the larger basis of the suggestion of bias in the social psychology of prejudice. This reluctance comes from a mistrust of large themes. They are forever snatched up by clear-eyed leaders who zealousy work for a better, brighter world. Instead they make converts from amongst us who, bemused by faith and with troubles unsolved, follow them. We follow them in compelling the unworthy, who do not subscribe to the cause, but only pay for it, to do as they are bid, or die early. The curious thing is that by the time the compelling is crushing the clear-eyed leaders have become the solid dense pillars of a new orthodoxy, and even the themes of health, justice, equality and freedom that they parade become the absurd legitimations of violence and complacency. What I am calling the 'larger basis' for removing the bias in the social psychology of prejudice is not new, and it is not enormous, and, after that last sentence, setting it down should not urge on anyone to cosmic certainty. This larger basis asks, if the prejudiced are recognized as people then why are their victims not equally recognized? And how shall we ever see all that we are, or might be, if we refuse to look, or, to consider what it may mean? We shall be the prisoners of our own narrower conceptions. We shall fail to notice what some people have done in situations that we would believe to be insuperably adverse. These few people have survived and much more, too. They vigorously demonstrate that human beings can be joyful and healthy, and strong and warm, not seeking power separately but celebrating life fully. This larger view is neither against social psychology nor independent of it.

We will, I believe, have a more complete human social psychology if those against whom prejudice strikes, and who are often very eager to utter and to offer their accounts of life, are not shut out, however unintentionally, on the grounds of being against the way things are now, or of some apparent experimental or observational ingenuousness. Social psychology has methods and substance to make the insights and experiences of the victims of prejudice and discrimination more specific and precise – but not meaningless – and it should get on and help. Those who are against oppression need to understand the experiences of its victims: their struggles may be better marshalled if more informed.

References

ABRAHAMS, R. D. (1964) (ed.), *Deep Down in the Jungle*, Folklore Associates, Hatboro, Pennsylvania.

ASCH, S. E. (1955), 'Opinions and social pressure', *Scientific American*, vol. 193, pp. 31–5.

BETTELHEIM, B. (1970), *The Informed Heart*, Paladin.

BETTELHEIM, B. (1971), *Children of the Dream*, Paladin.

BLANKENSHIP, A. B. (1938), 'Memory span: a review of the literature', *Psychol. Bull.*, vol. 35, pp. 1–25.

CLARK, K. B., and CLARK, M. P. (1947), 'Racial identification and preference in Negro children', in G. E. Swanson *et al.*, *Readings in Social Psychology*, Holt, Rinehart & Winston.

CLARK, K. B. (1965), *Dark Ghetto*, Gollancz.

FANON, F. (1967), *The Wretched of the Earth*, Penguin.

GRIFFIN, J. H. (1969), *Black Like Me*, Panther.

HERSEY, J. H. (1946), *Hiroshima*, Bantam.

JENSEN, A. R. (1969), 'How much can we boost IQ and scholastic development?', *Harvard Ed. Rev.*, vol. 39, pp. 1–123.

LABOV, W. (1972), 'The logic of nonstandard English', in P. P. Giglioli (ed.), *Language and Social Context*, Penguin.

MALCOLM X (1970), *The Autobiography of Malcolm X*, ed. A Haley, Penguin.

MILNER, D (1971), 'Prejudice and the immigrant child', *New Society*, vol. 18, pp. 556–9.

NCCL (1971), *Evidence to the Select Committee on Race Relations and Immigration*, vol. 2: *Police/Immigrant Relations*, pp. 618–39, National Council for Civil Liberties.

SARGENT, W. (1957), *Battle for the Mind*, Pan.

SEALE, B. (1970), *Seize the Time*, Arrow.

WRIGHT, R. (1970), *Black Boy*, Cape.

12 Mass Communication and the Construction of Meaning
Graham Murdock

The making and taking of meanings in everyday life

Traditionally social psychology has concerned itself with the forms rather than the contents of social action, and has concentrated on observable behaviour to the neglect of subjective meanings. What mattered was how people's actions looked to the psychologist and not what they meant to the people themselves. In addition, by detaching people from their on-going everyday relationships and encapsulating them within controlled experimental settings, the prevailing methodology effectively isolated the study of action from its appropriate social context. The attempt to redress these imbalances constitutes one of the main departure points for a growing body of recent work both in social psychology, and increasingly in sociology as well. This work attempts firstly to map out the categories and concepts through which people impose meaning on their experience and make sense of their situation; and secondly, to explore the ways in which meanings are constructed, sustained and modified in the course of everyday social interaction.

To the extent that this shift of emphasis opens up a neglected and fruitful field of study it is to be welcomed. At the same time, however, an over-emphasis on subjective meanings and on the immediate situation of interaction can lead to a drastically reduced consideration of the overall social context of action. The authors of one recent text, for example, have argued that 'social structure cannot refer to anything more than members' everyday sense of social structure since it has no identity which is independent of the sense' (Filmer et al., 1972, p. 54). This sort of foreshortened focus by-passes any consideration of the fact that the various settings within which everyday interactions take place are themselves embedded in a wider system of social and symbolic relations erected on the basis of systematic inequalities in the distribution of property and wealth – in short, a social class structure. The dynamics underlying a general economic process such as inflation are immensely complex, and consequently it is scarcely surprising that they 'will frequently be opaque to actors in their everyday lives' (Goldthorpe, 1973, p. 457). However, the fact that people may have an understanding of 'inflation' which is muddled, incomplete, or just plain wrong, does not prevent them from experiencing its consequences very directly in the form of rising prices. Similarly, it is true that when asked many people will tend to deny or devalue the importance of class inequalities. But the fact that 'class' does not seem to be a salient category through which these people make sense of their situation does not mean that class inequalities do not exist or that they do not impinge on their everyday life. On the contrary, whether they acknowledge it or not, a person's class situation as mediated through the kind of job they do and the sort of house and neighbourhood they live in intervenes decisively to determine not only their basic standard of living, but also to circumscribe the nature and range of their social relationships, and their access to systems of meaning. It is this last point particularly which I want to explore in this present paper.

The essential starting point is the recognition that those groups in society which occupy positions of the greatest power and privilege will also tend to have the greatest access to the means of communication with the result that their particular definitions and explanations of the social and political situation will 'tend to become objectified and enshrined in the major institutional orders' (Parkin, 1972, p. 83). Given the pervasiveness of these dominant meanings and their insistent institutional backing, it is scarcely surprising that they should provide at least some of the frameworks and categories through which those on the receiving end of class inequalities make sense of their situation. However, it is one thing to assert that the meaning system of the dominant group provides the dominant meaning system for the society as a whole, but it is quite another to show how this process actually works out in concrete practice. It is at this juncture that a consideration of the role of the mass media in relaying dominant meanings becomes crucial.

The mass media permeate everyday life in two very important ways. Firstly, contact with the various media provides the majority of the population with their dominant leisure activity. Secondly, for most people this contact constitutes their main source of information about, and explanations of, social and political processes, and also a major fund of images and suggestions concerning modes of self-presentation and general life styles. The mass media therefore represent a key repository of available meanings which people can draw upon in their continuing attempts to make sense of their situation and find ways of acting within or against it. At the same time, however, the operation of the media organizations is circumscribed by the general economic and political contexts within which they are embedded, with the result that the range of information, imagery and interpretive frameworks they relay tends to be restricted, repetitive and ultimately consonant with the interests of dominant groups (Murdock and Golding, 1974). The mass media are therefore, simultaneously, both a key resource for the everyday construction of meanings, and a significant constraint on the range and direction of such constructions. This present paper sets out to explore varying levels of this relationship between everyday constructions and contextual constraints, drawing on concrete illustrations from the two main areas of mass-media output: news and entertainment.

There is a considerable body of evidence now accumulating showing that the majority of people get most of their information about general social and political processes from media news coverage. This situation raises two important questions. Firstly, what are the mechanisms through which newsmen come to select certain happenings in the everyday world for processing and presentation as news, and how far do the resulting accounts coincide with, and support, the interests of dominant groups? Secondly, how far does the audience simply take these news accounts as given, and to what extent do individuals and groups differentially situated in the social structure remake these media-relayed meanings, deleting, highlighting and modifying elements in line with localized meaning systems erected on the basis of specific social experiences? These two questions are considered in the next section. The crucial relationship between situated and media-relayed meaning systems is then taken up again in the third section, and explored with reference to recent studies in the field of leisure.

Defining the situation: the reproduction of dominant meanings

So far, I have talked about the dominant meaning system as though it was more or less monolithic. Clearly, this is too simplistic and glosses over the undoubted differences in outlook between the various sectors of the dominant class. Despite these variations, however, dominant groups tend to share a common view of the social and political structure which legitimates their own privileged position and solicits the consent of the less privileged. Essentially, this view entails the denial of permanently structured inequalities in the distribution of wealth and power and the assertion of a 'national' interest as having greater reality than sectional interests; the denial of fundamental conflicts over ends and the assertion that residual disputes over means can be accommodated within the existing machinery of representation; and the labelling of any radical challenge to these assumptions as numerically insignificant, illegitimate, or ephemeral. The mass media in general, and the news media in particular, constitute the major means through which these consensual notions which form the core of the dominant meaning system are reproduced and relayed for public consumption. Of course, it is possible to offer an explanation of this situation in terms of direct manipulation. But this ignores both the relative political autonomy of news organizations and also the fact that news presentations are the outcome of a cumulative process of independent selection and meaning construction on the part of newsmen. Even so, news accounts do tend overall to support the consensual notions underpinning the dominant meaning system. In order to explain this coincidence, however, it is necessary to trace the operation of oblique rather than direct constraints, and more particularly to examine the ways in which the routine practices of news production and the professional assumptions which support them are circumscribed by the general economic and political context within which news organizations are embedded.

Newspapers and news bulletins are inextricably tied to time. They have to reproduce themselves once every twenty-four hours. This means that situations which can be conveniently covered and processed within this time-span are much more likely to become news than situations which take longer to unfold. Thus a strike will probably become news whereas the steady deterioration of working conditions which preceded it will not. This immediacy of news coverage necessarily concentrates attention on the form of events, on what happened and who was involved, to the neglect of the underlying content and causes. As a consequence, radical challenges to consensual assumptions are emptied of their political content and appear as sudden and ephemeral happenings, rather than as manifestations of structured inequalities in the distribution of wealth and power (Murdock, 1973a). In this way news accounts reinforce one of the key consensual notions underpinning the dominant meaning system.

Having selected an event for presentation as news, newsmen face the problem of placing it within a context that will render it meaningful to the majority of their audience. Necessarily, therefore, news presentations must work with meanings and imagery which are both widely available and generally understood. The authors of a recent study of the press coverage of race relations in Britain, for example, have pointed to the frequent evocations of the colonial context. By way of illustration they cite a *Daily Express* story about a group of illegal Indian immigrants discovered hiding in a Bradford cellar, which was headed 'Police Find Forty Indians in "Black Hole"', an immediately recognizable allusion to the 'Black Hole of Calcutta' (Hartmann and Husband, 1971). Once selected, a framework will structure the subsequent coverage. That is, events which are consonant with the basic image are likely to be given prominence whereas contradictory developments will tend to be played down or excluded altogether. A study of the news coverage of a large demonstration against the Vietnam War provides an interesting instance of this process in practice (Halloran *et al.*, 1970). The dominant image of the event was set in an initial story printed some weeks before the demonstration. The story drew an explicit parallel between the expected situation in London and the widely publicized confrontations between police and student demonstrators in Paris and Chicago earlier that year, and predicted widespread street fighting. Subsequent coverage elaborated this basic image of the event. On the day, however, the demonstrations were predominantly peaceful. Nevertheless, the news coverage continued to structure its presentation around the original image, highlighting incidents of confrontation and depicting the police as representatives of the consensus successfully coping with the challenge of militant outsiders.

This habitual presentation of news within frameworks which are already familiar has two important consequences. Firstly, it recharges and extends the definitions and images in question and keeps them circulating as part of the common stock of taken-for-granted knowledge. This, in turn, further increases their chances of selection as frameworks for future stories. Secondly, 'it conveys an impression of eternal recurrence, of society as a social order which is made up of movement but no innovation' (Rock, 1973). Here, again, by stressing the continuity and stability of the social structure, and by asserting the existence of a commonly shared set of assumptions, the definitions of the situation provided in news accounts coincide with and reinforce essential consensual notions. This last coincidence has been further cemented by the recent intensification of the economic pressures acting on news organizations.

In recent years, newspapers, particularly the 'populars', have found themselves competing for a declining readership against a background of spiralling costs. Nor have television companies been immune from economic pressures. Steadily rising costs, coupled with the fact that the audience has now reached its numerical ceiling, have intensified the competition for viewers and made news bulletins important counters in the ratings game. In their ensuing attempts to encapsulate the widest possible audience, news presentations have tended to define the situation in terms of a basic set of generally shared concerns and values, a 'National Interest', which transcends and takes precedence over the interests of specific class groupings. In the case of television news organizations, this fundamentally consensual definition is underscored by their statutory obligation to remain impartial, which means in practice locating the probable truth and the reasonable solution somewhere in the space between the two accredited sides of the case (Hall, 1972). However, as one prominent commercial television executive has noted, 'impartiality does not require putting the case for things which have already earned the disapproval of the majority consensus'.

The incessant pressures of time and the consequent problems of resource allocation and work scheduling in news organizations can be reduced or alleviated by covering 'pre-scheduled' events; that is, events that have been announced in advance by their convenors (Tuchman, 1973). However, one of the consequences of adopting this solution to scheduling problems is to increase the extent of newsmen's dependence on news sources, willing and able to pre-schedule their activities. In effect, this means an increased reliance on élite sources such as official announcements, political speeches and diplomatic exchanges. Thus a symbiotic relationship arises between newsmen and the élites, particularly the political élite, through which readily processable information is exchanged for publicity. This concentration on parliamentary events and political speeches is further reinforced by newsmen's conception of themselves as a 'Fourth Estate', acting as an indispensable channel through which the decisions and doings of the political élites, including their mistakes and miscalculations, are made known to the people at large. By making the debates between legitimated power holders a major category of everyday coverage, however, news presentation serves not only to publicize dominant definitions of the situation, but also to reinforce the key consensual notion that such conflicts as do exist can be adequately accommodated within the existing representative machinery without altering the basic distribution of wealth and power.

The cumulative outcome of the factors outlined here for the definitions of the situation conveyed by news presentations is well illustrated by a recent study of the press coverage given to race relations in four national daily newspapers (*The Times, Guardian, Mirror* and *Express*) during the period from 1963 to 1970 (Hartmann and Husband, 1974). This elongated time-span enables the authors to trace the cumulative build-up of definitions. Throughout the period one of the predominant themes of the coverage was the question of coloured immigration into Britain. The numbers coming in, the legislation introduced to regulate entry, and Enoch Powell's anti-immigration views all figured prominently as categories of news, and served to define coloured people as a problem. This basic problem-definition of the situation was amplified by the coverage of black–white relations within Britain. During the period examined in the study coverage of coloured people's relationship to the major social resources of jobs, housing and education (which constitute the major structural bases of white hostility) became overshadowed by the increasing concentration on specific manifestations of prejudice and conflict and on the legislation introduced to regulate these matters. These findings provide an interesting illustration of the way in which news accounts tend to concentrate on the immediate forms of situations rather than their underlying causes in structured inequalities, and to underscore the ability of existing channels of representation to regulate conflict. Taking the coverage as a whole, the authors conclude that it defined the situation as one in which coloured people presented a problem to be coped with and accommodated within a basically white society. Finally, they argue that by presenting race and racial conflict as significant dimensions of social structure and social process, and by reiterating the communality of interests involved in 'the British Way of Life', the coverage effectively served to deflect attention away from the continuing centrality of class inequalities.

Having outlined the basic framework of meanings underlying the news presentation of race, the authors go on to examine how far this framework underpins the definition of the situation which people actually hold, and how far the meanings relayed by the media are subject to re-negotiation on the basis of situational experience and individual attitude. The information in this part of the study was gathered principally through detailed personal interviews with 415 white, mainly working-class adolescents, aged between eleven and fifteen. To maximize the difference in respondents' personal experience of racial situations, half the sample was drawn from areas of high immigration in the Midlands and West Yorkshire, and the remainder from areas of low immigration in Teesside and Glasgow. Respondents' general definitions of the situation were elicited through a series of open-ended questions, while their personal attitudes towards coloured people were assessed by means of a specially constructed Likert-type scale.

As might be expected, both individual attitude and personal experience did act as mediating influences, leading respondents to emphasize different aspects of the situation. Thus, respondents with a generally hostile attitude towards coloured people tended to stress the fact that they caused or occasioned problems for whites. However, while those in areas of low immigration tended to reiterate this point in very general terms, those living in areas of high immigration were more likely to mention concrete instances such as that blacks were threatening housing opportunities for whites. Similarly, the less hostile respondents were more likely to be aware of the problems faced by coloured people themselves; but whereas those in areas of low immigration framed this situation in general terms, those in areas of high immigration tended to cite specific situational instances of prejudice and discrimination. Individual attitudes and situational experiences did therefore have some mediating influence on respondents' definitions of the racial situation. But, at the same time, and this is the crucial point, the authors argue that their evidence tends to indicate that these mediations operate *within* the general framework of meanings relayed by the news coverage. That is, despite the differences of selection and emphasis, all the respondents shared a common overall definition of coloured immigrants as constituting a 'problem', tended to feel that there were 'too many coming in', and anticipated 'trouble' as a likely consequence.

Over and above the intrinsic interest of the specific findings, this study raises two very important points. Firstly, it underlines the importance of exploring people's overall definitions of the situation, and indicates that no matter how competently done, the conventional kind of attitude scale that form many social psychologists' stock-in-trade cannot adequately tap this key dimension of meaning. Secondly, it points to the centrality of media-relayed frameworks in providing pervasive and authoritative definitions of general social situations, and suggests that the meanings derived from situational experience are more likely to work within rather than against these definitions, modifying and negotiating rather than challenging and rejecting them.

In view of the limitations stemming from the relatively restricted subject matter and the reliance on one-off interviews as a means of mapping respondents' meaning systems, this study should be regarded as suggestive rather than conclusive. Nevertheless, despite these limitations, by highlighting the central role of media-relayed meaning systems in framing people's accounts of general features of social structure and social process, this study marks a decisive advance on previous research, and opens up a key topic for future investigation. In the meantime, however, we can gain some further insight into the relationships between situated and media-relayed meaning systems by examining another key area of media output, entertainment.

Living in leisure

Historically, studies of the media audience have been dominated by the question 'What are the media doing to people?' Consequently, research has mainly concentrated on tracing the effectiveness of particular messages in inducing behavioural responses. Most typically, this has involved investigating the impact of advertising on subsequent purchasing behaviour and assessing the 'effects' of exposure to portrayals of aggression and violence on the later behaviour of children and adolescents. From the 1940s onward, however, a significant counter-tendency has developed, based on a reversal of the standard assumptions. Instead of starting from the message content and tracing the effects of this stimulus on audience responses, these researchers started from the disposition with which individuals approach ed the media. The emphasis therefore shifted from reaction to interaction, and the key question became not 'What are the media doing to people?' but 'What are people getting out of the material they choose to consume?' To the extent that this approach views people's involvement with specific media materials as the result of an active process of selection and meaning construction, it represents a significant and welcome advance over the simplistic stimulus–response models underlying 'effects' studies. However, by focusing on the individual, it effectively abstracts this process from its overall social context, and thereby produces a foreshortened analysis. This 'uses-and-gratifications' approach to the media–audience relationship has recently stimulated a good deal of discussion and research (Katz *et al.*, 1973), and consequently it is necessary to consider it a little more fully.

The leading British exponents of 'uses-and-gratifications' research base their work on the premise that: 'social experience gives rise to certain needs, some of which are directed to the mass media of communication for satisfaction' (McQuail *et al.*, 1972, p. 144). Unfortunately, however, by formulating the problem in this way they create several problems for themselves. The first problem is that the basic 'needs' which supposedly underlie particular patterns of gratifications can only be inferred from an individual's statements about these gratifications themselves. So that if a person claims to like quiz programmes because he finds the close finishes exciting, it is inferred that he has a need for excitement, and that this 'need' leads him to search for excitement in quiz programmes. Clearly this is a circular argument. Secondly, although they explicitly state that individual 'needs' are a product of specific social experiences, in the absence of a sufficient analysis of this experience or of the individual's overall response to it, they are unable to provide a systematic explanation of the considerable variations in media uses indicated by their own findings. In order to provide anything like a satisfactory account of the relationship between people's mass-media involvements and their overall social situation and meaning system, it is necessary to start from the social setting rather than from the individual; to replace the idea of personal 'needs' with the notion of structural contradiction; and to introduce the concept of subculture.

A situation can be viewed as contradictory when elements in it are simultaneously affirmed and denied. Typically, contradictions take the form of gaps between what is supposed to be happening and what is actually happening; between what has been promised and what is actually being delivered. Subcultures are the meaning system and modes of expression developed by groups in particular parts of the social structure in the course of their collective attempt to come to terms with the contradictions in their shared social situation. More particularly, subcultures represent the accumulated meanings and means of expression through which groups in subordinate structural positions have attempted to negotiate or oppose the dominant meaning system. They therefore provide a pool of available symbolic resources which particular individuals or groups can draw on in their attempt to make sense of their own specific situation and construct a viable identity.

Historically, class situations have provided the primary social bases for the generation of subcultures, and locality the main mediation. 'Cockney culture', for example, can be seen as one localized variant of the more general subculture of the urban industrial working class. Over the last fifteen years or so, however, age groupings have assumed an increasing importance as social bases for subcultural styles, and a considerable amount of work has focused on the notion of 'youth culture'. This notion rests on two interlinked assertions. Firstly, that generational membership has displaced social-class situation as the key determinant of social experience and social consciousness; and secondly, that the generational consciousness of adolescents is sustained and expressed through the mass entertainments aimed at the youth market, and more particularly through pop music. By ignoring the continuing and decisive importance of class inequalities, these assertions simplify and distort the process of post-war social change. More particularly, they gloss over the increasingly complex interplay between the youth-oriented symbols and styles relayed by the entertainment media and the situational meaning systems and subcultures of particular class groupings. Rather than displacing class factions, age groups have become an increasingly important mediating context through which contradictions in class situations are experienced and resolved (Murdock, 1973b). It is exactly this complexity which makes youth subcultures particularly relevant to the present argument.

The fullest illustration of the approach advocated here is provided by P. Cohen's (1972) exploratory analysis of youth subcultures among the 'respectable' working class in the East End of London. He points out that whereas previously a boy leaving school could expect to follow his father or uncle into a trade, the decline in the traditional craft industries of the area has reduced the number of openings in skilled jobs. Hence, lacking the necessary academic qualifications for entry into the newer industries, increasing numbers of school leavers have been relegated to routine manual jobs. Their work situation therefore makes it impossible to uphold the notion of 'pride in the job' which formed the cornerstone of the traditional work ethic, and which constituted an important component in the male self-definition. Faced with a dull and boring work situation offering little or no intrinsic satisfaction, and lacking the means to change it, leisure time assumes a decisive importance as the key area within which they can construct a meaningful life-style and a viable self-identity.

From the beginning of the 'rock-and-roll' era, the styles of teenage leisure sponsored by the mass entertainment industries provided the most glamorous and widely publicized manifestation of the 'affluence' theme announced by Harold Macmillan in his celebrated 'Never had it so good' speech. However, as Cohen points out, these new media-relayed symbols and styles were laid over the top of pre-existing class subcultures and over-specific structural contradictions, both of which 'framed' the direction of the selections actually made. He then goes on to suggest that the successive East End youth subcultures such as the mods and the skinheads can be considered as 'variations on a central theme – the contradiction at an ideological level between traditional working-class puritanism, and the new hedonism of consumption; at the economic level between a future as part of the new socially mobile élite, or as part of the new *lumpen*' (Cohen, 1972, p. 23). Each subculture therefore represents a way of working through, within the sphere of leisure, the possible resolutions to contradictions in the situation of the skilled working class. The mod life-style represented an attempt to explore the option of upward mobility into the white-collar class, while the skinhead style explored the *lumpen* option of downward mobility into the unskilled manual strata. At the same time, however, these explorations took place within the context of the overall meaning system provided by the pre-existing class subculture. Typically, therefore, youth subcultures combined elements drawn from the mass entertainment media with elements derived from situational subcultures. For example, whereas the music and dress styles incorporated into the mod style were drawn from the media-relayed milieux of the West End boutiques and discotheques, the characteristic styles of language and gesture were rooted in the class-based meaning system which permeated everyday life in the family and locality.

Another illustration of the relation between media-relayed elements and class-based meanings is provided by the results of a pilot study of pop music preferences among middle-class adolescents (Murdock and McCron, 1973). Theoretically, these pupils are 'free' to involve themselves with the whole range of current pop music. In actuality, however, the great majority chose to involve themselves most closely with those particular styles which they classified as 'progressive'. This term was typically applied to performers who were perceived to be breaking with, or 'progressing beyond', the standard pop formulas, through such devices as personalized lyrics, individual improvisation and experimental instrumentation. In order to explain the direction and meaning of this preference, however, it is necessary to explore the ways in which their choices are circumscribed by class-based meaning systems.

Everyday life within the family and local neighbourhood is permeated and underpinned by the patterns of meaning through which previous generations have negotiated their shared experience of a common class situation. Through the process of socialization, particularly within the family, these class-based meaning systems are reproduced within the rising generation and come to constitute the basic framework of assumptions with which they approach their social experience. Consequently we can suggest that one of the factors framing adolescents' media involvements and subcultural identifications will be the extent to which the available symbols and styles are capable of containing and resonating with these previously assimilated patterns of meaning. Hence the 'successful' pupils' high valuation of 'progressive' performers who 'do their own thing' can be seen as a logical extension of the middle-class emphasis on self-development and individual achievement. Similarly, Davis has suggested that the consistent preference and valuation of LSD as against Methedrine among the middle-class 'hippies' of Haight-Ashbury can be viewed as a negotiated version of the basic values of self-exploration and self-improvement among the American middle class (Davis and Muroz, 1970).

It would, however, be a great mistake to see youth subcultures as explicable entirely in terms of their class context. On the contrary, once formed, they assume a degree of autonomy and the relations of opposition and antagonism between them become important in determining the media-relayed elements they will incorporate. For example, in addition to relating the heavy-duty denims, braces and industrial boots worn by the skinheads to the basic situational values of masculinity and toughness, it is also necessary to see them as representing a decisive rejection of the sexually ambiguous dress styles which characterize the middle-class 'hippie' subculture. To a considerable extent, therefore, 'the demarcations and oppositions between different youth subcultures may be seen as versions of the divisions and conflicts within the wider class structure, transposed into the specific context of youth' (Murdock, 1973b). The situation is not quite as simple as this, however, as oppositions occur not only between, but also within, class groupings.

An interesting instance of intra-class opposition is provided by Monod's study of youth subcultures in a working-class suburb of north Paris during the mid 1960s (Monod, 1967). He concentrated on two groups: a younger group of fourteen-year-olds and an older group aged eighteen and upwards. The older group had adopted the 'snob' style in which the dress and hair length of the Rolling Stones constituted key elements. Incorporating this explicit reference to contemporary pop music served several functions. Firstly, it marked them off from the local homosexuals whom they otherwise resembled in their general appearance and mannerisms. Secondly, and more importantly, it separated them from the younger group who based their *voyou* style on the black leather jackets and slicked-back hair of the early rock-and-roll era. In addition to symbolizing the separation of age groupings within the contemporary situation, the opposition between the two styles also served to confirm the older group's repudiation of their own support for the *voyou* style when they were themselves fourteen. By counterposing the contemporary elements of the 'snob' style against the *dépassé* elements of the *voyou* style, therefore, the older group symbolically encapsulated their own biographies.

The oppositions between different youth subcultures are not necessarily entirely conditioned by forces within the specific situation however. Demarcations and antagonisms may be intensified by the way in which certain styles are taken up and presented as news. The fullest available account of this process operating in practice is Cohen's pioneering study of the imagery surrounding the mods and rockers (S. Cohen, 1973).

The subcultural styles of the mods and the rockers represented two solutions to the shared contradictions in the situation of working-class youth. Initially, Cohen argues, these solutions were simply different; they were not opposed. On the Easter Sunday of 1964 many East End adolescents made the traditional day trip to Clacton. Faced with abnormally cold and wet weather, they were thrown on the town in search of amusements, and finding very few facilities some attempted to create their own diversions. Those with motorbikes rode up and down the Front; there was some vandalism and some minor scuffles. The subsequent news coverage greatly exaggerated the amount and scale of the damage and disturbances, and interpreted the clashes between different youth groups in terms of an image of warring 'gangs' of mods and rockers based on the scenario familiar from *West Side Story*. In fact initially the main division was between the local youths and the day trippers from London. Once established by the original news stories, however, this imagery of mods versus rockers was amplified as subsequent coverage consistently presented acts of vandalism and violence within this basic framework. The imagery was taken up and further elaborated by commercial entrepreneurs who applied the label 'mod' to a wide range of entertainment goods, dances and dress styles. Not surprisingly, this imagery of polarization permeated the self-image of group members, with the result that elements of style which had previously been neutral became foci of intergroup antagonism and conflict. This conflict in turn served to confirm and further amplify the original image.

For the sake of convenience I have discussed news and entertainment separately in this essay. However, as the mods-and-rockers example makes clear, in actuality there is a constant interchange of imagery and symbolization between the two spheres. Consequently, instead of continuing to concentrate on the reception of particular 'messages' as most research to date has done, future work should seek to do justice to the complexity of people's total experience of media-relayed meanings.

Conclusion

In a letter written towards the end of his life, Engels argued that although 'men make their history themselves, they do so in a given environment which conditions it, and on the basis of actual relations already existing' (Marx and Engels, 1968, p. 705). Taking this general proposition as a starting point, this brief paper has attempted to explore the relationship between situational choices and contextual constraints drawing concrete illustrations from the field of mass-media studies. Obviously, given the relatively sparse and fragmented nature of the evidence currently available, the arguments outlined here must be regarded as tentative. Nevertheless, if social psychology is to reconstitute itself as a comprehensive and genuinely social study of everyday life, it must necessarily take the issues raised in this paper as a central topic for further investigation. That is, starting from the premise that a man is never totally conditioned and constrained by the social situation in which he finds himself, and 'can always make something out of what is made of him' (Sartre, 1969, p. 45), social psychology must explore the complex and multi-layered interplay between intentional social actions and their conditioning contexts. More particularly it must examine the circumstances in which people cease to act within these contexts and begin to act against them.

References

COHEN, P. (1972), 'Subcultural conflict and working-class community', *Working Papers in Cultural Studies*, no. 2.

COHEN, S. (1973), *Folk Devils and Moral Panics*, Paladin.

DAVIS, F., and MUROZ, L. (1970), 'Heads and freaks: patterns and meanings of drug use among hippies', in J. D. Douglas (ed.), *Observations of Deviance*, Random House.

FILMER, P., *et al.* (1972), *New Directions in Sociological Theory*, Collier-Macmillan.

GOLDTHORPE, J. H. (1973), 'A revolution in sociology?', *Sociology*, vol. 7, no. 3, pp. 449–62.

HALL, S. (1972), *The External–Internal Dialectic in Broadcasting*, paper to the Manchester Broadcasting Seminar.

HALLORAN, J. D., *et al.* (1970), *Demonstrations and Communication: A Case Study*, Penguin.

HARTMANN, P., and HUSBAND, C. (1971), 'The mass media and racial conflict', in D. McQuail (ed.), *Sociology of Mass Communications*, Penguin.

HARTMANN, P., and HUSBAND, C. (1974), *Racism and the Mass Media*, Davis-Poynter.

KATZ, E., *et al.* (1973), *Utilization of Mass Communication by the Individual*, paper to the Conference on Directions in Mass Communications Research, Arden House, New York.

MARX, K., and ENGELS, F. (1968), *Selected Works: In One Volume*, Lawrence & Wishart.

McQUAIL, D., *et al.* (1972), 'The television audience: a revised perspective', in D. McQuail (ed.), *Sociology of Mass Communications*, Penguin.

MONOD, J. (1967), 'Juvenile gangs in Paris: toward a structural analysis', *J. Research in Crime and Delinquency*, vol. 4, pp. 142–64.

MURDOCK, G. (1973a), 'Political deviance: the press presentation of a militant mass demonstration', in S. Cohen and J. Young (eds.), *The Manufacture of News*, Constable.

MURDOCK, G. (1973b), *Culture and Classlessness: The Making and Unmaking of a Contemporary Myth*, paper to the Symposium on Work and Leisure, University of Salford.

MURDOCK, G., and McCRON, R. (1973), 'Scoobies, skins and contemporary pop', *New Society*, vol. 23, no. 547.

MURDOCK, G., and GOLDING, P. (1974), 'For a political economy of mass communications', in R. Miliband and J. Saville (eds.), *Socialist Register 1973*, Merlin Press.

PARKIN, F. (1972), *Class Inequality and Political Order*, Paladin (especially ch. 3).

ROCK, P. (1973), 'News as eternal recurrence', in S. Cohen and J. Young (eds.), *The Manufacture of News*, Constable.

SARTRE, J. P. (1969), 'Itinerary of a thought', *New Left Review*, no. 58, pp. 43–66.

TUCHMAN, G. (1973), 'Making news by doing work: routinizing the unexpected', *Amer. J. Sociol.*, vol. 79, no. 1, pp. 110–31.

13 In Quest of Post-Industrial Man
Denis Pym

Emancipation provides the one continuing thread of idealism in psychology. But even emancipation has fallen on hard times of late. True, when challenged most of us still offer social justifications. But it is not without embarrassment we mumble of studying behaviour to help *man* understand himself, be freely responsible, exert personal control and influence the shape of his own society. The ideal has seldom received more than lip-service because it is politically self-defeating. Its pursuit does little good for the occupational territories labelled 'psychology'. Some of us may argue that the notion 'helping people to help themselves' is a contradictory nonsense anyway but success, if there is any risk of that, would spell the end of psychology. Somewhere, at some preconscious level perhaps, each one of us knows there is a much greater risk of achieving emancipation by leaving men alone. A return to idealism necessitates the recasting of psychology. Leaving it to rust away is not enough; there are too many psychologists around.

The crisis of professional territory and approach is most striking and most difficult to deny for those who carry psychology into the economic system itself. In this arena the forces of reality cannot easily be contained and the supply lines are weak. Our allies in personnel departments and welfare functions are politically inconsequential. In such circumstances, it has always been easier and outwardly more rewarding for psychologists to ditch ideals in wordy rationalizations and reinforce human dependence. We are on the side of *society* and its institutions. For a start men seem to prefer it that way. It pays financially and politically too. The psychologist's legitimization of *status quo* or timely advance of panacea, yesterday 'management training' today 'participation' to meet the latest call for help, keep him on the winning side. As a person he may lose his soul but there are other rewards.

An even more serious failing is our active pursuit of human bondage in concepts and concerns where our conduct is less easy to excuse. Notions like 'group', 'leadership' and 'social class' among a hundred others, useful as they may be in explaining behaviour, serve also to reinforce the authority of leader, class and group. They reflect our anti-personal politics. In the world of man–machine systems nobody would argue that the person should be free to do as he likes but in our obsession to *predict* we blunder into domains where prediction matters little except to provide institutional control. Furthermore, success in prediction locks men into their subservient relationships with machines just when failure might free them. In this respect those we often despise have the edge on us. The European boss, for example, cannot rely on his African worker to demonstrate the machine-like qualities of his European colleague. That sick joke – 'Give the African the job and he'll finish the tool' – is double-edged after all.

Problems of territory

The category 'occupational psychologist' makes the point clearly enough. The space and time carved out by 'work' invokes other territories – leisure, school, home – which break life into unrelating bits. In the process living dies a little. Yet we defer to the dominant framework of industrialization and the support of those with most to gain from it. We want to improve man's *working* life instead of just having *better lives*. This objection may appear trifling. Nevertheless, it is fundamental to the view I now hold that selection, training, vocational guidance, improving working conditions and rewards in pursuit of better 'performance' and more 'satisfaction' no longer provide a viable arena for the occupational psychologist.[1]

Let me argue first as an occupational psychologist. In my researches I reveal myself as a romantic optimist. Suffering terrifies me. I prefer the illusory world of 'the winners'. I have asked people in employment – managers, professionals and manual workers – to identify excellence in their colleagues and then I try to find out more about those so defined at first hand. Among a number of features that might enable us to identify 'the winners' is their preference when and wherever possible to ignore society's divisions of time and space. Activities normally differentiated by clock, ruler and alphabet still bear their personal stamp. For example, they do not distinguish clearly in their conduct between work, learning and leisure.

My principal objection to improving working lives carries on from this observation. The word 'work' is misleading. Occupational psychologists study man in the condition of Employment. We devote our energies to improving performance or satisfaction in Employment. Work is about creating wealth and providing service. Employment embraces some work, an ever *decreasing* amount, and much beyond which is to do with social

1. I have no intention of defining terms. With apologies to Dodgson, they mean what you, the reader, want them to mean.

control and the rituals of industrial man. The proliferation of coercive ritual in the name of work comes with the possibility of creating wealth and service without keeping man in the servile condition of Employment.

Several factors are responsible for the declining relevance of Employment in creating wealth and providing service. These include advances in technology, broadening views of 'wealth' and 'service' and limitations inherent in Employment which lead to the expansion of wealth-creating and service activities outside Employment. To illustrate this last point. More and more people now question the adequacy of our institutions in a range of social services, e.g. local government for meeting community needs, prisons for prisoner treatment, schools for education, housing agencies for homes. Along with these criticisms have risen voluntary community groups like Friends of the Earth, Release, Shelter, the squatters and communes whose frequent hostility to the institutions of Employment introduces a competitive basis to 'services for the community'.

Now take a long step and consider for yourself the role of Employment in our current problems – alienation, inflation and the overconsumption of scarce resources, pollution and competitive waste. What if Employment has became the cancerous condition of industrial society? It doesn't help to argue that most people have it and even more believe in it. Cancer is about dying not living. In medieval times people believed in God in much the same way that we believe in Employment. Early scientists who preferred not to find a place for God in their theories and explanations suffered exclusion from society and even death. Yet, on balance, God's exclusion from scientific endeavour has increased the understanding of ourselves and the world around us and widened our range of choices.

If Employment could become dispensable in the pursuit of 'better lives' we psychologists might make a more valuable contribution to this concern than we do.

Take another look at what occupational psychologists do. We are with few exceptions caught in our own closed-systems traps, dickering around with the mechanics of Employment. Wasting our souls on improving selection procedures for non-jobs or training people for spurious work. Designing the lay-out of glass-house head offices to facilitate the rituals of industrial man. We are experimenting in and preaching the wonders of Employment through job enrichment, participation, flex-time, theory Y, O D, performance appraisal, each designed to rescue 'the need for achievement'. For the most part we pursue these concerns in large undertakings and contexts where the need for achievement has no chance of or reason to survive. Finally we evaluate our contributions in terms of those non-sensical concepts – productivity, cost-reduction, profit and growth. In short we number among the high priests of industrial society, missionaries for the Gospel of Employment.

Unfortunately it doesn't help the cause of 'better lives through emancipation' to stand up and cry out that God doesn't exist particularly when most people need him. But maybe the seeds of doubt will germinate the transfer of attention from the processes of employment to examining the problematic relationship between man and work. In my view there are economic as well as personal and social gains to be had in shifting authority away from Employment.

Problems of approach

Our territorial strait-jackets and anti-personal politics are inextricably bound with the dominant 'empirical' approach to the study of man. Essentially the failure of empirical psychology is its failure to be empirical. The stress on so-called value-free science and logical, sequential orders leads us to focus on what is objective rather than subjective in man and on that which is reducible to written words and numbers, i.e. on the trivial. Employment is more or less an objective state, almost as tangible as a wall that separates two rooms. But leisure and work can be defined most usefully by the doer in the same way that 'involvement' is inherently subjective. Unfortunately, this doesn't prevent captains of industry from making claims about involving their employees in decision-making.

Accepting the subjectivity of meaningful experience does not necessitate the rejection of shared frameworks but it does require a preparedness to work with simple and crude definitions, let us say, *low definition*. The coolness of low definition shifts authority in communication from the message sender *towards* the message receiver. It conflicts directly with the hot authoritative approach that equates advance with 'new' and 'better' labels and definitions and all those other additions to the over-differentiated jungles of contemporary life. The tradition of empirical psychology has denied the subjective to the point where adherents communicate among themselves as though we could have research without researchers and thinking without thinkers. Yet close examination of any research tells us more about the assumptions, beliefs and frames of reference of the researcher than of the researched. All inquiry is first and foremost a political act, a way of imposing our views on the world we pretend to study. Once we can accept this fact distinctions between research and application or theory and practice fade into insignificance.

Psychologists are not on their own here. History tells us most about the frameworks and structures of its perceiver. The Dark Ages are so described by literary historians because civilizations of that period left few written records. Tomorrow's historian armed with carbon 14, time thermometers and a mass of electronic gadgetry will literally illuminate the Dark Ages and no doubt cast ours into the shadows. Analyse for yourself some interview tapes and then ask yourself – whom have I learned most about, interviewer or interviewee ? Sociologists can prove the very *embourgeoisement* thesis they set out to disprove by getting workers to submit to the dictates of literacy. The academic Marxist's property is his writing and the writing he has inherited from the spiritual father. In defence of these 'words' he betrays the whole range of behaviour he condemns in his arch rival but blood relation, the capitalist. Literacy is a powerful instrument of the middle classes. The 'non-directive' trainer watching in icy silence the activity of the 'T' group exercises an influence over proceedings second to one. If he could make himself invisible as well, he would indeed be playing God. Those of us who prefer to study the world from the safety of our offices define ourselves no less. We ask people to fit themselves into our boxes and categories and then claim we are finding out about them. Much can be learned about the intimate lives of experimental psychologists by studying what they have to say about the sex life of the laboratory rat. In the studies of organization theorists the desire to reaffirm the wonders of bureaucracy are evident in attempts to reduce all social behaviour to the nonsense language of printed words and numbers.

Empirical psychology, 'value-free' science and positivism in all its forms strive to reduce man's perceptual mechanisms from five to one by imposing a language of the eye on hearing, feeling, tasting and smelling. The intelligence test is a popular illustration of this bias. Its tasks typically set in visual, verbal and numerical symbols are solved by rational thinking. It measures acuity in visual perception. The intelligence[2] test is also a political instrument used by those who enjoy advantage in visual acuity – white, middle-class, male – against those who do not – non-white, working-class, female. The same bias is evident throughout our arsenal of professional weapons. In short we advocate a form of sensory colonialism which may well be what alienation and employment are all about.

Towards a personal creed

So persuasive is the ideology of empirical psychology that it took me some ten years to come to terms with the mirror my own inquiries provided.

2. Incidentally tests like the Raven's matrices though they are still visual offer alternative methods of problem solving precisely because they are non-verbal. As these alternative methods, e.g. pattern recognition, become common practice in problem solving so the test norms deteriorate and the test loses its discriminatory powers.

My interest in identifying the characteristics of people who perform 'best' in ambiguous, less well-defined circumstances eventually became a search for post-industrial man (PIM) which is as near as I can get to advertising for myself. It does not help to discard such work in terms of mere projection. The labels we give to the behaviour of others we never use to enslave our own.

This romantic entity, the chap who is having all the fun, I wished to be myself. He has been around before. We usually notice him in times of transition, between the orders that send him underground: the yeoman in the crises of medieval society, the merchant in the demise of medieval society, the millwright in the great industrial thrust that became visible in the eighteenth century. These were men whose trade and business kept them near the margin of society and so free from many of its controls. They enjoyed a freedom of action and movement not widely shared. Their position at the time of their rise in the middle ranks of the social order offered additional cover and freedom of movement and association. The people we envy in economic life today, the ones who seem to be having the fun, I found to have much in common with yeoman, merchants and millwrights as I recall them through the jaundiced percepts of my needs.

Post-industrial man is cool, invisible and therefore not easy to categorize. Our confusion is his salvation for it enables him to preserve and renew that personal identity men lose when they go public i.e., when their roles account for all the variance in their behaviour. Though you and I may define him as 'a winner', he for his part does not believe in the faith of losers – winning and losing. He works long hours and yet exhibits more diverse leisure interests. He is highly aroused, mentally if not physically. His desire to define time and space his way takes him to the margins and across boundaries. He is a boundary-rider rather than a fence-sitter for he holds points of view not necessarily acceptable to his society. His attraction to ambiguous roles is the key to his survival. From such vantage points he gains his superior perception of reality. He enjoys associations with outsiders and those who are not mirror images of himself. He has learned to live with the anxieties that derive from his aloneness.[3]

Very briefly, what does it mean to accept and work with the subjectivity of experience? Start with the Lewinian formula – behaviour is a function of personality and environment ($B = fPE$) – and observe in current practice the way psychologists ($b = fPe$) and sociologists ($bfpE$) interpret that formula. To re-establish our interest in behaviour (B) we might concentrate our attentions on the *ways* in which the person relates to his environment:

3. This brief, banal description has something in common with Norman Mailer's (1962) exotic and exciting description of the Hipster.

$B = fPXE$. There is however a contradiction inherent in acting out this view, of which those who adopt systems approaches do not seem the least aware. The more we elaborate on personality and social environment the less we can be concerned with their interactions. Dissociation or differentiation runs counter to integration. In pursuit of subjectivity and reality I prefer the low-definition view described earlier, i.e. $B = fpXe$ which enables the observer to concentrate his attention on connections.

In conjunction with this view I acknowledge the political nature of inquiry and so strive in my relationships with those I claim to study to maintain their political advantage. I meet them on their territory, on their terms and work on their problems. I use the psychologist's traditional tools but sparingly. One cannot deny one's past. I spend considerable time observing, talking and just hanging about. This does not prevent me asserting myself or them from throwing me out. It is a stressful and often wasteful strategy. It undermines my professional ties to the point where communicating with fellow professionals seems irrelevant. But it carries me closer to what men do.

In conclusion and reuniting the issues of territory and approach, I observe that the gulf between what men do and say is as great as it ever has been. In studying the anatomy of critical events engaging executives and professionals who occupy middling positions in large organizations I find that their major information sources are mostly marginal to the issue, their communication patterns lateral, informal and face to face and short in time span. They make little use of written materials, vertical chains of command, formal meetings and formal information sources nor does the year 2000 loom large in deliberations. Such observations heighten my interest in the rituals of Employment. Indeed my questioning of Employment is strengthened by exchanging perceptions with those I meet in business and government. They frequently confirm in private what they cannot yet admit in public. The god of Employment is a false god.

References

MAILER, N. (1962), *Advertisements for Myself*, Deutsch.

My reluctance to use 'references' is not an oversight. The reference requires a date but no mention of place. Either we are expected to gain a good knowledge of the context from the article or book in which our quoted fact or observation occurs or, alternatively, we are to assume that all contexts are the same, rigorous scientific conditions perhaps? Since professional papers quote on average a dozen or so authorities we can only assume that all contexts are assumed to be identical. Time is clearly a more significant variable. But the 'time' of the reference is linear, sequential and accumulative. Source A (1973) has advantage over source B (1903) in accumulated knowledge. In 1973 we know *more* than they did in 1903 or do we? More about what? There were things around then that we were unable to observe and there are things going unrecorded today, maybe more now than then. To quote Freud, Weber or Marx is to quote them out of context. Today they might even see things differently. References have become a professional game, part of the ritual of THE SCIENTIFIC METHOD, just another deception.

Part Three
Approaches

So far in this book, we have criticized methodology and certain topic areas in social psychology, and suggested some alternative lines of development. Now we come up against the question: are these alternatives at all coherent? In Part Three, we have six essays that outline plausible and coherent alternatives. Although they do not form a unified whole, there are again common strands that are worth drawing out.

In the introduction to Part Two, I put the main stress upon values in relation to social psychology. But *what* values? The values of our society are not a random selection from all possible values but the values of a particular sort of society at a particular point in history: a technocratic, hierarchical, capitalist society, inching its way towards social democracy on the one hand and state regulation on the other. Such a society stresses efficiency and competition, individualism and success, rewards and profit, power and control, acquisition and materialism, performance and the intellect, ends rather than means, at the expense of other values that would stress our common humanity and imply a wider vision of human possibilities.

And this society is run by people, some cooperating in the process more enthusiastically than others. These people have values which tend to correspond to where they are placed in our society. Social psychologists are people, people who on the whole are placed in institutions of higher education, social service and production. We are paid well by the state or private industry to think, talk and research about social-psychological issues. But what gets to be a social-psychological issue? In my view, the social situation of university social psychologists ensures that our issues are remote from the concerns of most people, and instead reflect the interests of ourselves and increasingly our present social class (technocratic middle-class, aspiring to some 'influence' over events).

Similarly, the social situation of 'practical' social psychologists (in schools, social-services departments, hospitals, industry) ensures that their issues are those of their employers, rather than of the people processed by these institutions. What constitutes an issue worthy of employing a social psychologist is decided by the 'authorities' (e.g., truancy, vandalism, drop-outs, family distruption, communication channels, absenteeism); the social psychologist *may*, if he is lucky or devious, carve out some influence over the way the issue is approached.

We are social psychologists of one sort or another, who are trying to carve out some influence for ourselves over what constitutes social psychology, and hope that the issues we formulate are not so much in our own interests or those of our pay-masters, but in the interests of people who do not hold élite positions in our society. Most of the approaches in Part Three criticize the connections between capitalism (used as shorthand for a more complicated social order) and social psychology, and go on to suggest more adequate conceptualizations that grasp the influence of capitalism while striving to be free of it themselves. John Heritage mentions the manipulative uses of assessment procedures and unravels how the values of our society get built into these procedures. Henrietta Resler and Paul Walton review the inadequate conceptualization of capitalism (shorthand) by several approaches to social psychology, while David Triesman looks at the difficulties of using official (capitalist) data. Finally, David Ingleby suggests how psychology as a whole incorporates capitalist norms and values into its 'universal' laws.

As far as alternatives go, Martin Richards argues that, in explaining the formation of a person, any social psychology should take biological structure and development into account in a way that integrates with the more commonly studied social influences. John Heritage expounds ethnomethodology as a way of comprehending people that does not do violence to our everyday assumptions and is not amenable to manipulative uses; Henrietta Resler and Paul Walton put together the bare bones of a materialist, class psychology; David Triesman believes that, with adequate theory, official data can be used to help oppressed groups in their struggles; and David Ingleby sketches a theory of how the problems of living under capitalism get reproduced in a distorted (ideological) form in psychology. Here, then, are some materials for reconstructing social psychology.

But what general principles would a reconstructed social psychology follow? I think I have identified several already in the previous intro-ductions, but would like to add two more that are inherent in the present six essays; an emphasis upon shared definitions and meanings, and a genuine focus upon the individual–society dialectic (two-way, developing relationship). These two principles represent an effort to overcome the impoverished treatment of the 'social' for which we criticize conventional social psychology. To recap briefly, social psychology individualizes its issues in the same way as general psychology. The root causes tend to be seen in human nature rather than in society. This individualization itself reflects a central capitalist value, and is reflected in the way social psychology treats the 'social' as 'interaction between organisms leading to differences in behavioural output, these organisms being abstracted from any on-going, real-life social context and processes' (see p. 13, this volume). It has no conception of how the phenomena conventionally studied by sociologists bear upon individual behaviour and group processes, which is part of the reason why the links between sociology and social psychology have never really been forged. Similarly, many sociologists have no idea that some social psychology might just be relevant to what they are doing.

The importance of shared definitions and meanings has already been mentioned by Martin Roiser and myself in Part One and by most of the contributors to Part Two. Here we find John Heritage exploring the common-sense knowledge of everyday life, but stressing that the shared nature of this knowledge is a tentative, for-practical-purposes thing, that can never be finally 'established'; Henrietta Resler and Paul Walton ask where the shared ideas come from and answer in terms of class and material conditions; Rom Harré provides a detailed account of what a social psychology that deals with *social* action and meaning would look like; and David Ingleby returns to the question of *whose* ideas are the ruling ideas, and what their functions are in a class society.

The dialectic between individual and society has also been broached in previous essays, particularly my own and those in Part Two. This line is developed more fully and systematically here. Martin Richards concentrates upon the interplay between the biological and the social spheres and shows how the definitions and interpretations of other people must be seen in the light of the biological preadataptions of the growing person.

Henrietta Resler and Paul Walton build their essay around the false separation of individual and society, and David Triesman stresses the necessary role of radical *theory* in bridging the gap even at the 'empirical' level; David Ingleby's essay contains one example of the sort of theory that might do the job. Although John Heritage and Rom Harré are operating rather at the sub-institutional level (interaction processes not directly connected with the major institutions of our society), their frameworks leave plenty of room for asking 'where do the meanings, definitions and rules come from and how do they operate in the major institutions and society at large?' In their essays, however, they are both trying to formulate the individual–society dialectic at a micro-social level. In doing this, they touch on many of the points raised in previous introductions: the defects of positivism and determinism, the importance of meaning and human agency in social action. They then present systematic outlines of how they would do things better.

14 The Biological and the Social
Martin Richards

Social psychology, as an academic training and research activity, has
developed as a self-contained and inward-looking discipline which has
not only become separated from the phenomena it sets out to analyse but
is also sterile as a source of human understanding. It has adopted the
ethos and methodology of mainstream psychology and applied them to a
restricted series of topics and problems – predominantly those constructed
by the manipulation of small groups of people ('subjects') in artificial
laboratory situations. Such theory as has been produced can always
suggest new experiments, which provide new permutations and embroidery
on the old themes, so that the social psychologists can always be seen to be
busy. But busy at what?

The field became inward-looking and esoteric because the language of
its discussions was not comprehensible to the main body of experimental
psychologists, and because little that went on seemed to have any bearing
on the outside world. This latter point is not simply one of relevance,[1]
but is even more seriously related to the generality of the findings. All too
often, what seemed to be a common feature of behaviour in laboratory
situations has been found not to hold in the real world. So, for example,
the ease with which 'attitudes' may be manipulated in a laboratory small
group seems to have few parallels in everyday life.

It is not too difficult to see why social psychology should have developed
in this way. Its practitioners have always had the lowest status within
psychology and they were left with the problems that were regarded as
peripheral by the higher-status psychologists. These latter people, while
concentrating on the topics most amenable to the methodology of classical
physics and chemistry, were happy enough to see social psychology
exist, for they could hardly deny the existence of a social world; but they
always looked down on it as the 'soft' end of the subject. In a situation
like this it was predictable that the social psychologists should try to gain

1. Recent attempts to demonstrate the relevance of this kind of social psychology
by applying it to everyday situations have only served to underline its triviality
(see, for example, Swingle, 1973) and show that it is perhaps a very pompous way
of stating the obvious.

status by aping the experimentalists – by trying to out-psychologize their more secure colleagues. So the methodology became everything and produced a subject that was all form with no function or, to adopt an analogy from psycholinguistics, it is all performance with no competence. Elaborate experimental designs and sophisticated statistics were used in studies of phenomena that might have no importance – or even reality.[2]

In recent years this picture has begun to change. Being the most vulnerable, social psychology was the first discipline to crumble in the face of attacks on mindless empiricism. At the same time interest in the problems of social life has been growing and not unnaturally people have been asking what academic psychology has to offer. So social psychology is being reconstructed. It is my aim in this chapter to argue that if these attempts at rebuilding are to be successful, they must take account of both the social *and* the biological nature of man. To do this I will use a discussion of early development and socialization as illustration.

Social scientists have had a longstanding prejudice against biological views of man which has been fed and justified by numerous misleading doctrines about human nature that have arisen from the theories of the biologists. The identification and analysis of these has become a major theme in the history of science (e.g. Young, 1973) and I have only space to mention a few of the more obvious.

The false translation of theories about evolution into Social Darwinism was but one phase in a long tradition which has used organismic analogies for society. In this particular version, the notion of natural selection was used to justify, and make seem inevitable, social divisions within society and the exploitation of man by man. Here, as so often seems to be the case, the biological analogy was not used to explore or analyse the structure of society or the processes acting within it but simply as a justification of a *status quo*. This same process may be found in the attempts to see cultural and social differences between individuals or groups of people as an inevitable product of biological differences, a tradition that runs from nineteenth-century anthropology through to the current debate about the heritability of IQ (Richardson, Spears and Richards, 1972). Here, as well as a misunderstanding about the social nature of social action, there is a misconception about the role of genetic differences in the development of individual characteristics. Those that have argued in this way have not understood that epigenetic processes specify means and not ends, and that therefore genes do not *determine* anything.

Another widespread biologism is obvious in 'explanations' of human

2. In passing, we may note how often in psychology departments the social psychologists are in charge of statistics teaching.

action that involve postulating a series of innate drives or instincts. Theories of this kind gloss over all problems about the meaning of behaviour (see Becker, 1972) which they see as being immanent in particular configurations of muscle movements. So behaviour is not distinguished from action and such accounts are unable to cope with fundamental questions about intention, the self or self-consciousness.

A final vice that should be mentioned is the use, or rather over-use, of accounts of animal behaviour in discussions of our own species. If these arguments are not based on both a full biological understanding and an appreciation of the social world constructed by man, they will always tend to reduce man to a complex animal–machine. They will underplay the species-specificity of our own behaviour and so ignore the human attributes of language, self-reflection and social communication (Bernal and Richards, 1973).

In a justified attempt to save their concerns from a reduction to biologisms of these and other varieties, many social scientists have moved in the other direction and have constructed entirely social theories of social action and it is this tendency I hope to counteract. Any complete account of man must be able to come to terms with both his social and his biological natures.

A human infant is born with a predisposition to become both adult (Trevarthen, 1972) and social (Berger and Luckman, 1967). Given both the biological structure of the infant and the social world in which he lives and which is necessary for his survival, a social adult will be formed during development. If the biological structure of the infant did not play an essential role in this process, any living organism should serve. But, of course, we find that attempts to rear even our closest biological relatives, the great apes, as children fail to produce people. Similarly, deprived of human companions, a human infant will not become a person. In order to understand socialization, the process whereby an infant born into a society becomes a full adult member, we must analyse the contribution of biological structure to the process. What is it about an infant that allows him to become a person?

One of the first things to notice about a human infant is his inability to survive on his own and so his absolute dependence on other members of his society which will last for several years (Bruner, 1972). During this time, even his most basic biological needs (for food, for warmth) can only be satisfied by the active intervention of others. So the essence of socialization becomes communication, for it is only insofar as other adults perceive and understand an infant's needs that these can be met (Macmurray, 1961, especially chapter 2). From birth onwards, adults are involved in a process of interpreting an infant's behaviour. It is through these interpretations, the actions of adults towards him, that an infant is able to perceive the consequences of his activities, and this allows him to develop an intentional structure for his own activities. Through this process, his behaviour becomes intentional action. This is a line of theoretical speculation which is grounded in the philosophical work of G. H. Mead (Morris, 1934; Strauss, 1956; Miller, 1973). Until recently, this work has largely been ignored by developmental and social psychologists and much more detailed theoretical analysis and empirical research is required before we can get beyond the most general statements. But its great advantage and potentiality lies in the fact that it opens the way to a truly human view of social development which may be married with an adequate theory of developmental biology.

However, there are some areas where our knowledge of development is already sufficient for us to see some of the details of the processes by which the social and the biological interact with one another.

The infant's biological structure provides a selectivity in the perceptual processes so that attention is focused on features that form part of adult communication modes and therefore allow the formation of agreed channels for communication between adult and infant.[3] From an early age one can observe rudimentary dialogue between infant and adult in which there seems to be agreement about how communication is to be effected even if the nature of what has to be communicated is little more than a mutual acknowledgement that there is another person there. Infants selectively attend to faces. This seems so natural to us adults that we seldom pause to consider either the complexity of organization that makes this possible or the enormous importance of this biological pre-adaptation for socialization and the richness of the face as a source of information about a person's state. Another example of this kind of pre-adaptation is the infant's preference for speech-like sounds. This provides a structure in (and of) the world for the infant; he does not have to begin from scratch trying to classify all sounds as if they all might have biological and social importance for him. Through this adaptation he is led towards relevant sounds and so into an agreed channel of communication which will culminate in the acquisition of language and his entry into his linguistic community.

To establish communication one needs not only agreed channels or modes, but also rules about the temporal use of the channels. Recent observational studies of infants have shown that their behaviour is structured in time and that they are very sensitive to the timing of the alterna-

3. This is described in much greater detail elsewhere (Richards, 1974).

tions and reciprocations of their social partners in communication episodes. Within the first few weeks of life, they come to expect that responses will arrive at particular points in sequences and, if they do not, the sequence may well be cut short. Abilities of this kind are, of course, essential before speech may be developed as a mode of communication, and yet again the indications are that they are made possible by the existence of a human biological structure.

The fundamental role of these biological preadaptations to social life can easily be appreciated if you perform a thought experiment on yourself. First fix in your mind a picture of an infant – say a nine-month-old. Picture his social actions, his powers of communication and understanding, his abilities to make his intentions known to other people. Then consider how these might have developed taking a traditional view of the infant as a creature which is essentially a *tabula rasa*, with a few reflexes and the rest of his behaviour a series of random movements. Add to this the postulates of any stimulus–response learning ('behaviour') theory. Then explain how the infant grows up into the nine-months-old you pictured at the beginning. . . . Of course, it won't work. Even if one assumes an enormously structured environment, a glorified conditioning laboratory constructed with the sole purpose of ensuring the learning of a vast array of specific attributes, it still does not seem possible. But even that is ruled out. Observation of the environments of infants provide no evidence that parents systematically respond to their children in the ways that are required by learning theory. No; the infant must play a major role in structuring and organizing his own environment and learning particular things about it, and clearly he is endowed with a biological nature that makes this possible.

However, this biological endowment does not determine outcomes – it provides means and not ends. Human development would not be possible without a social world. This is something that is missed by theorists who argue that the infant is a social being and that his behaviour patterns such as crying and smiling constitute social behaviour. Implicit in this view is the idea that the behaviour pattern determines its own social meaning (as it is seen as the determinant of the adult's response to the infant). In contrast to this, I would argue that the infant's behaviour pattern is of biological origin but it is made social by its recognition and interpretation by adults.[4] Its meaning is negotiated by those who interact with the infant.

This difference is much more than a quibble, because if one believes that a behaviour pattern arrives with a ready-made meaning, there is no room

4. This theme is elaborated by John Shotter (pp. 53–69).

left for the development of autonomy and self-reflection by the infant. Furthermore, the infant's signals (his crying, smiling, and so on) would become a kind of biological imperative and any adult who failed to respond to them would have to be regarded as biologically as well as socially deficient. Of course, these infant signals are not randomly associated with his internal states and conditions. Nobody seems to regard smiling as a signal of discomfort nor is crying seen as a sign of contentment. But in responding to the infant's signals an adult must interpret them, decide what they mean and what, if anything, is to be done about them. As cross-cultural studies have demonstrated, these interpretations vary across society and embody each culture's belief system.

In this discussion I have deliberately concentrated on some of the features of the earliest stages in the process of socialization, because it is here that the role of biological structure is perhaps clearest. But all the later stages rest on these beginnings. Often this is forgotten, and accounts of socialization emphasize later childhood and the role of school and other institutions. If these alone are considered it is easy to provide a superficially complete account without mentioning biological structure. However, this only touches the surface of the matter because, though a child may change while a member of a school, the total of such changes do not together make up the whole of socialization. These one-sided accounts take as unproblematic the formation of a person and merely consider the rather superficial processes that result from participation in particular social institutions. The central issue in the problem of socialization is the formation of a person.

In this brief essay I have only had space to sketch out a few points of an extremely complex area, but I hope I have established two things. That theories in social psychology must take account of man's biological structure: without this they are incomplete or, worse still, they will tend to drift off, unanchored, in an endless sea of social definitions. And that biological considerations need not lead to reductionism or to any denial of the social nature of social life.

Given the fragmentation of our academic life, in both research and teaching, into the various disciplines, it is extremely difficult to find positions from which to bring together those things that are traditionally kept in isolation. Here, I think, social psychology is ideally placed, and in its reconstruction the way is open to build a viewpoint that will cut across traditional tendencies and provide a holistic vision of man.

References

BECKER, E. (1972), *The Birth and Death of Meaning*, Penguin.

BERGER, P. L., and LUCKMAN, T. (1967), *The Social Construction of Reality*, Allen Lane The Penguin Press; Penguin, 1971.

BERNAL, J. F., and RICHARDS, M. P. M. (1973), 'What can the zoologist tell us about human development?', in A. S. Barnett (ed.), *Ethology and Development*, Little Clinic Clubs in Developmental Medicine, no. 47, Spastics Society and Heinemann.

BRUNER, J. S. (1972), 'The uses of immaturity', in G. V. Coelho and E. A. Rubinstein (eds.), *Social Change and Human Behavior*, National Institute of Mental Health.

MACMURRAY, J. (1961), *Persons in Relation*, Faber.

MILLER, D. L. (1973), *George Herbert Mead: Self, Language and the World*, University of Texas Press.

MORRIS, C. W. (ed.) (1934), *G. H. Mead: Mind, Self and Society*, University of Chicago Press.

RICHARDS, M. P. M. (1974), 'The first steps in becoming social', in M. P. M. Richards (ed.), *The Integration of a Child into a Social World*, Cambridge University Press.

RICHARDSON, K., SPEARS, D., and RICHARDS, M. P. M. (eds.) (1972), *Race, Culture and Intelligence*, Penguin.

STRAUSS, A. (ed.) (1956), *The Social Psychology of George Herbert Mead*, University of Chicago Press.

SWINGLE, P. G. (ed.) (1973), *Social Psychology in Everyday Life*, Penguin.

TREVARTHEN, C. B. (1972), 'Behavioural embryology', in E. C. Carterette and M. P. Friedman (eds.), *The Handbook of Perception*, Academic Press.

YOUNG, R. M. (1973), 'The human limits of nature', in J. Miller (ed.), *The Limits of Human Nature*, Penguin.

15 Blueprint for a New Science
Rom Harré

Science as explanation

The demand that we should develop an academic discipline more relevant to life than that to which we have become sadly accustomed demands a shift both in our idea of what it is to be scientific and in our conception of man and the nature of his social life. The first step in sketching the outlines of a new socio-psychological science will be to explain the realist idea of a scientific explanation and to contrast it with the neo-positivist conception of science under which psychology has gone so tragically astray. It will then become clear how releasing the change to the realist conception can be.

I ask the reader to imagine a scientific theory in its natural state. This will be rather different from the way it appears, neatly drawn up, in the scientific journals. We shall be interested in the form an explanation takes in the thinking of scientists and in the accepted knowledge of the scientific community. I shall develop a scheme which represents the various components of a scientific theory. The demand for a theory begins with the discovery of certain patterns in nature. For example, if we record the way blue and brown eyes are distributed from generation to generation we find that the distributions of eye colours form very definite patterns. Suppose we begin with two people, one with blue eyes and one with brown. The children of such a couple will usually all have brown eyes. In the next generation, a couple each of whose parents were the offspring of such a couple will probably have three brown-eyed children for every one whose eyes are blue. That is an example of one kind of pattern we observe in nature and, of course, one of Mendel's laws describes that pattern. To the educated eye non-random patterns appear everywhere from the behaviour of falling bodies to the exchanges of social life. Social customs have a very striking source of regularity. Every person I met in Belgium on a recent visit put out his or her right hand to be shaken. In Italy, *prego* follows *grazie* with a regularity which even a Newtonian determinist would envy. In America, a similar pattern can be heard in 'thank you', with the standard response, 'you're welcome'.

The regularities seen in social customs turn out to be even more accurately predictable than those in physics. Once they are set in train their completion follows almost without exception. On a recent visit to America I observed something like five hundred examples where saying 'thank you' was followed by 'you are welcome' without exception. One can predict the reply with certainty.

The neo-positivist idea of science was that the compilation of a catalogue of laws describing such regularities completely exhausted the content of a science. Theory consisted of a formal deductive system, from the axioms of which the laws of nature could be deduced. In science proper there was nothing but the study of the patterns of nature, their formulation in laws and the construction of a deductive system, from the axioms of which the laws could be deduced. This has been called the 'Covering-law' theory of scientific explanation. The sole virtue of a theory, on this view, is to bring order into the mass of observational and experimental data. Provided that order is produced, neo-positivists are not much concerned with the meaning of those concepts which appear only in the theory, since they refer to states of affairs which cannot be observed, at least then and there. Most theories can be interpreted either neo-positivistically or from the point of view of realism. Thus, 'cognitive dissonance', introduced to explain a wide range of attitudes and behaviour, can be treated merely as a device for bringing order into the data of attitude change, or it can be treated as the name of a real state of mind whose phenomenology can be actively explored, and upon whose real existence the theory can be judged.

Except for the most general branches of physics, the natural sciences are interpreted by working scientists according to the realist point of view. A real scientist tries to discover what produces patterns which he observes; that is, what mechanisms are responsible for them. He requires that his theories have a certain kind of *content*. A real scientist should ask what produces the pattern of hand-shaking in Belgium, and of polite responses in the United States. What is responsible for the structure of pattern of this kind of interaction? It is at this point in most sciences that observation temporarily comes to a halt, and for the next step we are forced to resort to the scientific imagination. Unlike the artist's or layman's use of his imagination, the work of the scientific imagination is under a rigorous discipline. It is a controlled use of the imagination by which we construct our ideas of those things and processes we cannot observe which produce and so explain the patterns and structures we do see.

For the most part, the realist theory of science is concerned with the study of how the imagination would be controlled by a real but ideally rational scientist. It is no good just imagining any kind of process that might produce observed patterns. To be scientific one must imagine processes and generative mechanisms which are proper and appropriate to the problem in question. The problem of a scientist's imagination is a model of the unknown processes of pattern production. Since we do not know what the generative mechanism of some pattern actually is, we imagine something that it is like, in that it performs the same function, or behaves in the same way. The model and the unknown real mechanism must be functionally equivalent.

Imagine we are in the situation of a Gregor Mendel. He did not know what mechanism produced the pattern of inheritance he had observed, so he imagined something which would produce a similar pattern. Any mechanism he imagined would have to be functionally equivalent to whatever is the real cause of the pattern of inheritance, and of course, as we know, he imagined the mechanism of genetic factors and dominant and recessive genes. In creating ideas of hypothetical mechanisms we imagine something which we hope is like something in the real world. But we do not know, at least in the early stages of a science, whether what we imagine is exactly the same as the productive structures of the real world. So at least in the beginning of a scientific development, our ideas of the mechanisms of nature are at best functionally equivalent or analogous to what is really there.

How do we know what kind of model to construct? Remember that these are not models in the sense the mathematician uses the term. Scientific models are iconic; that is, they are imagined things, processes or structures. They may, of course, be very remote from pictureable things. To get a

Table 1

patterns	generative mechanism	model	sources	
			empirical	meta-physical
distribution of eye-colour		dominant and recessive genes	chemical atom	invariant material atoms and the void
gestures and words used in greeting		rule-following and meaning-interpreting	formal ceremonies	man as intelligent agent

satisfactory iconic model we have to control for plausibility, physical in the physical sciences, psychological and historical in the human sciences. To achieve this plausibility, we must have a suitable source for our models. The hypothetical mechanism we imagine as producing some observed pattern will bear some sort of analogy to its source. For example, in simple chemistry, atoms are imagined as something like electrically charged lumps of matter. But iconic models may become extremely abstract, as, for instance, in the concept of the field of potential as used in physics, which is a bare structure in space, modulating its form with time.

A theory considered in all its details has a very complicated structure but we need all of this to understand anything scientifically.

Nothing simpler will do. The task of psychology as a science, just like chemistry or physics, is to identify patterns in its subject of study, and to try to conceive of the means of production of those patterns by the use of a suitably disciplined imagination. In this chapter I shall be constructing the outline for a theory of social psychology which uses this structure. To adopt such a conception of science requires a very radical departure from the simple-minded positivist methodology of dependent and independent variables, of statistics and correlation coefficients. It demands, as we shall see, a return to the idea of a human being as a responsible agent, capable of constructing and managing his social world. And it involves a corresponding change in the kinds of patterns we look for. In this chapter I shall be concentrating on patterns of meaningful action, abstracted from the mass of mere behaviour. But one might equally select the patterns of experience, abstracted from all the influences to which we are subjected, and which are generated by an interaction between our interpretative skills by which we make sense of our experiences and those mechanisms in society which produce human social experience. This interaction is exceedingly complex and by no means fully understood.

The genesis of action

We must be as radical in the way we structure our thinking about the psychological processes which are productive of human social behaviour as we have just been about the nature of a psychological science. To make the next shift of thought clear, I must introduce another philosophical idea, but one of a very different kind from the extension of the logic of theories advanced in the previous section. In thinking scientifically we come to a problem with our ideas about the world and the nature of things already fairly well fixed. The nature of these ideas is crucial since they control both what we perceive and the explanations we offer of what we have perceived. Sciences are structured around certain concepts or ideas of the natures of things and productive processes. These ideas do not come from observation of phenomena, but are already in the very language in which the scientist has been educated. They are implicit too in his social and historical background. They form a cognitive, complicated structure, with which he controls and gives sense to his experience. It is partly included in, and partly an extension of, the system of ideas and images, with which any human being tries to make sense of his situation. A prominent feature of the approach we are advocating is the respect we pay to the intellectual capacities of ordinary human beings as managers and interpreters of the social world. Everyone is, in a certain sense, a fairly competent social scientist, *and we must not treat his (or her) theory about the social world and his place in it with contempt*.

In discussing the genesis of action we must pay particular attention to one of these controlling ideas, namely, the concept of causality. Our problem is: how are our social actions produced? In this paper I want to concentrate on the *psychological* components of the causes of social happenings leaving the interactive social components to other contributors. There are two main concepts of causality in the contrast between which the old and the new ideas of the genesis of human action can be clearly delineated. Suppose I am giving a talk in what I hope is a systematic and coherent fashion. How is that achieved? How am I kept going to produce the appropriate pattern? Am I continuously prompted by the reward of the listeners' approval, or by reinforcement from some other environmental contingency? There is a well-known theory in psychology associated with Skinner (1953) according to which the only kind of causes to be sought in a scientific psychology are efficient causes. That is, for example, the stimuli to which I am subjected and which trigger my responses. What keeps me talking, according to Skinner, are the rewards stemming from the listeners' behaviour. The audience is giving me positive reinforcement. They are looking at me, smiling a little; some are not following terribly well because I am introducing an unfamiliar line of thought, but they are generally showing by little signs of posture and gaze that they are concentrating and trying to understand. According to Skinner, what keeps me speaking is the 'control' (in the particularly Skinnerian sense) of environmental contingencies. But that is quite false of this kind of case.

What keeps me talking to an audience is something very different. What keeps me talking is my plan – my prepared scenario for the talk. It is the potency of the plan which leads me on to say one thing after another. Like most speakers, I keep on going even if there's a riot. I know what I want to say and could be stopped only by physical force. Even if the audience goes to sleep some heroic souls continue to lecture. Why? They must realize their plan, or to put it more accurately, their plan must realize itself in actual pattern of speech. *I* make the plan (or acquire the habit) and through it I mediately control the action.

The ideas of efficient causality, controlling variable and positive reinforcement are not sufficiently subtle for the explanation of such events as an academic lecture, or indeed any extended piece of social action such as a greeting episode. A quite different kind of causality must be invoked. It is the causality of what can be called the 'powerful particular'. It is something like the old idea of a formal cause but with the idea of agency added. This is an idea fairly new to modern philosophy. Let me introduce the idea with a non-psychological example. In a tank of water, the water is continuously exerting pressure at every place within it. At any point, even when there is nothing there except water, there is a potentiality for physical action. The water in the tank is a powerful particular. It is always capable of crushing something. If a small box, empty except for air, is put down sufficiently deep, the water will crush it. Thus we show that the water had a power or a potentiality to crush such a box at that particular point. The water is, in a way, the physical bearer of what a physicist would call a field of potential.

We can use the idea of the powerful particular in explaining what it is that is controlling, shaping and organizing the material in the flow of human social action. Part of what we need in an improved psychology is a range of ideas of suitable, powerful particulars. I will use the general terms 'plan' and 'rule' for the powerful particulars that shape social action. A 'plan' is, if you like, a kind of field of potential. It is a synchronically organized structure; that is, a plan is something which can exist at a moment in time. Each point of the plan is potent in shaping action and each stage of it is ready to become operative when the action has passed through the previous stages. A plan is realized in a diachronic pattern of actions; that is, in a structure whose component parts exist at different times. There are, of course, certain relevant environmental contingencies involved in the processes which generate these patterns. But they are not enough to explain the production of the coherent form of the action in all its details.

This idea is part of a general theory of human social action which I would like to convey with a rather childish but, I hope, striking image. Imagine a factory manufacturing spaghetti. It is a fairly primitive factory in Southern Italy. This is how it works. There is a bucket full of pasta on the first floor. A tube runs down to a little old man in the room below. He has a box of different dies. He screws a die on the end of the tube. It has a certain pattern of holes. It is, let us say, a spaghetti die. There is a macaroni die, and a vermicelli die in the box too. The old man pulls a handle and the pasta starts to run down the tube. It keeps on coming, always moving down through the die and out on to iron trays. There are some little old ladies in black headscarves who collect the trays and who rush them off to the oven. Notice that the pasta keeps on coming and it is the die that makes it into spaghetti. After a while they do not need any more spaghetti, so they screw on the macaroni die and out comes macaroni. These dies are, in a way, like those powerful particulars I have called plans and rules. They control the form of the product and shape the continuous flow of pasta. There is no question of looking for an explanation of the differentiation of spaghetti from macaroni or vermicelli wholly in terms of efficient causality. There is always some product emerging from the factory because the pasta is coming down the tube all the time. The same general process goes on all the time. The question is: what differentiates the shape or form that the product takes? And the answer to that question is given in terms something like this – there is a specific die which puts structural form on to the continual flow of undifferentiated material. And there are two further questions: where does the stock of dies come from? And what prompts the little old man to change one die for another?

We are to imagine human life as something like a spaghetti factory. We are to imagine people continually generating a stream of activity. It begins when one wakes in the morning. But human beings play out some important sequences of the action in their imagination, particularly in the early morning and late at night. On the general theory that I am advocating, there is no sharp division between thought and action. Some actions are thought made concrete and many thoughts are themselves continuous with and thus part of the patterns of action. Indeed, some thoughts are actions, in those cases like ordering or forcing oneself, where one acts upon oneself. According to the spaghetti-factory theory, the fact of action does not call for a psychological explanation. No psychological explanation of why a human being does one thing after another is required. We assume that human physiology is such that a person is continuously busy. It is a matter of energy exchange and biochemistry to explain why a human being is always in action. Why someone is doing *some*thing is not an interesting psychological question. The interesting psychological question, particularly the social-psychological question, is why is he doing *what* he is doing? It is not the business of psychologists to explain *that* something is being done, but why *that* thing is being done. This question will have a sequence of answers passing through the psychological states and cognitive structures of individuals, out into the history of that individual and of the society in which he is embedded.

The history of a person's social milieu, and his personal history in it, is an essential part of the explanation of social action, as we conceive it, since it supplies the answer to the problem of the origin of just that stock of dies with which every social spaghetti maker is equipped. There is a deep and unresolved scientific question about that stock of dies. How much are the forms of patterns of action universal and immutable, deriving from inherited structures, or biological necessities, such as the fact that parents are for some time bigger and always older than their children?

Contemplation of the spaghetti-factory image suggests that an answer to the central psychological question is to be sought by trying to find something corresponding to the dies. They must be powerful particulars, which are synchronically structured and capable of diachronically controlling the flow of thought and action, giving form to this continuous flow at the appropriate moment. The concept that I shall be developing for explaining the shaping of action by human beings and thus developing the theory is that of a rule or plan. A rule is something which is like a die which itself is in a way a kind of rule. It is a rule for the flowing pasta. It tells it how to behave if you like. The die exists permanently. It is always there in the little man's box. When he wants to make spaghetti, he pulls out a particular die and screws it on. Correspondingly, I know of some rules which prescribe the actions to be performed when I meet people. When I am on the continent of Europe I use them in deliberately shaping my actions. One rule is: 'shake hands firmly, with everybody – man, woman or child'. To say I know the rule is to say that I have it ready, and when the appropriate situation occurs I use it to shape whatever I am doing at that particular moment. I do not need to explain the fact that I am doing something but what I need to explain is *what* it is that I am doing. The rule or plan that an ethogenist is going to look for is the psychological powerful particular.

But what has all this got to do with the realist theory of science? The answer is simple. The realist theory of science bids us imagine possible generative mechanisms of the patterns we observe, controlling our scientific imagination by modelling our imagined generative processes upon mechanisms and processes we already know. The message is clear. We must develop hypotheses about the generation of patterns of social action by analogy with those cases where we consciously create a pattern of action by following a rule. The imagined rules are hypothetical powerful particulars. Thus, on this view, I am to see both my social habits and my conscious social manipulations as patterned according to rules. In the former case these are like the rules of language, a system of norms whose expression in explicit statements awaits the grammarian of the social world, the new-style social psychologist. In the latter, they are like rules of etiquette, or maxims of acceptable behaviour, which a person consults deliberately. I shall be enlarging on these matters in a later section of the chapter.

Preserving the level of meaning

In order to pursue the question of the causality of social patterns we must be equipped with an analytical device by means of which we can identify the elements or units or component parts of such actions. A valuable maxim for controlling the analysis that we make of social patterns for psychological purposes was offered many years ago by the great Russian psychologist Vigotsky. The maxim is this: never analyse a psychological process into units which are below the meaning level of the original phenomenom. Now I can illustrate the force of this maxim by an example, though for illustrative purposes I shall choose a simpler example than any social process is likely to be. Suppose I am concerned with analysing the following: 'the cat'. It is a fragment of language. How should I analyse it? According to Vigotsky (1962), I must analyse this for psycholinguistic purposes into units of meaning. But I must choose a level of analysis appropriate to the kind of meaning which the phrase has as a fragment of language. For illustrative purposes we might say that the word 'the' would be one elementary unit and 'cat' would be another. That is, the analysis would yield two units and the total meaning of the phrase would be a function of the meaning of those units. If someone were to raise the question, 'What about the meaning of the individual letters?' one might be inclined to reply that they had not understood the point of the analysis. The *letter* 't' and the *letter* 'c' are not meaning units in the sense in which the phrase 'the cat' has meaning in a linguistic context. If analysis proceeds to the point of such units as the individual letters, the analyst has missed the point. It is an analysis which fails to observe the mode of meaning of the original phenomena.

But such an analysis is not wholly pointless because it would be appropriate for solving another type of problem. Suppose the problem were to encode the sentence fragment 'the cat'. We might make up a code with the form:

t = 17, h = 3, e = 12, space = 4, c = 8 and a = 27.

If one were trying to operate with the phrase at the level of linguistic meaning, say, for example, if one were translating the phrase into Spanish, it would be useless to attempt the translation by carrying out a unit by unit substitution at the encoding level of an analysis. To translate into Spanish one would have to make a meaning-unit analysis, and by substitution, one would get the phrase *el gato*. The fact that the Spanish phrase is *el gato* is extremely convenient for purposes of this illustration, since there is certainly no one-to-one letter correspondence by which 'the cat' can be transformed into *el gato*. This is, of course, an obvious point about language. But precisely the same maxim which would be taken for granted by any linguist applies to all other human-constructed forms of which meaning is an essential feature.

Psychologists have frequently supposed that one can divide up socially meaningful phenomena into basic non-meaningful units between which they have sought the kinds of correlations which Boyle and Hooke found between the pressures and volumes of gases. Let me give you an example. There have been studies of the development of liking between human beings. Psychologists have sought to investigate this process by identifying elementary features of the liking-generating process and studying them independently of all other features of a real situation of liking. They have isolated the frequency with which a person is confronted with another person as an element in the formation of liking between people. And then they have attempted to study the effect of frequency of meeting on the development of liking in an apparently 'pure' case. To this end, people were asked to report on the way in which their liking of nonsense syllables had changed with the frequency of presentation of such syllables.

It should be clear that the most elementary examination of the social interaction which produces feelings of liking or disliking between people involves intimately and inextricably other elements besides mere frequency. Frequency is equivocal in social meaning. The notion of frequency by itself is not a social concept. It is an element which lacks the level of meaning at which liking and similar concepts apply. We have to know what the social meaning of the frequency of interaction is. Is it an accidental co-occurrence of two people on the morning bus? Is the propinquity forced upon the interactants, and so on? A great deal will depend upon what a frequency of interaction means to the individual people involved.

It is essential in doing social science to distinguish between two distinct levels of human interaction. There is the physical interaction by which, say, the noises made by one person affect the ears of another; and there is the message conveyed; the study of the vehicles and of their meanings. Both are legitimate subjects for study, but in social matters the universal patterns which science seeks are to be found among the meanings. For example, a ceremony of parting is a socially meaningful act and it may be achieved by a widely differing variety of physical forms, from shouts to kisses and waves.

The analysis of social action

In order to apply the general theory to the construction of a particular explanation of the social behaviour of human beings, it will be necessary to devise an analysis of social life which does not violate Vigotsky's maxim. The analysis will lead to units of social life to which we give the technical name 'episodes'. Any coherent fragment of social life is an episode. A lecture by a visiting lecturer with introduction, thanks and ritual meal to follow would be an episode. To enter a university, study for five years, take your degree and join lay society once again would be an episode. To go to a restaurant, eat, pay and leave with expressions of civility would be an episode. To get married and divorced would be an episode. All these are life units of a certain kind. The idea of an episode is, then, very general, involving some coherence of meaning in a pattern of actions.

We have introduced a new word for the kind of psychology which concentrates on a meaning-and-rule analysis of episodes. It is the adjective 'ethogenic', from which comes the noun 'ethogeny'. The word is patterned on 'ethology', the new-style animal study associated with Konrad Lorenz and Niko Tinbergen (1969) in which the lives of animals are studied as they are really lived. 'Ethogeny' is the study of human lives as they are really lived, not in the strange and impoverished world of laboratories, but out in the streets, at home, in shops and cafés and lecture rooms where people really interact. The word 'ethogenic' expresses the idea of the psychological component of social science as a search for the origin or genesis of human social actions. Actions are not just behaviours. They are meaningful, and sometimes purposeful performances.

An ethogenic analysis of episodes, that is, an analysis which pays attention to the mode of genesis of the actions and the origin of their patterns which make up the episode, yields a three-fold division of patterns of social action into the formal, biological and enigmatic.

A formal episode is created by the performance of a pattern of actions by the participants knowingly and deliberately following the rules which lay down the order and character of the component actions.

A very important feature of the rule-following theory is its insistence that even though *all* the rules may not be free human constructions, because of the universality of some biological constraint, a human being is *always* a free human agent, with respect to the rules of formal or ceremonial episodes. Anybody consciously involved in a formal episode can abrogate or abort the process at any stage provided he, or she, is prepared to pay the social penalty. It is always possible to get up and go away, except perhaps for such social events as executions. To abrogate the rules is to go in for what we call 'a proof of autonomy'. To prove that one is a free and autonomous human being one can best select some formal situation and then refuse to follow the rules.

Biological episodes involve a quite different relation to consciousness. In a biological episode the pattern of behaviour is produced by physiological mechanisms, of the action of which we are only spectators. Consider a case of influenza. There is nothing the patient can do about it consciously speaking. He must simply stand by and observe what goes on in his body. He is not capable of a proof of autonomy with respect to that pattern of happenings. This is true of a number of physiological processes such as digestion and heartbeat. Breathing is an interesting intermediate case. But the category of purely biological episodes covers only a very small part of human life.

Most of human life is neither formal nor biological. It is enigmatic. We do not know whether the patterns are the direct result of the operation of biological mechanisms, or whether they stem from some form of rule-following. We just do not know what is going on to produce the pattern that we observe. Let me give you an example. Imagine you are at a formal academic lecture. You are watching the speaker, conscientiously taking notes, listening attentively from time to time, properly dressed in the style which is now *de rigeur*. Why are you doing all those things? Isn't it a strange thing to find about fifty people sitting quietly for an hour while one person talks? I will guarantee that you cannot stay silent in a normal home situation for more than five minutes. How do we explain this enigmatic episode?

If you walk down the street, why don't you bump into people? How is it possible to make your way with all those people milling about? It is neither an automatic biological process, nor a piece of conscious rule-following. An enormous amount of social life is enigmatic and particularly the social matters most important at any individual level. If you become friendly with someone, was it a biological episode, or was it achieved by following rules? It seems to be neither of these. It is, therefore, enigmatic, though – and here is an important clue – there are manuals or rule-books for achieving social constructive acts like making friends; for example, the famous manuals by Carnegie (1953) and Potter (1970). We shall see how this is possible.

There would be no psychological component of social science if there were only the formal and biological kind of episode. The reason why we need a psychological component in social science is because there is a vast variety of episodes, the genesis of the patterns of which we do not understand. We do not know how they are produced nor how they are maintained. Ethogenic social psychology produces a revolutionary change in attitude to the investigation of such episodes.

For the last thirty years social psychology has taken the physiological genesis of biological episodes as a model and tried to construct concepts for the enigmatic from it. For example, in the work of R. B. Zajonc (1969) you will find exactly the use of the physiological basis for explanations of the enigmatic. He speaks of getting friendly with someone as 'decline in response competition'. Now a decline in response competition is a physiological concept and he conceives of the process of getting friendly as something like this: the less your responses to the person as stimulus object are in competition with one another, the more friendly you are likely to be with him. But it is easy to see that the sense in which you respond to someone as a friend is, at best, a tenuous analogue of 'response' in the sense of, say, the 'galvanic skin response'. How you respond to your friend is mediated by meanings, upset by misunderstandings, maintained by constructive forgiveness for occasional coolness. It is a complex and elaborate structure of custom, skilled action and interpretation of meaning in which each person is an agent. The explanation of why all this elaborate and unstable structure is thought capable of being crammed into the one-dimensional functional relation between feeling friendly and decline of response competition is that the idea behind the psychological theory is derived from a physiological conception. Biology is taken as the model for the explanation of social patterns. The ethogenic revolution in social psychology is expressed in the principle 'Try to understand the enigmatic by means of development of the concepts appropriate to the explanation of the patterns of formal episodes'. Let us try to understand the enigmatic region of human behaviour by reference to imagined processes conceived on the model of rule-following, meaning-endowing and grasping; in short, of intelligent forms of action.

We already possess a vast storehouse of information and principles of explanation for the understanding of many enigmatic episodes. This is the ordinary system of concepts and the ordinary mode of explanation which is found, I suppose, most fully deployed in the phenomenon of gossip and has been refined and developed by novelists, playwrights, clinical psychologists, lawyers, policemen, judges and so on. A very sophisticated conceptual apparatus is utilized by such people in the explanation of patterns of social behaviour. For example, a very widely applicable law exemplified from day to day, both amongst children and adults, is the principle that people often attempt to ameliorate their own shortcomings by transferring the blame for failure from themselves to some other person significant to them. Part of the programme of ethogenic social psychology is the systematic rescue of such explanatory principles from scientific obscurity. A start in this direction has been made by Opie and Opie (1959) in their study of children's social order, but a great deal more requires to be done. I also believe that in the work of Erving Goffman a considerable start has been made in the more systematic exploration of what we should call the ethogeny of enigmatic parts of social life. For example, in his recent book *Relations in Public* (1971) amongst many other aspects of social behaviour he and his students have analysed the processes by which people organize their passages through a crowded street and, not surprisingly, it turns out to be a mixture of habitual following, of convention and intelligent evasive action, according to rule. Common-sense explanation is a social psychology which deserves to be taken seriously, at the same time as we recognize that it is often an unexamined element in the identification of social phenomena by the psychologists and sociologists.

But to proceed systematically, we have to construct models of the processes which are generating our social behaviour and we look, at least for a beginning, for a source for these models in the processes by which formal episodes are generated by conscious rule-following. Here we have a clear, though not as yet fully explored, idea of the generative forces at work in the translation of the fully specified rule into a determinate pattern of action. There are two very characteristic sorts of formal rule-following episodes in which we all engage and these will be the basis of the most general category of models. These formal episodes can be broadly divided into those which are ritualistic and those which are agonistic – that is, in which there is some form of rule-bound competitive action. Sometimes the latter sort have been called games. A ritual is a cooperative sequence of actions performed by several people in which some social act is achieved. A game is a competitive interaction between several people which similarly serves to perform a social act. For example, a quarrel can be treated on the agonistic model, where a rule-bound, competitive episode is seen as the performance of a social act, such as the establishment of a social micro-hierarchy. On the other hand, getting married is a ritualistic way of changing the social order. Once the ceremony has been performed a profound change has taken place in society, ramifying out through hundreds of people. The two getting married are just the focus and centre of a very complex network of changes in relationships. A new element in the social order has been created and the ritual of marriage is a co-operative way of proceeding to do it.

The utility of the adoption of these broad categories of models can be illustrated by the light they throw on what happens inside the family.

The social function of rule-bound competitive processes may be that of setting up a family hierarchy. Quarrels will have a totally different interpretation if they are seen in this context than if they are seen simply as the product of an abrasive emotional conflict. Once one conceives of the family as organized into a hierarchy which was created by quarrels which have been won and lost from time to time, one can understand other actions by the members as challenges to this hierarchy. Very frequently a small child will challenge for control of the family, and indeed may well succeed in organizing the status hierarchy to his own advantage. The very earliest days of a marriage have agonistic elements in them which are involved in the setting up of a status hierarchy which may have very great resistance to change.

Similarly, much of family life has a ritualistic form. The distribution of food is often ritualistically carried out, in that the meals are at set times and will have little to do with the biological necessities of the nourishment of a family. In many families there are special ways of distributing the food, which serve to reflect family structures in a formal way. It is not necessary to visit the remoter New Guinea tribes to see the captured animal being divided up and apportioned in a wholly ritualistic way. The same can be seen at almost any Anglo-American dining table.

We must now turn to the problem of developing the outlines of a psychological theory to explain the genesis of the kind of micro-social interaction which can be seen to occur in human life when we take the ethogenic viewpoint.

An individual psychology of social action

When we analyse social life by treating social persons and the actions they engage in as fundamentally ceremonial and under the control of rules and conventions, we will find that we can express our knowledge of the rituals and games that we identify in terms of certain systems of rules, and our knowledge of the appropriate personas in certain principles of deportment and maxims of good behaviour. But social analysis is not the only way of discovering hypothetical rules.

Most of the time, most people live out their social lives successfully simply by having certain social habits; that is, we do not usually reflect on what we are doing and consciously control it. We only start to think about what to do when we are uncertain of ourselves. Only in the situation when the rules are unknown or when the rules run out, do we consciously attend to our actions and become aware of our social habits. Finally, and very importantly, conscious attention to social habits and the maxims and principles of our actions also becomes important when what we have done or propose to do is under challenge and some justification is required from us. Characteristically in that situation we refer to the rules.

We must, then, conceive of a system of concepts appropriate to the analysis of an individual psychology of rule-following. Complementary to the notion of a rule is, of course, the requirement that the situations to which the rule is to be applied have been recognized for what they are, that is, recognized socially. The complementary concept to rule is then that of social meaning. We must be able to identify the social meaning of a situation before we can properly act on the appropriate rule. The ethogenic movement supposes that the rule-following process can be broadly described in terms of four general concepts. First of all, a person has to try and decide what it is that is happening. This can be comprehended under the concept of 'situational definition'. Let me give you an example. Suppose one were to reach out one's hand towards a stranger. Provided that the stranger recognizes the situation as the initiation of a greeting ceremony, he is likely to shake it. However, should he mistake it for the opening move of a karate encounter he is likely to respond in a wholly different fashion. Or indeed, he might simply slip five new pence into one's hand supposing that the gesture was that of a beggar. Social action can only begin when the situation has been defined. This idea is of considerable antiquity, having been revived in recent times by the unjustly neglected sociologist and psychologist W. I. Thomas (1928).

The second element in the psychological processes creative of social action is that of the choice of appropriate social persona. In the previous example I spoke of a gesture being socially identified as being an act of begging. Now those who beg are beggars. There is, therefore, a very close connection between situational definition and individual identification. Identities are created in interactions. This is the basis of the so-far unexploited work of Simmons and McCall (1966). It is also a key part in Goffman's theory of the social self (1970). He sees it as constructed by and identified in the manner or style in which social interaction is performed. And of course, if we reflect again on the outstretched hand, it is the manner of its outstretching that identifies it as an aggressive karate opening or a deferential begging gesture.

But social action is not always the immediate response to a direct and immediate challenge for performance. It is very often the product of some antecedent thought. A third element enters into the psychology of the individual in social action through the existence of preparatory run-throughs, particularly those made in the imagination. In fact, such trial runs of action are often performed in the mind's eye before a particular person who serves as the arbiter or judge of the propriety of the social action. If one is preparing one's performance at a committee one probably bears in mind the reactions of a certain individual for whom that performance is primarily put on. This element we call 'the judge'. Of course 'the judge' is not a particular envisaged person in every case but we are inclined to believe that the personification of the rules of social propriety in the imagined social reactions of particular people is a much more common phenomenon than one might think. There is some strong empirical evidence from recent studies of fetishism to suggest that accounts, that is excuses and justification, are prepared by the fetishist to justify his odd behaviour for those whose opinions he takes to be socially significant.

The final element is, of course, the rules that are known to the person explicitly or are enshrined in social habits: rules to which we might refer should those habits be challenged.

Table 2

situations	personas	arbiters	rules
s_1	p_1	j_1	(r_1)
s_2	p_2	j_2	(r_2)
—	—	—	—
s_n	p_n	j_n	(r_n)

The matrix laid out in Table 2 is intended to represent schematically a very much more complex actual structure. Each element is itself complex. That is, a situational definition is a cognitive structure of considerable elaboration as is a social persona. We would regard it as reasonable to pursue the empirical filling out of each of the key elements by the use of the methods that Kelly has recommended for the discovery of cognitive structure – that is, linkages between key elements in the microstructure of the leading concepts constitute the cognitive resources of the individuals involved in a particular interaction.

Now it is part of the ethogenic revolution to insist that each human being is not a single socio-psychological individual, but a complicated set of such individuals. In fact, ethogenists think of each human being, each biological individual, as having a set of such cognitive structures as could be expressed under the four concepts of situational definition, social persona, arbiter or judge and rule system. The social-psychological analysis of a human being involves the attempt to discover what are his available social resources; that is, what repertoire of definitions, personas, arbiters and rule systems does he have at his disposal. Social action is then, in our view, skilled action, and I share the idea of social skill with Argyle. I part company with him, however, in insisting that the skills that are involved in the deployment of these conceptual resources are not to be conceived on the model of motor skills but are rather of intellectual skills directly deployed in the attempt to solve a continuous sequence of problems presented by the appearance of other human beings in situations in which interaction is inevitable.

Finally, one must notice that this operational structure is qualified throughout by a flux of emotions and moods. But from an ethogenic point of view emotions and moods are seen as the products of a meaning endowing interpretation of the states of excitation etc. of the human system. To return to the spaghetti-factory image, they represent the rate of flow of the pasta through the factory, not by a raw datum, but as interpreted by the workers in that establishment. A sudden gush will be treated in many different ways, depending on whether it is thought to come from the malice of the pasta-mixer, or to be due to a blockage in the tubes or whatever.

Scenarios and the reconstruction of reality

A change to a realistic conception of science involves not only the shift of structure that was outlined in the first section but a shift of aim as well. The advanced sciences are very much less concerned with prediction than has been assumed by those who have sought to copy them in setting up an apparently scientific psychology. As a major aim, prediction is almost confined to the sciences of astronomy and to terrestrial branches of mechanics. In the other sciences, prediction is only a subsidiary ideal for the scientific enterprise. For *most science* the aim is explanation. This aim is achieved by an understanding of the generative mechanisms by which patterns of nature are produced, as outlined in the first section. But how do we know that we have succeeded in achieving adequate knowledge of such mechanisms? Here we had best abandon the model of physics and turn to chemistry for a guide. A chemist considers that he has achieved a successful understanding of a compound on the basis of the discoveries he has made of its structure and components in the course of his analysis. Chemistry then turns from analysis to synthesis. It is part of our recommendation for the reform of social psychology that it too should turn from the predictive experimental model for empirical studies to the analysis/synthesis conception that is found in classical chemistry.

The object of a social psychology conceived on the model of chemistry is to obtain so detailed a knowledge of the rules, conventions, situational meanings and so on, by which skilled and intelligent actors manage their social lives, that any particular fragment of social reality can be reconstructed. The art then of the social-psychological investigator comes closer to that of the playwright than it does to that of the astronomer or the mechanician. A playwright, in successfully creating social life before us on the stage, is deploying a vast amount of social-psychological knowledge. It is that knowledge which we wish to tap. The empirical method which will replace naïve experimentalism is then the method of scenarios. We attempt to create the psychological conditions by acquainting our interactants with the sort of knowledge which they ought to possess for skilled social interactions, as well as placing them in situations which they will define in certain ways.

A brilliant beginning of the new empirical style has been made by Mixon (1972) in his now famous reconstruction of Milgram's equivocal experiments (1963). Milgram, investigating the degree to which obedience could overcome moral scruples, found, or seemed to find, that something like half the people he studied were prepared to obey an experimenter to such a degree as to endanger the life of another person involved in the experiment. The peculiarity of this result has led to all kinds of bizarre speculations. However, Mixon was able to show that by introducing the neglected dimension of social meaning, and by paying careful attention to the definition of the situation, he was able to replicate any degree of obedience from total disobedience to perfect conformity. He was able to construct scenarios and to instruct the participants in his investigations in the kind of knowledge that sufficiently filled out their cognitive resources to allow an exact replication of reality. Do not mistake this for successful prediction. Of course, as a by-product, Mixon was able to predict with complete certainty what his participants would do, but this was, as Francis Bacon would have put it, only one of the troupe of effects which followed from a thorough understanding of the nature of the interaction involved in the Milgram experiment.

It is part of our purpose, then, to urge psychologists to follow Mixon into a new realm of empirical research.

References

CARNEGIE, C. (1953), *How to Win Friends and Influence People*, Cedar Books.

GOFFMAN, E. (1970), *Stigma*, Penguin.

GOFFMAN, E. (1971), *Relations in Public*, Allen Lane The Penguin Press.

MILGRAM, S. (1963), 'Behavioral study of obedience', *J. abnorm. soc. Psychol.*, vol. 67, pp. 371–8.

MIXON, D. (1972), 'Instead of deception', *J. Theory soc. Behav.*, vol. 2, pp. 145–77.

OPIE, P., and OPIE, I. (1959), *The Lore and Language of Schoolchildren*, Oxford University Press.

POTTER, S. (1970), *The Complete Upmanship*, Hart-Davis.

SIMMONS, J. L., and McCALL, G. J. (1966), *Identities and Interactions*, Free Press.

SKINNER, B. F. (1953), *Science and Human Behavior*, Free Press.

THOMAS, W. I. (1928), *The Child in America*, Knopf.

TINBERGEN, N. (1969), 'Ethology', in R. Harré (ed.), *Scientific Thought, 1900–1960*, Oxford University Press.

VIGOTSKY, L. (1962), *Thought and Language*, MIT Press.

ZAJONC, R. B. (1969), *Experimental Social Psychology*, Wiley.

Further Reading

ARGYLE, M., *Social Interaction*, Methuen, 1969.

FILMER, P., PHILLIPSON, M., SILVERMAN, D., and WALSH, D., *New Directions in Sociological Theory*, Collier-Macmillan, 1972.

GOFFMAN, E., *Interaction Ritual*, Allen Lane The Penguin Press, 1972.

HARRÉ, R., and SECORD, P. F. *The Explanation of Social Behaviour*, Blackwell, 1972.

HARRÉ, R. *The Principles of Scientific Thinking*, Macmillan, 1970.

VIGOTSKY, L., *Thought and Language*, MIT Press, 1962.

ZAJONC, R. B., 'Social facilitation', *Science*, vol. 149, pp. 267–74.

16 Assessing People[1]
John Heritage

Most of us in our daily lives are concerned with assessing people. Often we may have a direct purpose or interest in mind when we make these assessments. We may want to know how someone will vote in an election, how they might behave in a committee or whether they will keep a secret; we may try to guess whether someone will marry us or refuse us, whether they will help or hinder us, whether in the last analysis they are for or against us. In our more abstract moods, we may wonder if there are any general explanations for the things people do like biting their nails or smoking; we may even wonder what makes people 'tick'. Although assessing people and explaining and predicting their actions are very complicated activities, I want to try to compare the ways in which psychologists and ordinary people set about doing them, and to ask firstly how adequate the psychological methods of assessment are for their task, and secondly, is there some way for social psychologists to study how ordinary people do assessing, predicting and explaining? I will start by looking at psychologists.

Despite the idea propagated by philosophers of science that explanation and prediction are interdependent elements in an ongoing process of scientific understanding, in psychology explaining action and predicting action tend to be handled by different branches of the discipline. Explaining why people act is usually seen as the province of motivation theory, whilst predicting how they will act tends to be a rather piecemeal affair dominated by psychologists who concentrate on devising various types of assessment techniques and then making predictions on the basis of their results. Unfortunately, the relationship between the results of the tests on the one hand, and the various explanatory motivational variables on the other hand is by no means clearly understood at present. So, as my title implies, I want to ignore the rather large topic of motivation theory, and focus on psychological assessment, and in particular on personality and attitude measurement.

Psychologists and assessment

In their ongoing effort to predict the activities of ordinary people, psychologists have tended to concentrate on perfecting their measuring

1. I would like to thank Jeff Coulter, Nigel Armistead and Tim Lang for their detailed criticisms of an earlier draft of this paper. My errors remain my own.

devices. The devices which I have chosen to concentrate on – personality tests and attitude tests – all consist of answering questions. All of them also embody the broad assumption that there is some relationship between what a person says (about himself, an ink blot, a TAT card, a union, a racial minority and so on) and some subsequent activity which he or she might undertake. As my examples indicate, the questions which are asked vary a great deal from test to test, and correspondingly it is also true that the answers are used in a wide variety of ways by psychologists. For instance, depending on the style of analysis adopted, an answer to a question about unions may be used to evaluate a person's personality, or his self-conception or his attitudes. Thus the particular inferences which are drawn from a person's responses tend to vary with the theoretical ideas of the investigator in charge. The point I want to make here is that psychologists use all kinds of questions to evaluate people's personalities and attitudes, that psychologists' conceptions of 'personality', 'attitude' and 'self-conception' are quite diverse, and that their methods of inference from the data to the theoretical constructs are also pretty varied. These are points which are worth bearing in mind.

Attitudes

For Gordon Allport, the attitude concept is 'the primary building stone in the edifice of social psychology'. Allport defines an attitude as

a mental and neural state of readiness, organized through experience, exerting a directive or dynamic influence upon the individual's response to all objects and situations with which it is related (Allport, 1935, p. 844).

However, despite Allport's somewhat rhetorical reference to 'neural states', it remains true to say that attitudes have always been measured via *verbal* responses. Now regardless of the particular items that make up an attitude test, three major problems dominate the field as a whole:

1 The problematic empirical relationship between verbal responses and overt actions;

2 The problem of the actual nature of the link between a score on an attitude test and the tendency to act in a particular way;

3 The problem of validity.

I will proceed to the first two problems immediately, but defer discussion of the third issue until personality assessment is in the picture.

1. Words and deeds. The idea that what people say and what they do should correlate is perhaps as old as language itself, yet its self-evident flavour is eroded by the equally obvious truth that people may lie about their views, they may have ulterior motives for concealing their ideas and so on. Thus paradoxically, it is the *failure* of the self-evident connection between saying and doing which in part provides the impetus to do attitude research. This failure has been well documented by psychologists themselves. Thus Lapiere's classic study of the attitude–action relationship in racial prejudice revealed a 90 per cent *negative* correlation between expressed attitudes towards Chinese-Americans and the action taken towards them. The fact that people will say one thing and do another thus leads psychologists to ask numbers of questions in the hope that if patterns of answers develop there will be more likelihood that the person will act in the way the pattern indicates. This hope has not by and large been realized. Thus Wicker's survey of studies on the attitude–action relationship came to highly negative conclusions:

Taken as a whole, these studies suggest that it is considerably more likely that attitudes will be unrelated or only slightly related to overt behaviours than that attitudes will be closely related to actions. . . .

The present review provides little evidence to support the postulated existence of stable underlying attitudes within the individual which influence both his verbal expressions and his actions (Wicker, 1969, pp. 161, 173).

As both Wicker (1969) and Blumer (1969a) have pointed out, this lack of correlation between attitudes and overt actions is hardly surprising in view of the very large number of contingencies which affect actions. These contingencies affect not only a person's choice of an action, but also his expression of an attitude and, as Taylor (1972) has recently demonstrated, his description of his inmost motives. Summing up, it is clear that *both* the expression of attitudes *and* the concrete actions of ordinary people are subject to a range of contingencies which we have hardly begun to study, let alone analyse satisfactorily.

2. Attitudes and actions – the nature of the link. The second major issue in attitudes studies concerns the nature of the relationship, if one exists, between attitudes and actions. Here, as Defleur and Westie (1963) point out, there are two front runners: a 'probability' conception and a 'hidden-mechanism' theory. The 'probability' conception of attitudes is basically a refusal to theorize about the relationship between attitudes and actions. In keeping with the theoretical parsimony of S–R research (with which the probability account of attitudes is sometimes connected), the 'probability' researcher simply records the correlation of a score on a test with a tendency to act in a particular way. The 'probability' viewpoint and its associated theoretical underpinnings have been extensively criticized by Harré and Secord (1972) and their criticisms will not be repeated here.

However, the ultimate justification of the 'probability' model lies in its utility: thus if it were the case that constant correlations between test scores and actions had been found (and they have not been so far), the result would be a useful predictive tool. Yet even if this were established, the inductive 'theory-less' status of the model militates against its effectiveness because it demands an entirely *static* relationship between a score on the fixed attitude test and the predicted action. If for some reason the relationship were to alter (for instance, because of some autonomous change in general social opinion), not only would the predictions be nullified, but also our atheoretical psychologist would be left in no position to understand or allow for this altered state of affairs. This basic defect in atheoretical assessment may seem relatively unimportant in view of the general empirical failure of the programme. However it does articulate with a further problem in this type of research, namely, its orientation to the psychological subject.

As a number of contributors to this volume and to *Rat, Myth and Magic* have made clear, the research machinery and theoretical outlook of S–R theory have been fundamentally *manipulative* in orientation. This manipulative orientation is compounded by the absence of adequate validation of attitude–action correlations, and the inability of atheoretical models to deal with the fact that the correlations could vary over time in line with general secular changes in social life. Such failures as the above result in an overall absence of safeguards against the manipulative tendencies of the assessment enterprise as a whole. These manipulative tendencies develop in the following way. Firstly, lay organizations in society such as the Army, large corporations and so on are encouraged to accept the view (which is largely unsubstantiated) that psychologists can predict the performance of recruits to their enterprises using attitude and personality tests. In the absence of adequate validation (whose methodological problems will be dealt with below), the tests tend to develop into self-fulfilling prophecies: the person who did 'well' on the test 'turned out all right on the job', whilst the person who did 'badly' on the test 'would never have been any good anyway', whilst at worst the tests, whose operation is permeated with social and ideological assumptions (see below), are merely successful in identifying a person's political and social beliefs.

It may be that many social psychologists will find these assertions tenuous either because they are unwilling to recognize the circular operation of definitions in social processes or because they feel that psychological assessments could not be involved in such processes. Yet those who are unconvinced need only look at the data relating to self-confirming social processes in the apparently more 'objective' area of I Q testing (Rosenthal and Jacobson, 1968) to see the possibilities of a parallel process in the general field of psychological assessment, whilst the history of our understanding of working-class potentialities in relation to the educational system illustrates the problems on a societal scale (Jackson and Marsden, 1962). In view of this kind of evidence, it is clear that if the results of atheoretical attitude and personality testing are taken seriously by laymen in the future, one major result will be a greatly increased incidence of 'self-confirming' predictions by psychologists. The rigid operation of 'probability-oriented' attitude and personality tests will undoubtedly be highly conducive to the future involvement of both psychologists and practical people in a vicious circle of self-fulfilling predictions mediated by the manipulative structures in our society.

The second approach to the relationship between attitudes and actions which Defleur and Westie (1963) outline is the 'hidden-mechanism' approach. This approach postulates an underlying, unobservable but causal and directive mechanism which provides a stable basis for activity by mediating between events in the world and people's reactions to them. Although a causal model of the role of attitudes is assumed to hold, the proponents of the 'hidden-mechanism' theory typically remain unclear about the nature of both the causal mechanism and its effects. As Blumer points out in a study of this problem, the demonstration of the causal role of attitudes is a complex and difficult operation. Thus:

Instead of merely correlating the two ends of the act – the tendency and the overt behaviour – one would trace out in a step-by-step manner how the tendency played into the developing act, shaped wishes and impulses, fashioned perception, determined selections and dictated decisions (Blumer, 1969a, p. 94).

Blumer is subsequently able to demonstrate that no social psychologist has been able to trace through this causal chain, and also suggests that such a chain of inference is itself decisively counter-intuitive. As Coulter has indicated, the problems of attitude testing revolve around the fact that

both self-conception and attitude define possible tendencies to act, but some knowledge of either in a social situation is not sufficient for us to assert that self-conception or attitude actually direct any given activity (Coulter, 1973b, p. 54).

To see why this is the case we must return to the basis of an attitude survey: the questions. Following a suggestion of Louch (1966), I want to argue here that the kinds of statements which make up attitude (and personality) questionnaires are primarily *moral* statements; that is, statements which people use to entitle, justify or excuse a *particular* action in a *particular context*. If this is true, then it follows that the use of such statements to explain and predict actions in a causal and *indiscriminate* way (i.e. independent of context) can only end in failure. Curiously enough ordinary people themselves intuitively grasp this difficulty: as any interviewer will tell you, people just do not want to answer specific-sounding questions in general terms (see Roiser, this volume); their attitude is enshrined in the interviewer's bugbear 'it all depends'.

Now it is partly because of this problem, and partly because people do not act in the way their attitudes suggest, that psychologists compile a wide variety of questions to present to people in the hope that their questions will tap the main dimensions of a wide variety of related issues. This move would appear to be entirely sensible, yet it compounds the problem of the particularity of moral statements in the following way. The various questions are aimed at tapping a variety of moral issues in accordance with the logic of attitudes understood as an underlying causal structure, and the results of the questions are typically aggregated into scores on unidimensional scales like the tough/tenderminded scale for instance. Now if, as I shall argue later, the attitude items do not relate to an underlying causal structure, but in fact have their own socially sustained logics and relevances to social participants, the aggregated results simply succeed in destroying the intricately structured and differentiated patterns of inference and judgement which are employed by people in the various cognitive domains tapped by the questions. On this reading, the score which finally eventuates is as useful in predicting social activity as the chemical analysis of superheated DNA would be in locating the structure and function of genes. In both cases the effect is the same: the structure which contains the information is smashed into a 'soup' and the knowledge which we retrieve is reduced to banality. Using attitude studies as a psychological tool is rather like trying to understand genetic codes when all our techniques can tell us is that genes are made up of carbon, nitrogen and oxygen. Perhaps this is why ordinary people find the results of attitude tests to be elementary, and complain that we spend far too much money proving the obvious.

Summing up here, we might say that the scientifically respectable conception of attitudes in probabilistic terms may or may not generate useful manipulative measures, but that their utility is far from stable (because the attitude–action relationship may change with the climate of opinion), nor is it scientifically established. The 'hidden-mechanism' approach to attitudes is less respectable because its problems are more obvious: the operation of the causal links is entirely unclarified and is conceptualized in a counter-intuitive way. Both approaches share the flaw of 'denaturizing' the way we see and evaluate the world by turning the way we do these things into a kind of 'soup' which can then be summarized by a number. It is hardly surprising then that under these conditions attitude *research* flourishes – it solves policy makers' problems and is an easy Ph.D. area, whilst attitude *theory* is non-existent. Since theory is the hall-mark of the mature sciences, our conclusion can only be that psychologists' scientific methodology has – in this area at least – left them without a scientific enterprise. Finally, it is clear that the idea that answers to questions can be used to index some invariant and causally operative structure is one which is not supported by current research results.

Personality assessment

Personality assessment is also enmeshed in a wide variety of difficulties (Bannister, 1970). Some of these difficulties are shared with attitude testing because both sorts of tests use similar techniques. Unfortunately the consequences of these difficulties in terms of inadequate evaluation are more serious for the subject of a personality assessment. This is because whereas attitudes are usually thought of as subject to change, 'personality structure', being more 'fundamental' and 'underlying', is seen as less flexible. The result is that if the subject's replies to questions are construed as an assessment of his 'personality', he is likely to be trapped within a more final and total evaluation than if they were regarded as an assessment of his 'attitudes'.

Rather than repeat earlier arguments which hold with respect to both attitude and personality assessment, I want to turn to some methodological problems which also have relevance for both types of assessment technique. These methodological problems turn on the issue of the 'contamination' of psychological tests and experiments by social factors. For example, it is well known that the social setting of an experiment, or even that the experiment is *known* to be an experiment, will 'contaminate' (introduce variance) the results. Now despite one or two notorious cases[2], the contamination of psychological *tests* is not generally believed to be a serious problem. In fact, however, social factors contaminate psychological tests at every stage of their production and administration. They contaminate the constitution and construction of the tests, the assessment of the relationship between the answers of subjects and their projected later activities (i.e. the selection of the questions), the nature and dimensions of the (theoretically interpreted) 'facts' which the subject's answers or actions are seen as indicating (the coding procedures), the construction of the results by psychologists themselves, and the meaning of those results to ordinary people. Let me briefly review a few of these assertions.

2. The standard example is perhaps H. J. Eysenck's *The Psychology of Politics*.

The starting point in this review is the realization that personality assessment starts and finishes in the realm of ordinary language and the concepts and meanings that this ordinary language enshrines. Thus, bluntly, personality assessment starts with questions; questions like:

Are you inclined to be quick and sure in your actions?
Are you inclined to take life too seriously?
Does it embarrass you to do the wrong thing in a social group?
In social conversations are you usually a listener rather than a talker?
Were you ever 'the life of the party'? (Eysenck, 1960, p. 199)

Now some of these well-known question are idiomatic, some may even invite the respondent to lie, but the over-riding feature of these questions is that their meaning is extremely vague, or to be more technical they employ open-textured concepts. By 'open-textured' here I mean that the questions have no final or precisely formulable meaning, and a respondent could in principle ask us to elaborate the meaning of the question *ad infinitum* or at least until we got fed up with him (Garfinkel, 1967, p. 35–44). By the same token, answers to these questions do not take the form of mathematical expressions or numerically measurable statements (compare 'Do you take life too seriously?' with 'What is your height?'). In general we could reasonably expect highly variable types of answers to the list of questions above: an answer could be monosyllabic, or it could be so complicated that we could warrantably describe the question as 'initiating a psychoanalytic session'. It is precisely this variability in both the meaning of the question and the way in which the answer is expressed that Eysenck attempts to foreclose when he demands a simple Yes/No answer. What does this emphasis on the open-textured quality of concepts and questions mean for personality assessment? It means at the minimum that the person framing the question and the person answering it may have different ideas of what the question means. To quote Cicourel:

The researcher cannot assume that he and the actor enjoy the same community of subjective meaning structures for assigning cultural significance to an event or object (Cicourel, 1964, p. 199).

More generally, the open-textured quality of concepts and questions means that even where there is a general agreement on the meaning of a question the agreement is 'for practical purposes' or 'without getting too philosophical about it', rather than an agreement on an operational definition of something (e.g. voltage). Thus the meaning held in common will not provide a strong enough basis for mathematical measurement and quantitative operations. Where such measurement is undertaken it thus becomes what Torgerson (1958) has termed 'measurement by fiat'.

Now the questions at the beginning of the personality investigation are not its only imprecise and socially contaminated feature. Let us look at the end of the test and consider what your parents or any practical person would do when they were told that you had scored highly on a neuroticism scale. First of all, they will have to imagine what 'neuroticism' is, and to do this they will remember what some 'neurotic' acquaintance of theirs once did – perhaps the acquaintance drank too much or ran away from his wife. Sociologists usually call this process 'consulting one's common-sense knowledge' of, in this case, neuroticism. Cicourel describes the general process which is involved in your parents' understanding of neuroticism in the following way:

I am suggesting that labels designating a range of features . . . are used . . . as practical language games for simplifying the task of summarizing a visual field and complex stimuli that are difficult to describe in some precise detailed way. This means that the labels do not recover the appearances and imputations subsumed by the participant unless imagined details are supplied by an auditor during the course of the interaction. . . . This elaboration supplied by the actor – an elaboration not subject (by him) to verification – serves his practical interests (Cicourel, 1973, p. 25).

Thus a further source of social contamination develops at the end of the assessment because people who are told that you are neurotic fill in this description in ways which are both imprecise and unchecked by the methods of natural science. The time-honoured defence against this process is to argue that 'neuroticism' is what the C scale measures, yet it is clear that this argument is hardly relevant to your parents who do not know the items on the C scale, could not grasp them all at once if they did, and in any case could hardly evaluate the effects of mathematical techniques like 'rotation'. For practical people 'neuroticism' means a more or less permanent disposition to act in unusual and anti-social ways – you might find them reacting to you accordingly.

Clearly these points could be multiplied and elaborated for every stage of processing in a personality test. By way of example, I will look at two more areas, the coding of open-ended questions and researcher-generated bias, before evaluating the basic and classic defences erected by psychologists against these troubles.

In all questionnaires or interviews involving open-ended questions – these particularly arise in sociological research and in psychological tests such as the TST, TAT and Rorschach – there arises the problem of coding responses. One aspect of the coding process that studies of coding procedures have shown to be centrally important is the finding that no matter how well trained coders are, and no matter how detailed the

coding instructions are, an invariant feature of coding activity is the practice of 'ad hocing'. In the 'ad hocing' procedure, the coder discovers
'what is really meant' or 'the rock-bottom meaning' of a response by
matching the response with their socially organized knowledge of (or
socially organized psychological knowledge of) 'what the question is
about'. This matching process is *never* entirely precise (because of the
open-textured nature of the concepts involved) and the 'adequate coding
match' is thus a practical achievement decided on 'for now' in response
to the practical exigencies of coding. Thus the *ad hoc* devices of 'et cetera',
'let it pass', 'it will do for now' have to be used in the face of open-textured questions just to get the job of coding done. Thus coders of open-
ended questions do exactly what Cicourel is talking about (above) *just
to get a set of coded answers*. Here again then pure knowledge is unavoidably contaminated by loosely structured common-sense knowledge,
although 'contamination' is hardly the right word here, because, as
Garfinkel points out, the coding could not be done at all if common-sense
knowledge was not appealed to in this way. In relation to this issue,
Garfinkel comments:

Nor is it the case that *ad hoc* practices such as 'et cetera' or 'let it pass' are controlled or eliminated in their presence, use, number or occasions of use by making
coding instructions as definite as possible. Instead, *ad hoc* considerations are consulted by coders and ad hocing practices are used *in order to recognize what the
instructions are definitely talking about*. *Ad hoc* considerations are consulted by
coders in order to recognize coding instructions as 'operational definitions' of
coding categories. They operate as the grounds for and as methods to advance
and secure researchers' claims to have coded in accordance with 'necessary and
sufficient' criteria. . . .

To treat instructions as though *ad hoc* features in their use were a nuisance, or
to treat their presence as grounds for complaint about the incompleteness of instructions, is very much like complaining that if the walls of the building were
gotten out of the way one could see better what was keeping the roof up (Garfinkel, 1967, p. 22).

Garfinkel's last point can hardly be of much comfort to the social psychologist of personality who uses open-ended questions, since if his coders are
continually invoking *ad hoc* common-sense knowledge about 'personality'
to grasp 'what is really meant' by the responses, the results can only be
circular: that is, the coders' own common-sense knowledge (or psychological knowledge) about 'personality' is continually being built into the
results.

A further source of social 'contamination' ironically comes from the
researcher himself. This is because even the researcher is involved in the

process described by Cicourel when he evaluates the significance of his results, and therefore must bring socially generated assumptions into his evaluation of their meaning and significance. The commonly accepted use of mathematical techniques to collect co-varying items is of little help in evading the problem because ultimately a point will come when some evaluation has to be made. As Weber pointed out seventy years ago, this process involves the translation of mathematical expressions into a set of socially meaningful categories and conclusions. Such a process can never be entirely neutral, and the attempt to ignore its 'one-sidedness' can only result in the mystification of psychological research.

In this discussion I have pointed out a few of the many points at which socially organized knowledge is *necessarily* incorporated in an *unavoidably* loose way into the results of psychological tests. Since socially organized knowledge is very frequently ideological knowledge possessing built-in evaluative dimensions, its necessary incorporation into psychological results decisively weakens the claim of psychology to be a value-free discipline. Similarly the open-textured quality of the knowledge involved seriously vitiates the possibilities of psychology as a deductive–nomological enterprise.

Pre-coding and operational definition

The major devices used by social psychologists to eliminate the kind of 'contamination' I have been discussing have been the 'pre-coding' of questionnaire items using criterion groups, and the development of operational definitions. In the first method, groups of persons selected in terms of some characteristic (e.g. 'neuroticism'), or in terms of their representativeness of some wider group, are given an extended selection of items which are deemed (again in terms of common-sense knowledge) to relate to the area under study. The items to which they respond in a uniform and significant way are then selected for the questionnaire that will be administered to the wider population. Here it is clear that a great deal of socially organized knowledge gets built in during the selection of the criterion group. The researcher basically has two options:

1 He can select his criterion group (e.g. neurotics) from his acquaintances – they might be people whose hands shake at parties or who hate interviews for jobs;

2 He can select a group of people officially diagnosed as neurotic to help him.

Clearly his own common-sense knowledge of 'neuroticism' is involved in the first approach, whilst his second option places some strain on the objectivity of psychiatric diagnosis. Without going into detail here, it is clear that studies of psychiatric diagnosis do not give credence to the idea that there exist universal and unambiguous signs of psychiatric illness. Diagnoses are practical affairs which vary between psychiatrists, and often appear to depend on complexes of socially sanctioned inferences (Coulter, 1973b, p. 8). Once again then we are back in the realm of open-textured, evaluative common-sense knowledge as not simply a contamination in social psychological tests, but a foundation on which they are built and evaluated. In sum, the method of pre-coding questionnaire items is a device aimed at developing and validating complex and mechanically structured schemes of inference such that once the responses are obtained, they can be analysed 'untouched by imprecise and subjective human bias'. As I hope I have demonstrated, this illusory goal is only 'achieved' by building in the imprecise, evaluative social assumptions at the start.

The psychologist who rests his case on operational definitions is quite indifferent to the sorts of processes I have been outlining. As a pragmatic man, he is content with a correlation between a score on a scale (no matter how the score is arrived at) and some kind of observed action. His position would be entirely defensible if it were not for three points. Firstly, the poor predictive powers and low validity of both attitude and personality tests have been a source of concern since the tests were first evolved. Operational definition is a device which can only be legitimated by practical results, and these are rather thin on the ground. In this connection, some of the points I have raised so far militate against the very *possibility* of the kind of precision and validity that the operationally orientated psychologist is searching for. Secondly, the anti-theoretical aspects of operationalism turn it into a purely inductive operation incapable of generating theoretical scientific knowledge. Finally operationalism achieves consistency at the cost of cutting itself off from the world of common-sense. This is because the measurements bear no specifiable relation to whatever was thought to be the target of the measurement procedure in the first place (Blumer, 1969b, 1969c). Operational definitions therefore tend not to translate back into the world of human meaning within which (and only within which) they achieve significance.

Summary

Clearly the various difficulties outlined in the previous pages do not *all* apply to each and every assessment of attitude and personality: however there is a common thread of criticism running through all the points. It is this:

Psychologists involved in the business of assessing people are essentially trying to improve on the inaccurate 'hit-and-miss' assessment procedures that ordinary people use in everyday life. Yet these supposedly superior assessment methods have open-textured, common-sense knowledge built into them right from the start – they are thus less than entirely scientific or mathematically grounded. Equally their results only acquire meaning and validity during a process which involves the matching of scientific psychological results with intuitive common-sense assessment (for instance, whether someone has done 'well' in his job). Psychologists are thus caught in the ironical position of setting up their studies as *superior competitors* to common-sense, yet having to demand validation from the very same *inferior* source. The contradictions of this enterprise develop luxuriantly in the studies characterized by operational definition. These studies which most consistently embody psychologists' ambitions to transcend the everyday ultimately succeed in divorcing psychological results from basic human meanings. The net result of this programme is a psychology which is so out of joint with common-sense reality that its results are unintelligible. The problem is compounded by the parallel attempt to generate general, context-free descriptions of personality or attitudes which can be summarized by numerical scores. This process has only resulted in the reduction of socially structured subjectivity to a 'soup' from which only banalities are retrievable.

As a way of pointing up the problems associated with these methods, we might recall the definition of validity associated with George Kelly: 'validity is the capacity of a test to tell us what we already know'. If we accept this definition, and realize that the basis of our ordinary knowing in the social world is inherently open-textured and highly complex, then it becomes apparent that the attempt of attitude and personality testers to side-step socially organized knowledge in order to achieve numerical measurement in a world of open-textured concepts can only end in the production of spuriously mathematical and, very frequently, covertly ideological knowledge. This would be of only academic interest if it were not for the fact that psychology plays an increasingly important role in the assessment of people in our society. Coming back to those people, it is clear that the kinds of theory and measurement extant in personality research do violence to the multiplicity, complexity and particularity of human life. To explore the extent of that damage, you need only ask yourself whether you would use a personality inventory or an extended description to describe your lover to your parents.

Ordinary people and assessment

So far, I have implied that psychological assessment is rather more common-sensical than psychologists care to admit. I have also suggested that it uses ordinary socially structured knowledge in a number of covert ways. Equally, a further implication is that ordinary social actors use socially structured knowledge in artful ways to arrive at assessments of their fellows, and this implication contrasts with the mechanical concept of attitudes and personality which dominates the psychological assessment literature. It is now relevant to ask: what are ordinary people doing when they go about the business of assessing people and how do they do it?

Firstly, as I argued in the introduction, people assess their fellows within a context of pragmatic concerns: they want to know how some feature of a person's attitudes or personality will affect that person's willingness or ability to help in some activity or other. This simple fact has some far-reaching consequences for psychologists and sociologists, because it implies that assessments in everyday life are practical, *ad hoc* affairs which are *not* predicated on deductive–nomological theoretical knowledge. Given that people act on such assessments, and as social psychologists we try to study both their assessments and the actions they take, it follows that we are logically precluded from generating deductive–nomological data about this aspect of their activity. This is not to deny that *aspects* of human activity can be studied by purely natural scientific procedure but it is to assert the functional autonomy of motives, of social assessment and social activity. Here it is relevant to add that since ordinary *ad hoc* assessments are not strictly logical (i.e. necessarily disproved by counter-instances), our descriptions of them must necessarily have a degree of flexibility built into them (see Gross, this volume). Again this kind of flexibility is not consistent with deductive, nomological schemes of knowledge.

Assessments of people then are *ad hoc* affairs closely tied up with the business of practical prediction in social life. As descriptions of dispositions to act, they embody open-textured concepts which for ordinary people are tied up with action in a *prima facie* way; concepts like purpose, intention, motive, belief and attitude. A major feature of these types of concepts is that in addition to explaining actions and putatively predicting them, they also justify or entitle actions (Louch, 1966), often in the sense of moral approbation and sometimes in the more technical sense of providing for the 'ownership' of actions – thus jealousy provides for the 'ownership' of the act of murdering an unfaithful lover.

This last feature of these concepts – the fact that they have this entitling property in everyday life – is closely linked with the curious way in which they are used. As we have seen, they are used to predict actions but the assertions expressed in the concepts (e.g. 'he was jealous') are not invalidated if the predictions turn out to be incorrect; equally, on the other hand, the concepts are used to explain actions after the event even though their explanatory power does not rest on any general law. Instead their capacity to explain rests on a fitting together of an explanation and a social context in a plausible way. If this analysis of ordinary assessment is correct, it follows that the stability we all see in one another's actions does not flow from some sort of natural scientific 'constant conjunction', but from the routine use of certain diffuse, open-textured rules and formulae which guide our perception of the social world. If this seems to be a curious way of putting things, think of what happens when a 'motiveless' murder occurs and the police are 'baffled', and compare this with a course of events in which a context (known infidelity) generates a motive (jealousy) and a search for persons who could be properly described as 'owning' the motive (husband or lover) leading to the detection of the criminal. The point I am driving at is that assessments of people are informed by routine, methodical procedures which involve assessments both of people and of the contexts in which they act. If the two assessments 'fit' together, then they are usually taken as confirmed. I want to argue further that the way to study the assessment of people by their fellows is to observe the operation of the (shared) routine procedures which form the basis of social assessment in everyday life.

Summary

In this short section, I have argued that assessing people is an integral and vital part of social interaction which gears in with the practical purposes of everyday life. Since ordinary assessment proceeds in a *non-deductive* way and yet people by and large reach agreement in their assessments, it is clear that this agreement is achieved by the methodical application of shared 'assessment procedures', and in turn it is clear that the methodical application of such procedures helps to sustain the predictable and orderly character of social interaction (Garfinkel, 1963). The orderly character of social life is thus predicated not on some kind of 'naturally' organized order of the type which can be seen to prevail in the physical universe, but on the rule-oriented procedures which inform ordinary people's social lives. Socialization is thus in part the teaching of these procedures; thus, for example, children are given rigorous and unremitting training in recognizing 'naughtiness', policemen are trained to distinguish between suicides and homicides and so on. Social assessments and the procedures which inform them are thus part of the socio-cognitive equipment with which we face the world and our fellow men; they are part of the 'stuff', so to speak, out of which social reality is constructed and as such they can be studied by social psychologists.

A paradigm for analysing assessment as part of social interaction

The paradigm I want to present as a basis for analysing social interaction has been developed by ethnomethodologists as a result of their preoccupation with many of the issues I have outlined in this paper. 'Ethnomethodology' covers a fairly wide range of substantive concerns and analytic styles, hence I propose to restrict myself to a few basic propositions on which the style of analysis rests, passing on to look at their significance for social psychology.

Basic propositions

1 Social actors are methodical. That is, their actions are informed by their views of the world which in turn can be socially substantiated or invalidated. Their actions are thus 'reasonable' or 'accountable' rather than be-haviouristically or mechanically generated. The accountability of actions in turn depends on *shared* access to common rationales and procedures through which the 'sense' and 'order' of events can be made inter-subjectively available. This last point is made here in explicit contrast with personal-construct theory, which provides that each actor sees the world through a unique system of constructs. If this latter outlook is taken seriously, it implies that there can be no communication between human beings, and equally that a world in common is impossible.

2 People should be studied 'naturalistically'. Data for analysis should not be generated via questionnaires or other means which deform the natural procedures through which persons and social settings are made describable. Ethnomethodologists share the ideal of naturalistic investigation with a growing number of psychologists, ethnographers, ethologists and workers in the communications field, who feel that artificial intervention in social-action scenes using experimental or questionnaire methods tends to destroy more information than it generates.

3 A corollary of the postulates of methodicity and naturalistic methods of study is the view that action must be explained in terms of some sort of competence model. This implies that social psychologists must specify the 'programme' or 'apparatus' out of which the action was produced before they can claim to have explained it. This corollary *definitely rules out* the substitution of the investigator's view of the situation and his logical modes of thought for the subject's, *no matter how open-textured, inconsistent*

and irrational the subject's construction of the world may appear to be.
In this connection, Garfinkel, whose writings furnish ethnomethodologists
with a common starting point, writes as follows:

a leading policy [of ethnomethodology] is to refuse serious consideration to the
prevailing proposal that efficiency, efficacy, effectiveness, intelligibility, consistency, planfulness, typicality, uniformity, reproducibility of activities – i.e. that
the rational properties of practical activities – be assessed, recognized, categorized, described by using a rule or standard obtained outside actual settings
within which such properties are recognized, used, produced and talked about by
settings' members.... All 'logical' and 'methodological' properties of action,
every feature of an activity's sense, facticity, objectivity, accountability, communality is to be treated as a contingent accomplishment of socially organized
common practices.

The policy is recommended that any social setting be viewed as self-organizing
with respect to the intelligible character of its own appearances as either representations of, or as evidences of, a social order. Any setting organizes its activities to
make its properties as an organized environment of practical activities detectable,
countable, recordable, reportable, tell-a-story aboutable, analysable – in short
accountable (Garfinkel, 1967, p. 33).

4 Natural languages have indexical properties. This proposition embodies
the idea that for fully socialized persons ('members') who have mastery of a
natural language, many of the things we say only have their sense against
the context or background in which they are said. Equally the sense of
statements is elaborated by some knowledge of the context in which they
are said. Thus the statement 'I am a social psychologist' will be heard to
have different 'fringes of meaning' depending on whether it is said, for
example, in a witness box, during a church sermon, at a psychology convention and so on. The addition of knowledge about the precise linguistic
context of the statement will provide a competent hearer with more im-
plicative detail. All of this detail however will be generated through
members' procedures of situated practical reasoning.

5 The open-textured nature of many natural-language concepts means that
even with the help of background contextual knowledge, we still cannot
establish a precise and final evaluation of the sense of a statement. The
reading which we arrive at is always a provisional reading established
'for now' in response to our practical problems, but always open to further
extension and elaboration. Propositions 4 and 5 are summarized by Garfinkel and Sacks as follows:

These properties are sometimes characterized by summarily observing that a
description, for example, in the ways it may be a constituent part of the circum-

stances it describes, in endless ways and unavoidably elaborates those circumstances and is elaborated by them (Garfinkel and Sacks, 1970, p. 338).

This process of endless elaboration is cut short however by the exigencies of practical circumstances.

6 Propositions 4 and 5 logically preclude the construction of manuals of instruction for disambiguating meanings, or context-free rule books for developing meaningful statements independently of members' methods for making those meanings available. Thus ethnomethodology is not oriented to providing a 'generative semantics' (Coulter, 1971, 1973a); in fact, the logical objections to such an enterprise also militate against computer translation of languages, and natural-language-competent robots.

7 The indexicality of natural languages is a massive stumbling block in the path of quantification in the social sciences, and in using mathematico-deductive schemata as the basis of theory. A basic implication is that we can never achieve finite descriptions or assessments of persons or events in the social world. Thus the decision to tolerate an assessment of someone's personality is achieved not by invoking some criterion of logical exhaustiveness, but by reference to the practical concerns of the assessor. As Bittner comments:

the ideal of objectivity embodied in the joint norms of *operational definition* and *formalization of inference* is unattainable ... because it fails to do justice to cultural reality (Bittner, 1973, pp. 116–17).

8 Actors' actions should be treated by the analyst as action-in-accord-with-a-rule. This 'methodological' precept follows logically from the idea that languages have indexical properties. The idea of 'rule-governed' action implies a mechanical, programmable property of action which is ruled out both by the indexical properties of natural languages and the open-textured qualities of social rules. In fact, it is these properties that logically provide for the possibility of freedom and change in social life. If we were entirely programmed by rules, we would be forced to make invariantly identical choices in given situations rather in the way a computer plays chess. Additionally the idea of 'rule-governed' action implies that the actor invariably has a pre-existing plan of action to which he rigidly adheres. Whilst it is true that actors may indeed have pre-existing plans of action on occasion, to say that actors' actions are rule-governed would imply that there are no cases in social life where an actor acts in an unplanned way and subsequently justifies his actions by *ad hoc* references to social norms. Since this is something that all of us do on occasion, it is unwise to rule it out *a priori*.

The set of propositions outlined above will, I am sure, seem rather outlandish to anyone who has received a traditional social-psychological training. In order to explain why they are important, I want to backtrack over some of the points I have made so as to tie them in more clearly with social-psychological perspectives.

The first point I want to repeat is that from the very start of our lives we are trained to make evaluative judgements and assessments of people and activities on a common-sense basis. Initially we receive a training in common sense (socialization), and this training is progressively built up until our 'primary socialization' is complete. This training involves the progressive learning of a natural language and the social practices in which that language is embedded and which it articulates and elaborates via the many forms of language use. What I am getting at here is the fact that common sense is the first thing we know and it is imposed on us unilaterally by societal members often by the use of arbitrary force (e.g. during our learning of 'naughtiness'). The common sense we learn in primary socialization in its turn becomes the basis on which other and more rarified areas of knowledge are built (work processes, human sciences, arts and so on).

What implications do these remarks have for social psychology? Firstly, they imply that social psychology is *grounded in* and *predicated on* common-sense knowledge. Social psychology is *grounded in* common sense because all its explanatory concepts are saturated with common-sense meaning: concepts like conformity, leadership, extroversion, dissonance and so on clearly have a common-sense basis – their meaning is supplied by common-sense rather than science. Social psychology is *predicated on* common-sense knowledge in the sense that the observer of social interaction waits to see that (for instance) 'conformity' has been *recognized by the parties to a situation* before he goes on to discuss the operation of factors affecting conformity, or conformity as a tactic. In other words, many social-psychological studies are parasitic on common-sense meaning and build up from the parties' own recognition of the situation, and then go on to attempt to establish some stipulative reading of the situation under study which flies in the face of the participants' own understandings. Thus in many cases the social psychologist's work is predicated on common-sense meanings, yet not only does he fail to acknowledge this simple fact, but also he goes on to build an account of a social-psychological event which is *competitive* with the participants' accounts yet is built out of them. Similarly the easy assumption by psychologists of the (unexplicated) operation of common-sense meaning and its irrelevance to psychological studies has been precisely the error which has enabled psychologists to erect the foundations of a deductive, nomological science which is totally inappropriate to the methodic character of common-sense judgements and their flexibility. In sum, the failure of psychologists to grasp the significance of common-sense knowledge has resulted in a misconception of the nature of psychological science.

A second implication of this position is that social psychologists both can and must analyse the operation of common-sense meaning as an area of study in its own right. The explicit study of common-sense reasoning, description and assessment would go a long way towards rescuing social psychology from the current theoretical *impasse* and associated sterility with which it is burdened. Finally I want to assert the human significance of such studies. For example, social-psychological investigations into the common-sense structure and logic of racialism are extraordinarily significant possibilities for research. To say this is not to deny the utility and worth of studies which locate people who affirm items reflecting racial prejudice, but it is to say that social psychology has so much more than this to offer. It is to say that the time has come for social psychology to transcend its own limitations.

Conclusions

At the beginning of this paper we questioned the adequacy of psychological assessment methods. Our conclusions, reached at the mid-point of the paper, were that psychological testing is not as 'scientific' as it appears, and that under its present conceptualization it is both ideological and manipulative in tendency. We also saw that the theoretical underpinnings of assessment methods involved psychologists in a fundamental misconception of the basic psycho-social phenomena they addressed, because they obscured the 'methodicity' of human action.

We then asked how social psychologists could study social assessment and social action whilst retaining this fundamental emphasis on 'methodicity' or 'rule-oriented' action. Our answer was that we could address these phenomena by using the ethnomethodological paradigm to begin studies of the situated use of common-sense knowledge. It is clear that this paradigm strikes at the heart of the positivist programme for psychology with its covert ideological assumptions, 'external' observation and 'mechanisms of decontamination'. This paper will have achieved its aim if it provokes you to look at some of the work listed below.

References

ALLPORT, G. A. (1935), 'Attitudes', in C. Murchison (ed.),
A Handbook of Social Psychology, Clark University Press.

ARMISTEAD, N. (ed.) (1972), *Rat, Myth and Magic: A Political Critique of Psychology*, Russell Press.

BANNISTER, D. (1970), 'Comment on Eysenck', in R. Borger and F. Cioffi (eds.),
Explanation in the Behavioural Sciences, Cambridge University Press.

BITTNER, E. (1973), 'Objectivity and realism in sociology', in G. Psathas (ed.),
Phenomenological Sociology, Wiley.

BLUM, A., and McHUGH, P. (1971), 'The social ascription of motives',
Amer. Sociol. Rev., vol. 36, pp. 98–109.

BLUMER, H. (1969), *Symbolic Interactionism – Perspective and Method*,
Prentice-Hall.

BLUMER, H. (1969a), 'Attitudes and the social act', in Blumer (1969).

BLUMER, H. (1969b), 'What is wrong with social theory', in Blumer (1969).

BLUMER, H. (1969c), 'The problem of the concept in social psychology',
in Blumer (1969).

CICOUREL, A. V. (1964), *Method and Measurement in Sociology*, Free Press.

CICOUREL, A. V. (1973), *Cognitive Sociology*, Penguin.

COULTER, J. P. (1971), 'Decontextualized meanings: current approaches to
verstehende investigations', *Social Rev.*, vol. 19, pp. 301–23.

COULTER, J. P. (1973a), 'Language and the conceptualization of meaning',
Sociology, vol. 7, no. 2, pp. 173–89.

COULTER, J. P. (1973b), *Approaches to Insanity*, Robertson.

DEFLEUR, M. L., and WESTIE, F. R. (1963), 'Attitude as a scientific concept',
Social Forces, vol. 42, pp. 17–31.

EYSENCK, H. J. (1960), *The Structure of Personality*, Allen & Unwin.

GARFINKEL, H. (1963), 'A conception of, and experiments with, "trust" as a
condition of stable concerted actions', in O. J. Harvey (ed.),
Motivation and Social Interaction, Ronald Press.

GARFINKEL, H. (1967), *Studies in Ethnomethodology*, Prentice-Hall.

GARFINKEL, H., and SACKS, H. (1970), 'On formal structures of practical actions',
in J. McKinney and E. A. Tiryakian, *Theoretical Sociology*,
Appleton-Century-Crofts.

HARRÉ, R., and SECORD, P. F. (1972), *The Explanation of Social Behaviour*,
Blackwell.

JACKSON, B., and MARSDEN, D. (1962), *Education and the Working Class*,
Routledge & Kegan Paul; Penguin, 1966.

LOUCH, A. R. (1966), *Explanation and Human Action*, Blackwell.

ROSENTHAL, R., and JACOBSON, L. (1968), *Pygmalion in the Classroom:
Teachers' Expectation and Pupils' Intellectual Development*,
Holt, Rinehart & Winston.

TAYLOR, L. (1972), 'The significance and interpretation of replies to motivational questions: the case of sex offenders', *Sociology*, vol. 6, pp. 23–39.

TORGERSON, W. (1958), *Theory and Method of Scaling*, Wiley.

WICKER, A. W. (1969), 'Attitudes versus actions: the relationship of verbal and overt behavioural responses to attitude objects', in K. Thomas (ed.), *Attitudes and Behaviour*, Penguin.

Further Reading

In addition to the Garfinkel, Coulter, Cicourel and Blum and McHugh references listed above, the following works contain ethnomethodological writing and commentary.

ATKINSON, J. M., and WATSON, D. R. (eds.), *Ethnographics: Studies in Ethnomethodology*, Robertson (forthcoming).

DOUGLAS, J. D. (ed.), *Understanding Everyday Life*, Routledge & Kegan Paul, 1971.

SUDNOW, D. (ed.), *Studies in Social Interaction*, Free Press, 1972.

GUMPERZ, J. J., and HYMES, D. (eds.), *Directions in Sociolinguistics*, Holt, Rinehart & Winston.

MCKINNEY, J., and TIRYAKIAN, E. A. (eds.), *Theoretical Sociology*, Appleton-Century-Crofts.

17 How Social Is It?[1]
Henrietta Resler and Paul Walton

Our concern here is with the reconstruction of social psychology. But before we begin, let us remember that 'social psychology' is constructed out of two words, and this is strange and rather telling. For what would a non-social psychology look like? Yet oddly enough this is how it is often dealt with, for in many university courses social psychology is taught separately from psychology. One might infer from this that social psychology is of a different order from psychology *per se*. The fact of the matter is that both psychologists proper and social psychologists, proper or otherwise, work from assumptions that split the individual and society into two conceptual halves. Try to imagine a science which attempts to understand the human psyche or mind; which builds its founding assumptions and theories upon experimental evidence drawn from work with pigeons, rats, mice and dogs. If you can imagine this, then grasp the problems involved when the same supposed science assumes that these theories and assumptions, with a little tinkering, will hold as explanations for human behaviour. Even if such a science was in any way sensible, it would be in no way 'social'.

It would seem then that the main task of reconstructing social psychology would not simply be 'to bring the men back in', as some have argued, but to construct psychology from evidence, assumptions and theories which have as their starting point the fact that people and society are not two separate and variable entities, but are one and the same thing (Homans, 1969). For it is impossible to conceive of a society without people, and people without society. Yet even the best of modern social psychology tends to delude itself into believing that individuals and society can be treated, for experimental purposes, as two separate and distinct phenomena. In the world of social psychology, there thus exists a fictitious dilemma in which groups of scientists, with hoards of naïve subjects and stooges, attempt to isolate the independent from the dependent variables and the so-called extraneous variables (the residual rubbish bin for the unknown and the unexplained).

What this in practice means is that the questions being asked, and the

1. We should like to acknowledge the help of John Westergaard who kindly commented on the draft.

problems being posed, come to be determined by the methods and techniques used for isolating and controlling the various 'relevant' variables. Thus the gap between the laboratory and the real world comes to be seen by such a science as merely involving the difficulties of conceptualizing, operationalizing and controlling variables. But this is in fact an attempt to resolve by method and technique what is essentially a problem of theory. What present psychologists are attempting to do is the impossible. They create artificial situations whereby they try to isolate and control phenomena, like aggression, by concentrating on techniques which will allow some rating or measurement at the individual level. Having done this they then bemoan the fact that the causes of aggression in the real world are so numerous as to render the scales useless for any predictive purpose. It is the theoretical split between the individual and society which is unreal; even the best methods and techniques would fail to put them together again. It is no accident that one of the more prominent radical psychology magazines is called *Humpty Dumpty* for the very good reason that if you split up the individual into bits, which you then divorce from society, then 'all the king's horses and all the king's men couldn't put Humpty together again'.

This is not merely a criticism of the worst of psychology, for even at its best its suppositions are similarly unworkable. Let's take Eysenck's scaling techniques for differentiating between introverts and extroverts as another example. Even if these scales were perfectly reliable and valid (which they are not) what would they tell us about the behaviour of individuals labelled extrovert or introvert acting in the real world? Eysenck tells us that a typical extrovert 'is sociable, likes parties, has many friends, . . . craves excitement, . . . tends to be aggressive and lose his temper quickly . . . and is not always a reliable person'. Whilst the typical introvert, he suggests, 'is a quiet, retiring sort of person, . . . seldom behaves in an aggressive manner, . . . is reliable, . . . and places great value on ethical standards' Eysenck (1970).[2] Eysenck obviously has a down on extroverts. But aside from this, even if people fell into these neat divisions, it should be apparent that everybody engages and exhibits these traits to varying degrees. The variation will depend on socialization and social context, rather than upon given, once-and-for-all, individual traits. It is no surprise, therefore, that psychologists' attempts at scaling and rating, based as they are on a search for individual predispositions (involving in Eysenck's case, and many others, a fool's search for the genetic,) fail miserably in a world where causes are many and usually social.

2. For a more extensive critique of this position see Taylor, Walton and Young (1973).

But even psychologists who don't consciously reduce social psychology to individual traits – like aggression or extroversion – still split society and the individual. They tend to leave the social unexplained or simply take it for granted. Thus even learning theorists, who start from the social fact that most behaviour is learned behaviour, slip rapidly into attempts to explain individual rather than social learning patterns. Such psychologists, looking at questions like homosexuality or alcoholism, tend to examine these as individual problems rather than as social phenomena. Learning or reinforcement theorists attempt to explain learned behaviour as the outcome of a sequence of positive or negative reinforcements which lead persons to act the way they do. This approach has led many psychologists working with homosexuals, for example, to take for granted that homosexuality (a) is a problem and (b) can be 'cured' by the correct application of learning theory. Working on the assumption that homosexuality must be unlearned, psychologists have subjected homosexuals to so-called negative reinforcement by showing them a variety of nude and semi-nude photographs whilst simultaneously delivering electric shocks. The same treatment has been given to alcoholics who have been shown bottles of drink, glasses and various photos, whilst negative reinforcement is delivered.

These horrendous experiments based on learning theory are ill-conceived, inhuman and profoundly unscientific. Even by their own criteria such learning theorists are in error. For they conveniently forget the balance of reinforcements at the societal level, and simple-mindedly concentrate on the individual. What little success they have had with individual homosexuals has been at the expense of the person's sexuality. So while in some cases they have succeeded in turning them off their own sex, they have yet to show that they can teach them to have relationships with the opposite sex. This is not surprising, for if we take the case of male homosexuality, the positive reinforcements and inducements to have relationships with women which exist in larger society far outweigh any that could be offered by the psychologists. Indeed, men who become homosexuals in our present, sexually unliberated society have to face massive social disapproval (i.e. negative reinforcement) long before psychologists have the inhuman audacity to administer electric shocks. Thus by treating homosexuality as an individual problem it is apparent that they not only deny the sexual strait-jacket of wider society, but they also deny the sexual authenticity of individuals. It should be clear to any thinking individual that homosexuality, in itself, is not a problem. It only becomes problematic in a society which rigidly sanctions a two-fold sexual division based on gender. The same goes for alcoholism; for what possible point is there in administering shock treatment to a few self-confessed alcoholics in a society where the social inducements to drink exist on every street corner.

Thus the major difficulty with learning theory is that few psychologists confront the questions of what the reinforcers are and where they come from. By lapsing into examination of reinforcement at the individual level, the larger social reinforcements are ignored and left unexamined. As Taylor (1971) has argued in another context, reinforcement theory can be compared to playing rather than questioning the existence of one-armed bandits.

It is as though individuals in society are playing a gigantic fruit machine, but the machine is rigged and only some players are consistently rewarded. The deprived ones then either resort to using foreign coins or magnets to increase their chances of winning, or play on mindlessly, give up the game or propose a new game altogether. But in the analysis nobody appears to ask who put the machine there in the first place and who takes the profits. Criticism of the game is confined to changing the pay-out sequences so that the deprived can get a better deal.

At its best present social psychology meets some of our criticisms. There has been a growing awareness in the past couple of decades of the need to move away from the individual level of explanation. Indeed, there has been a resurgence of theories which attempt to come to terms with the fact that people are social animals. However, these more recent developments also suffer from their own problems. Whilst most of them attempt to examine the relationship between the individual and society, they tend to do so at the micro level. The problem then turns upon what type of theortical framework will allow us to say something real and meaningful about psychological behaviour, but at the same time does not arbitrarily reduce this to either individual or societal determinates.

The favourite non-behaviourist approach of social psychologists has tended towards interactionism in various forms. From this perspective psychological change or psychological predispositions are worked out in various interaction sequences between the individual and larger society. Some psychologists choose to concentrate on the exchange of symbols, and thus come to be regarded as symbolic interactionists; others concentrate on social transactions and come to be known as transactionalists. This perspective tends to look at the way in which self-conceptions are built up or destroyed in society; that is, it concentrates on the creation and presentation of self and how that is validated or invalidated in given contexts. For example, there has been a great deal of work on role conflict, which has shown that in industrial society most people are expected to live out a large number of roles, each of which has differing expectations attached to it. The role of good father to a child can often conflict with the role of being the main wage earner for a family, if the man is required to work long and unsocial hours to earn a reasonable living. In situations such as these, social psychologists have been able to demonstrate that much family conflict is not psychological but socio-structural. Again, social psychologists working in the areas of crime and deviance have shown that public revelation and symbolic degradation in court have led some people to change their self-conceptions and, as a consequence, their behaviour, often in an undesired direction. If it is continually insisted that someone has to be treated as a thief, and is labelled as criminally inclined, it may well leave that person little option but to internalize that definition and act on that assumption.

The difficulty with most of this work is that it uncritically tends towards a liberal position whereby it is assumed that there are clear, and normal, ways of interacting or socializing in our society. At their worst, social psychologists working with these assumptions have concluded that the pathological, strange, deviant or mentally sick are the way they are because of something intrinsically wrong with them (whatever negative labelling adds to that), rather than examining the possibility that there is something wrong with the society. But even at its best, much of this work, whilst describing or examining interactional sequences and social pressures, still denies larger social conflicts by retreating to individualistic or special explanations. Lemert's treatment of radical behaviour in America is best seen as highlighting the inadequacy of such an approach. His attempt to explain radicalism leads him to suggest that 'a cross-sectional role analysis of the radicals in a given society will reveal not only a number of symbolically disordered persons, but also a large number – perhaps the majority – of persons who profess the extremist beliefs because of general or special situational pressures'.[3]

The danger inherent in this approach is that behaviour which is disliked or disapproved of by the psychologists in question is explained away in terms of symbolic disorder or as merely the result of special pressure. At the back of this analysis is the unstated assumption that there is a normal, good and proper way of going about life which will enable people to avoid disorder or pressure. But this simply is not true. For what is right, proper and good for one section of society may make little sense for another. As Gouldner (1973) and Mankoff (1971) have noted in examining the transactionalist approach to crime, deviance and the mentally ill, transactionalists and symbolic interactionists see these phenomena as emerging from the process of small-scale social interaction; they do not analyse the matrix of larger society. They do not see conflict and disorder as

3. For a detailed critique of this position see Walton (1973).

deriving from the specific master institutions of larger society; let alone expressing a sensible and rational opposition to them. Where social psychologists working within this tradition do analyse and criticize larger society, they tend merely to conceive of individuals as badly treated, as underdogs who need our sympathy rather than as rebels who may be correct.

Another position which is becoming increasingly popular and which at first sight seems to overcome some of these difficulties is the large amount of ethnographic work which is now being done by social psychologists and sociologists. Much of this work has been careful, ethnographic description which has tended to leave generalizations and theory to others.[4] More recently ethnographic work which professes theoretical imperatives has been undertaken by a group of primarily American researchers, who call their work 'ethnomethodology'. Ethnomethodology concentrates on the way that society's members construct and reconstruct reality within the limits of a given context. It studies the way in which 'members' create a world of social facts, which is treated by those same members as an organizing basis for their everyday activity. Harold Garfinkel can be said to be the chief practitioner of ethnomethodology. His work *Studies in Ethnomethodology* appeared in 1967 and has led to a popularization of a whole new approach to the study of social behaviour. Garfinkel defines the approach as follows: 'Ethnomethodological studies analyse everyday activities as members' methods for making these same activities visibly-rational-and-reportable-for-all-practical-purposes, i.e. "accountable" as organizations of commonplace everyday activities.'[5] Garfinkel and his followers argue that all so-called structural phenomena are, in fact, the emergent constituted products of a large amount of perceptual and judgmental work by members. The basic task of ethnomethodology therefore is to demonstrate that the structure and process of everyday life is reducible to and, in fact, is the same thing as 'members' methods for making these same activities visibly-rational-and-reportable-for-all-practical-purposes'. Garfinkel himself has done work on the achievement of sex status in an intersexed person, how jurors come to make decisions about guilt and innocence, and why there could be good organizational reasons for keeping bad clinical records. Undoubtedly his work is varied and insightful. His followers have done work on such things as the use of puns and dirty jokes in social interaction, turn-taking in conversations, queuing and various other phenomena of everyday life.

This work represents a great advance over learning theory or inter-

4. Erving Goffman's work is a good example.
5. For a detailed and careful critique see Taylor, Walton and Young (1973).

actionism in getting to grips with the real reasons that members of society give for going about the way they do. The ethnomethodologists correctly argue that conventional social psychology and sociology tend to endow actors with internalized attitudes, beliefs, and predispositions. They are correct, for most social psychology assumes that actors internalize or introject the roles, values and beliefs of larger society. Such assumptions leave unanalysed what advice, values and beliefs actors in given roles do take or internalize from larger society. Ethnomethodology aims to study the practical reasons that members have for believing what they believe or acting as they do. So for these ethnomethodologists the existence of a clear normative order, which is miraculously internalized, is to be treated as problematic. Normative order is to be treated as an achievement of every-day life, not an internalized pre-given.

Whilst this development represents an advance over static and cruder approaches, it too has its own weaknesses. For, by concentrating on practical reasoning, although it can reveal members' taken-for-granted assumptions, it has chosen to be uncritical of such assumptions. Garfinkel and others insist that objectivity is merely a practical accomplishment. For instance, they point out that any person has an infinite number of memberships – sex, age and religion being the most obvious ones. As the list is theoretically endless, the selection of criteria for categorization is a practical task. From this view-point, any objective description becomes impossible: one can only classify for the job in hand. Having thus argued that objectivity is a practical achievement, they go on to deny that it exists, insisting quite falsely upon the infinite variability of possible description. Ethnomethodologists recognize and study only one plane of social reality – individual consciousness. In rejecting general statements and concepts until they are reducible to members' consciousness, they falsely reduce meaning to the meanings held by individual actors. They believe that nothing is really fixed in the world, that the social world order is merely an ongoing, practical achievement of its members. But it is and it is not. Men create society, but not always in circumstances of their own choosing. Theoretically they deny the existence of a totality in the world, by denying the completeness of individuals.

In insisting that we examine the way members have internalized the values of a given social system, they have advanced social psychology. But when they go on to reject objectivity and thus the reality of structure, they lapse into metaphysics of idealism. In substance their project is atomistic; they see individuals as creating rules not social relationships.[6]

6. This section is heavily indebted to collaborative work undertaken by Taylor, Walton and Young (1973).

It is significant, therefore, that most of their work focuses on face-to-face interaction. For such action is apparently relatively unstructured.

Our approach so far has been critical and somewhat negative. But it is the case that the positions outlined above show a characteristic carelessness in moving from the individual to the social. This carelessness, common to apparently divergent and contradictory perspectives from Eysenck to ethnomethodology, has as its foundation a neutral or liberal view of social science. Despite differences among all these approaches with regard to the objectivity of social-psychological work; and notwithstanding their theoretical divides; and in spite of their efforts to examine entirely diverse kinds of phenomena, their work is united by their self-deception with regard to society. They share an inability to confront theoretically the limitations placed upon science in a society dominated and divided by class interest. Their blindness with regard to society is shown most clearly by the lack of any historical dimension in their work. For we are not dealing with a social psychology of all societies, but a social psychology of societies in a given historical period.

In our period the contours of advanced societies are determined by their relationship to the world market – a capitalist market. Thus, a social psychology which ignores these relationships and their impact on the psyche of the individual cannot be regarded as social. Therefore, in a capitalist society such as ours, where the economy is based on competition and accumulation, the inevitable outcome is to produce psychologies which see obedience, achievement and competitiveness as desirable qualities. One does not have to be a Marxist to realize that the shape and type of society that one lives in shapes and types the psychologies that emerge from it. It is no accident that in our society, the model of man chosen as rational by the economists is a man who acts and thinks in market terms. From this point of view, if a man is to be psychologically rational in our society, the criteria for his decisions would be market decisions, regardless of any social consequences.

Yet the liberal view of science refuses to examine or analyse the type of society we live in. It pretends to offer social-psychological knowledge which is derived from an unanalysed society, or in the case of ethnomethodology derived from particular contexts, whose own determinants are unexamined. In suggesting that social psychologists have to make judgements about the nature of the society in which they live for their science to be truly social, we are arguing that the liberal position has emasculated the political dimension of psychology and refuses to confront the major political forces which shape and determine the direction of our society. By being liberal and avoiding the political understanding of society necessary for its analysis, they obstruct the development of a social psychology and are consistently forced back to individualistic explanations. Social problems become individual problems; political questions become matters of individual pathology; and the healthiness of society is left unquestioned. What is necessary for the reconstruction of social psychology is to analyse people's psychic development and responses within a historical perspective, which recognizes that the limits on behaviour are shaped by the relations between power, politics and people.

There are few people working in psychology who have recognized that the type of society we live in produces by its nature certain types of people. Yet there are notable exceptions. In our own period the work of Laing, Cooper and Esterson on schizophrenia, and their work on the family, has led them to argue convincingly that diagnosis and treatment measures in psychiatry are derived from ethical judgements and social pressures. They have demonstrated that mental illness is in part a social construction; that psychiatry is a social institution; and that both incorporate the values and demands of larger society. They have highlighted the normative nature of conceptions of mental illness and have questioned the liberal complacency of psychiatry in larger society. Yet they have stopped short of a full-blown critique of society. They have called the modern nuclear family the concentration camp of modern society, but have left us without explanations of the necessity for such a bourgeois institution in a propertied society. And although they have seized on the value-laden, subjective and political elements of psychiatric diagnosis and treatment, they have implicitly attributed a value-free and apolitical character to medicine in general.

Even the best of these modern, critical thinkers are reluctant to push the logic of their work to its necessary outcome. As yet, few people have seen the importance of the position which Sedgwick (1972) has advanced, namely, that all sickness, illness or pathology is essentially deviancy. In other words, no attribution of sickness or psychological disturbance can be made without the expectation that there is some 'normal' state which is more usual and desirable. Because of their refusal to analyse and criticize society in all its aspects, psychologists, psychiatrists and doctors of even the radical variety have implicitly taken for granted the expectations of the present. Whatever is usual is thus regarded as normal and not pathological. Thus it is normal for the life expectancies of workers to be less than those of professionals. This is treated by ordinary medical practitioners as a fact of life, not the social effect of an abnormal division of labour. We could give many examples, drawn from the medical and other professions, of so-called facts which are taken for granted and left unexamined precisely because psychologists, sociologists, doctors – the professions in general – uncritically accept the norms of bourgeois society. But science advances as much by challenging accepted 'facts' as it does by producing competing theories. The shape and nature of industrial society is not inevitably and indispensably bourgeois. Many of the 'facts' of our society are taken to be eternal or at least a necessary product of industrial society, when in fact they can be shown to rest on domination and class division. Eliminate domination and class division and the 'facts' will change.

The reconstruction of social psychology thus requires as a precondition the thorough examination of all the norms and values of the society in which we live. We must sort out the essential from the inessential, the historically specific from the historically inevitable. One of the few attempts to carry out work in this fashion was undertaken by Wilhelm Reich and his followers in the 1930s. In his *Mass Psychology of Fascism* and in much of his other work (1946, 1973a, 1973b) he attempted to build a psychology founded on historical materialism. He argued that the radical movement must approach orthodox psychological work with caution. For Reich, and for us, official psychology has in our society the principal function of concealing and diverting attention from the economic basis of class society and the class struggle. From this perspective psychology is engaged in the business of mystification; it is an indirect instrument of social control. An example of this is the way in which personality tests are still used in determining the parole chances of prisoners, thus giving officialdom the excuse that they are refusing men their freedom on objective grounds. Reich provided the basis upon which we must begin to build a psychology which has its roots in historical materialism and has as its aim the building of a psychology which is immediately practical and useful. The usefulness of psychology, other than as a tool of social control, turns upon developing an approach which connects with the problems of human freedom. It must therefore be critical of present bourgeois society, for many of the so-called psychological problems here are problems whose sources are structural and political; they are endemic in a class society, not common to all possible societies. Until this work is begun in full, we can have no notion of its potential developments. Yet there are already some areas where a materialist, non-utopian, critical psychology can be of immediate use. Indeed, in a lay fashion, women's liberation and gay liberation movements have started to build – knowing or unknowingly – a radical and practical psychology. They have done so by refusing to see their identity problems as psychological problems, by insisting that sexual chauvinism is a problem of bourgeois society and that one must psychologically struggle to overcome this now.

The women's liberation movement has been able to move towards building a radical, materialist psychology because its struggle has involved exploring the female experience, beginning with the problems that women face by virtue of being women in a society which has been structured and dominated primarily by men. By examining their role as women in such a society, they were able to understand, and to examine, the forces which make for the degradation of women and the shaping of their personalities to quiescence and acquiescence. They came to understand that the frustrations and neuroses of women were an expression of their supporting role within a bourgeois, nuclear family. Their struggle is a struggle for equality in every possible area of social life. The end result of this is as we should expect: that women in general are less articulate, less sure of themselves, in fact – more repressed. In fact, the women's liberation movement have shown this repression to be a bourgeois oppression. The struggle, in a collective movement, to change this has given many women the hope of a totally new manner of living. Like any dominant and privileged group, men have reacted to this liberation movement at first with scorn, sarcasm and derision. But in areas where men were forced to confront this movement they have had to learn to hide their sexism and have made token gestures of compromise, in a manner similar to that in which the ruling class has attempted to accommodate workers' protest.

The difficulties of radical psychological work should be apparent. Every challenge to every norm, every questioning of every value, every upset to the *status quo* brings forth strong and sometimes violent reaction from the privileged. Even radical males who are nominally committed to equality have been known to resort to violent and abusive responses when confronted by such simple demands as the exclusion of men from women's conferences (Dalla Costa and James, 1973). Reich was very clear on this question and argued that:

It is very easy to be in favour of the sexual pleasure attainable at present – even the most extreme reactionary will be in agreement with that; but contributing in practical terms to the creation of the social and educational conditions which would in practice facilitate the full-blooded enjoyment of life for the mass of humanity leads directly to a confrontation with all the forces of conservatism including those in the revolutionary movement (Reich, 1973a).

The job at hand then is to construct a materialist psychology that has a clear grasp of history. To develop such a psychology we must jettison the false conceptual divisions that official psychology erects between individual and society; we must see people and society as forming a complex unity. We must aid all those whose condition is at present represented as a psychological problem. Above all, and consistently, we must struggle against those psychological inhibitions which originate from early socialization into a sick society. We must clearly demonstrate that attacks against authority, domination and oppression are not endeavours of the psychologically irrational, the genetically abnormal, the deviant and the sick, but can be seen as entirely rational. They are purposeful and comprehensible, without any psychological explanations. What does need explaining psychologically are the psychological inhibitions that *prevent* rational rebellion. We must psychologically explain and conquer the submission to authority, including the feelings of helplessness and dependency which are the result of the early authoritarian upbringing we all suffer in the bourgeois family.

We conclude with a quote from Reich, a man whose foresight and brilliance led him to face persecution, and, as a consequence, a rational paranoia. If we undertake the task of reconstruction, we must be aware that it is in no way an easy one.

Psychology can only be integrated into the revolutionary movement in one single way if it is not to cause harm but to be of use. Marx and Engels demonstrated that the social relations of men, and in particular their economic relations, are the basis on which all else is built – morality, law, state institutions, etc. But that does not explain how this economic basis works itself out in people's instinctual structure. Dialectical materialist psychology therefore has the task of investigating and grasping practically how the social existence of men influences the fundamental biological instincts of hunger and sexuality, and how in the different classes the concrete living individual develops out of this and not the abstract 'human nature' the bourgeois talk about (Reich, 1973a).

References

DALLA COSTA, M., and JAMES, S. (1973), *The Power of Women and the Subversion of the Community*, Falling Wall Press, Bristol.

EYSENCK, H. (1970), *Crime and Personality*, Paladin.

GARFINKEL, H. (1967), *Studies in Ethnomethodology*, Prentice–Hall.

GOULDNER, A. (1973), *For Sociology*, Allen Lane The Penguin Press.

HOMANS, G. C. (1969), 'Bringing men back in', *Amer. Sociol. Rev.* (1973).

LEMERT, E. (1951), *Social Pathology*, McGraw-Hill.

MANKOFF, M. (1971), 'Societal reaction and career deviance: a critical analysis', *Sociol. Q.*, vol. 12, pp. 204–18.

REICH, W. (1946), *The Mass Psychology of Fascism*, Orgone Institute Press.

REICH, W. (1973a), *Sex-Pol Essays 1934–37*, Socialist Reproduction.

REICH, W. (1973b), *What is Class Consciousness?*, Socialist Reproduction.

SEDGWICK, P. (1972), 'Mental illness is illness', National Deviancy Symposium, 10th Conference, University of York, unpublished mimeograph.

TAYLOR, I., WALTON, P., and YOUNG, J. (1973), *The New Criminology*, Routledge & Kegan Paul.

TAYLOR, L. (1971), *Deviance and Society*, Joseph.

WALTON, P. (1973), 'The case of the Weathermen: social reaction and radical commitment', in I. Taylor and L. Taylor (eds.), *Politics and Deviance*, Penguin.

18 The Radical Use of Official Data
David Triesman

Most students of Marxism are familiar with what are, arguably, among the best presentations of statistical data that have ever been made. I am referring to Marx's writing in various parts of *Capital*, particularly the chapters on 'The Working Day' and on 'Manufacture' and Lenin's 'The Development of Capitalism in Russia'. Both authors cite evidence that supports their theoretical structures from data generated by official agencies and presented, originally, in official statistics.[1] They did not of course stumble on their theoretical positions because of any theoretical insights lurking, as it were, immanent in the statistics themselves. Rather, they sought adequate data to support propositions which they advanced.

But if these same students are familiar with the debate in contemporary sociology and social psychology between empiricists and ethnomethodologists, they may find themselves in a confusing dilemma. On the one hand, in Marx and Lenin, they are presented with a manifestly revolutionary analysis made out with the assistance of empirical data. Marx and Lenin quote the sort of data which ethnomethodologists criticize as being generated by the most orthodox and ideologically moribund members of the social-science professions and official organizations. On the other hand, the tests of ethnomethodology themselves make the vociferous claim to represent a radical critique of empiricism, a fundamental re-establishment of the link between theory and method, and therefore to be in some measure revolutionary. For example, Cicourel (1964, p. 225) says in discussing John Rex's book *Key Problems of Sociological Theory*:

Rex's book contains a lucid discussion of differences in the substantive foundations of social theory and research. My own discussion bearing upon sociological theory ... will seldom deal with the kinds and varieties of substantive theoretical issues raised by Rex, but will be concerned primarily with 'basic theory' which I presume would *underlie* all the various substantive theories he describes.

These two positions suggest a contradiction. Can it be that the revolutionaries are using reactionary empiricism? Or can certain sorts of data be of value in making out a viable radical theory? In this paper, I will try

1. For example, the report of the Inspector of Factories and the reports of the Child Employment Commission.

to show that the contradiction is, in fact, non-existent because the use of the data by Marx and Lenin is not empiricist, and the critique raised by ethnomethodology is insubstantial. This is no part of an arid academic debate. There are large resources of material available to people who want to make out analyses which serve working-class and other oppressed people – women, racial and ethnic minorities, gay people and so on. The question is: what are these materials and how can we use them?

First, perhaps, why haven't we used them in the past or generated better data ourselves? Major companies, the media and the State itself are never at a loss to promote social-science research serving the aims of the dominant class and other dominant racial and sexual groups. It is painfully difficult for anyone who wants to work in conjunction with the struggles of oppressed groups to mount the kinds of work which would assist that struggle. Yet I still want to suggest that certain opportunities are missed in building theoretical structures which can at least contribute to the defence of working-class and oppressed group positions, and may even assist in carrying their struggles forward. It is no part of this argument that an élite corps of sociologists, psychologists or whoever are responsible for 'leading' or supplying the key ideological weapons in the struggles of oppressed people. It looks only towards what constructive assistance can be provided by social scientists both in the overall task of producing revolutionary theory – the analysis of the present conjuncture – and to the dilemma of defending the particular interests of the working class, racially and sexually oppressed people and communities in the struggle with their class enemies, with racists, sexists and the apparatus of the State.

Even rereading this last paragraph, I am aware that it poses suppositions about the necessity for struggle, and in a language which will undoubtedly be unpalatable to many people. But it is hard to doubt that most professional social scientists, and many of the students whose cheap labour they use, have worked principally in the interests of the bourgeois state. We have been, often in spite of radical posturing, the quislings of the ruling class. The Isaac Deutsche Prize Winner, Martin Nicolaus, outspokenly condemned this situation in sociology at the 1968 Annual Convention of the American Sociological Association:

This is the type of sociologist who sets the tone of the ethic of the profession; and it is the type of sociologist who is nothing more nor less than a house servant in the corporate establishment, a white intellectual Uncle Tom, not only for this government and ruling class, but for any government and ruling class!

It isn't difficult to discern the structural and ideological impediments to progressive work. In the first place, there are the traditions of the disciplines. In Britain it is usual to be taught to study 'social problems' without considering who defines them as such or why, and to regard them as quite discrete entities – separate from all other 'social problems'. The notion of common sources generating 'social problems' and the lack of analysis of their commonality militates against theoretical work which establishes just this, whether one is an empiricist or ethnomethodologist. Each problem is expressed as having a unique grounding and its solution requires a unique and limited intervention. The uniqueness, or individuality, of each problem is a burlesque reflection of the idea of the individuality of persons, the underpinning assumption of most schools of psychology, though it is well worth looking at those who oppose the assumption of the 'overweening conviction of authentic individual self-hood – the delusion of unique individuality' (Stack Sullivan, 1953).

The behaviourist learning 'paradigm', which does not, as Chomsky shows (1959, p. 35; 1971), amount to a theory at all, requires that only one individual can acquire any particular set of learned responses, since only that individual can have received appropriate stimuli with appropriate reinforcement in that particular order. Behaviour, therefore, can only be modified person by person. Ironically, phenomenologists, following Schutz, whilst introducing categories taboo in behaviourist parlance – meaning, choice, consciousness – equally emphasize the uniqueness of these structures for each person; hence the unreliability of 'common-sense' assumptions about shared meanings.

Thus both the abstract, black-box individuality of behaviourism and the relativism of phenomenology can be used to supply social-scientific credibility to the *assumption* about the primacy of individuals in a tradition central to the ideology of capitalism (MacPherson, 1962). 'Individuality' conveys the unique and necessary right to the ownership of personal property, whether capital itself (and here even a company is treated as an individual in law), or the worker's saleable property, his labour power. And the concept is readily enlarged to a 'collective individuality' like the actions of the firm in the free market, or to the 'collective individuality' conferred on all those designated as demonstrating the same 'personal' problem – homelessness, old age, drug addiction, delinquency or whatever.

But these questions of ideological problematic (Althusser and Balibar, 1970, p. 316), which have reduced everyone from psychology professors to first-year students to mouthing familiar formulae about the importance of theory (that is, of formulating the relationships between social phenomena and proposing which of the relationships is determinant), avoid theory like the plague. And this is not a matter of the psychological difficulties which they may experience. Not only do they inherit an intellectual tradition governed by what Alec Douglas-Home once praised as 'good horse sense', but they also must look uneasily over their shoulders to the bank manager in the living-room cupboard. The production of theory is decisively not what they are paid to do.

The most cursory glance at research funding in recent years as shown by the *SSRC Newsletter* shows that money comes in considerable volumes for 'solving problems'. Though where, like the Child Poverty Action Group, the funded workers are actively challenging aspects of the very *status quo* that supplies the money (by using the Test Case strategy), future fund availability becomes haunted with question-marks. Secondly, there seem to be more than a few pennies to rub together if what you have in mind is research in the social psychology of personnel management or in worker 'involvement', or some equally transparent project. Whether the problem is one faced by firms trying to keep their work force at the lathes, or social agencies desiring to see fewer alcoholics on the streets,[2] or welfare organizations testing how happily housewives can integrate small-component assembly with bed making, then 'real person' solutions to immediate 'problems' are what are required. And paid for. Thus even an institution with a respected record like the Tavistock Centre of Human Relations can produce scientific documents like *Attitudes towards Cosmetics* (February 1967) for the market-research firm Charles Barker & Sons, themselves acting for the advertising department of Barbar Gould Cosmetics. The psychologist who researched and wrote the report, Isobel P. Menzes, begins, 'Conservatism is characteristic of the mature woman because she is reconciled to an image of herself which is acceptable. It is an attitude conducive to brand loyalty.'

The task for many social scientists is to use acquired skills to sift the resources of official and commercial data to provide the evidence that can be used with revolutionary theoretical constructions that elucidate the present socio-economic situation. This involves two questions. Firstly, what data can safely be used and how does one discriminate? Secondly, how can one determine the priorities among the possible tasks?

Empirical data and the ethnocritique

An enormous number of official organizations and commercial enterprises collect 'data'. In essence their activity consists of assembling observable events under various headings, more or less relevant to their purposes. They are, to be accurate, engaged in the *production* of data and this production requires the use of a variety of tools or implements of production which are themselves produced in a special way. Rather than being

2. See, for example, LCC (1965, p. 5) or Home Office Working Party (1970, p. 5). These are quoted in an excellent article by Archard (1974).

produced by manual labour or by machines, except insofar as questionnaire schedules are typed on stencils, duplicated or printed, the instruments are produced by intellectual work. The form of this work it will be necessary to specify at a later stage, since the form the work is said to take by ethnomethodologists does not amount to a viable critique of it.

Categories into which observable events are to be grouped are stated with sufficient precision to allow trained observers to record observed events of the same kind under the same category head. Indeed, quite standard texts are used to illustrate the procedures to be adopted when framing the instrument of production of data (Moser and Kalton, 1971). From the universe of events that might be recorded or the 'population' of events, these same standard texts either recommend that all events are taken and categorized, or that a sufficiently large, appropriately drawn sample is selected and categorized. This is what some people call 'counting noses'. All those events observed which fall within the same category are added up, expressed as percentages of all events and manipulated in numerous statistical variations.

Further, on occasions, 'data' is collected of such a kind that the simple placement of an observation into a preordained category by a trained observer is not possible. This occurs where the observation is not directly of the type that can be rendered into numerals. It happens particularly with 'attitudes' and 'opinions'. Here, scales are devised which allow the self-reported or observed attitude or opinion to be placed on a scale of attitudes and opinions of the same kind, and thus given a scalar value. Then, like the data discussed above, the observations which have been given the same numeral value, or code number, are regarded as equivalent and counted as falling in the same category. For example, if two people are shown the statement: 'I am unhappy with my college psychology course' and they both – God forbid – state that they 'Agree very much', then they will both be recorded with all others who have said the same thing. All those answers will be regarded as equivalent members of the same category.

In short, those who publish statistics on various questions actively produce them by the use of specialized instruments, which have themselves been produced by intellectual work. The finished product is then used to state the scale of a particular phenomenon (as it is defined by the producer), and the rate of its occurrence among the general or more specialized populations. This mass of data is what is popularly regarded among the professionals who are, after all, paid to know about such things, as the 'objective facts' about society or people.

The critique made by social scientists like Garfinkel, Cicourel, Douglas,

Kitsuse, McHugh and others must be restated here to show that it does not provide an adequate rejection of empiricism. Their criticisms fall into four principal areas:

1 The categories used are inadequate;

2 The mathematization of events is absurd;

3 The placement of events into categories as a research task is impossible;

4 There is no reliability of the statistic which is arrived at.

The argument can be summarized in the following ways:

1 'The categories used are inadequate'

The construction of categories for analytic purposes is generally based on arbitrary and biased premises. Thus, for example, there is nothing inherently deviant in a person that leads to his classification as a deviant. Rather, that classification is contingent upon what a society states is deviant. Clinard (1963, p. 22) describes deviant behaviour as 'behaviour in a disapproved direction from the norms and sufficient in degree to exceed the tolerance limit of the community'. This behaviour, then, is no more than 'behaviour that people so label' (Becker, 1963, p. 9). It will already be apparent that the categories which are usually employed by the police or the courts to classify the type of people that commit certain acts are not accepted as unequivocal characterizations of the people classified. They may or may not have committed the act, but the only reason for them being placed in the category is that the category has been established to so categorize them. The allocation of the label is the consequence of applying the rule rather than the quality of the act itself, and to successfully apply the label (and place a person in the appropriate category), specifically structured social acts must be employed (Lemert, 1967, p. 42; Garfinkel, 1956, pp. 420–24), court-room trials, psychiatric interviews, etc.

A great deal of work has been undertaken in recent years to explore the construction of such categories and to question the assumptions that they make about the categorized acts. For example, in a recent article Maxwell Atkinson (1971, p. 187) discusses what type of events will be recorded as suicides rather than as other forms of death. He notes that there are taken-for-granted, common-sense ground-rules that enable coroners to pronounce cause of death where that might be equivocal. Further,

The shared definitions of suicidal situations prevalent in a society at any one time will also be shared, to a greater or lesser extent, by the coroners, the individuals who indulge in suicidal behaviour, the researchers, and those employed by the media of mass communication.

ethnomethodologists have argued that either the categories used in official statistics are simply reflections of reactionary common-sense assumptions about the nature of certain activities or structural locations, the situations people find themselves in, or they provide a type of framework which it is impossible to use, since human activity cannot be categorized at all.

2 'The mathematization of events is absurd'

Empiricist social science has always attempted 'the correlation with numbers of entities which are not numbers' (Nagel, 1931, pp. 313–33), trying to make possible the mathematical measurement of social phenomena which are in fact observed events by using mathematical numerals and scales. To do so requires that we assume logical continuity between such events and scales of measurement. Cicourel (1964), in particular, argues against the assumption made in such a procedure. In the first place, mathematization requires scales of measurement, and these are themselves not unequivocal scientific instruments, free of human intervention.

The qualitative assignment of objects to classes and the assignment of numbers to objects are two means at the disposal of the measurer for generating broadly applicable information. The striking consequence of such a proposal is that measurement is a decision-making activity and as such is to be evaluated by decision-making criteria (Churchman, 1959, p. 84).

To be brief, Cicourel argues that the assignment of numbers to social events requires three conditions: that there is no discordance about the commonly held perception of any event between all the parties to it; that any two events recorded in the same category must be fully equivalent (Breuer, 1958, p. 13); and that the imposition of scales must be seen as an imposition by fiat rather than a property inherent in the event which the scale purports to describe.

3 'The placement of events into categories as a research task is impossible'

It has already been indicated that there are seldom, in the view of ethnomethodologists, clear-cut grounds for the practical assignment of events to categories, firstly because the categories are not themselves clear-cut, and secondly, because the human actor who undertakes the task must make certain assumptions about the common-sense nature of the material being classified.

In the case of an official agency recording the occurrence of particular events, a number of constraints may face them.

In modern society, the socially significant differentiation of deviants from the non-deviant population is increasingly contingent upon the circumstances of situation, place, social personal biography, and the bureaucratically organized activities of agencies of control (Kitsuse, 1962, p. 225).

In the case of data collected by the field researcher, the framing of the questions asked, the comprehension of those questions by a respondent, and the interpretation of the answer of that respondent by the field researcher require the assumption that they share the same commonsensical meanings in the words used and the concepts employed. Douglas (1967) makes it clear that the observation of events (which would obviously include the hearing of utterances) is not simply a question of sensory judgement, but a complex sequence of applied social judgements about what is actually being transacted. Questions asked encode the researcher's background descriptions and cultural expectations which are never stated. Replies assume a shared system of interpreting these systems of assumptions and expectations. The replies then must be themselves decoded. What ethnomethodologists have asked is what is the warrant for assuming the existence of these common-sense assumptions. Indeed, this problem is so intricate that Cicourel concludes that language itself cannot be taken for granted:

Language, then, and the cultural meanings it signifies, distorts and obliterates acts as a filter or grid for what will pass as knowledge in a given era. Similarly, cultural meanings about such matters as afterlife, causation, physical events, social events, biological events, beauty, ugliness, pain, pleasure, and the like have their own grammar which may be expressed and/or influenced by language (Cicourel, 1964, p. 35).

For the ethnomethodoligst, two conclusions should be drawn. The first concerns the official production of statistics. Everywhere this takes place it is necessary to analyse the organizations which produce the statistics. Secondly, where the field researcher takes the interview schedule, with the precoded questions, there must be a full elucidation of the unspoken, supposed and common-sense understandings that actually, or are taken to, constitute the underpinning of the discourse. Garfinkel (1967, pp. 38–70) illustrates the depth and profundity of such underpinnings.

4 'There is no reliability of the statistics arrived at'

Because many of the assumptions which underpin the statistics gathered in the manner outlined above have never been validated, it becomes reasonable to conclude that they are unreliable. Equally, the studies which have taken place of official organizations which produce statistics suggest that the production process does not reflect the 'real' situation so much as the practice of the organizations.

The assumptions we make about common understandings will mean that events will arbitrarily be assigned to the same categories whether they accurately fall within them or not. It also means that we will assume mathematical equivalence between any two members of the same category. Neither assumption can be warranted.

In the case of organizations, as Cicourel elegantly demonstrates (1968), the decisions taken in practice by organizations determine who will or will not fall within the category. Thus, in the processing of a person into a delinquency statistic, a number of hurdles must be crossed. An offence must be recorded by the police who must *decide* not to ignore it, and if it has not been observed by them in the first place, it must have been reported by someone who took it sufficiently seriously to do so. The police must *decide* to act to detect and/or apprehend someone, who they must *decide*, on some basis of police practices, is an appropriate suspect. They must *decide* whether to charge him, and if so, what with, and the person must *decide* how to plead to that charge. The police *decide* how to construct their case, and this is in no small part determined by the willingness of others to *decide* to be witnesses. And then a court must *decide* on guilt and disposal. Then, and only at this stage, does the person who is recorded in the statistic appear in the category that we see only as the final tabulation. Thus the process of nets and filters is demonstrated by the statistic rather than the actual number of people who do anything in the first place. The decisions taken at each stage, which determine the outcome, are themselves guided by ideologies of good or bad policing.[4] Chambliss summarizes the position:

Those persons are arrested, tried and sentenced who can offer fewest rewards for non-enforcement of the laws and who can be processed without creating any undue strain for the organizations which comprise the legal system (1965, p. 84).

The ethnocritique criticized

We have seen that empiricist materials are criticized because the categories employed in analysis are taken-for-granted divisions of the phenomenal world, from the point of view of only one set of the social actors, the hegemonic class or their agents. The allocation of events to those categories by officialdom is unreliable and only analysis of the organizational procedures by which it is accomplished will account for the final 'objective facts'. Finally, the elucidation of unspoken contextual assumptions is necessary before events can be allocated to categories by researchers. All these provisos unquestionably give rise to essential caution in formulating

4. See Bittner (1967).

new data-gathering work, but they are not, of themselves, a substantive critique of empiricism, and they offer no guide as to what accomplished work we might reject or accept for our own theoretical purposes.

1. The categories employed may appear to be taken for granted, even to the actors themselves, but this does not mean that they are theoretically neutral. The difficulty is that no one takes the trouble to grasp the implicit theories in them – we are inclined to leave them untheorized. Analysis of the structure of the organization which uses particular categories to record events will not necessarily theorize these categories either. It is a separate and distinct task based on theoretical and not organizational analysis. The definitional rules which constitute the guides to recording particular phenomena under particular headings only stand in relation to alternative allocations, although those relationships are seldom stated. They generally assume hierarchy of some types of events over related others, the exclusivity of one event from related others, and most important, they assume that the interest in framing such an analytic procedure is common to all classes and groups. These tendencies obscure the *relationships* that exist at the level of theory, whilst at the same time they must presuppose that relationship.

For example, the Registrar General's Index of Employment sub-divides all forms of work, employed or employee, so that it should be possible to allocate any individual's work to a precise category. Since it must be possible to place any individual in one category, and in one only, there must be rules of inclusion and rules of exclusion. Or put another way, the rule that includes an individual in one category must be derived from those which also exclude that individual from all other categories. This relationship to other categories, the unspoken, unacknowledged theory is based in this case on a hierarchy of incomes and status perceptions, in which an individual must be subordinate to another on these dimensions; the status, income and power of the superordinate 'other' fills in the two sides of the relationship and makes clear its nature. Yet there is no indication in the Index showing the relation of any category to any other. Thus, at the same moment as it is obscured that an employee who falls in any category is only definable in that way because he is a particular relation to the employer who buys his or her labour time, the category suggests a realm of its own. But it only exists by relation to other realms. 'Class' vanishes under the misleading term 'stratification' at the same moment that the researcher who uses this guide uses it to impute class. It is possible to use the Registrar General's Index if the relations are fully theorized and determined to be *adequate* at the relevant level of theory. Whilst the obscuring of class differences will strike no one as surprising, perhaps another example will illustrate the point.

From a sociological point of view there is no 'objective' definition of illness; instead, it is necessary to ask in whose interest and with what purposes in mind illness is socially defined by different people, e.g. patients and doctors, and by different social classes and ethnic and religious groups (Dreitzel, 1971, p. vi).

To accomplish this, whilst study of the social organization is interesting, it is not *necessary*. Theorization allows the assessment of the utility of statistical materials quite apart from knowing anything about the organization that generated them because the theoretical criteria implied or stated by the research instrument must stand on their own feet, face their own critical analysis. The assessment as to whether we can use data generated on those *theoretical* premises is the only question. It is the question that Marx asked of the reports of the Inspectors of Factories, the Children's Employment Commission, the Public Health Board, and so on. Some information will be, by this judgement, useless, some useful.

2. The necessity for the elucidation of common-sense background expectancies where questions are asked by a researcher and answered by a respondent provides one useful insight and one logically impossible demand on research. The insight is that new research in aspects of social activity and meaning should be sufficiently well theorized as to allow for the elimination of much that is equivocal, and promotes the type of persistent, fully interactional study which has existed in some parts of social anthropology. But just as it recommends learning one's way into a culture, so it must equally recommend the application of both received and newly formulated theory of a specified kind when asking research questions of that culture. In short, a researcher may be inexperienced but there is no naïve status for any social actor, researcher or researched (MacIntyre, 1967).

But the problem raised by the critique seems, to me, to be logically insurmountable. If it were possible for the common-sense background expectancies to be fully elucidated, then it would seem to follow that it might be possible to use the categories proposed in a sophisticated piece of empiricist research. That ethnomethodological demand appears to be more one for the careful elaboration of counting and recording procedures than a call for their abandonment. But the ethnocritique is alert to this possibility. The demands it makes for elaboration of common-sense assumptions is so stringent that no extent of elaboration can apparently fill the bill. The search for the background expectancies and the day-by-day, held-in-common knowledge must be entirely rigorous since every interpretation of it by the social scientist does it violence. There is, here, an assumption that a pure, unadulterated form of the communicated event exists, if only it could be uncovered by researchers who rid themselves of sociological or psychological glasses, and look at the facts in themselves.

It is no accident that no researcher would be allowed by some ethnomethodologists to bring back an account of what they saw transpire in any event. They must bring back a tape-recording, which allows no distortion of either segmental (the words and sentences used) language and nonsegmental (the tone, pitch, etc.) language. Even this does not explain context, so the next step would presumably be the use of 360° of video coverage to establish the context. These 'tape-documents' would constitute the research report, since interference with them would do violence to the material collected. In fact, as Cicourel points out (see above), even language may be an impossible tool, since it too does violence to the data, which is, presumably, pre-linguistic, and not formulatable at all. This critique is a prescription for total relativism. As Atkinson shows in discussing Douglas's materials on suicide:

Douglas uses second-hand case histories drawn, for example, from other studies of suicide. Yet if, as he says, it is not valid to use coroners' reports as a source of data because they reflect the views of the coroners about what constitutes suicide, then it is presumably equally invalid to accept case studies taken from other writers. In other words, it can be argued that the sources of data used by Douglas are inadequate even according to his own criteria. Carried to its logical conclusion such an argument suggests that there are no valid sources of data on suicide and hence that no further research is possible (1971, p. 168).

The radical use of official data

We have suggested that even without studying the institutions that produce statistical data, we can reject the absolute relativism of the ethnocritique since it would exclude us from all research activity. In fact, the argument advanced is that with adequate theoretization of data categories, we can determine whether they are useful to us as evidence supporting revolutionary or radical theories. We have rejected the empiricist idea that statistics provide research 'findings', because nothing is 'found' at all. Data is research 'product', and the mode of its production by theoretical work is what informs us about its utility. The remainder of this paper will discuss one, hopefully useful, example.

Two years ago, I was asked by representatives of community groups in Covent Garden to look at the proposed GLC Comprehensive Development Plan for the area. It became clear at once that the plan was directed at displacing the remaining population described by the GLC Survey *Covent Garden Is Moving* as working class. From the planners' own data it was seen that although 'most of the respondents liked the area and wanted to stay' (p. 76), and that about half had lived in the area for more than twenty years, the proportions of middle-class newcomers was much greater than the proportion of working-class newcomers. In short, working-class people were being displaced by the process which Glass (1955) called 'gentrification':

Once this 'gentrification' starts in a district, it goes on rapidly until all or most of the original working-class occupiers are displaced and the whole character of the district is changed. . . . As land values rise, the scarce, expensive commercial space has to be allocated increasingly to the higher lords of managerial and executive staffs. In 1951, Central London already had a disproportionate share of jobs for men in occupations classified in the census as belonging to social classes 1 and 2. But as journeys to work became more harassing, it is such upper- and middle-class people, especially, who think of acquiring – and who indeed need and can afford to acquire – some sort of a home if only a *pied-à-terre* near their place of work.

In Covent Garden it was already clear that commercial pressure for this type of accommodation, *pied-à-terres* for fatigued businessmen hurrying towards their first premature coronary, and other high-monetary-yield land usage, was changing a substantially working-class area into a middle-class haven.

The immediate task that faces a radical social scientist in this situation is similar to the defensive work undertaken by trade unionists in *defending* the living standards of working people. Initially it is necessary to develop a theory which understands the social dynamic and, then, to provide the researched information that show the consequent probabilities of certain social actions unless there is political (mass) intervention.

In the case of the Covent Garden community, the task was to frame a theory accounting for the present solidarity of the class in the area, a theory capable of underpinning a variety of accounts of how it handled the range of connected phenomena of the type generally called 'social problems'. In short, it was necessary, and with reference to current conditions in the Garden area, to specify the nature of relations and persistent structures in working-class life that exist. To do so represents no sentimental hungering after the days of back-to-back slums, days in many cases still with us, but an analysis of the living community of working-class people which Marx and Engels indicate is called into existence by the capitalist mode of production.

If a theory of these historical structures can be formulated, then it becomes possible to hypothesize the consequences of the dispossession of the geographic location on any one set of these working-class community relationships, literally, to specify the consequences of alienation from the location and structure of community. The theoretical proposition framed was, in outline, that the alienation from specific community structure would become visible in adverse social outcomes for the people in Covent Garden. To test this proposition, it was necessary to look at a British working-class area in which this had happened, to specify a definition of some of those adverse outcomes and to demonstrate the relationship of them to the alienation from the relationships of working-class life. There are a number of interrelated consequences of community disruption – growth in rates of 'official' delinquency, unwanted pregnancy, separation of family and kinship groups, instances of communicable disease and in the rate of diagnosed mental illness, to name a few. A variety of uncritical sociological and social-psychology studies have 'found' these occurrences.

In the Covent Garden area, it was decided to hypothesize what would take place in terms of the rates of diagnosed mental illness. The basis for doing so was that Faris and Dunham (1966) have suggested that certain forms of community disruption are closely associated with certain mental illness diagnoses. What they found, in summary, was that cases of mental disorders as plotted by residence of patients prior to admission to public and private hospitals generally show a regular decrease from the centre of a city to its periphery. This pattern is similar to patterns of distribution shown for various social and economic phenomena like poverty, unemployment, juvenile delinquency, adult crime, suicide, family desertion, infant mortality, communicable diseases and general mortality. This allows for the probability that if the existence of one can be established, that one may indicate the likely presence of the others. Secondly, they showed that it was possible to relate paranoid schizophrenia, catatonic schizophrenia, manic-depressive psychoses and senile psychoses to a variety of urban conditions, many of them directly emanating from the destruction of working-class communities.

If one wanted to establish that the patterns would also hold for British cities, then the question arises as to which official statistics would provide the appropriate evidence. It is clearly the case that there is enormous disagreement among medical personnel, as well as among laymen, as to the *adequacy* of the definitions used to designate 'schizophrenia'. Statistics recording schizophrenic illnesses are completely untheorized, and may include an enormous variety of behaviours to which the definition has been applied. In fact, a search of the statistics gives no indication of the criteria used for putting a patient in a particular category, other than the 'clinical opinion' of the doctor. On the other hand, in a particular locality, the relatively small number of consultant psychiatrists tends to reduce between-diagnosticism variance, and suggests that those who appear in a limited number of hospitals may well be showing some kind of pattern of social distress ('mental illness') which the consultants in question call 'schizophrenia'. Because the statistic does say how many *diagnoses* there are, as a gross rate, it indicates the prevalence of a 'type' of distress, consistently identified by a small number of doctors. It is unnecessary to fully theorize 'schizophrenia' in this context since whether it is a disease is not in question. Further, the degree to which doctors vary in their allocations of people to categories by routine criteria, albeit both criteria and allocation having been determined in part by fiat, can itself be measured on the basis of tests of variance.

During the 1960s, central Liverpool was redeveloped, fundamentally changing the character of the area (land usage, residential building format, etc.). Abstracting the reported mental-illness diagnoses in central Liverpool from the hospital records for the relevant catchment areas, it is possible to chart the changes in rates and types of 'official' diagnosis. These figures were compared with another British city, Sheffield, which had been redeveloped on an entirely different basis involving participation in strategy by the local people. Sheffield could be seen to have similar class and income patterns to Liverpool. 1957 was taken as a baseline, when all the old catchment areas were more or less intact, and it emerged that the Liverpool rate of diagnosed mental illness in the catchment was 148 per 100,000 people. Midway through the Liverpool redevelopment, the figure had reached 455 per 100,000, though Sheffield's figure was well under half of this, and remained close to the national rate. By 1968, the end of the decade, the Liverpool population were being diagnosed as mentally ill and needing inpatient treatment in 1006 cases in each 100,000 of the population. Thus, whilst the Liverpool rate showed an increase of 750 per cent, the remainder of Britain, including Sheffield, showed a growth rate of just double the figures from a decade before. As we have seen, there is good reason to believe that other signs of crisis for the working-class population will equally be present.

Moreover, as Faris and Dunham would have predicted, given the types of urban change and rates of movement from one dwelling to another, 95 per cent of the diagnoses were made up of illnesses related to such changes, of schizophrenia, depressive psychosis, psychoneurosis, involuntary melancholia and senility. Given the patterns of change envisaged by the Covent Garden planners, the population there might well look forward to a similar rate of crisis related to the alienation of them from their self-produced and preferred community. However, the planners had determined that the working-class way of life (and this even more than the housing conditions was redundant, that progress could not be impeded by 'sentimental' attachments to homes, ways of life, street, community, networks of persistent relationships from child-minder to school to youth club to workmate, neighbour. . . .

The material from this piece of work, together with other calculations made from the survey conducted by the Covent Garden planners themselves, showing the discrepancies between the two, and the areas they had not considered at all, were placed at the disposal of the community organizations. The first decision was to present them as evidence at the Inspector's Committee of Inquiry. At this level, they were, with other material researched by social scientists, effective in obtaining a postponement of the redevelopment scheme, and its reference back to the planners. They, needless to say, made minor readjustments to the plan, preserving rather more of the old buildings, instead of the old community, but they were forced to a public confrontation on points which they had scrupulously avoided. The materials have subsequently been used in community papers and leaflets, at public meetings, and as resource material for courses and alternative planning sessions mounted by staff at the Architectural Association, who, working very closely with community representatives, have played an exemplary role in contesting the plan. Given the ammunition, there is no question that these battles will go on. If Covent Garden is finally bulldozed, the basis for protecting the next area, in this urban Domino Theory situation, namely, Piccadilly, and then Soho and the British Museum environs, will be far more effectively established. The key to the process, however, must remain intact: the strategy for using the researched, and all other materials, is the prerogative of the local community organization and not the social scientist.

Prospects

This brief description of a relatively long piece of work is used only as an example of the use of available materials to construct, in this case, defensive research on behalf of a particular oppressed group. Other work might well go onto the offensive. It is quite impossible to do such work in the rarified atmosphere of the sociology/social psychology department. It is brought into being by long-term work with the people experiencing economic and ideological oppression. They call for its accomplishment and regulate its use. The development of a theoretical perspective on these forms of oppression is immediately given concrete content by the people involved in the struggle. This entire task is an act of production: theory is not 'received' by any party to the production, but rather is constituted by the parties to it. It is from this constitution that the practical work-tasks will develop. 'Everyone knows that without a corresponding scientific *theory*', Althusser comments, 'there can be no scientific practice, i.e. no practice producing new scientific knowledge' (1971, p. 74). He goes on to illustrate why it is that oppressed people will find it easier to grasp both the theory and the practice, and their relation in praxis, than many intellectuals will.

The opportunities to move from Uncle Tomdom to direct work with oppressed groups, an opportunity made available by the continual development of organization and militancy in those groups, now becomes an opportunity for the radical social scientist. But it is only possible to do so in a structure that denies him or her resources, precisely because of what we want to do with those resources, and if we can learn to use what is already available. Ours is the task of overcoming phoney scientism or crippling relativism, of recognizing that theoretical work is not a luxury and that atheoretical work is a shroud.

References

ALTHUSSER, L., and BALIBAR, E. (1970), *Reading 'Capital'*, New Left Books.

ALTHUSSER, L. (1971), *Lenin and Philosophy and Other Essays*, New Left Books.

ARCHARD, P. (1974), 'Sad, bad or mad: society's confused response to the skid-row alcoholic', in R. Bailey and J. Young (eds.), *Contemporary Problems in Britain*, Heath.

ATKINSON, M. J. (1971), 'Societal reactions to suicide: role of coroners' definitions', in S. Cohen (ed.), *Images of Deviance*, Penguin.

BECKER, H. (1963), *Outsiders*, Free Press.

BITTNER, E. (1967), 'The police on skid-row', *Amer. Sociol. Rev.*, vol. 32, pp. 699–715.

BREUER, J. (1958), *Introduction to the Theory of Sets*, Prentice-Hall.

CHAMBLISS, W. (1965), *Crime and the Legal Process*, McGraw-Hill.

CHOMSKY, N. (1959), 'Review of *Verbal Behaviour* by B. F. Skinner', *Language*, no. 35, pp. 26–58.

CHOMSKY, N. (1971), 'The case against B. F. Skinner', *New York Review of Books*, December.

CHURCHMAN, C. W. (1959), 'Why measure?', in W. Churchman and P. Ratoosh (eds.), *Measurement*, Wiley.

CICOUREL, A. (1964), *Method and Measurement in Sociology*, Free Press.

CICOUREL, A. (1968), *The Social Organization of Juvenile Justice*, Wiley.

CLINARD, M. B. (1963), *Sociology of Deviant Behaviour*, Holt, Rinehart & Winston.

DOUGLAS, F. (1967), *The Social Meaning of Suicide*, Princeton University Press.

DREITZEL, H. (1971), *The Social Organization of Health*, Recent Sociology, no. 3, Macmillan Co.

FARIS, R., and DUNHAM, W. (1966), *Mental Disorders in Urban Areas*, Harper & Row.

GARFINKEL, H. (1967), *Studies in Ethnomethodology*, Prentice-Hall.

GARFINKEL, H. (1956), 'Conditions of successful degradation ceremonies', *Amer. J. Sociol.*, vol. 61, pp. 420–24.

GLASS, R. (1955), 'Urban sociology in Great Britain', *Current Sociology*, vol. 4, pp. 5–19.

HOME OFFICE WORKING PARTY (1970), *Habitual Drunken Offenders*, HMSO.

KITSUSE, J. I. (1962), 'Societal reactions to deviant behaviour', *Social Problems*, vol. 9, pp. 247–56.

LCC (1965), *Report on Crude-Spirit Drinkers*, London County Council.

LEMERT, E. (1967), *Human Deviance, Social Problems and Social Controls*, Prentice-Hall.

MACINTYRE, A. (1967), 'The idea of a social science', *Proc. Aristot. Soc.*, supplementary volume 61.

MacPherson, C. B. (1962), *The Political Theory of Possessive Individualism*, Oxford University Press.

Moser, C., and Kalton, B. (1971), *Survey Methods in Social Investigation*, Heinemann.

Nagal, E. (1931), *Measurement*, Erkentnis.

Stack Sullivan, H. (1953), *Conceptions in Modern Psychiatry*, Norton.

19 The Job Psychologists Do
David Ingleby

I am his Highness' Dog at Kew
Pray tell me Sir, whose Dog are you?
Alexander Pope, *Epigram Engraved on the
Collar of the King's Dog* (1737)

What has somehow earned itself the label of 'empirical psychology' has
been the target of particularly determined attacks in the last few years, not
just in the social psychology departments but wherever it is practised. Yet
it is not at all easy to see what either its proponents or its critics are
getting at: the debate, if it can be called that, resembles a battlefield on
which skirmishes are breaking out apparently at random, it being hard to
discern which soldiers belong to whose army, how many armies there are,
and what it is they are fighting over. This paper is an attempt to make some
sense of the situation, and to add to it by defining a few causes I think
worth rallying round. If this seems a broader task than my title suggests,
do not feel misled: for I shall try to show that the job psychologists do –
their role in society – is, in the last analysis, what the conflict is about.

My starting-point – and the stimulus behind much of what follows – is a
book which presents the position of those calling themselves empiricists
elegantly and with some *de facto* authority, Broadbent's *In Defence of
Empirical Psychology* (1973). (I have refrained from speaking of 'the empiricist position', because it has yet to be established which of its defenders
are wearing proper uniforms and which are in fancy dress.) Two important
points are quickly established in Broadbent's book: first, that the conflict
is not simply about the correctness of particular findings, but also about the
value-systems held to be associated with them; and second, that it has a lot
to do with the historical situation of the various protagonists.

I shall pursue these two points below, but I would like first to deal
with another attitude expressed by Broadbent, that the criticisms of empirical psychology represent 'the last kicks of an outdated culture' (1973,
p. 9). This remark needs to be taken more seriously than its offhand manner
of delivery suggests. It communicates two things: firstly, the overt belief
that the criticisms are inspired by outside influences, rather than being a
product of psychology's internal problems; and second, the covert wish
that the critics were, in fact, dying, and moreover as the result of some act
which leaves them kicking. I do not think it would be taking the point amiss
to infer that the critics have aroused a – literally – murderous hostility;

Broadbent's remark is the urbane academic equivalent of Khrushchev's famous 'we will bury you', and those whose livelihood does in fact depend on doing psychology do not need its implications spelt out for them.

I think that such a reaction is not only unfair but unwise, for it seems to me that most of the criticism originates, not from subversive influences outside or troublemakers within, but from the shortcomings of empirical psychology itself; moreover, a great deal of it is informed by that discipline's own standards and findings. To blame Sartre or Laing – to name a couple of favourite scapegoats – is merely to adopt the tactics used by the press in 1968, when an obscure academic called Herbert Marcuse was 'discovered' as the evil genius behind the trouble the students were making. It is psychology's internal problems which are responsible for the current spate of criticism, and accordingly, its critics do not need to look to third parties for their supplies of ammunition, but can find most of it in the tenets of empiricism itself; for those who have pioneered the application of scientific methods to psychology have all too often used them 'like horse and mule, without understanding'.

Let me give a couple of small but revealing examples. We find, for instance, Eysenck (1957) quoting the results of his factor-analytic personality studies with six-digit accuracy, without considering the accuracy of the figures themselves – thus rendering most, if not all, of his smart regiments of digits empirically meaningless: clearly, they are there not to provide information, but to *look scientific*. Past the first digit or two, the numbers have the same sort of function as the shaving-foam with which the six-year-old will plaster his face in emulation of his father. Again, I have heard Slater (1973) trying to impress upon his audience the vastness of individual differences in intelligence by referring to 'this great span of variation, going all the way from below 55 up to, say 200' – neglecting the fact that the size of these figures was fixed quite arbitrarily by the psychologists. (Presumably, had the tests been scaled with a standard deviation of, say, .01, we should have been forced to accept that all men are pretty well equal.)

To regard these as minor lapses would be misplaced charity: for they are the tell-tale signs of the methodological bemusement which has brought psychology into its present plight – the tendency to fetishize the *representations* of reality (i.e. graphs, tables, numbers, symbols and theories) while losing sight of the reality they represent. The point of these examples is the staggering unawareness they show, quite simply, of the meaning of numbers. Moreover, they do not come from first-year students, but from men who, in terms of their influence, are the giants of their profession: Eysenck (1970) boasts that he has trained over thirty Professors of Psychology, while Slater, on the above occasion, was introduced as the man who through his textbooks had educated half the world's psychiatrists. In what, one may ask, was the training and the education?

The current debate, of course, is not about how many decimal places one should record or how many IQ points constitutes a lot. If it were, it would never have got further than the experimental literature. But the realization that psychologists have very often *not* been practising empirical science leads naturally to the question: what have they been doing? What is the point – for we may take it, I think, that Eysenck and Slater are too intelligent for their lapses to be merely accidental – of this pseudo-science? My answer will be that the shortcomings of the human scientist reflect the contradictions of his social role: that he fails to discover truth because he is paid (in part) to conceal it, just as the welfare agent fails to help people because he is paid (in part) to hinder them. I shall argue that the key to the current debate is the question – for whom does the psychologist work? What interests is he paid to further, and what value-judgements does his work embody in consequence? Sartre provides the key word: it is the *universality* of psychological knowledge which is in question.

The technicians of practical knowledge develop, or utilize by means of exact disciplines, a body of knowledge which, in principle, serves the welfare of all. Naturally this knowledge aims at universality: the doctor studies the human body *in general* in order to cure anyone. But the technician of practical knowledge can just as well be an engineer, a scientist, a writer or a teacher. In each case the same contradiction is found; the corpus of their knowledge is conceptual, that is to say, universal, but it never serves *all* mankind: in capitalist countries it serves *above all* certain categories of people belonging to the ruling class and their allies. Thus the application of the universal is never universal, it is particular, it concerns *particular individuals* (Sartre, 1972, p. 608).

In the same interview, Sartre also raises the question of why this kind of concern should manifest itself now: with 1968 in mind, he says:

It was the students who first experienced the real problem; basically they were going to be made into salaried workers for capital, or into bureaucratic policemen who were to help run business more smoothly. Those who saw this said to themselves: we don't want this, or more precisely, we don't want to be intellectuals: we want the knowledge we acquire to be used for the benefit of everyone. At the time of the Vietnam base-group committees the students came to realize that the fact that their studies led to their becoming watch-dogs for the bourgeoisie was in no way compensated for by their belonging to a Vietnam group. It was not simply by organizing demonstrations that one can alter the essence of the nature of the intellectual in our society as someone who is in perpetual contradiction insofar as he is condemned to do the opposite of what he wants and to contribute to the oppression of those whom he should be helping (1972, p. 609).

The chronology is important, and Broadbent is likewise alluding to a relevant fact when he identifies himself as a member of 'the so-called "silent generation" which returned to universities from World War Two, and which in contrast to their fathers or their sons, raised no protests, went on no marches and issued no manifestos' (1973, p. 5). I suggest that the chief difference between 1945 and today is that the Boche has disappeared (he is, in fact, a valuable trading partner); there is no clearly identifiable aggressor 'outside', compelling us to close ranks and, in addition, enabling us to project all our internal wrongs elsewhere. Nothing ensures peace at home so effectively as all-out war. To say this is not to ridicule the mentality engendered by those years, so unimaginable (if we are honest) to my own generation: indeed, it is only thanks to that solidarity that we can enjoy the luxury of questioning our own. But we have all met the type of person who spent his best years fighting for the defence of freedom, and the rest of his life objecting to its manifestations: the mentality that sees conflict as essentially external in origin, and critics as nuisances, is useful only on rather special occasions. To perpetuate it now – in whatever space of time remains before that kind of solidarity is forced on us again – is truly to adhere to an 'outdated culture'.

What we are witnessing now is, in my view, an attempt by psychologists to wake up from the trance of their own unquestioning professionalism to a realization of who they are working for and what their real job is – or, as Pope would say, whose dog they are: and the answer is not, ultimately, to be found anywhere in their contracts, even in the small print. My hypothesis is that their unwritten contract is to maintain the *status quo*: and in what follows I shall attempt to show, in very general terms, how they do it.

I shall not be concerned here with the obvious ways in which psychology is used to secure the advantage of those in power, although there are plenty of issues of this type for organizations such as the British Society for Social Responsibility in Science to take up. My analysis will be at a different level: I shall argue that the applications of psychology have formed the concepts to such an extent that psychology can only be used to perform the tasks for which it was fashioned. Thus, psychological knowledge cannot claim the same 'conceptual' universality as, say, engineering (nor, as I will try to show, can medicine); it is not just its applications which serve particular interests – it is the form of the knowledge itself. Sartre, like the sociologist Martin Nicolaus in his famous 'Eyes down, hands up' speech (1968), seems to take the scientists' word for it that their knowledge is universal. Ironically enough, if both men had been experimental psychologists they might not have been so readily taken in; for it is this tradition above all which has taught us to think of knowledge as a selective, pragmatic process of construing, and thus to call in question the pragmatics and the selectivity of psychological knowledge. (My own questioning was partly inspired by the theories of one D. E. Broadbent, who was pursuing lines laid down by the late Sir Frederick Bartlett: nothing could more effectively refute Broadbent's simple 'us/them' model of the situation, with something called 'empiricism' at one end of the football pitch and something called 'existentialism' at the other.)

Now ideological criticism of this type is not something scientists are used to, and tends to be misunderstood. Slater made it clear, on the occasion referred to above, that, for him, psychology's ideological critics are simply saying 'your findings make difficulties for our political beliefs, therefore we reject them', citing Liam Hudson's book *The Cult of the Fact* as an example. But the criticism is, of course, the other way round. Hudson may be to blame in that, by not putting inverted commas round 'Fact', he appeared to subscribe to the notion that psychological orthodoxy is indeed 'fact', and thus allowed Slater to get the impression that the title meant truth was a bad thing; but it is not reality which is currently under attack – it is psychology's systematically distorted representations of it. There are many ways of locating the distortions, but the essential issue from an ideological point of view always comes out as the same one: *the incorporation of social norms into the laws of nature.*

The fallacy involved in representing social norms as laws of nature is, of course, that the former can be altered if we so wish, but the latter cannot: and if this fallacy becomes incorporated into scientific orthodoxy, the latter becomes an obvious instrument for maintaining the *status quo*. Such 'reification' is what I set out to analyse in an earlier paper (Ingleby, 1970): a paradigm case in bourgeois economics is the 'law of supply and demand', which (as Lenin put it) tries to disguise a relation between people as a relation between things. (If the reader feels uncomfortable at the mention of such foreign notions, I would refer him – as I did in the earlier paper – to the refutations of the 'naturalistic fallacy' given by our own chaps, David Hume and G. E. Moore, which – compared to Lenin – make up in philosophical elegance what they lack in political acumen.) The fallacy has its root in the much deeper problem of how to deal scientifically with the specifically human aspect of human beings: *agency*. Psychologists have tended either to deny the phenomenon of agency altogether, like Skinner, or to deal with as much human behaviour as possible in terms that do not involve it. Broadbent, who represents the latter approach, is fond of using the example of pilot error to show that fundamentally mechanistic consid-erations can be far more relevant than questions of agency: and indeed, in the type of situation he cites, it is clear that dealing mechanistically with the pilot's perceptual apparatus would be much more helpful than merely making him try to fly more carefully. (It is ironic that Broadbent's latest version of this story appeared at about the same time as the proceedings of an air-crash inquiry which suggested that more old-fashioned kinds of human factors on the flight-deck might be capable of defeating the best ergonomic design: a psychology inspired by the fate of the Trident Papa India would probably take a very different form from one based on that of Viscount G–AORC.) However, sooner or later psychology had to come to grips with the notion of agency. Perhaps the most thorough proposals are those of Harré and Secord (1972), who claim to put forward a paradigm for psychology which accommodates the traditionally neglected features of human beings with complete adherence to scientific principles – though to my mind, their presentation of man as a rational, conscious, self-governing agent is as much an overstatement of the case as Skinner's is an understatement, describing an *ideal* way of behaving which is seldom the actual one (Ingleby, 1973b).

Fortunately, however, it is not necessary to venture very far into this treacherous territory to show the lack of universality, and hence of scientific status, in much psychological knowledge; we need only look at the way in which thoroughly conventional empirical concepts have been misused. I believe the most important way in which psychology has incorporated the norms of its own society can be defined very simply: the use of variance ratios (or correlations) as if they were regression co-efficients, and variables as if they were constants.

A *variance ratio* tells us the proportion of observed variation in X that can be accounted for by changes in Y: its value depends not only on the sensitivity of X to changes in Y – the regression of Y on X – but on the amount of variability present in Y in the sample under consideration. The phenomenon measured by X may be very sensitive to changes in Y, but if Y varies little in the sample studied, the proportion of variance in X that it accounts for will be small. It follows that if we use a variance ratio to gauge the sensitivity of X to Y, as psychologists habitually do, we run the risk of being misled by the unknown parameter – the variance of Y. Nowhere is this more true than with the so-called 'heritability constant' – the percentage of variation in I Q due to heredity. This figure is, by its very nature, descriptive of a specific population in specific conditions: as well as heredity, it depends on the extent of environmental differences in the population studied. (Usually, in fact, it depends on the extent of the differences between the environments in which pairs of separately-reared identical twins grow up: an even more obscure parameter.) Yet it is used as if – like a regression coefficient – it told us the *intrinsic* vulnerability of I Q to environmental change: this use is of course fallacious, as not even a scale of 'environmental difference' exists. The same applies to similar estimates made of the vulnerability of any psychological phenomenon to environmental change – for example, Slater's own studies on neuroses and psychoses.

More generally, however, because psychologists collect data on society as it exists, they are easily misled into producing causal theories embodying the covert assumption that the existing social order is the only possible or desirable one – a constant, and not a variable. This follows from the pragmatic nature of the concept of 'cause' itself. When we say that X is caused by Y, we generally mean – because human phenomena are capable of being affected by a wide range of factors – that Y is the 'loosest' variable in the set of factors affecting X; thus, if we wanted to know the cause of someone's death, we would usually be satisfied with the explanation that he was suffocated. We would be surprised to be told that he died from having a body temperature of 98.4°F: and yet this fact would be equally responsible for his death, since at a lower temperature he might easily have survived the degree of anoxia contingent on suffocation. The second is of course a silly answer, because the most practical way of avoiding death would have been not to get suffocated: but it is just as true, as an explanation, as the first.

Now the conservative bias inherent in the way psychologists set about looking for 'causes' is that, when it comes to factors determined by the way society is organized, they treat these as given – i.e. as constants – and not as variables. This is why psychological knowledge cannot claim the universality, at present, of physical knowledge: and I shall argue shortly that it is a direct consequence of the social role that psychologists have – because for them the facts of social life *are* constants, in the sense that their brief does not allow the possibility of varying them. I would go further and suggest that medical knowledge suffers from the same flaw. The doctor is, by the nature of his job, not empowered to change the way people live: in his role as a consultant to society, he therefore takes the client's way of organizing life as a constant and proceeds to look for cures which will remove the problem by other means than changing it. This is why he usually ends up treating symptoms rather than causes – because he is not allowed to consider normal life as the pathogenic condition it so often is: it is not part of his job, whether he practises physical or psychological medicine, to do so. But there is no reason why he should allow his clinical *role* to distort his empirical *perspective*: theories of causation cannot be universal if they depend on pragmatic considerations. In many ways they do, perhaps the paradigm case being the concept of 'death by natural causes'; when a doctor issues a certificate to this effect, he is including in the concept of 'nature' (whose laws, as we know, cannot be altered) a whole host of variables – conditions of work, housing, nutrition and social relations – which are to a very large extent not part of 'nature' at all, but part of that man-made artefact we call civilization.

To sum up: the bias which the psychologist's role gives rise to in his theories can be located in the practical meaning he gives to the abstract concept of a 'variable'. A 'dependent variable' comes to mean one which *must* be varied (the problem he is paid to manipulate), and an 'independent variable' one which *may* be varied. Any other factors acquire the status of constants, and like other constants – the speed of light for instance – become imbued with the inviolability of laws of nature. We can see most clearly how theory is moulded by the role of the person making it by taking as our paradigm a scientist whose function is quite overt: the industrial psychologist, whose understanding of human beings is invoked to improve their efficiency at work. It is easy to show that this understanding will be far from universal, either in the sense of being valid in all contexts or being equally geared to the interests of all involved.

Firstly, it is the company that the industrial psychologist works 'for': he is paid by it, and not by its employees, so that their welfare is only his concern insofar as the company's depends on it – and no further. To be sure, he will want the workers to be contented: but what the company requires him to *maximize* is not their contentment, but their productivity. Thus, what he tries to predict – the dependent variables – will be determined by his function.

Secondly, in constructing predictive models as a tool for increasing efficiency, he will only be interested in those causal factors that the company's policy will allow to vary: he would be wasting his employers' time if he investigated factors which are, for policy reasons, constants – such as the basic power-structure of the company, or indeed of the economic system as a whole. He will therefore turn his ingenuity to discovering variables which will produce as much effect as possible within his own terms of reference. So his independent variables will also depend on his role, and what his role does not permit him to vary will acquire the status of a constant and the sanctity of natural law.

The case of the industrial psychologist is thus relatively straightforward: few would claim that he is in a position to provide anything more than a highly task-oriented understanding of the situation. We are brought up to believe, however, that this is an isolated case: that psychologists working in the welfare or education systems are, by definition also, impartially promoting the good of all – so that this kind of bias cannot enter into the research that informs their efforts.

This belief, unfortunately, rests on a failure to appreciate the role of these systems in society as a whole. For the premise underlying the Welfare State is that the basic power-structure of society is constant: 'welfare' is a system for providing piecemeal remedies for the human problems created by this constant structure, in ways that remove from it the threat of change. So the constancy of social structure becomes an axiom for the psychologists employed by the Welfare State, and the knowledge they produce is little use as a guide to how the structure might be altered in the common interest.

The goals of social work, medicine, education and the penal system are thus heavily bound up with the efficient regulation and protection of a particular political structure; and only the most naïve or optimistic of my readers will believe that this goal is synonymous with 'the general good'. (Even if one does, what I have to say about the consequent lack of universality in the knowledge these systems utilize is unaffected: the only difference is that he ceases to be disturbed by the possibility that any of it is true.) We are all industrial psychologists: and our knowledge is moulded by our role in precisely the same ways as that of the psychologist whose contract describes him as such. What is regarded as a 'problem' is to be that which threatens the efficient working of the existing political system, rather than human unhappiness or disease *per se*. Adaptation of people to the social structure is our yardstick, not the adaptation of social structure to people: providing human beings who will act out their required roles efficiently and without making trouble. Education becomes primarily a matter of training, and welfare a matter of avoiding lost working days and social unrest; we are not primarily concerned with whether people actually have a worthwhile existence – as witness what we allow to happen to them when they grow too old to be productive or threatening. The psychologist's (and doctor's) job is to service the institutions of family, school and work in the particular form that the existing socio-economic system requires them to take – not in any other, hypothetical forms: correspondingly, he will take as his independent variables those that can vary independently of that system, and will hunt around for causal factors which have nothing to do with the actual form of our civilization. In education, different strategies of learning; in clinical psychology, different attitudes to one's situation; in medicine, different drugs or operations.

From what I have said, it would appear that psychological knowledge is more likely to obscure than to clarify the actual conditions of human life: in the rest of this paper, I shall advance the proposition that this activity of obscuring is, in fact, an important unwritten part of the psychologist's job, and moreover that by studying the smokescreen itself we may learn a lot about what it is there to conceal. What I have in mind is that psychology can perhaps be understood as having the same role socially as the conscious ego has individually: at both levels, since (as T. S. Eliot put it) 'human kind cannot bear very much reality', the symbolizing mechanism will be engaged in constructing defences against the experience of things as they are – but the form of the resulting distortions, once we know the code, will point to the facts of life against whose perception they are defences. Properly speaking, this applies not only to psychology, but to all the ways in which man represents to himself his own activities: what follows is therefore a tentative theory of ideology, in which psychology is situated as one component. Insofar as it is a psychological theory, of course, it runs the risk of circularity – i.e. of invalidating itself by its own conclusions: I shall try to minimize that risk by introducing the political considerations which traditionally emasculated versions of psychology sought to ignore – in other words, by expressing Freudian principles in Marxian terms rather than vice versa. At this point the empirical psychologist will no doubt feel the rot is setting in: all that is happening, however, is that we are pursuing the implications of the empiricist credo stated by Broadbent (1973, p. 187), that 'our processes of thought reflect very largely the particular structure and dynamics of the world in which we happen to find ourselves'. The point of departure is that we do not make any assumptions about how accurate the reflection will be.

What Marx wrote about ideology was directed chiefly at the religious, literary and philosophical effusions of his own time. If we apply his words to the human sciences today, however, their relevance is striking: and this indicates the extent to which psychology and its related disciplines are doing the same job. The spaces in the educated man's bookshelf which would have been filled in the last century by sacred tracts, novels and philosophical treatises are now occupied by works on psychology or sociology – produced by the same people, 'the thinkers of the [ruling] class . . . who make the perfecting of the illusions of that class about itself their chief source of livelihood' (Marx and Engels, 1970, p. 65). The basic themes – the human condition; men's needs and the way the social system caters for them – are the same, but the vocabulary has changed and the formerly overt moral standpoint has been covered by the somewhat perforated fig-leaf of scientific objectivity. Over and above the practical uses of psychology, then, we must recognize its purely *conceptual* utility, as a source of ideas which will tend to reinforce and justify the *status quo*.

Therefore, the distortions residing in empirical psychology are deter-

mined in two ways – by their applied origin and their ideological accept-
ability. One might conclude from this that we would be better off without
all those books, but this is not so: for even rose-tinted spectacles are better
than none at all, if we have the right filter to put over them. The human
sciences, if interpreted in parts as a sort of social phantasy-system – i.e. as
rationalizations or consolatory fictions – may reveal in latent content what
they do not utter in manifest content. What we need to understand are
therefore the mechanisms through which our thought-processes reflect
'the structure and dynamics of our world' – i.e. the laws governing the
transformations: what Freud, Marx and modern cognitive psychology all
have in common is that they refuse to take people's statements about
themselves as data which are true by definition, as philosophical idealism
and the introspectionist method tended to do, but instead treat them as
selective, prejudiced and pragmatic *acts*, following patterns which are
capable of being abstracted and defined. 'If in all ideology men and their
circumstances appear upside down as in a *camera obscura*, this phenomenon arises just as much from their historical life-process as the inversion
of objects on the retina does from their physical life-process' (Marx and
Engels, 1970, p. 47).

Such an approach would imply that ideological illusions are not so much
the sources of repression as 'the return of the repressed': for the experience
of living within a particular set of power-relationships cannot be eradicated,
and if it is not construed in political terms it will re-emerge construed in
some other terms – systematically distorted, as in a dream, but containing
all the necessary clues to the nature of the realities being repressed. In other
words, I do not think that psychologists are simply insensitive to their
political situation: rather, they are talking politics much of the time without
knowing it. What is needed, to salvage this material, is to decode the
language-games played by psychologists in the same way that the psycho-
analyst decodes the nursery-games played by children – in terms of the
underlying preoccupations they reveal; Freud required a whole bunch
of transformational 'keys' to do this – displacement, projection, condensa-
tion, and so on – and we are unlikely to require less. Lacking the keys,
I am obliged to try and put my meaning across by giving a set of examples:
the reader himself will have to discover what, if anything, they have in
common.

My paradigm is what Marx did for Hegelian metaphysics, when he
pointed out that the lofty system of universal relationships the latter
secreted from his own brain was in fact merely a depiction of the workaday
realities of contemporary European society: the most important case being
Hegel's claim that the master/slave relationship is an inevitable con-

sequence of the tendency of 'consciousnesses' to annihilate each other. Substitute for this the observation that most people are engaged in competitive economic relations, and it is clear that Hegel's conclusion is the nineteenth-century way of treating variables as constants, and representing social norms as laws of nature. Its closest modern counterparts are psychoanalytic and 'ethological' theories about the instinctual origin of aggression, which ignore the extent to which anxiety and the urge to compete are carefully fostered in the culture of family, school, work, class and nation; or, indeed, any type of psychology which sees in individual or family structure forms that are actually determined by socio-economic relations. (See, for example, Joan Busfield's contribution to the present volume.) In fact, the picture that emerges from most 'scientific' studies of animals as well as men is heavily overlaid by the projection on to innocent reality of our own, exceedingly primitive, political mentality: it is as if we can only discern those parts of nature which conform to the relations we ourselves are subject to. The view of men (and rats) as machines which exist to be mastered, as passive consumers and producers, and as perpetual threats to each other's existence, has a certain ironical truth-value – for instance, in the uncanny resemblance between Skinner's rat and Jules Henry's 'virtuoso consumer': but it is as treacherous a guide to reality as any schizophrenic's delusions.

Another similarity between the functions of phantasy and of ideology can be illustrated by analogy with the mass media. It is remarkable how newspapers, radio and television all manage to dwell constantly on the image of people inflicting hardship on each other, while seldom touching on the concrete hardships experienced daily by the readers and viewers, and their political origin. After a day renouncing his own needs and impulses, the average office- or factory-worker will turn to the media to 'read all about it' – 'it' being exploitation, not in the forms he is caught up in, but in the phantasy-material of murder, rape and theft, which succeeds in absorbing his own preoccupations while taking his mind off their origins. Through such images he is permitted to experience, by a process akin to displacement, all his feelings about his employers, educators, family and landlords – the people who constitute his interface with the political system.

The forms which moral indignation often takes – especially that which is fostered by the mass media – also seem to achieve, by displacement, the same ends. For instance, it is to my mind an oversimplification to ascribe passionate feelings against pornography to a repressed desire to indulge in the activities depicted. Those of the anti-pornography brigade who manage to state any coherent case at all (e.g. David Holbrook) usually rest it on the principle that people should not be treated as objects, and actions should not be divorced from feelings; in other words, that exploitation and alienation are a bad thing. Personally, I agree: but what is noteworthy is that the same people seldom seem to have much energy left over to attack the forms of exploitation and alienation that most people are subject to *as a way of life*. Like murder, rape and theft, pornography is a live issue precisely because of its quantitative insignificance, not in spite of it: it lends itself ideally to the politically necessary displacement of feelings. One could bracket with the issue of pornography much of the current concern about ecology or environmental pollution – which, however valid, serves all too often as a red herring alongside the fundamental question of the relationship between those who have power and those who are affected by the way it is exercised.

From mass media and moral indignation it is but a short step back into psychology: this time, however, the point I want to make is that when psychologists actually *do* attempt to confront the problems of human nature and human needs in earnest, they – like the pigeon, who sees things worst head-on – are most hampered by the need to conceal political actualities. What I am trying to account for here is the curious air of unreality about most discussions of the nature and the vicissitudes of 'being human'. The 'third-force' movement in psychology, for example, promotes eagerly the values of self-realization, creativity, fulfilment, etc., while hardly ever mentioning the concrete obstacles that obstruct most peoples' pursuit of these ideals: 'becoming a fully human being' thus becomes not a universal right, but a middle-class leisure activity. (Anyone who uses public transport in London has the true politics of 'creativity' literally in front of his nose: you may paint the buses in any garish pattern you like, as long as you are advertising Wimpy Bars or the *Evening News*; but if you wish to render the Blues on your own behalf in the caverns of the underground, you are liable to be marched off to the cells of the nearest police station.)

Secondly, the tradition of conceptual analysis which lies behind Harré and Secord's bold pronouncements about human beings is conducted in a political vacuum: 'freedom' thus becomes an abstract property of human beings, rather than a socially determined parameter of their situations. So, for example, Harré and Secord's discovery that it is logically only possible to be a person to the extent that one is recognized as a person by others, comes out as a purely conceptual observation, with no hint of its profound political implications.

Lastly, the applied psychologist in the most acute state of contradiction is the person employed to restore people's humanity to them without touching on the inhumanities of their situation: I mean the social worker,

probation officer or therapist, whose task is to raise his client's consciousness of the dynamics of his situation, while carefully preserving the split
between 'personal relationships' (which are variable and demand a human
approach) and 'social realities' (which are constant and thing-like in nature)
– see Ingleby, 1973a.

My conclusion is not as pessimistic as these examples might suggest.
It *is* possible to practice a psychology which does something more than
reproduce collective illusions, just as it is possible to escape from one's own
phantasies into relationships with real people: in both cases, the prerequisite of losing one's illusions is renouncing that which creates the need
for them – the refusal to apprehend certain disturbing facts of life. What is
therefore necessary is for psychologists to try and hold political realities
and psychological problems in focus at the same time: the result may not
be a 'radical psychology' – any more than the renunciation of racialist
genetic assumptions produces a 'radical biology' – but at least it will not be
a reactionary one. I suggest, then, that what we are currently witnessing in
empirical psychology are not 'the last kicks of a dying culture', but the
first kicks of something which is gestating within the body of psychology
itself: and nothing can be achieved by ignoring the pregnancy or denying
the parentage, except a painful birth and a lost inheritance.

References

BROADBENT D. E. (1973), *In Defence of Empirical Psychology*, Methuen.

EYSENCK, H. J. (1957), *The Dynamics of Anxiety and Hysteria*, Routledge & Kegan Paul.

EYSENCK, H. J. (1970), 'Programme research and training in research methodology', *Bull. Brit. Psychol. Soc.*, vol. 23, pp. 9–16.

HARRÉ, R., and SECORD, P. F. (1972), *The Explanation of Social Behaviour*, Blackwell.

INGLEBY, J. D. (1970), 'Ideology and the human sciences', *Human Context*, vol. 2, pp. 159–80; reprinted in T. Pateman (ed.), *Counter Course*, Penguin.

INGLEBY, J. D. (1973a), 'The psychology of child psychology', *Human Context*, vol. 5, pp. 557–68; reprinted in M. P. M. Richards (ed.), *The Integration of a Child into a Social World*, Cambridge University Press.

INGLEBY, J. D. (1973b), 'New paradigms for old', *Radical Philosophy*, vol. 6, pp. 13–19.

MARX, K., and ENGELS, F. (1970), *The German Ideology*, ed. C. J. Arthur, Lawrence & Wishart.

NICOLAUS, M. (1968), 'Sociology liberation movement', in T. Pateman, *Counter Course*, Penguin.

SARTRE, J. P. (1972), 'The nature and social function of intellectuals', interview reprinted (trans. George Gross) in *Human Context*, vol. 4, pp. 608–18.

SLATER, E. (1973), 'Biological differences and social justice', *New Statesman*, vol. 6, April.

Postscript and List of Contributors

This book has emerged out of a circular letter I sent to people I knew or had heard of who might want to say something about a better sort of social psychology. We have tried to produce the book as democratically as possible, with authors circulating drafts for comment and criticism, and decisions at least being open to anyone's influence. Some of the money from the book will go towards expanding the 'critical psychology movement' that has been emerging over the past year or two. We hope that paperback publication will ensure the book a wide distribution, and that it will act as a stimulus for others who are dissatisfied with their social psychology to explore new areas, new ideas, new approaches.

Some of us have doubts about the value of a 'reconstructed social psychology'. Given what we know about the irrelevance of social psychology to most people, and the uses to which it can be put both practically and ideologically by the ruling class, perhaps we had better abandon it and get on with something more useful. However, if you are stuck with a social-psychology course for a few years and want some ammunition, we hope that you will find a little in these pages. We also hope that people will write to us with any comments, criticisms, suggestions, requests that they may have.

Nigel Armistead — Department of Sociological Studies, The University, Sheffield S10 2TN.

Peter Sedgwick — Department of Politics, The University, Heslington, York Y01 5DD.

George Gross — Anabas Research Project, The University, 23–4 Buccleuch Place, Edinburgh EH8 9JT.

John Shotter — Department of Psychology, University Park, Nottingham NG7 2RD.

Don Mixon — Department of Psychology, College I, University of Massachusetts at Boston, 100 Arlington St, Boston, Massachusetts, 02116, USA.

John Rowan — 28 Redbourne Avenue, Finchley, London N3 2BS.

Martin Roiser — Division of Psychology, Ealing Technical College, St Mary's Road, Ealing, London WS5 RF.

Geoffrey Pearson   Department of Social Administration, University College, P.O. Box 78, Cardiff CF1 1XL.

Joan Busfield   Department of Sociology, The University of Essex, Wivenhoe Park, Colchester, CO4 3SQ.

Tim Lang   Carr Farm, Low Snowdon, Askwith, Nr Otley, West Riding, Yorks.

Godfrey Harrison   Department of Psychology, University College, P.O. Box 78, Cardiff CF1 1XL.

Graham Murdock   Centre for Mass Communications Research, 104 Regent Road, Leicester LE1 7LT.

Denis Pym   London Business School, Sussex Place, Regent's Park, London NW1.

Martin Richards   Unit for Research in Medical Applications of Psychology, 5 Salisbury Villas, Station Road, Cambridge CB1 2JQ.

Rom Harré   Sub-faculty of Philosophy, 12 Merton Street, Oxford.

John Heritage   Department of Sociology, University of Warwick, Coventry CV4 7AL.

Henrietta Resler   Department of Sociology, London School of Economics, Houghton Street, London WC2A 2AE.

Paul Walton   Department of Sociology, Adam Smith Buildings, The University, Glasgow W2

David Triesman   Addiction Research Unit, Institute of Psychiatry, 101 Denmark Hill, London SE5 8AF.

David Ingleby   MRC Unit, London School of Economics, Houghton Street, London WC2A 2AE.

Rat, Myth and Magic is a 64-page political critique of psychology written by a collective of students over the summer of 1972. It has now been revised and costs 30p. Cheques to N. D. W. Armistead at above address.

Humpty Dumpty is an occasional magazine of about twenty pages that aims to criticize psychology in practice outside academia, and if possible to suggest and construct alternatives. There have been four issues so far which cost 15p each. Issue no. 1 is out of print. Cheques/postal orders to *Humpty Dumpty*, c/o 28 Redbourne Avenue, London N3 2BS.

R. D. Laing in Penguins

Knots

Laing works out the deadly dialogues that silently mar relationships.

The Politics of Experience and The Bird of Paradise

Laing postulates that the schizophrenic may simply be someone who has been unable to suppress his normal instincts and conform to an abnormal society. The whole concept of 'normality' is questioned in this book.

The Divided Self

By investigating case studies of schizophrenic patients, Laing is able to offer a rich existential analysis of personal alienation.

Sanity, Madness and the Family
R. D. Laing and A. Esterson

This book suggests that madness may largely be a social creation and its symptoms no more than the tortured ruses of a person struggling to live in an unlivable situation.

Self and Others

Laing and Anti-Psychiatry
Edited by Robert Boyers and Robert Orrill

This book establishes the context of Laing's unique role of 'psychiatrist as prophet' and reviews in searching and critical essays the performance of that role from the first writings on severe mental disorder to Laing's recent, more general assault on the foundations of modern civilization.

Erving Goffman in Penguins

Interaction Ritual: Essays on Face-to-Face Behaviour

This volume contains six papers written since 1955 which amount to the groundwork for a sociology of occasions.

Encounters

Two studies in the sociology of interaction: fun in games and role distance.

The Presentation of Self in Everyday Life

An investigation of the structures of social encounters, the roles which we enact and the use we make of job-situations, houses and clothes. The author poses the moral and philosophical questions to which such performances give rise.

Relations in Public: Analysis of Face-to-Face Behaviour

Stigma

A study of situations where abnormal and normal meet, and of the ways in which a stigmatized person can protect his precarious social and personal identity. Using extensive quotations from autobiographies and case studies, the author argues that stigma is stereotype, and that both are related to the unconscious expectations and norms which act as unseen arbiters in all social encounters.

Asylums

Four essays on various types of closed community, all of which seek to mould their inmates to some socially approved purpose.

Two books on deviance

Images of Deviance
Edited by Stanley Cohen

A collection of essays by prominent sociologists on deviance as it exists in this country. The problems discussed range from drugs and hooliganism to suicide and industrial sabotage.

Politics and Deviance
Edited by Laurie Taylor and Ian Taylor

A collection of essays by members of the National Deviance Conference, this book is a follow-up to *Images of Deviance*. It includes discussion of popular novels, the hippie movement, relationships between crime and penal sanction, social control in revolutionary society and politics of housing.

Race, Culture and Intelligence
Edited by Ken Richardson, David Spears and Martin Richards

Are differences between black and white people in the kind of intelligence that I Q tests measure due to genetic inheritance? Can social-class differences be explained in the same way?

Few questions have stirred so much heated debate as the controversy, revived by an article by Arthur Jensen in 1969, over the origins of mental ability – and no question has graver implications for the individual, for educational policy and for social justice.

No answers, counter-questions (not least perhaps about the reasons for the question itself) can be attempted without first grappling with the concepts that lie behind it. The aim of *Race, Culture and Intelligence* is to do just that: to disentangle in turn the four central notions of intelligence, race, heredity and environment in contributions from psychology, biology and sociology that do not falsify the complexities of the issues, yet offer guidance that the non-specialist can follow.

'A useful survey and discussion of the varying approaches to the subject'
The Times Educational Supplement

'This collection of essays by an expert team is a comprehensive and stimulating production' *Social Survey Quarterly*

Ken Richardson and David Spears are members of the Neurobiological Research Group at The Open University. Martin Richards is University Lecturer in Social Psychology at Cambridge University.